W. M. Torrens

Empire in Asia, how we came by it

a Book of Confessions

W. M. Torrens

Empire in Asia, how we came by it
a Book of Confessions

ISBN/EAN: 9783743306400

Manufactured in Europe, USA, Canada, Australia, Japa

Cover: Foto ©ninafisch / pixelio.de

Manufactured and distributed by brebook publishing software (www.brebook.com)

W. M. Torrens

Empire in Asia, how we came by it

EMPIRE IN ASIA

HOW WE CAME BY IT

A Book of Confessions

BY

W. M. TORRENS, M.P.

LONDON
TRÜBNER & CO., 8 & 60 PATERNOSTER ROW
1872

CONTENTS.

		PAGE
I.	INTRODUCTION,	1
II.	A FOOTHOLD NEAR THE SEA,	9
III.	BEGINNINGS OF AGGRESSION,	17
IV.	PLUNDERFUL TIMES,	40
V.	THE DEWANNY,	53
VI.	PLIGHT OF THE PEOPLE,	66
VII.	WARREN HASTINGS,	81
VIII.	PUNCHAYET AND ADAWLUT,	98
IX.	THE ROHILLAS,	114
X.	BENARES AND OUDE,	129
XI.	HYDER ALI,	140
XII.	RIVAL INDIA BILLS,	153
XIII.	TYRANNY ON ITS KNEES,	169
XIV.	TIPPOO SAIB,	184
XV.	THE LAND SETTLEMENT,	197
XVI.	LORD WELLESLEY,	210

		PAGE
XVII.	THE MAHRATTAS,	237
XVIII.	THE SWORD IN THE SCABBARD,	252
XIX.	SCINDIA AND HOLKAR,	268
XX.	THE PEISHWA,	282
XXI.	LORD WILLIAM BENTINCK,	294
XXII.	AFGHANISTAN,	307
XXIII.	THE AMÍRS OF SCINDE,	317
XXIV.	PUNJAB AND PEGU,	330
XXV.	ZULM,	358
XXVI.	TAKING IN KINGDOMS,	377
XXVII.	TO-DAY; AND TO-MORROW?	392

EMPIRE IN ASIA.

CHAPTER I.

INTRODUCTION.

"It would be an ill lesson indeed for the people of India, that while they are subjects to Vizier or Soubahdar we will protect them in their rights, that while they hold of him we will stand forth in their favour. If he attempts to oppress you, we will rescue you from the hands of your lawful master; but if by conquest or by any other means we become your sovereign, remember there is none can guarantee the treaty between you and us. The power of the sovereign is all, the right of the vassal is nothing. You are persons without right, engagement, or any political existence, but our will and arbitrary pleasure. That this doctrine is unjust, that it is inequitable, that it is monstrous, that it is detestable, is so clear that I am almost ashamed of having misspent time in showing how impolitic it is."[1]

—CHARLES JAMES FOX.

AT the beginning of the seventeenth century, India may be said to have been, to the people of Europe, an unknown land. Save to the learned who had read of its ancient fame, or to such as listened to the wonder-weaving legends that now and then made their way from the shores of the Levant, its name was a sound that woke no echo of individual hope or national solicitude. It was out of reach; it was out of sight: from the cupidity of Christendom it was safe. The command which said, "Ye shall not

---

[1] Speech on the Benares charge; impeachment of Warren Hastings, 22d February 1788.—*Speeches in the Trial*, edited by E. A. Bond, vol. i. p. 197.

covet," spake of a neighbour's goods; for it is those things that are pleasant to the eye to see, and pleasant to the lip to taste, that stand chiefly in need of its inhibition.

But distance, which had hitherto left fair Hindustan secure from European lust, seemed to lessen year by year, after the Portuguese and Dutch mariners had proved that the Cape of Storms could be safely passed in ships of heavy burthen. The prolific isles of the Eastern Sea were speedily lit upon by these birds of adventure; and the loud satisfaction they were heard to express, invited by degrees successive migratory expeditions of the rival or kindred dwellers in the colder regions they had wandered from. Finding on their arrival that there was room enough for all, certain of these latter set about the business in a more methodical way, and strove by various regulations, charters, laws,—and, whenever needful, forgetfulness of laws,—to establish for themselves the most lucrative and gigantic monopoly that the annals of commerce contain.

In the accomplishment of this gradually formed and slowly developed plan, they were eminently successful. By degrees they drove the Portuguese, or first discoverers, completely from the field; and the Dutch, who came somewhat later, and who made a harder fight for their share, were eventually reduced to so low an ebb, that they continue now rather by sufferance than by any inherent power of self-defence to retain a remnant of their once great possessions. The Spaniards were engrossed with their acquisitions in the West, but the French were easily led to put faith in fortune in the Eastern seas; and, at a later period, fair promises of factories and fortresses, influence and dominion, in Asia, seemed likely to be realised. The English, for a time, lagged slowly in the race of gain and glory. They had come last, and they stood long at disadvantage. Civil dissensions and the want of a strong and wise Government at home left them without material support; and they had to be content, from the accession to the overthrow of the house of Stuart, to chaffer and bargain as best they might with the rulers and people of the land.

The bravest hearts and clearest heads among them during the seventeenth century, never dreamed that they were marking the site, if not laying the foundation, of an empire —not of the ocean merely, or its isles,—not of trade alone, with its infinite produce,—but of territory won by the sword for its own rich sake, and kept by the same for the like reason.

Southern Asia, in the days of Walpole and the elder Pitt, was still ruled, like Western Europe, by a number of distinct and independent Governments differing in origin, creed, power, and civilisation; frequently at feud with one another, and often suffering from overweening vanity and ambition, just as if they had been blessed with the paternal sway of most Christian kings, august and apostolic kaisers, or most religious and gracious sovereigns of immortal memory: but they were practically self-ruled and locally free. Even where the loosening ties of fealty to Moslem or Mahratta suzerain rendered states of a secondary rank dependent in diplomacy or war upon the superior will of Peishwa or Padishah, the people of each separate province still saw in the midst of them the camp and the court of the prince whom they obeyed; and, whatever may have been the burthens on their industry, they could not be unconscious that its produce was lavished or husbanded within their borders.

The whole of the vast region lying between the Affghan hills and those of Burmah, and from the Himalayas to Cape Comorin, 1,500,000 square miles, with upwards of

200,000,000 of inhabitants, consists to-day of revenue districts under an English Minister, or of mediatised states dependent for their continuance in that equivocal condition on his will.

No change like this, effected within a single century, is to be found in the chronicles of conquest. It may be said to have been begun in 1757, when India was but a geographical expression, identical with no political unity, and to have been completed in 1858 by the proclamation that her present Majesty assumed thenceforth the rights, duties, and responsibilities of sovereignty throughout the wide domains partially or perfectly brought beneath her sway. As foreshortening is in art the means whereby the most vivid sense of reality is imparted, it is even so in history. The infinitely varied lights and shades that fall upon events as they unfold themselves in succession, render it difficult, if not impossible, to realise as one the aggregate of facts which we know to be indisputable. But it is instructive as well as startling, to place for a moment the beginning and the end of recent and contemporary changes in the degree of proximity, wherein from afar they will by and by appear in the view of the historian. How will our acquisition of empire in the East, and our actual position there, look in the sight of those who shall come after us? How does it look in the sight of Heaven?

These are not merely curious questions fit to amuse the speculative or idle. If public morals be a reality, and if there be such a thing as national conscience and national accountability, it behoves us, as a free people, to consider how we came by Asiatic empire, and how, for its sake, and for our own, we ought to deal with it.

If the attempt of Napoleon to subjugate Europe to his authority may be said to have begun at Campo Formio, and if we can imagine the course of victory rolling onwards at his bidding until it reached at length the shores of the Dardanelles and those of Lapland, the banks of the Vistula and the mouth of the Tagus, we shall have something like an accurate parallel, as far as space is concerned, and the variety of creeds and Governments existing in that space, to that which is now presented to the world by the spectacle of British India. Great and manifold as are the discrepancies between the two, there are points of analogy not ascribable to accident. Napoleon, when he conquered, did not always or generally annex or seek to crush the memory or the spirit of separate political existence. He pulled down kings and set up his nominees in their room; but he left Naples, Spain, Holland, and Westphalia the titular dignity and the municipal freedom of separate states, and was prudently content with the absorption of comparatively limited acquisitions, and their incorporation as provinces of France. No scruple would assuredly have withheld him from adopting an indiscriminate policy of imperial amalgamation. But we know from his public acts, and from his private after-thoughts in captivity, that his ambition was not to be head constable, but Lord Paramount of Western and Southern Europe. He was a fearless and a selfish man, but he had the discernment, foresight, and magnanimity of genius; and to him it would have seemed purblind impolicy and greedy blundering to have affected to establish, for such widely-scattered realms, one centralised administration in Paris. On the contrary, he spent no end of time and toil in replacing firmly, as he thought, the foundations and the outworks of separate and local government in nearly all the subordinated states over which his power extended. His aim was to be suzerain—appellate judge in peace, generalissimo in war. But he thoroughly understood that the vigour of the gigantic system he essayed to form, and the chance of its prolonged existence, rested upon the degree in which it might be possible to reconcile loyalty to empire with the preservation of traditional and progressive ideas of separate nationality and local self-rule. That this was his splendid dream is demonstrable not merely from his words, but from his actions; and in truth, no other supposition is intelligible. Nor is there in any of his numerous confessions of error and miscalculation, a trace to be found of misgiving as to the wisdom of this characteristic portion of his conduct. He fell through other causes, not from this; and the fact that his vast designs perished ere they were complete, ought not to blind us to the lessons that may be gathered from the manner in which he made use of partial success.

The spirit of conquest breathes so fearlessly through every page of England's history, that it would probably be reckoned by the majority of her people rather absurd to attempt, by any timid or ingenious paraphrase, to hide from view the real nature of an attribute whereof they are nationally not a little proud. From the earliest times, they appear to have cherished a longing for foreign possessions; and from the days when Edward and Henry devoted all the flower of English knighthood, and all the contributions of English trade, to "the conquest of France," to those when the red Indian of America was proclaimed a usurper of the hunting-grounds his forefathers immemorially had enjoyed, the love of territorial acquisition has been deemed by most of our distinguished, royal, and noble authorities, worth gratifying at any cost which the nation from time to time might be brought to think it could afford. That many notable attempts ended in memorable discomfiture is indeed most true. "Such," as court chaplains preaching for a bishopric were wont to utter with a sigh, "are the ways of Providence!" But the history of European Governments must be re-written ere Christendom can honestly disclaim the practical belief that it is pleasant, glorious, and profitable, when you can, to hold down a neighbour by the throat, and take his sword and money from him. The longing for forbidden fruit seems to be ineradicable, and few of the great names we are accustomed to recall with admiration are wholly clear from the charge. The pen that signed reluctantly, after six years' costly and disastrous war, the recognition of American independence, traced an enlarged scheme of territorial compensation for the loss, in Hindustan.

Though Chatham in opposition scandalised all good society by exclaiming that "he rejoiced to hear the Colonies had resisted," Chatham in office never would agree to let them go. His greater son was by temperament averse from war, and disapproved, he said, of encroachments in the East; but he never gave back anything his subordinates had got by fair means or foul. In later times, English statesmen have indeed taken credit for greater magnanimity; and Lord Castlereagh in particular has been praised for restoring Java to the Dutch, and Sicily to the Italians. But if in this respect, in Europe, he made a great character, in Asia he took care to spend it like a gentleman. It would be useless to multiply examples, worse than useless to set up invidious contrasts and recriminations. Our duty is not to judge others, but ourselves; to beware of covetousness, and of being betrayed into passive complicity by unpardonable laziness to seek, or still more despicable cowardice to own, the truth. We cannot undo what is done, but for that we are not accountable. We are accountable, as a free-speaking and freely represented people, for all that may hereafter be done in our name; and if upon investigation—which with honour and in conscience we are not at liberty to elude—we are convinced, with Burke and Fox, with Cornwallis and Bentinck, with the elder Mill and Richard Cobden, that a great debt of reparation is due to India by this country, we are bound to use every just and fair occasion to press for restitution to individuals of such rights and benefits as can be restored to them, compatibly with justice to others equally claiming our care, and for such restitution of local self-rule to the nations of the East as may not be incompatible with the preservation of peace amongst them, and the maintenance of that suzerainty in the English crown, which they, in common, never acknowledged as due to any other single authority.

It will be necessary that we should briefly recall the commencement of the intercourse between England and the Eastern peninsula. Nor will it, perhaps, be thought waste of time if we try to retrace the stealthy steps by which strangers got a permanent footing in the country, and how they stood, contrasted with the people and the native Governments of India, at the period when, properly speaking, the struggle for ascendancy began.

CHAPTER II.

A FOOTHOLD NEAR THE SEA.

1500—1700.

"I cannot think that, if all the ranks of the different communities of Europe and India are comparatively viewed, there is just ground for any arrogant feeling on the part of the former."
—Sir J. Malcolm.[1]

IN the reign of Emanuel, King of Portugal, a fleet of four armed vessels was sent forth on an expedition of discovery, and the command of it was given to Vasco de Gama. Steering his venturous course beyond Madeira and the coast of Guinea, he reached at length the southernmost point of Africa; and believing that a path to India lay through those waters, whose insincere repose invited him to trust his weary fleet upon their bosom, he spread his sails once more, and with a prosperous voyage attained the coast of Malabar. After a brief stay, De Gama returned to Europe. His countrymen were intoxicated with joy. The key of the East was found. Infinite wealth, imperishable fame, was theirs. Let new fleets be equipped and launched without delay. Who or what should hinder their prosperity?[2]

This was the morning time of Eastern discovery, and every object wore a glittering and exaggerated form. Ignorance lay like a soft haze over all things, and in the distance anything might dwell, waiting to be revealed.

[1] Memoirs of India.   [2] Reynal's Indies, book I.

As the clearer light of information grew, the dreams of dawn passed reluctantly away. There were no treasures to be had for merely asking; but there was abundant scope for industry and enterprise. The people of Hindustan were not timid savages, capable of being robbed or swindled by whoever chose to try; they were a great and intelligent race, acquainted with commerce and the arts, and ready to exchange the various produce of their skill for objects of Western workmanship. By degrees these soberer but far more lucrative advantages arising from the discovery of De Gama became understood, and the Portuguese succeeded in establishing relations of commercial friendship with the minor princes of the East, and finally with the imperial court of Delhi. They confined their ambition to mercantile pre-eminence, and engaged in naval warfare only with those European powers who sought to interfere with them.[1] Among these, the Dutch for a while were the most conspicuous, and eventually the most successful. In 1611, they worsted the Portuguese fleet, and forcibly took possession of Surat. By degrees they gained a complete ascendancy over their forerunners, and they would probably have sought more extensive continental possessions than those adjoining their factories at Ormuz and at Goa, had not their attention soon after been engrossed by the culture of those garden isles that stud the Indian Sea. Meantime the English and French began to seek their share of a traffic which promised to be so profitable. The design of an East India Company[2] was among the many schemes of Colbert for developing the maritime power of his country; and, though ill-conducted and sustained, the plan of establishing a like association was not forgotten by the Ministers of England.

[1] Anderson's History of Commerce, and Reynal.   [2] In 1644.

Little more than two centuries have elapsed since a few English merchants humbly solicited from the princes of India permission to traffic with their people. "Our dominion now embraces nearly the whole of that vast region which extends from Cape Comorin to the mountains of Thibet;"—such are the significant words in which the great historian of English power in India opens his narrative. The first charter to a Company trading to the East was granted in the year 1600. Its provisions are in no way remarkable, but it may be recalled, as an apt illustration of the exclusively mercantile character of the undertaking, that when the Government of that day endeavoured to impose a court favourite upon the first expedition as a sinecurist, the committee of the Company declared that they desired "not to employ any gentlemen in any place of charge, and requested that they might be allowed to sort their business, with men of their own qualitie."[1] For many years afterwards, they were content with fitting out a few vessels, adapted to the commerce of the East; and they deemed themselves fortunate when their annual adventures proved remunerative. The Portuguese and Dutch, their only rivals, possessed several factories or entrepots of trade on different parts of the Indian coast. It became an early object with the English Company to gain similar places of security for their goods; and as the jealousy between them and the Dutch grew warm, their anxiety to get a footing on the continent increased. James I. addressed a letter to his "illustrious brother," the Mogul, commending them to his protecting care. Jehangîr suffered them to found settlements at Surat, Cambay, and Ahmedabad, and in 1613 issued a firman confirming them in these possessions.

Sir Thomas Roe was sent as ambassador to the court at

[1] Mill's History of India, I. book I. vol. i.

Delhi in 1615, and was received with honour and hospitality there. Another factory was founded in the following year. In 1616 the Company had established themselves at Calicut and Masulipatam. In 1624 they obtained a grant of jurisdiction over their own servants,—it being as difficult to keep order in a distant factory, amidst a foreign community, as among the crew of a ship at sea. The Padishah, being a just man and wise, understood their needs, and yielded what they asked, little dreaming that the time would come, when, from such root of title, they would claim jurisdiction over his subjects and successors, and, as the penalty of resistance, decimate the one, and imprison the other for life as guilty of rebellion.

In 1639 Fort St George was founded, and eventually raised into what was called a Presidency or residence of those who were intrusted with the chief direction of the Company's affairs in those distant regions. From the outset the Company maintained the strictest principles of monopoly. Any ships but their own, whether manned by their countrymen or by foreigners, were causes of complaint, and, when unarmed, of pursuit and capture. They grumbled at being undersold by the Dutch, and the English who ventured on independent traffic they designated and treated as pirates. The horrors of this system have been often told. The Dutch resented the cruelties practised upon their countrymen, and every school history recounts how several Englishmen were put to the rack at Amboyna. But the truth, says an old chronicler, founding his statements upon English authorities of the period, was, " that they themselves at this very time were in the habit of perpetrating tortures upon their own countrymen, even their own servants. Before they were intrusted with the powers of martial law, *they made it a rule to whip to death or starve to death* those of whom they wished to get rid; and the power of executing for piracy was made use of to murder private traders."[1]

When Bombay was overrun by the Mahratta chief Sivají in 1664, the English, under Sir E. Oxenden, the governor, successfully defended Surat, and thereby laid the basis of their reputation for constancy and prowess in the East. Aurungzebe, who reigned at Delhi, sent to compliment them on the courage they had shown, and volunteered further privileges as their reward. In the reign of Charles II., Bombay, which had been a Portuguese settlement, was ceded to the King of England, as part of Princess Catherine's marriage portion; and it was thought of so little value, that the open-hearted monarch conceded it to his open-handed subjects the Company. Thus, in the progress of the first eighty years of their intercourse with the East, they contrived to make some money, to establish themselves as colonists in several important places, to commit an infinity of misdemeanours of various degrees of enormity upon friends and foes, but not as yet to excite the jealousy of the Oriental powers.

Some years later, their rash and offensive demeanour at Bombay provoked the Mogul also to wage war against them. He issued orders declaring that it was no longer compatible with the safety of his dominions that they should be suffered to remain for their purposes of encroachment. They were driven from Surat; Bombay was besieged; and possession was taken of their factories at Visigapatam, and other places; but they had already learned to diplomatise, and "stooped to the most abject submissions."[2] The Emperor yielded to entreaty, and suffered the restoration of Surat. He deemed the loss of their trade

[1] Note to Mill, I. book I. chap. ii.   [2] Mill, book I. chap. v.

likewise a consideration;[1] and in the recent consciousness of having brought them to the verge of extinction, he relapsed into false security, believing that in case of renewed danger he might easily at any future day bridle their presumption again.

The chiefs of Bengal appear to have been more upon their guard than the rest of their neighbours. They viewed with alarm the insidious progress of the strangers in founding and fortifying new positions along their shores. The advantages of augmented revenue and trade they suspected might be bought too dear; and after numerous petty misunderstandings with the Company, matters came to an open rupture. Of the rights of the immediate quarrel we are uninformed; and it should be carefully borne in mind that, until a very modern period, we are totally destitute of statements upon any side but one. All we know is the result of unwary admissions, or of the comparison and translation into vulgar truth of official documents. Thus we may be satisfied that, however dark the colouring seems throughout the strange and eventful history we are entering upon, it is lighter than the revelation of much that can never be dragged into the view of this world would render it.

Hitherto the Company had everywhere professed to be the humble servants of the princes of the East; but when they fell out with the Nawab of Bengal, a new scene opened. They ventured to question whether disguise had not been worn long enough, and whether the policy they had found so successful with their own countrymen and with the Dutch, might not answer also with the native powers. Accordingly, in 1685, they fitted out their first invading expedition, and sent it forth with orders to seize

[1] Mill, book I. chap. v.

Chittagong, and to do such further violence as might be practicable to those amongst whom they had hitherto dwelt in peace. This premature attempt at open aggression failed; had it succeeded it might have opened the eyes of the Governments generally in Hindustan to the danger and folly of temporising conduct. But it was fated otherwise; and after seizing the island of Jujellee and burning the town of Balasore, the raiders suffered a severe reverse; and the loss of their factories at Patna and Cosimbuzar reduced them to seek for terms of accommodation.[1]

From that day the designs of the Company were changed from the mere pursuit of commerce to those of territorial acquisition. In the instructions sent out from England in 1689, we find the following significant expressions:—" The increase of our revenue is the subject of our care as much as our trade: it is that must maintain our force, when twenty accidents may interrupt our trade; *it is that must make us a nation in India;* without that we are a great number of interlopers united by charter, fit only to trade where nobody thinks it their interest to prevent us." And undeviatingly were these instructions followed by successive generations of "Company's servants," as they were styled. Thenceforth trade was valued less for its own sake than as a diplomatic agent, or a well-appointed pioneer to prepare the way for dominion. The experience which had been lost upon the Padishah in their recent conflict with him was not thrown away on them. In 1699 they persuaded him to grant them liberty to found several new factories, and to erect forts beside them. "This, however," says their historian, "they began cautiously, so as not to alarm the native Governments."

The closing days of the century were spent by the

[1] Mill, book I. chap. v.

Company's servants at the mouths of the Hooghly in establishing themselves in three villages, Chuttanatti, Calcutta, and Govindpur, which had been granted them as a jaghire on the customary terms of fealty and tribute by Azîm-shâh, when Soubahdar of Bengal. A rich present had induced the grandson of Aurungzebe to make them this concession; and, with or without his leave, they lost no time in erecting works, to which, in compliment to their sovereign at home, they gave the name of Fort William.

Since the wolf's cub leaped over the mud wall on the banks of Tiber, nothing so pregnant with consequences had happened in the history of empire-building; yet few things attracted less of notice among the Whig politicians of St James's, or the Tory politicians of St Germain;—so little, indeed, that the date is erroneously given in many popular histories, the matter not having been thought apparently worth accurately searching out. The Mogul, living far inland at Delhi, probably heard no more for some time of his new tenants-in-fee, who had come over the dark waters, and humbly craved his permission to squat near the sea-shore. If he was told of their planting stockades, and putting a sort of fortification there, why should he trouble himself regarding it? Likely enough his native subjects around them were jealous and disposed to be quarrelsome. Why should not Feringhees defend themselves as best they might? Poor people! they had come a long way, and seemed to work hard—he would not interfere.

CHAPTER III.

BEGINNINGS OF AGGRESSION.

1701—1756.

"A new scene is now to open in the history of the East India Company. Before this period they had maintained the character of mere traders, and by humility and submission endeavoured to preserve a footing in that distant country, under the native powers. We shall now behold them entering the lists of war, and mixing with eagerness in the contests of princes."

—JAMES MILL.[1]

AT the beginning of the eighteenth century, the ties which had held together the dominions of Aurungzebe were visibly beginning to decay. As in the dependencies of Spain under Philip II., the infatuation of proselytism had tended only to work the disintegration of the scattered realm. In Bengal especially this species of impolicy had served to shake the loyalty of the people. The poorer and more ignorant sort yielded to the harsh dictates of their masters, and to some extent conformed to the Mohammedan faith. The more subtle intellects of the Brahmins resorted to evasion, and the wealthier classes were able to purchase the luxury of keeping a conscience, and of transmitting to their children the traditions of Vishnu. Elsewhere the bulk of the population adhered to the rites and tenets of their fathers; but throughout Southern India, the silent process of alienation had set in.

[1] History of British India, book I. chap. ii.

Wherever the Mahrattas came, they unfurled the flag of religious deliverance; and to drive them back, the great lieutenants of the empire found it expedient to revert to the old ways of toleration.

From the death of Aurungzebe the strength and unity of the empire thawed more rapidly. His successors were still honoured with the title of "the Sun," but the power to wither or bid flourish they had once possessed grew feebler day by day. Large and remote provinces became unmanageable; and being handed over to individuals of influence and ability, were governed by them as tributary States. The title of Soubahdar or viceroy and the language of political trusteeship, were scrupulously preserved; but inquiry into misrule was too easily evaded, too easily defied, to be attempted frequently; and the reality of control was silently abandoned by the Imperial Durbar, in the hope of preserving the fragile show of supremacy. Taking advantage of the circumstances of the time, and of the errors of their suzerain, the Soubahdars gradually sought to become more independent of the court at Delhi. The Nizam, who ruled over the Deccan, the Vizier of Oude, and the Nawab-Nazim of Bengal, aspired to found viceregal dynasties in their respective provinces. They never tried to throw off their allegiance to the Mogul, to refuse him tribute, or to question the validity of his acts of occasional interference and supreme interposition; but, like the African Beys of our own time, they succeeded in asserting a qualified independence within their respective pashalics. They took the title the Padishah conferred on them, not that of Majesty, which would have been incompatible with the idea and duty of their station; but practically they exercised over their people all the real authority of government. The English at Madras found that it was with the Nizam primarily and principally they must deal if they would dwell securely; and their fellow-countrymen at Calcutta understood, in like manner, that a good understanding with the court of Moorshedabad or of Lucknow was of more importance to them than friendship, however unruffled, with that of Delhi.

In each of the Presidencies, power had been given them to employ civil servants in their foreign settlements, to raise such troops as might be necessary for their defence, and to determine, without previous reference to the Government at home, what native powers were to be regarded as enemies or friends. The continual wars between England and France had led both Governments to send, from time to time, portions of their disposable force to India; and thus were the means afforded to the ambitious governors in those remote possessions, of intermeddling in the contests of the native chiefs. To reckless and irresponsible men with arms at their disposal, a pretext will not long be wanting for employing them.

The French were perhaps the first to conceive the project of founding a territorial empire in the Indian peninsula. For a long period their settlements were presided over by Dupleix, a man thirsting for power, and eminently qualified, by his subtle and adventurous disposition, to extend the dominion of his employers. He had married a native of rank, who beside her fortune brought him the accession of local knowledge, and acquaintance with the ways and aims of the subordinate courts of the empire. Her natural abilities, it is said, were good; and, educated in a school of political intrigue, she was able to conduct for her husband the daily correspondence and diplomacy which no European at that time could have attempted. The struggle for ascendancy between the English and French settlers was long and sanguinary. Le Bourdonnais had, in 1746, worsted the fleet of his opponents and taken Madras. But quarrelling with Dupleix, he was ordered home, where, unable to withstand the calumnies raised against him, he soon after perished in the Bastile. For a time the genius of Dupleix prevailed. Meddling openly in the strifes of the Deccan, he espoused the cause of Chunda Sahib as claimant of the throne of the Carnatic. The reigning prince sought help from the English; and Arcot, the capital of the province, was more than once taken and retaken.

Among the earliest allies of the English on the Coromandel coast was the Rajahj of Tanjore. In 1742, the reigning prince had been deposed by domestic revolution, and Pretab Sing obtained the throne. The authorities at Madras having no concern in the event, acknowledged the new prince without hesitation. Their correspondence with him was continued without any interruption, and mutual expressions of fidelity and confidence were interchanged for more than seven years. At the end of this period, Sahuji, the exiled rajah, solicited their aid in effecting a counter-revolution. He offered, by way of recompense if they should succeed, to grant them the fort and Jaghire of Devecotah, and undertook to pay all expenses of the war. They accepted the offer. Pretab was their ally; they had recently sought his assistance against the French; they had no pretence of provocation to urge against him; nevertheless "they despatched an army to dethrone him."[1]

The expedition failed, but a second was resolved on. They determined, however, says their apologist Malcolm, "that the capture of Devecotah, not the restoration of Sahuji, should be their first object."[2] The fort was accordingly invested and taken. And no sooner was this

[1] Mill, book IV. chap. ii.   [2] Memoir of Lord Clive, vol. i. chap. i.

accomplished, than they entered into a negotiation with Pretab Sing—agreed to desist from all further hostilities—not only to abandon him for whom they pretended to have theretofore fought, but engaged to secure his person and to receive a fixed sum for his maintenance, on condition of being suffered to remain undisputed masters of Devecotah and the circumjacent territory.[1] This was the beginning of the conquest of Hindustan.

In 1751, the French were successful everywhere; then fortune veered: fresh troops were sent out from England, and unobservedly a young adventurer about the same time threw down his writer's pen in one of the Company's offices in Madras, and asked leave to join the ranks. It was that young man who changed the destiny of the East. Robert Clive was, in 1740, an idle and passionate boy, engaged chiefly in acts of petty plunder, and other mischief done and suffered at his hands by the quiet folk of Market Drayton. His father being able to make nothing of him, got him a clerkship in the Company's service. The dull routine of commerce was ill suited to his bent; he was not indifferent to gain, but his love of excitement was greater. He fought from time to time a good many duels, but this afforded him only casual occupation; and, gladly seizing the opportunity of escape from innocuous employment, he went with enthusiasm to the wars. His intuitive skill and versatile daring were soon recognised; and it is not too much to say that he was the means of saving his countrymen from extirpation during the period of Dupleix's victories.

The general peace of 1754 left the rival intruders in possession of no great increase of territory. But in the course of the struggle the all-important truth had broken

[1] Mill, book IV. chap. ii.

on the minds both of natives and Europeans, that the hosts of the former were unable to contend with the arms and discipline of the latter. "No valour could equalise the combat, and the impressions produced by defeat were rendered tenfold greater by a comparison of numbers. The well-commanded and well-trained battalion moves amidst myriads of opponents, "like a giant with a thousand hands which defend and strike according to the dictates of one mind,"[1] and to whom an ill-disciplined multitude fighting hand to hand can offer effectually neither injury nor "resistance." On the other hand, it is true, to use the words of Malcolm, that "Hindustan could never have been subdued but by the help of her own children."[2] At first it was Nizam against Arcot, and Arcot against Nizam; then Mahratta against Moslem, and Affghan against Hindu. Nor should it be forgotten that to the early conviction of the amazing odds which European arms and discipline secured, much of the anxiety of the native princes to engage their assistance must be traced.

When peace was signed in 1754, the first article of the treaty bound the Companies of both nations "to renounce for ever all Indian government and dignity, and to interfere no more in the differences that might arise between the princes of the country."[3] Chunda Sahib was dead, and Mohammed Ali, the friend of the English, was acknowledged Nawab of the Carnatic. By way of assuring the unambitious equality of the rival colonies, the French consented to relinquish four valuable districts of which in the course of the war they had acquired possession. But hardly was the ink of this compact dry, when Mohammed Ali

---

[1] Memoirs of Clive, vol. i. Introduction.
[2] Political History of Central India, by Sir John Malcolm.
[3] Mill, book VI. chap. ii.

tempted the servants of the English Company with half the spoil which might be won, if they would help him against certain feudatories, whom he represented as owing him large arrears of tribute. The promise of booty dazzled them, and they agreed. The French expostulated and appealed to the terms of the treaty, and to their surrender of the four districts as a pledge of their desire of peace; but all in vain. They were driven once more to arms. But Dupleix was no longer at the head of their affairs, and the only officer of ability they possessed at the time in that quarter of the world, was engaged in maintaining a perilous position in the Deccan. Their affairs grew desperate, and would have been lost without further struggle, had not events still more important suddenly called the attention of their opponents to another and more memorable scene.

Azîm-shâh, son of the Emperor, filled for a season the post of Soubahdar of Bengal. After him it was occupied successively by Sujah Khan and Seraffrez, his adopted son. Aliverdy Khan, one of the Omrah of Sujah's court, had for his ability been appointed Naib of Behar, and eventually he rose in 1739 to the dignity of Soubahdar. His personal qualities were such, that though inexorably firm as a ruler, the hand of resentment was never uplifted against him. His government for eighteen years was one of prosperity and peace. He quelled the insubordination of lesser chiefs, and acquired a reputation for wisdom and humanity greater than most of his contemporaries. While the Company kept to their proper business as traders, he steadily befriended them, protecting their rights, and extending their privileges; but he brooked no disregard of his authority, and permitted no exaction or ill-usage of his people to go unredressed.

In 1749, the merchandise of certain Armenian and

Hindu traders had been seized by the King's ships in the Indian Sea, on the real or alleged ground that it belonged to the French, with whom we were then at war. Complaint was made to the Nawab, who thereupon wrote to Fort William a peremptory demand for restitution. "These merchants were the kingdom's benefactors. Their imports and exports were an advantage to all, and their complaints were so grievous, that he could not forbear any longer giving ear to them. As the Company were not permitted to commit piracies, he wrote them that, upon receipt of this, they should deliver up all the merchants' goods and effects to them, as also what appertained to him, otherwise they might be assured of due chastisement, in such manner as they least expected." The Nawab appeared to be terribly in earnest; for we find the Company's agents recommending the gift of a fine Arab horse to his Highness, and nuzzurs to his courtiers, to "keep him in temper." The President at Calcutta tried to cajole the Armenians into signing a paper expressive of satisfaction with the Company's procedure, under threat of expulsion from the settlement if they did not comply; but this they stoutly refused to do; and Aliverdy having seized the English Factory at Cosimbuzar, the dispute was only settled, after much negotiation, by the payment as damage of twelve lacs of rupees. He had other differences with the Company; but regarding them as valuable customers, with whom it was not for his interest absolutely to quarrel, he took care never to press matters to extremity; and during his reign their opulence increased, though they had encroached but little beyond the narrow confines allotted them at the beginning of the century.

According to the custom of adoption, Aliverdy, being childless, designated his nephew, Suraja Dowla, as his heir;

and the court of Delhi, grateful for long and faithful services, agreed to recognise him as the future Soubahdar. A despatch to the Court of Directors, September 18, 1752, informs them that Suraja had been waited on at Hooghly by the French, Dutch, and English Governors—the last of whom he had received with especial courtesy and distinction. The usual presents were made, and the Governor and his coadjutors returned from the interview exceedingly well satisfied. They wrote, " We flatter ourselves that the expense we have been at on this occasion has procured you great favour, and will be the means of your honours' business being conducted without any interruption from the Government for some time to come." [1]

Although not born in the land, these wise men of the East were glad to bring their gifts of gold; nor was the frankincense of flattery forgotten. Condescending to particulars, they have set down the cost of these propitiatory offerings at 15,560 rupees (£1556) in ready money alone. [2] Their anticipations of future favour were, however, doomed to disappointment. The young Prince, though educated, it is said, with especial care by his uncle, inherited few of his high qualities; and on his accession to the Nizamut in April 1756, he was thrown without experience into circumstances that might have tried a judgment more mature. He has been accused of innumerable vices, and it is probable he had his share. But it is somewhat remarkable that his enemies, who had an interest, if ever men had such, in establishing their eager accusations, failed to make out the enormities which their invectives lead us to anticipate. Whatever may have been the defects of his disposition or understanding, the sudden height of power to which he

---

[1] Despatch to Court, September 18, 1752, par. 3.
[2] Long's Indian Records, vol. i. p. 34.

found himself raised, the hoarded wealth of which he became master, and the homage paid to him as sovereign of a great and populous domain, were little calculated to teach him patience, caution, or forbearance in the exercise of authority: and he had abundant need of them. The Company possessed several prosperous factories at Calcutta, Cosimbuzar, and other places; and the French had settlements also at Hooghly and Chandernagore. Just then the prospects of the former were by no means hopeful. The new Nawab was jealous of their position, and the French were about making a vigorous effort to attack their rivals in Asia. An expedition was known to be preparing at L'Orient for that purpose. The force at Calcutta was small, recruiting in England difficult,[1] and the long expensive voyage made it impossible to reinforce the garrison to any important extent. On December 29, 1756, we find the Directors writing out, "We must recommend it to you in the strongest manner, to be as well on your guard as the nature and circumstances of your Presidency will permit, to defend our estate in Bengal; and in particular, that you will do all in your power to engage the Nawab to give you his protection, as the only and most effectual measure for the security of the settlement and property." But ere these instructions arrived, the affairs of the Company had fallen from bad to worse. Suraja Dowla was not begotten in the likeness of his wise predecessor. The activity then being shown in fortifying Calcutta aroused his suspicions, which the explanation that they were intended to keep out the French did not allay. In the midst of this distrust, an officer of rank, who had been detected in malversation, sought and found protection at the English town. Suraja demanded the extradition of the fugitive; the Governor not only re-

[1] Letters from the Directors.

fused, but treated his envoy with open contumely. Incensed at this demeanour, he declared he would consider perseverance in such defiance of his power as a declaration of hostilities. The Calcutta Council persisted, and without further warning the Nawab took the field with several thousand troops on the 30th May, and seized the factory at Cosimbuzar. He does not seem on this occasion to have incurred the reproach of wanton bloodshed. Mr Watts, Mr Warren Hastings, and the rest of the Company's officers, were detained as prisoners, but were otherwise well treated.

The panic caused by this event at Calcutta is described as being great. The garrison numbered but two hundred regulars, and the militia, though more numerous, were imperfectly armed, worse trained, and without competent commanders. A resolute and guiding spirit was indeed their greatest want. The Council, with one exception, slunk away on board ship to a safe distance from the place they were impotent to save, and thus made confusion worse confounded. Mr Holwell, who alone bravely remained, made a futile effort at organising a defence, but no one seconded his efforts; and the troops, getting possession of the liquor stores, became drunk and unmanageable. He therefore threw a letter of capitulation over the ramparts, and on the 20th June 1756 Fort William was surrendered without a blow. The fallen Councillor and his friends were taken bound into the presence of the Nawab. With a humanity that ill accords with the ferocity imputed to him, he ordered their bonds to be removed, and pledged his word as a soldier for their personal safety. The catastrophe which followed in a few hours, if not the result of accident, does not clearly connect itself with him as its deliberate author. At night, when it became necessary to secure Mr Holwell and the other prisoners, 146 in all, no place was, or was said to be, available but the garrison prison, or "Black Hole," a cell only eighteen feet square, and ventilated by two small windows securely barred. Into this dungeon the 146 victims were thrust to pass the hours of a tropical night. Tears, entreaties, persuasions, bribes, could not move the pitiless sentries. In the morning, only twenty-three emerged from the cell, survivors of the suffering of that memorable night. One hundred and twenty-three victims perished by the stupid cruelty of an unauthorised prison-guard: a sad sum of human misery not to be forgotten—of inhuman violence not to be extenuated. But if history is anything better than an old wife's tale, it must keep accounts by double entry, and keep them fairly. Men were still living at the time who could remember how, by the orders of a Secretary of State, the unsuspecting inhabitants of a peaceful glen in Argyleshire were beguiled into admitting a party of king's troops into their dwellings, and were by them, at dead of night, butchered in cold blood, and their wives and little ones flung out to perish in the snow. History does not record that any inquisition for blood was made, or that any of the princes, lords, and gentlemen who, before and after the fact, were accessories thereto, were called upon to suffer for the same. Precedent will not justify crime; but when excuse is sought for invasion, conquest, and the permanent disfranchisement of a people, in one rash and ruthless act, perpetrated without premeditation or authority, the historian, if he be a true and faithful witness, will turn back a leaf or two, and say, "Let those that are without sin amongst you cast the first stone." The melancholy fate of these persons may be justly deplored; but it is neither just to distort or misrepresent facts, as too frequently has been done. There is no evidence that the Soubahdar knew of this transaction until it was past and irremediable; and there is direct testimony that no indignity or hurt was either before or after suffered by any of the prisoners at Calcutta or Cosimbuzar. Why, if he desired the death of these helpless individuals, should the Nawab have suffered three-and-twenty of them to go free to circulate the appalling tale? The hands are unfortunately not clean that bring the revolting charge. They who subsequently were at such pains to raise an uproar of pity, were those by whose disgraceful abandonment the sufferers were exposed to their doom; and we shall presently see how quickly they could forgive, when a selfish purpose was to be gained, the calamity for which they were in some degree answerable.

Tidings of the fate of Calcutta rapidly reached Madras, and for the moment diverted all thoughts from Carnatic affairs. A force of 900 Europeans and 1500 sepoys under Colonel Clive, with five of his Majesty's ships under Admiral Watson, was collected for the recapture of the Bengal settlement. They arrived in the Hooghly on the 20th December, and found the fugitive members of Council and a few others at Fulta, a small town a few miles from Calcutta. The few remaining days of the year were occupied in the capture of a fort, in establishing a base of operations, and concerting measures for the assault on Calcutta, which was retaken on the 2d January 1757. After further defeats in the open field, finding the military prowess of the Company's troops under Clive too much for him, Suraja Dowla was glad to make peace. He agreed to restore to the Company all their privileges of trade, to make compensation for the losses sustained by his occupation of Calcutta, and to offer no impediment to the completion of the ramparts. The treaty was signed on 9th February 1757, as Clive wrote to the Directors, on "honourable and advantageous terms." In the same month an offensive alliance was ratified; Mr Drake and the runaway Council were restored to their posts; and, being well paid for the damage done to their property in the siege, were comforted. Clive's account of these gentlemen is amusing. Writing confidentially to the Governor of Madras, he bids him be on his guard "against anything they say, for they are bad subjects, and rotten at heart. Their conduct at Calcutta finds no excuse, even among themselves, and the riches of Peru would not induce him to dwell amongst them."[1] Ah, Clive! don't be too virtuous. The riches of Peru (being at the other side of the world) might not tempt thee, but think of the riches of Bengal—here under thy hand, with nobody looking at thee, except these comrades of thine—"rotten at heart." Might not these rotten hearts induce thee to stay thy departure, and closer intimacy blunt thy chivalrous contempt of them? What a pity we made peace so soon! True, the Soubahdar is our ally now; he has been prompt to fulfil every promise; he is saluted in all letters, speeches, and addresses as "our friend." What of all this, if we can find some new excuse for getting at his treasures,—said to be innumerable? We have been paid, to be sure, and shaken hands of amity. But then, is he not very rich?—that is to say, is he not a tyrant? Ought we not to take humane and philanthropic counsel together on the matter? And all the rotten-at-heart responded—Yea.

When Suraja Dowla's attack on Calcutta was impending, though France and England were then at war, the Council, in their terror, applied for succour to the French as well as to the Dutch, with whom we were at peace. The latter bluntly declined. The former agreed, if the Company

[1] Memoirs of Clive, vol. i. chap. ii.

would exchange the settlement of Calcutta for theirs at Chandernagore. The Council had no powers to entertain such a proposition, and help at such a price was declined; but though an alliance on the part of the French with the Soubahdar at this juncture would have been highly embarrassing, and might have gained for them material advantages, they generously declined to aid in exterminating their old competitors. They also wished to enter into a treaty of neutrality with the Company, and articles of agreement were actually drawn up to that effect. But Admiral Watson, in command of the British naval squadron, refused to be bound by any such agreement. Fearing that the chagrin of the French at the failure of the treaty would lead them to join the Nawab, Clive recommended the ruthless alternative of surprising and destroying the settlement of Chandernagore. Admiral Watson did not quite relish the proceeding, and at first actually opposed it.

Clive wrote the Council on the 4th March 1757 :—[1]

"The immediate attack of Chandernagore becomes in my opinion absolutely necessary, if the neutrality be refused. Do but reflect, gentlemen, what will be the opinion of the world of these our late proceedings. Did we not, in consequence of a letter received from the Governor and Council of Chandernagore, making offers of a neutrality within the Ganges, in a manner accede to it by desiring they would send deputies, and that we would gladly come into such neutrality with them? and have we not since their arrival drawn out articles that were satisfactory to both parties, and agreed that each article should be reciprocally signed, sealed, and sworn to? What will the Nawab think? After the promises made him on our side, and after his consenting

---

[1] Unpublished Records of the Indian Government, by the Rev. J. Long, vol. i. p. 88.

to guarantee this neutrality, he and all the world will certainly think that we are men of a trifling, insignificant disposition, or that we are men without principles. You may be assured the instant the French find their offers of neutrality refused, they will immediately assist the Nawab in all his designs against us, if he has the least intentions of not complying with the late articles of peace. It may then be too late to wish Mr Watson had been pleased to pay more attention to our representations. I must therefore request you will join with me in desiring Mr Watson a third time to ratify the neutrality in the manner agreed upon, and if he refuses, to desire he will attack Chandernagore by water immediately, as I am ready to do by land with the forces under my command." So, as the Admiral would not consent to an armed neutrality with our French neighbours in the East, the next best thing to do was to fall upon them suddenly and smite them hip and thigh. The Admiral agreed, and the return for French forbearance and desire for peace was to be their extirpation from their factory, and the demolition of their dwellings at Chandernagore. But the French were living peaceably in the Nawab's dominions, under the express guarantee of his protection; and it was necessary to obtain his sanction to this breach of the peace. On the 1st March, Mr Watts, the Resident at Moorshedabad, was directed to sound the Nawab on the subject. He justly refused to recognise the pretext that the expulsion of the French was necessary for the Company's safety in Bengal. Admiral Watson ingeniously suggested that they were bound by the treaty to aid one another. "You are going to Patna—you ask our assistance; let us take Chandernagore, and we will go with you even to Delhi if you will. But have we not sworn reciprocally that the friends and enemies of the one should be regarded as such by the other?

and will not God, the avenger of perjury, punish us if we do not fulfil our oaths?"[1] The Soubahdar had never contemplated such an interpretation of the compact when he signed it, and he refused to aid or countenance the deceit. Cajolery failing, threats were tried. On the 7th March, the Admiral wrote that "he had sent for more troops; and he would kindle such a flame in the country as all the waters in the Ganges should not extinguish."[2]

Unwilling so soon again to hazard the chances of war, Suraja yielded so far as to say that he would not interfere in any measures the English might take "which were strictly indispensable to their safety." This was deemed sufficient leave, and Chandernagore was taken and sacked, only a few indigent widows' houses being left standing. The Nawab was greatly incensed, and made little secret of his sympathy with the French. He gave the fugitives from Chandernagore an asylum, corresponded with the French commanders, calling the Company "the disturbers of his country," and expressing himself unable to "write about their perfidy."[3] That there was no just ground of complaint against him, is evident from the confidential letters of Clive, who said he "had performed almost every article of the treaty; he had paid Mr Watts three lacs of rupees (£30,000); he had delivered up all the factories, with the money and goods taken in them, and little or nothing was wanting."[4] To the Durbar of Moorshedabad very different language was addressed. Clive, who was now the dominant spirit in the Calcutta Council, was bent on acquisition of territory and political power; his appetite for conquest was whetted, not satisfied, and the

---
[1] Memoirs of Clive, vol. i. chap. iv.   [2] Ibid.
[3] Intercepted Letters, *vide* Long's Records, vol. i. pp. 110, 111.
[4] Memoirs of Clive, vol. i. chap. ii.

Nawab was to be goaded into hostilities. The destruction of the other French factories was demanded. Suraja's answer was an indignant refusal, accompanied with vehement reproaches. Next day his resolution wavered, and he recalled the messenger with expressions of regret. Again he refused, and again consented. The dark shadows of his fate began to haunt him. He believed he was betrayed, and that the Company would be satisfied with nothing short of his ruin. Yet, urgent and natural as these misgivings were, he would have started had one whispered in his ear that they were literally and speedily to be realised. It was clear that Suraja Dowla would be no pliant partner in schemes for the aggrandisement of the Company. Early in April, therefore, Clive proposed to the President and Council of Calcutta that they should enter into a secret engagement with certain disaffected courtiers at Moorshedabad for the purpose of hurling their sworn ally from the musnud of Bengal.

Ungifted with the stability of mind and administrative talents of his predecessor, Suraja's reign had not been one to please his people. Discontent was widespread, and at Moorshedabad he was surrounded by false friends and dissembling favourites. Like James II., his chief officers and nearest kinsfolk were ready to abandon him. Nor were there wanting features of resemblance in the means employed and methods used to compass revolution. Until assured of foreign aid, none were inclined to stir, but a comparatively small force would be joined by half the army, and the contemplated change might be effected without any real struggle. Many persons of distinction were engaged in the combination, at the head of which was the most influential member of the reigning family. Here it was the nephew who was to be set up—there the uncle. Mir Jaffir

Ali Khan had married the sister of the late Soubahdar. He was commander of the forces, and to him it was proposed that he should take the place of Nawab-Nazim of Bengal. When all was ripe for action, it was arranged that Clive should suddenly take the field, and that Mir Jaffir should draw off a large number of the Nawab's troops.[1] Meanwhile, it was necessary to lull the suspicions of him who was to be deposed; and Clive's letters written during the plot give evidence of the pains that were taken for this purpose, as well as of the diplomatic dexterity of the writer. In one epistle he talks of "the perfect harmony and friendship which subsisted" then between them;[2] and on the very eve of the crisis, lest the Soubahdar's fears should be inconveniently excited, he mentions that he wrote him a letter "which would calm his resentment." Resentment,—what for? Were there, then, wrongs to resent? The Council became uneasy as the correspondence was protracted, and on one occasion wrote to Clive beseeching him to employ confidential agents, and to commit nothing to paper; but he was not to be scared by the peril of exposure, and laughing at the fears of the "rotten at heart," he went his dauntless way. At length, on the 13th June, all the preparations were ready, the march on Moorshedabad was commenced, and Suraja, roused too late from his dream of doubt and indecision, advanced to meet his enemies. It had been arranged that Mir Jaffir should join the forces under his command with those of the Company at Cutwa; but on arriving at the rendezvous, Clive was perplexed to find only a letter from his confederate, promising to join him on the field of battle. The treacherous suspected treachery, and a council of war decided on retreat, fearing that their small force might be surrounded and entirely cut off; but Clive, though he at

---

[1] Mill, book IV. chap. iii. [2] Memoirs of Clive, vol. i. chap. v.

first wavered in his resolution, took counsel with himself, resolved to trust his ally, and to stake all on the chances of a battle. Pushing forward with his little army of 1000 Europeans and 2100 sepoys, he reached the village of Plassey a little after midnight, where he found the Nawab's army, numbering 50,000 foot, 18,000 horse, and 50 guns, securely posted behind intrenchments. The battle was begun soon after dawn of the 23d June by an attack on the part of the Nawab's troops, who thus left the shelter of their intrenchments; and it had not lasted long, before Mir Jaffir was observed moving off with a large body of horse. The critical moment had arrived, and Clive ordered an advance of his small but resolute corps. The ill-trained numbers of the Soubahdar, disheartened by the defection of their comrades, scattered in confusion, and he himself fled the field with 2000 men. At Moorshedabad, his fallen fortunes left him but few friends, and quitting the palace in the disguise of a fakir, accompanied by two servants, he endeavoured to reach the French, who were advancing to his aid. But he was discovered at Raje Muhl, taken back to the capital, and there put to death.

The prey had fallen; it remained to divide the skin. Clive, at the head of a select body-guard, entered Moorshedabad on the 25th June, and on the 29th, Mir Jaffir Ali Khan was duly installed as Nawab-Nazim of Bengal, Behar, and Orissa. The bill of costs presented by Clive and the Council for their assistance in his elevation was a heavy one: 1,280,000 rupees was demanded and actually paid to the members of Council for their personal share, of which Mr Drake and Colonel Clive received 280,000 rupees each, and Watts, Beecher, and Kilpatrick, 240,000 rupees each. Clive also took an additional present of £160,000 from the new Soubahdar. When, in later years, he was questioned before a committee of the House of Commons[1] touching this princely donation, he recalled the gem-crowned piles of gold which he had seen in the treasury of Moorshedabad, and swore he was astonished at his own moderation: and his biographer accepts this as a satisfactory proof that Clive was not influenced by sordid or mercenary motives. The settlement of so nice a question may be left to the metaphysicians. Less subtle intellects would deduce from the story, that civil war must have been a speculation worth pursuing when it yielded sums so handsome for promotion-money. Besides the twelve lacs of private spoil, the Company were to be paid 10,000,000 rupees; the European inhabitants of Calcutta, for damage sustained in the late occupation, 5,000,000 rupees; the Armenian residents, 2,000,000 rupees; and a further sum of 5,000,000 rupees was to be divided amongst the army and navy. The total amounted to £2,697,750 sterling; but the exchequer of Moorshedabad was wholly unequal to such demands, and after much wrangling, the amount of the compensations was subsequently reduced to one half, which was paid, all but five lacs, in specie and jewels.

The fitting climax of the drama yet remained. Associated with Mir Jaffir in the revolution were Omichund and Jugget Seit, two of the rich bankers who enjoyed so much favour and influence with the Governments of the East. The notoriety of their opulence, the habitual security in which they lived, and their great political power, is in itself a comprehensive refutation of the ignorant pretence that these Governments were the mere transient and capricious alternations of despotism. Credit is brittle ware at best, and needs all the care and shelter of what is esteemed the subtlest system of civilisation to preserve it unharmed;

[1] Evidence before Select Committee in 1772.

and banking is precisely that part of the credit system most susceptible of injury from the breath of violence, and most sure to perish at the very apprehension of arbitrary usage. The bankers of India could no more have accumulated their vast wealth, and maintained their importance in the State, had they not been exempt from the fear of outrage, than the exotics we have borrowed from their land, whose luxuriance we protect in houses of glass, could gain or preserve that luxuriance if exposed to the rude caprices of our fickle weather. The universal safety of Oriental bankers is still more instructive when we learn that their riches generally lay in securities of various kinds, which they held of men of every class, from the trader to the prince. Without their aid, no Government ventured to undertake permanent or expensive schemes. Their friendship was courted by the Minister, and purchased by favours from the throne. They had better means of intelligence than any other men; they were the best of political agents, and the least easily deceived. Hence, the wish of all the confederates against Suraja Dowla to engage Jugget Seit, who carried on business at Moorshedabad, and Omichund, whose house was at Calcutta, as participators in their design. The avarice of Omichund was keenly excited. He entered readily into the whole intrigue, and soon gained knowledge which rendered him indispensable. He had the ear of the Soubahdar at all times, and felt that, having both sides in his power, he could exact from each his own terms. Under the threat of betrayal, he claimed an immense sum as his share of the spoil, and peremptorily demanded that a clause guaranteeing him should be inserted in the treaty between Mir Jaffir and the Company. Omichund was master of the situation, and the Council felt there was no alternative but compliance. Clive, fertile in expedients, came to the rescue. Two treaties were drawn up—one on white paper, the other on red. One contained the grant to Omichund, in the other it was omitted. Both papers were signed by all the parties except Admiral Watson, who declined putting his signature to the cheat. The omission would have raised suspicion, and Clive made all safe by forging Watson's name. The unsuspecting Hindoo was satisfied; but when the time came for settling accounts among the conspirators, Clive bade an interpreter inform the old man of the trick of which he had been the dupe—that the treaty containing his name was a sham, and that having asked too much, he was to have nothing. Stunned at this ruin of his golden dreams, Omichund fell to the ground insensible. He slowly recovered, but remained for the rest of his days an idiot.

When the news of the retaking of Calcutta and the conclusion of peace reached England, public satisfaction was naturally great. But when the Court of Directors and the Ministry announced the subsequent events, exultation and rejoicing knew no bounds. The English public were kept long in ignorance of the truth; they were dazzled by the glittering trophies of acquisition. It were well for their own memory, and for the character of the nation thus deceived, if the court of George II. or the East India Company could have pretended that they were equally uninformed.

CHAPTER IV.

PLUNDERFUL TIMES.

1757—1764.

" Then was seen what we believe to be the most frightful of all spectacles, the strength of civilisation without its mercy. To all other despotisms there is a check, imperfect indeed, and liable to gross abuse ; but still sufficient to preserve society from the last extreme of misery. A time comes when the evils of submission are obviously greater than those of resistance, when fear itself begets a sort of courage, when a convulsive burst of popular rage warns tyrants not to presume too far on the patience of mankind. But against misgovernment such as then afflicted Bengal, it was impossible to struggle. The superior intelligence and energy of the dominant class made their power irresistible. A war of Bengalees against Englishmen was like a war of sheep against wolves." —LORD MACAULAY.[1]

THE terms on which Mir Jaffir obtained the co-operation of the Company were not allowed to remain in the insecure form of spoken promises ; they were embodied in a solemn treaty of thirteen articles, dated June 1757 ; sworn to by "God and the Prophet" on one side, and declared on the Holy Gospels and before God, on the other. Colonel Clive, Admiral Watson, Governor Drake, and Mr Watts, were the signataries on behalf of the Company, whom they bound to "assist Mir Jaffir Khan Behander with all their force to obtain the Soubahship of the provinces of Bengal, Behar, and Orissa, and further to assist him to the utmost against all his enemies whatever, as soon as called upon to that end." On his part, the Nawab agreed to an offensive

[1] Historical Essays—Warren Hastings, vol. iii.

and defensive alliance with the Company; to possess them of all the effects and factories belonging to the French, whom he was not to permit again to settle in his Soubahdary; to pay the pecuniary compensation already mentioned; to give them several tracts of land within, and 600 yards extent beyond, the ditch of Calcutta; to give them the zemindary or leasehold of revenue of all land to the south of Calcutta; to maintain their troops when in his service; and not to erect fortifications below the Hooghly. But the fine gold of this agreement soon grew dim. Mir Jaffir had the Company's friendship while he could pay for it; but he soon found that the glove of a friend may cover the mailed hand of a foe. India, at its best, was not the mine of fabulous wealth that covetous Europeans fondly imagined. Foreign invasion and domestic strife had seriously crippled the industrial resources of the country, and hence the payments guaranteed by the treaty fell into arrear. Mir Jaffir was a soldier, not a financier, and he knew not how to meet importunate demands save by fresh exactions from an overburdened people. His troops were mutinous for pay, disquietude was general, and the whole machinery of government was out of gear. Yet the importunities of the Council of Calcutta were unremitting, and their demeanour became such at last as to extort bitter reproaches from the impoverished Prince, whom they professed to treat as the ruler of Bengal. On a threatened invasion by the Shahzada, heir-apparent of the Great Mogul, they furnished, at the Nawab's request, military succour, in accordance with the terms of the alliance, and the Vizier of Oude was repulsed with great loss by Colonel Forde, Clive's favourite lieutenant. These events tended still further to confirm the prestige of British prowess in the eyes of the natives, and to exalt still higher in their own esteem the handful of intrepid adventurers who had broken in the ivory doors of power. For his services in this campaign Clive was created an Omrah of the viceregal court. By his own account of the transaction, it appears that he demanded an estate to support his new dignity, and the Soubahdar conferred on him a jaghire valued at £27,000 a year.

Meanwhile, on the Coromandel coast, fortune had veered round. Lally, a man of versatile genius and romantic courage, had undertaken to retrieve the losses of the French, and for a time he seemed likely to keep his word. Fort St David surrendered, and Madras was besieged, until relieved by Admiral Pocock, after the battle of Condore, in which the French were signally defeated. Forde then laid siege to Masulipatam, which was taken April 7, 1759, with much booty. Eventually, with a territory extending eighty miles along the coast, and twenty in the interior, it was retained as a permanent possession, with the acquiescence of the Nizam.

If Mir Jaffir had to endure the mortification of appearing, in the sight of his subjects, too much indebted to his foreign allies for military support, and with having mortgaged for it too deeply the immediate revenues of his country, he might at least console himself with the belief that his own pre-eminence and that of his family were secure. He could hardly have believed that already those in whom he trusted, not wisely but too well, were privily planning how he might be superseded, and his lineal descendants set aside. There is a letter from Clive to Mr Pitt, then First Minister, bearing the date of 7th January 1759,[1] wherein he depicts the weakness of the Nawab's administration; hints that they could easily find a pretence for breaking with him; describes his son, Meeran, as so

---

[1] Memoirs of Clive, vol. ii. chap. x.

inimical to the English "that it would be unsafe trusting him with the succession; and that 2000 Europeans would enable the Company to take the sovereignty upon themselves." He then combats the notion of the project being too vast for execution; urges its importance as being the groundwork for still further acquisitions; and finally appeals to the prospect which the possession of so rich and populous a kingdom would afford of diminishing the national debt. This notable epistle was delivered by Mr Walsh, Clive's private secretary; and that gentleman gives an account of the Minister's observations on the subject, in an official interview. He seemed averse to the enterprise being undertaken in the name of the Crown, lest the objection should arise of the King being likely to obtain thereby an income independent of Parliament. It is probable, moreover, that he discerned the jealousy with which the aristocracy of birth would regard any scheme endangering the exclusiveness of that political ascendancy which they had enjoyed for the threescore years and ten that had elapsed since the Revolution. How easily their jealousy of rival wealth, derived from foreign ventures and possessions was aroused, when fortunes acquired in Asia began to attract notice by emulous display and the purchase of parliamentary influence, was not long afterwards seen.

Clive quitted India in February 1760, to enjoy at home the rest and renown he had earned by his marvellous exploits. The Directors voted him a diamond-hilted sword. George III. created him an Irish peer, and expressed the highest admiration of his conduct and achievements; and Mr Pitt, in his place in Parliament, pronounced upon him one of his most elaborate eulogies. Possessed of an income of £40,000 a year, he expended no little portion of his suddenly acquired wealth in the purchase of rotten boroughs, and at the head of his nominees, in 1761, he entered the House of Commons.

He had left behind him as President at Calcutta his friend and confidant, but feeble imitator in the ways of aggressive rule, Mr Vansittart. Under this gentleman's guidance the Council concerted a *coup d'état* for the purpose of deposing the Nawab from the active authority of government, which they designed to put into the hands of his son-in-law, Mir Kasim. Access to the Prince at Moorshedabad was easy and unquestioned, and the visit of the President, attended by a numerous body of troops, excited no surprise. While the escort surrounded the palace to cut off aid or exit, the aged Soubahdar was formally requested to relinquish the reins of administration in favour of his younger and more pliant relative, while retaining the title and income of Nawab. Bewildered by this unexpected blow, and bereft of all means of resistance, Mir Jaffir, it was thought, would have quietly succumbed. But the old man did not forget his dignity. He scornfully repelled the proposal, bitterly denounced the treachery with which he had been treated; and, without hesitation, chose in preference to quit his capital and retire to a private residence at Calcutta, rather than submit to play a nominal part in the Government where he had hitherto been supreme. Addressing the President, he said, "You have thought proper to break your engagements. I would not mine. Had I such designs, I could have raised twenty thousand men, and fought you. My son Meeran forewarned me of all this. Send me either to Lord Clive, or let me go to Mecca; if not, let me go to Calcutta, for I will not stay in this place." His intimacy with Clive led him to imagine that he would do him justice, and he clung to this delusion to the last, leaving him in his will a sum of £60,000.

These shameless proceedings were not, indeed, unanimously approved of in the Council. A minority warmly objected, and those who persisted deemed it necessary to frame some plausible excuse. On November 10, 1760, a memorial, drawn up by Mr Holwell, set forth "the causes of the late change in the Soubahship." In this document the Nawab is charged with almost every enormity, but particularly with wanton taking of life without justifiable cause. Eight persons of distinction are specially mentioned, and over seventy others are stated to have been put to death by his capricious orders. Six years later, and when Mir Jaffir was no more, the Council admit they had ascertained all this to be fabrication. Addressing the Directors on 30th September 1766, they say, "In justice to the memory of the late Nawab Mir Jaffir, we think it incumbent on us to acquaint you that the horrible massacres wherewith he is charged by Mr Holwell in his address to the proprietors of East India stock, are cruel aspersions on the character of the Prince, which have not the least foundation in truth. The several persons there affirmed, and who were generally thought to have been murdered by his order, are all now living except two, who were put to death without the Nawab's consent or knowledge; and it is with additional satisfaction we can assure you, that they are lately released from confinement by the present Soubahdar, which fully evinces the entire confidence he reposes in the Company's protection against all attacks on his Government."

The iniquity of this transaction finds few apologists even among those who have taken upon themselves to dress and to enamel Oriental deeds for European view. The treaty with Mir Jaffir still subsisted; and measured by the elastic rules of that convenient code of public morality which conquerors in all ages have striven to pass off under the guise of international law, there was no pretence for such behaviour. He was the sworn and blood-knit ally of the Company; and if ever men were bound by decency to maintain at least the forms of good faith, the Governor and Council of Calcutta were so bound. Yet, being so, for the sum of £200,000, to them privately paid, and for the cession of three rich and populous provinces, they sold their too confiding friend and ally. The terms of their service to Mir Kasim were formally drafted in a treaty, which, as far as the advantage he derived from it, was only to be for life; but to the Company was surrendered wholly and for ever the fertile districts of Burdwan, Midnapore, and Chittagong. For their dexterity in cozening Mir Jaffir he paid Mr Vansittart £58,000, Mr Holwell £30,937, Mr Sumner £28,000, General Caillaud £22,916, and proportionately smaller sums to other members of the Council.

The necessary firman of investiture was obtained from Delhi, a detailed account of the revolution was transmitted to the Directors and Government in England, and the Nawab-Regent entered upon the exercise of his functions. He quickly displayed a capacity for government which bid fair to reconcile the people to his authority, to restore the country to health and vigour, and, if it were possible, to vindicate his share in the acts whereby he had been raised to power. By a rigorous economy of the public revenues, he was able to satisfy the arrears long due to the army, and to increase its efficiency. He rapidly acquitted the Company's claims. He made himself master of the wants and weaknesses of his subjects, and took prompt measures for the redress of their grievances. It was not long before his energy in this direction brought him into collision with his allies. At an early period of their settlement in Bengal, the Company had obtained a firman exempting them from customs, dues, and the payment of tolls along the roads and navigable rivers, on the transit of their goods. The dustuck (certificate) of the heads of their factories had the virtue of an imperial permit. They had also established the vicious custom of paying their servants in the East a nominal and insufficient salary, with the liberty of engaging in private trade. The liberty thus accorded gradually grew into a license to neglect the Company's trade on the one hand, and to oppress the natives on the other. An official free pass was made to cover the goods of private individuals all over the country. When the toll-collectors questioned the validity of the dustuck, and stopped the goods, as they were rightfully entitled to do, they were arrested, imprisoned, loaded with fetters, and even beaten. The Company's servants, for their own private profit, were thus getting into their hands the whole trade of the country, and were practically drying up one of the sources of public revenue. Every subordinate English agent assumed the airs and profited by the prestige of participation in the joint-stock of power. Vast fortunes were accumulated rapidly, none knew how, for there were none whose business it was to inquire. Individualised spoliation ran loose, and only came home to rest when weary of the burthen of booty, or spent with predatory toil. Not content with the advantage wrung from this injustice, they went even further, and turned general dealers inland, which trade they also exercised free of duty. In every village and market they undersold the native shopkeeper in rice, paddy, fish, straw, bamboos, and other commodities. They compelled the natives to buy and sell at their own price, and enforced their will with personal violence. The harassed and dismayed inhabitants seldom ventured to resist. Grievous complaints of these enormities reached Mir Kasim from all quarters, and he presented the strongest remonstrances against them to the Council.[1] Mr Ellis, the Resident at Patna, was among the most prominent in the violation of fiscal authority, and most of the Council were too much implicated to be the willing authors of a reformation. They affected to doubt or deny the existence of the injury, and declared the Nawab's remonstrances to be an evidence of ingratitude which ought to be reproved. When he offered to agree to a transit duty of 9 per cent., though it was much less than that paid by the natives, they met him with a reluctant offer to pay $2\frac{1}{2}$ per cent. on salt alone. At last the negotiations ended in a compromise, and a treaty was signed in December 1762, binding the Company to pay a small fixed duty on their internal trade. But the majority of the Council were jealous of the popularity and success of the Regent. He would not wink at their frauds or suffer their violence, and it was necessary, therefore, to pick a quarrel with him; and this they did by publicly annulling the treaty, declaring that the President had no authority to sign it. Indignant at being thus trifled with, the Nawab issued a decree abolishing all internal duties, thus putting all classes in the country on an equal footing. The Council demanded its revocation, and preparations for hostilities were made on both sides. Some boats containing arms were stopped by Mir Kasim's orders; they were afterwards released, yet this was made the pretext for the plunder of Patna by a European force. But reinforcements arriving, the native Governor turned the scales on the following day, and compelled the aggressors to capitulate, Mr Ellis, the obnoxious Resident, being of the number. The imprisonment of every Englishman in the province

[1] Mill, book IV. chap. v.

was also ordered; but only in the case of Mr Amyatt, who had been acting as mediator between the two Governments, was any life sacrificed; and his death was occasioned by the indiscretion of his escort, who drew upon themselves a volley by which he was killed.

Though Mir Kasim had been at some pains to organise and equip his army after the European pattern, victory did not declare in his favour. Moorshedabad was taken on 19th June, and he was again defeated in a general engagement at Geriah, on the 2d August, after such a resistance as the invaders had not encountered before in any struggle with native troops. He made another stand at the pass of Oodwa, and for a whole month defended it with judgment and resolution. Mongheer, which he had made his capital, fell in October; and now, finding his resources exhausted and fortune against him, in a paroxysm of rage and despair he ordered the execution of Mr Ellis and the prisoners from Patna, to whose conduct he mainly ascribed his downfall. He then took refuge for some time in Oude, and died at Delhi in 1777, in obscurity and indigence. When the Company found that Mir Kasim would not make his country's interests subservient to theirs, they entered into negotiations with Mir Jaffir for his resuming active authority; and, on the 10th July 1763, a new treaty was signed, by which the Company engaged to reinstate him in the full exercise of all the executive powers, rights, and functions, of Soubahdar. On his part, Mir Jaffir ratified the previous treaty of 1757; granted afresh and confirmed to the Company the chucklas (districts) of Burdwan, Midnapore, and Chittagong, for defraying the expenses of their troops; "confirmed their privilege of trading free from all duties, taxes, and impositions, except in the article of salt, on which 2½ per cent. was to be levied on the Hooghly market-price;"

gave them half the saltpetre from Purnea, and allowed no others to make purchases of that article; and gave them half the chunam (lime) prepared in the district of Sylhet for five years. He agreed to "maintain 12,000 horse and 12,000 foot in the three provinces, and besides which, the Company's troops were to attend him whenever they were wanted;" to receive, wherever he should fix his court, a Resident or political agent, and to appoint a like official on his part at Calcutta; to reverse and annul the free-trade edict of Mir Kasim, the differential tolls and duties to be levied on the natives as before; to "give thirty lacs for defraying the expenses of the war" with the superseded Regent; to reimburse losses incurred by private individuals, either in money or by assignments of land; and not to "allow the French to erect fortifications, maintain forces, hold lands, zemindaries, &c.; but to make them pay and carry on trade" as formerly. Experience had taught the aged Prince that the pledges and promises of his allies were not trustworthy, and he sought to obtain some higher guarantee for the fulfilment of these new covenants than that afforded by the signatures of the ever-changing Council at Calcutta. The terms of his demand, appended to the treaty, and accepted by all the members of the Council, are worthy of historic note. There they stand full to the brim with reproach of broken faith.

"I now make this request, that you will write in a proper manner to the Company, and also to the King of England, the particulars of our friendship and union; and procure for me writings and encouragement, that my mind may be assured from that quarter that no breach may ever happen between me and the English, and that every Governor, Councillor, and chiefs of the English that are here, or may hereafter come, may be well disposed and attached to me."

He then proceeds to enumerate many ways in which mutual forbearance and respect by subordinates on each side ought to be enjoined and enforced. It has never been even pretended that, by him or his successors, any attempt was made to depart from the stipulations of this treaty; yet, by degrees, one after another of its covenants have been infringed and frittered away by the stronger party, to the detriment of the weaker, until at last it has been coolly proposed, in a suppressed recommendation by a Secretary of State, that the whole substance and spirit of this fundamental treaty should be set at nought, and that the very existence of a Soubahdar of Bengal, from whom we were glad in 1763 to accept grants of land and privileges, should, after the lifetime of the present Prince, on grounds of financial expediency be publicly denied.

Suja-ul-Dowla, the Vizier of Oude, warmly espoused the cause of the fugitive Regent, and to threats of the Company's hostility returned a dignified rebuke of their ill-concealed designs. "To what," he wrote, " can all these wrong proceedings be attributed, but to an absolute disregard of the court (of Delhi), and to a wicked design of seizing the country yourselves. If these disturbances have arisen from your own improper devices, deviate from such improper behaviour in future ; interfere not in the affairs of government; withdraw your people from every part, and send them to their own country ; carry on the Company's trade as formerly, and confine yourselves to your own commercial affairs." Shah Alum also began to be alarmed at the state of affairs in Bengal, and with the Vizier he entered the province at the head of a powerful force in 1764.

For some months desultory skirmishes greatly harassed the European army, but a pitched battle was finally fought at Buxar, in which they were victorious. The Vizier sued for peace, which the Company would only grant on condition of Mir Kasim's expulsion from Oude; the Padishah opened separate communications with the victors, with whom he made his own terms. Ultimately peace was concluded by the cession of the districts of Allahabad and Korah by the Vizier to the Padishah; and while the negotiations lingered, in January 1765, Mir Jaffir died, and was succeeded by his son, Nudjum-ul-Dowla.

CHAPTER V.

THE DEWANNY.

1765.

" In consideration of the services of the English Company, we have granted them the Dewanny of the provinces of Bengal, Behar, and Orissa, as an ultumgau (free gift). It is requisite that the said Company engage to be security for the sum of twenty-six lacs a year for our royal revenue, which sum has been appointed from the Nawab Nudjum-ul-Dowla Behauder; and as the Company are obliged to keep up a large army for Bengal, we have granted them whatsoever may remain out of the revenue, after remitting the sum of twenty-six lacs, and providing for the expenses of the Nizamut."
—FIRMAN OF SHAH ALUM.[1]

WHEN the partakers in the first harvest of spoil returned to England, laden with unlooked for riches, wonder, curiosity, envy, and emulation filled the minds of men. Dreams of speculation and adventure, such as had quickened the popular pulse after Raleigh's voyage of discovery, or when the city had been bewitched by the golden promises of Law, once more occupied the thoughts of youth and age, of the well-to-do and the runagate. Clive was looked upon as another Cortez, who had, for the benefit of his countrymen, broken into a distant storehouse of exhaustless wealth. The way was opened for the attainment of treasure without toil, and the enjoyment of power without the waste of years in apprenticeship. Who would not go

[1] Firman of Gift of Dewanny to the Company, 12th August 1765.

for a share in the Indian lottery? The scene was distant, the passage long, the climate tropical, and the manners of the natives strange. But every wastrel who had courage left—every bankrupt whose credit was run out,—every reckless soldier who had neither money or interest to secure promotion,—every daring seaman who was impatient of the rough nights and scant wages of winter voyages in the German Sea,—every younger son of quality who, bred in ease and pleasure, despaired of finding a fat living or a place at court, a legal sinecure or an heiress for a wife, began to meditate exploits in Bengal or the Deccan :—

> "To spill a few bright drops of blood,
> And straight rise up a Lord."

The hope of Oriental spoil spread like an epidemic; and, like other diseases, its taint once generally diffused, it became, among certain classes, families, and connections, normal and hereditary. Reasoning, where all the elements of calculation were illimitably vague, seemed but waste of time; and scruples about international or individual right or wrong, were of course regarded as mere sentiment. The tone of political society in England, at the accession of George III., was eminently propitious to the growth of such ideas. To the unchecked corruption of the previous reign, was added the development of arbitrary notions, encouraged by the Court. The Church was fast asleep, and the religious revival led by Wesley had made but little way. The slave trade and West Indian slavery, with their showers of golden fruit, were the tallest trees in the fashionable orchard; while the hardy growths of American industry were regarded with comparative disdain by the statesmen and courtiers, jurists and critics, who advocated the appropriation of their unpretentious fruit to eke out means of prodigality at home.

It was the fittest season and the fittest field in which the seeds of a new kind of fillibustering could be sown, and every year, it was said, would prove as plenteous as the last, or yet more abundant.[1] The incidents of Asiatic adventure, and all the ideas suggested by its successful prosecution, became interwoven alike with those of public and of private life, and they may be traced as a new source of illustration in the philosophy and literature of the day. In comedy, the forgotten scamp constantly turned up in the third act, under the title of Nabob, to rescue the mortgaged inheritance, or deliver some despairing fair from the arms of a high-born suitor whom she loathed; and the climax of charity-sermons consisted of an adulation to munificence, addressed to Dives, to whom providence had mercifully given wealth, that otherwise would have been offered to idols.

Mr Vansittart's administration was eminently successful for all who were concerned in it. It was the heyday of rapine, and if *coups d'état* at Moorshedabad, and wars on the frontier were not as plunderful as before, they secured personal opportunities greater than ever to those who made haste to be rich. The hapless ryots cried and there was none to help them. The richer classes, Rajahs, Polygars, and Talookdars, shuddered in silence at the progress of expropriation, but knew not how to make their complaints heard in England. What they could not do for themselves, was done for them by their tormentors, who were incessantly quarrelling amongst one another, and recounting the enormities they had witnessed in the East.

All this would probably have mattered little, but for one

---

[1] Annual Register, 1767, p. 40. See description, written probably by Edmund Burke.

unpardonable fault of the system in the eyes of the Directors: it did not pay. Individuals were continually returning home laden with riches; and of despatches there was no stint, full of glorious victories over ungrateful Moslems and the hated French. But the remittances did not improve. Too much was spent in salaries, perquisites, and riotous living. Sumptuary rules and reductions of expenditure were all in vain. At every shearing, the golden fleece seemed to be appropriated amongst them by the Company's servants, and little was left for the Company but the goat's wool. It was clear that unregulated spoliation did not yield the proper percentage. But how to economise and regulate it ?—that was the question.

Men's eyes turned once more on Clive. He was just beginning to enjoy the ease and luxury of the position he had won. His house in Berkeley Square, his equipage, and even his dress, betrayed his daily exultation. He had a dozen votes in Parliament at his command, and rival statesmen, therefore, sought his society. He was the only living commander who had actually won pitched battles, so he was made much of at the Horse Guards. He was the only Englishman who had added to His Majesty's dominions without adding to the national debt, so George III. liked to talk to him at levée. Though quizzed by the fops of St James's Street, and laughed at as ill-bred by women of fashion, he was regarded by the multitude as a hero, and by politicians as an administrator of signal power. If he could be only persuaded to return to Bengal, all would be sure to go well. So thought the proprietors of India Stock. The Chairman, Mr Sullivan, was, however, his personal adversary, and many of his colleagues shrank from submitting to one whom they knew would prove to be their master. But bad tidings grew worse, and shortcomings grew shorter.

How was a 10 per cent. dividend to be paid? After a stormy debate at the India House, in which Clive insisted on Sullivan being deposed, he was deputed to resume the reins of government at Calcutta, and was named by the Crown, General-in-chief of all the English forces in Asia.

While he was at home, Clive had doubtless interchanged views with those who held office under Bute and Grenville as to the future direction of the Company's affairs in relation to the Princes of the East. How far his own views of further encroachment were systematised or matured at this period, it is impossible to tell. Immersed in pleasure and intrigue, it is not likely that the Ministers of George III. bestowed much deliberate care upon forecasting the future of India. Clive went forth a second time to feel his aggressive way; but he was not long in determining on the path to tread. In a private letter addressed to one of the Directors, Mr Rouse, he thus writes—" We are at last arrived at that critical period which I have long foreseen, which renders it necessary for us to determine whether we shall take the whole to ourselves; for it is not hyperbole to say, To-morrow the whole Mogul Empire is in our power. After the lengths we have run, the Princes of Hindustan must conclude our views to be boundless; they have such instances of our ambition, that they cannot suppose us capable of moderation. The very Nawabs whom we might support would be jealous of our power. We must become *Nawabs ourselves*, in fact, if not in name."

On the death of Mir Jaffir, Mr Vansittart retired from the Presidency, which was temporarily filled by Mr Spencer from Bombay, pending the arrival of Clive. The accession of a young and inexperienced Prince to the Soubahdarate offered an opportunity of further encroachment not to be neglected. A new treaty was entered into accordingly with Nudjum-ul-Dowla on the 20th February 1765, which, ratifying that first made by his father in 1757, repeated most of the provisions of the alliance of 1763. Besides this, however, it secured the appointment of a friend of the Company, Mahomed Reza Khan, the Naib of Dacca, in the office of Chief Minister. Nuncomar, a rich Brahmin, who had held this office under the late Soubahdar, was not deemed well-disposed to the Company's interests, and hence the desire to have him superseded. For the defence of Bengal against the Mogul and the Vizier of Oude by the Anglo-Indian forces, Mir Jaffir had paid at the rate of five lacs a month. This sum his successor agreed to continue; and, moreover, as he "esteemed the Company's troops equal to the defence of the provinces, and as his own," he would only himself maintain such in addition "as were immediately necessary for the dignity of his person and Government, and the business of his collections throughout the provinces." The Company thus became contractors for the military defence of the country, but for that only; judicial and fiscal authority still remained in native hands. In spite of the positive injunctions of the Directors at home to put an end to the scandalous system of inland smuggling, until an equitable and satisfactory plan "could be arranged with the free will and consent of the Nawab, so as not to afford any just ground of complaint," Mr Spencer and the Council inserted in the new treaty a clause which gave the Company, and every servant of theirs trading in his private capacity, immunity from tolls and dues, except $2\frac{1}{2}$ per cent. on salt. The young Soubahdar, and his Minister, as usual, paid liberally for the Company's friendship, in sums ranging from one to over two lacs, given under the name of nuzzurana to different members of the Council.

Clive arrived at Calcutta 3d May 1765, accompanied by Mr Sumner and Mr Sykes, who, with himself, General Carnac, and Mr Verelst, were appointed by the Directors a Select Committee, invested with extraordinary powers, to inquire into abuses too notorious, and to take measures for restoring "order and tranquillity." This supercession of their authority provoked attempts at resistance among the Council, but Clive showed a resolute front, and while they murmured, they submitted. The first act of the Committee was one of official reform. The Directors, with a view to check the scandal caused by their servants exacting enormous presents from wealthy natives, had prepared forms of covenant to be subscribed, pledging them not to accept any land, rents, revenue, or other property, beyond a small amount, without special permission previously obtained. Though these documents had arrived in January, the Council absolutely ignored them in their dealings with Nudjum-ul-Dowla and Reza Khan, intending also to remonstrate against the inhibition. The Committee at once set about enforcing compliance; and, by dint of dismissals, suspensions, and retirements among the refractory, order and decorum were for a time restored.

The aspect of military affairs had improved, and Clive was, perhaps, disappointed that no immediate opening presented itself for the exercise of his unusual powers as diplomatist or general. But he had not long to wait. The Vizier of Oude, who had sought the aid of the Mahrattas to conquer Bengal, had sustained a crushing defeat, and sued for peace on any terms, to arrange which Clive proceeded to the camp. It was not thought advisable to press the vanquished too hard, and he was mulcted only in a war-fine of fifty lacs, and the relinquishment of the districts of Allahabad and Korah; which, instead of being appropriated, were used as a bribe wherewith to obtain new and valuable concessions from the court of Delhi. A separate peace was negotiated, whereby, in consideration of these territories and the Company's guarantee of twenty-six lacs of yearly tribute, Shah Alum agreed to issue a firman appointing the Company his farmers-general of the revenues of Orissa, Behar, and Bengal—provision being carefully made that nothing therein contained should imply any derogation from the authority and dignity of the Nawab-Nazim, the maintenance of whose Government should be a permanent charge, and should be fully defrayed before anything was appropriated to their own profit by the new collectors. This notable transaction is what has been called the transfer of the Dewanny, and from its singularity and importance, it is not surprising that it should have been variously misunderstood and misrepresented. It was, in fact, the realisation of a scheme conceived seven years before. In 1758 the Council wrote home that their late successes had acquired for them so great a reputation with the Emperor, that his Ministers wished for their good offices at Moorshedabad to secure the more punctual payment of the imperial tribute. Their diplomatic agent, Sitab Roy, more than hinted that if they would guarantee the annual payment, they might have the function and title of Dewan. "The Dewan is the second man of rank," they say, "in the kingdom; and such a dignity annexed to your Presidency would give extraordinary weight to the Company in the Empire, which nothing would be able to remove. The accepting this employ might occasion jealousy on the part of the Soubahdar, and we are unwilling to cause him any dissatisfaction at a time when our small force is engaged another way, especially as you gentlemen give us so little hopes of reinforcements from home."[1]

[1] Long's Records, vol i.

But times had changed, and the reinforcements were now come. The encroaching lodgers clutched at the latch-key, which gave them henceforth the run of the house without let or hindrance or question. In its ultimate consequences, the transfer of the Dewanny proved to be, no doubt, the turning-point of India's fortunes; and in whatever aspect viewed at the time, it is impossible not to regard it as a proof of the political imbecility into which the Durbar of Delhi had sunk. For the sake of ready money to sustain its lavish and luxurious expenditure, a concession was made to encroaching and ambitious foreigners, who had recently been open foes, incompatible with all our notions of imperial self-respect, patriotism, and policy. But it is idle to pretend, looking at the terms employed in the firman, the stipulations it embodies, and bearing in mind the confidential language used regarding it by the concessionaires, that it ever was proposed or granted, asked for or accepted, as tantamount to a transfer of the dominion or government of the three provinces to the Company. That it was used and abused to that end, at first stealthily and slowly, and then rapidly and ruthlessly, is true. But it is not true that any such purpose was breathed until the deed was done. Let those who found a claim of forfeiture upon this so-called act of expropriation by the then acknowledged paramount power, consult the private correspondence of M. de Barillon, wherein the payment of secret pensions and gifts from Louis XIV. to Charles II. are carefully chronicled, with the receipts and acknowledgments given by English peers and diplomatists, and similar documents from noble lords and right honourable gentlemen in Parliament, for like gratifications and benefits from the King of France; and then let them think what would have been said had any one attempted to construe such transactions as a mortgage of the soil of England, reducible into possession at the pleasure of the mortgagee. Yet, between the two bargainings, the moral difference is unspeakable. Want of money by a sensual and prodigal court is the one feature of identity: everything else is different, the difference being in favour of the Asiatics.

The Council could not contain themselves for joy; and sped their congratulations by the next mail to London. The hills were now about to drop fatness; and for the first time they felt as if they could afford to keep a conscience. The contentions about tolls and duties, wrung from the natives, but not exacted from their own people, and all the corruptions and crimes incident thereto, suddenly had become scandalous in their eyes. They declared they had just discovered that the only way to put an end to all such evils was to take away the bone of contention, and to become tax-gatherers themselves. Their solemn effrontery cannot be appreciated in paraphrase. "The perpetual struggles for superiority between the Nawabs and your agents, together with the recent proofs before us of notorious and avowed corruption, have rendered us unanimously of opinion, after the most mature deliberation, that no other method could be suggested of laying the axe to the root of all these evils, than that of obtaining the Dewanny of Bengal, Behar, and Orissa for the Company. By establishing the power of the Great Mogul, we have likewise established his rights; and His Majesty, from principles of gratitude, equity, and policy, has thought proper to bestow this important employment on the Company, the nature of which is the collecting all the revenues, and, after defraying the expenses of the army and allowing a sufficient fund for the support of the Nizamut, to remit the remainder to Delhi, or wherever the King shall reside or direct. But as the King has been graciously pleased to bestow on the Company for ever such surplus as shall arise from the revenues, upon certain stipulations and agreements expressed in the Sunnud, we have settled with the Nawab, with his own free will and consent, that the sum of fifty-three lacs shall be annually paid to him for the support of his dignity and all contingent expenses, exclusive of the charge of maintaining an army, which is to be defrayed out of the revenues ceded to the Company by this royal grant of the Dewanny. And, indeed, the Nawab has abundant reason to be well satisfied with the conditions of his agreement, whereby a fund is secured to him, without trouble or danger, adequate to all the purposes of such grandeur and happiness as a man of his sentiments has any conception of enjoying. More would serve only to disturb his quiet, endanger his Government, and sap the foundation of that solid structure of power and wealth which at length is reared and completed by the Company, after a vast expense of blood and treasure.' Already, however, they began to devise how this new privilege might be stretched to work a defeasance of the general authority of the Soubahdar; and they proceed to indicate their meaning in unmistakable terms. It is worthy of note that the Directors in their reply [1] broadly and significantly distinguish between their appreciation of the value of the Dewanny, and their entire disapproval of its perversion to political ends. "We entirely approve of your preserving the ancient form of government in upholding the dignity of the Soubahdar. We conceive the office of Dewan should be exercised only in superintending the collection and disposal of the revenues. This we conceive to be the whole office of the Dewanny. The admin-

[1] Despatch, 17th May 1768.

istration of justice, the appointments to offices, zemindaries, —in short, whatever comes under the denomination of civil administration, we understand is to remain in the hands of the Nawab or his Ministers."

In compliance with the terms of the imperial rescript, fifty-three lacs of rupees were agreed to be paid annually out of the taxes for supporting the expenses of the Nizamut—seventeen lacs being for household charges, and thirty-six lacs for guards, police, and other purposes requisite to maintain the state and dignity of the Soubahdar's Government. The gross receipts of the three provinces were estimated at no less a sum than two millions sterling; and Clive concurred with the Directors in declaring that all the details and functions of collection should be left, as before, in native hands. When in England, he had strongly urged upon the Directors the necessity of putting a check on the private trade of their servants. " The trading in salt, betel, and tobacco" having been one of the causes of dispute, he hoped these articles would be restored to the Nawab; and the Company's servants absolutely forbidden to trade in them : " the odium of seeing such monopolies in the hands of foreigners need not be insisted on." Under a tropical sun his good resolutions, however, all dissolved away, for before he had been out a month he had become a partner with Messrs Verelst, Sykes, and Sumner in the salt trade. It was said that he devoted his profits derived from the traffic to the relief of needy relatives and dependants, and that personally he obtained no benefit from them. Possessed of a vast fortune, drawn from the resources of native princes, he could hardly appropriate more from that quarter, and he had creditably aided in putting an end to the system of exactions under the name of presents, where his successors were concerned; but the orders of the Directors were equally imperative for the cessation of private trade. He chose, notwithstanding, to disregard those orders, and to stultify his own previous professions, for the advantage of those about him.

In May 1766, the Nawab Nudjum-ul-Dowla died, and was succeeded by his younger brother, Syef-ul-Dowla. A new treaty between him and the Company was made, which ratified that first made with his father, and also that made with his brother the year before. The viceregal guards had been kept up at a cost of eighteen lacs a year,[1] but overtures were made for their disbanding, in order that their pay might be saved, and their duty performed by the Company's sepoy battalions. The occasion was thought propitious for effecting this further change; and in the new treaty, the fixed sum for Nizamut expenses was reduced from fifty-three to forty-one lacs. The credit which the Governor took to himself for this piece of economy was not readily acknowledged at home. The Directors wrote,[2] "As the reduction of the stipend to the Nawab arises from striking off the pay of an unnecessary number of his sepoys, and does not affect the allowance for support of his dignity in the Government, we approve what you have done in it; but we direct you never to reduce the stipend lower, being extremely desirous that he should have sufficient to support his public character, and appear respectable to his subjects and to foreigners."

[1] Long's Records, vol. i. p. 419.
[2] Despatch from the Directors, 16th March 1768.

CHAPTER VI.

PLIGHT OF THE PEOPLE.

1767—1770.

"English historians, treating of Indian history as a series of struggles about the Company's charter, enlivened with startling military exploits, have naturally little to say regarding an occurrence which involved neither a battle nor a parliamentary debate. Mill, with all his accuracy and minuteness, can barely spare five lines for the subject. But the disaster which, from this distance, floats as a faint speck on the horizon of our rule, stands out in the contemporary records in appalling proportions. It forms, indeed, the key to the history of Bengal during the succeeding forty years."
—Dr Hunter.[1]

THE second administration of Clive, who was sent from England to consolidate the acquisitions somewhat awkwardly achieved by Vansittart and his Council, lasted about two years. After that, Verelst and Cartier filled successively the office of President of Bengal, and being calm, unambitious men, few events of historical importance occurred. It were perhaps more accurate to say, that few striking or sudden changes took place in the supreme relations of the State during that period. For events of historical importance are of two kinds, the silent and the noisy; and all things considered, the silent are of much more consequence than those whose taking place clamours for observation. In Bengal, a great event or coming forth into light of a new fact on the scroll of human destiny noiselessly revealed itself; no less a fact than that of an

[1] Annals of Rural Bengal.

attempted Government by two separate and unlike powers —the one native, and hitherto paramount; the other alien, and hitherto tributary, but fast becoming irresistible and dominant. All the old respect and native predilection looked after the waning lustre of the Soubahdar's court; all the hope of profit and the fear of oppression looked towards the Presidency. The feelings of the community were instinctively devoted still to native rites, usages, and laws; their apprehensions were daily riveted more inquiringly upon the strange and unintelligible commands of Calcutta. How the pretensions of superior force came by degrees to be submitted to as irreversible, how acquiescence in the course of years grew into a sullen habit of obedience, it would take long to tell.

External force has sometimes been hailed as a deliverance from petty tyranny and internecine feuds; and when separate chieftainships and principalities have been swept away, the lot of the community at large has been benefited by the change. This has only been, however, where local rights, the securities of property, and the immunities of personal freedom have been maintained or strengthened. Instances are not wanting of substantial benefits having been at first conferred by a high-handed exercise of alien authority, which by degrees came to be recognised by their recipients as more than counterbalancing the affront to native pride involved in the manner of the gift. But such instances are rare, and there is, perhaps, not one in which such gratitude has ever been felt, or has ever been fairly earned, in which the irresistible power of the intruder has attempted to uproot the customary laws of the country regarding the administration of justice or the possession of land. By violent mutations of the royal power, the happiness of the many does not always suffer—not immediately or perceptibly, at least. Government is much more palpable, and to the community is much more influential, in the performance of its daily administrative duties than in its intercourse with foreign states, or in its internal exercise of what may be termed national functions. It is true that a gradual and exact subordination of powers to the supreme authority is indispensable; and that such as the one is, such the subordinate many are ever likely to be. But it usually takes time to discern this. Practically, the conviction can only be realised by habit and reflection. Instances there may have been where the subtlety and care and wisdom of an alien Government have introduced improvements and reformations appealing to the sense, if unable to engage the affections, of the people; and however shortlived and unstable such advantages may be, we can imagine men so sick and weary of domestic misrule as to hail with reckless but real joy the questionable aid of foreign interposition.

In the story of Asiatic conquest, we have, however, no task of nice discrimination to perform. Not only was the sovereign authority of each state subverted, but the subordinate, and perhaps more important, institutions of law, property, and taxation, were subverted also. To understand, clearly, the causes which precipitated these social and municipal changes, it is necessary to recall the condition of the Company's affairs in England, and the action of Parliament respecting them. The acquisition of the Dewanny caused the Company's stock to rise considerably; and in a Court of Proprietors a resolution was carried by a large majority declaring that the dividend should be in future 10 instead of 6 per cent. Government cast wistful eyes upon the splendid progress making by the Company in revenues, which no longer could be in any sense classed under the head of commercial profits. The Duke of Grafton had, on quitting office, told the Chairman and Deputy Chairman that the time was come when our dealings with the rulers and traders of the East must be taken in hand by Parliament as a national concern. But his Grace had not time to develop whatever ideas might have been put into his head upon the subject; and when Chatham for the second time became First Minister,[1] one of the great measures of reform which he hoped to carry was that respecting India. At his instance, Alderman Beckford, whose character for mercantile knowledge and probity stood high, moved in the House of Commons[2] for a committee to inquire into the state and condition of the East India Company. The motion was resisted by those—and they were many—who directly or indirectly were interested in its management being left uncontrolled; but 129 votes against 76 were told in its favour. A fortnight later the House ordered that copies of all treaties with native powers between 1756 and 1766, both years inclusive, as well as of all correspondence relating thereto, and an account of the state of the Company's territorial revenues, should be laid before them. It was understood that this step was but preliminary to the development of a comprehensive plan regulating our course and conduct in the East, and for turning into the imperial treasury the streams of affluence theretofore engrossed by individual or joint-stock enterprise. The committee of inquiry did not go to business until the end of March 1767; and it had made little progress when a General Court of Proprietors, on the 6th May, in a paroxysm of cupidity, voted that the dividend on their stock should be raised to $12\frac{1}{2}$ per cent. This was too much for even the most languid parliamentary conscience; and on the following day the House of Commons called in threatening terms

---

[1] 30th July 1766.   [2] 25th November 1766.

for the proceedings which had resulted in this vote. The Court quickly re-assembled, and repeated substantially what they had done before, by declaring that a dividend of less than £400,000 a year would not satisfy them. Parliament was offended at this apparent intention to challenge, if not to resist, its authority; and Mr Fuller, chairman of the committee, forthwith moved to bring in a bill limiting the dividends of the Company to 10 per cent., which, after many warm debates, was read a third time on the 28th of May, and passed. In the Upper House it was denounced by Lord Mansfield and other peers as an infraction of the rights of private property; but public feeling ran high, opposition was unavailing; and before the session closed, another bill was passed which bound the Company to pay £400,000 a year into the exchequer out of their revenues in Bengal, as a condition of the renewal of their charter. It was thus made plain for whose benefit the collection and administration of the revenues of the Nawab-Nazim had been transferred from native to foreign hands. In the scramble between Westminister and the City for a divison of the spoil, the weightier matters of justice, judgment, and mercy seem to have been forgotten. The darkening shadows had fallen upon the mind of the great statesman who then nominally held the reins of administration, but who, secluded in his villa at Hampstead, refused for months to attend Parliament or Council, to answer letters, or even to receive visits from his colleagues. Chatham, towards the close of the year, gave up the Privy Seal, and returned no more to power. Politicians occupied themselves with more pressing affairs in Europe and America, and the new owners, as they had virtually become, of Bengal, Behar, and Orissa, went their way.

In the session of 1769, the agreement made for three

years between Government and the Company had to be revised. Lord North now led the House of Commons in his pleasant off-hand style. He offered the Company a new lease of their Eastern-hunting grounds upon the old terms. No stipulations, political or social, administrative or legislative, were proposed. But a new voice was to be henceforth heard in the affairs of India, whose lofty and passionate protests against wrong have not yet ceased to thrill the hearts of all who love the honour of their country wisely and well. Three years before, the Member for Wendover had entered Parliament, and had rapidly asserted, by the unhelped force of courage, eloquence, and independency of thought, a position such as no man without birth or wealth had before attained in that assembly. With ineffable wonder and disdain, Burke noted this mere perfunctory discharge of the great duties of State, and rebuked warmly the absence of all policy and prudence displayed in such official conduct. "This bargain," he exclaimed, "is not an agreement but a ransom. Without calculating the revenue, without allowing for risk, without inquiring into circumstances, to make a great commercial Company pay £400,000 to Government is but a robbery."[1] His vehemence in conversation and debate suggested in the meaner minds around him only the suspicion, genuine or feigned, that he must have some personal motive for engaging so earnestly in a subject that did not ostensibly concern him or his country-town constituents; and not a few of his political friends were rather chilled than kindled by zeal which never slackened in or out of season. His prophecies of evil were not believed, his too accurate prognostics, his too prescient insight into consequences, were unheeded. If they squeezed the Company in this blind fashion, they but

[1] Cavendish, vol. i. p. 266—Burke's Speeches.

incited them to squeeze their servants in the East, and that only meant that they should squeeze the native victims of their rule. But he seemed to them as one that mocked. How could they know what was really happening, or might possibly happen, at the other side of the globe? and at heart what did they care? Though he spoke like an angel, the House laughed,[1] and few divided with him. Then he grew angrier and less convincing. Nature, which had lavished on him so many of her choicest gifts, had forgotten tact when he was made. Tact he had none, and the want of that species of instinct cannot be supplied by learning, discipline, or even by experience. Few sympathised enough with the poor and plebeian man of genius to risk his ill-humour by telling him the truth of what was said or insinuated in his disparagement. The Duke of Richmond, who had both good-nature and good sense, on one occasion frankly told him the truth, taking care to add, that for himself he did not believe him to be swayed in the least by any personal motives. But the haughty spirit of Burke was not to be influenced by hints however delicate, or advice however kind. He had his work to do, and, after all, he could only do it in his own way. Justice to India became to him an Egeria, whom he loved to commune with in the silent hours of night, and from whom, most truly, he received inspiration.

The musnud remained, but the sceptre had been taken away. The dignity of native rule still subsisted, and still wore the ancient embroidery of power; but power to protect, control, defend, or guide, was gone. After ten years of foreign rule, what was the plight of the people? Did they grieve like the Hebrews of old? or if unmoved by national sentiment, had they physical cause to feel that "their inheritance was turned to strangers, and their houses

[1] Life of Burke, by Macknight, vol. ii. p. 18.

to aliens; that they drank their water for money, that their wood was sold unto them; that servants ruled over them, and that there was none to deliver them out of their hand?"[1]

The rice crop of 1768 had been scanty throughout Bengal, but "the revenues were never so closely collected before." Prices rose, and the poorer cultivators of the soil had consequently little to spare for seed. Nevertheless, in the spring of 1769, the export of rice went on; for customers at Madras and elsewhere could afford to pay high, and no one in authority cared about consequences. The rains fell as usual in the spring, copiously enough to do even harm in the Delta. But the clouds of autumn came not as usual, and failed to drop fatness. Everywhere the crop withered, and the rice-fields became prematurely fields of straw. Governor Verelst did not deem the matter worth mentioning when writing home; and except for the troops, no care was taken to lay up provisions in store. The only question indeed was about the troops; for as once was said of another neglected dependency by a statesman of our own time, Bengal "was occupied, not governed." Mr Cartier mentioned incidentally late in January 1770, that one district was suffering severely for want of food, but he adds the consolatory assurance that "they had not yet found any failure in the revenue." What no failure of revenue means, when people are famishing, it can hardly be necessary to explain. Subsequently it occurred to the Governor and Council that if some relaxation in the collection of the land-tax were conceded, that was the utmost that could be expected of them; but as for taking measures to save the lives of the community, they naturally thought nobody expected that at their hands. In seasons of drought it had

[1] Lamentations of Jeremiah, v.

not been uncommon for native rulers to suspend the land-tax, and to make advances to ryots; and measures of this kind were proposed at Fort William, but "except in a few isolated instances they were not granted."[1] In April, the pulse harvest, though scanty, was secured, and about the same time an addition of 10 per cent. was made to the rent-revenue. But destitution deepened, and in the middle of May the reports of suffering came from far and near. "The mortality and beggary exceeded all description. Above one-third of the inhabitants perished in the once-plentiful province of Purneah, and in other parts the misery was the same."[2] From every native official who had still been retained earnest representations poured in of the dire calamity that had befallen the people. Sympathy and selfishness alike inspired these representations. Even Mussulmans, Tusuldars, and Hindoo police might be credited with pity and compassion; while whatever tribute they still were able to send in, would entitle them to all the more praise when it was known under what difficulties it had been collected. There were no disorders, outbreaks, or threats of violence among the peasantry. The habitual reticence and domestic privacy of Bengalis is well known. Even the charitable who sought out objects of benevolence, found it often difficult to reach the inner chambers, where debilitated and despairing women and children slowly perished for want of food. Cattle were sold, tools pawned, and seed-grain eaten; then children were offered for sale, till purchasers could not be found; and finally the Government were informed by their subordinates that the living were known to prey upon the dead."[3]

At length all traditional reserve gave way. Troops

---

[1] Hunter's Annals of Rural Bengal, p. 23.
[2] Despatch, 9th May 1770.   [3] Letter of 2d June 1770.

of famished peasants, worn and wan, came crowding into the towns, bringing with them pestilence, in various forms, small-pox, dysentery, and fever, and spreading terror and dismay among rich men and rulers. Death did not heed being told to begone. Its carnival was come, and the ghastly revel was prolonged from week to week and from month to month, till the gravedigger was weary and the jackal and vulture grew lazy and tame.

The testimony of an eyewitness whose veracity has never been questioned, and who afterwards rose to the highest post in Bengal, confirms what a despatch of the Council, so late as the month of September, expressly set forth, that it was "scarcely possible that any description could be an exaggeration of the prevailing want and woe." Mr Shore was nothing of an enthusiast, and in every act of his life he was a loyal and trusted servant of the Company. Punctilious, careful, plodding, and exact, he was of all men the least likely to overstate any case where the credit of the Government was concerned. Yet he owned in after years that nothing could obliterate from his recollection the horrors of that dreadful time—

> "Dire scenes of horror, which no pen can trace,
> Nor rolling years from memory's page efface."

A certain show of compassion was made at Calcutta when the evil was at its height. An embargo was laid for several weeks on the export of grain, but the total amount contributed by the Calcutta treasury to alleviate wretchedness so unparalleled did not exceed £4000. The native landlords must do the rest, if they would and could. For the most part, they were not unwilling, but the means were wanting. Their own resources had wholly failed, and they could only borrow at high usury, or become defaulters to the exchequer. Instances are recorded of the sacrifices they made, and of the suffering they subsequently endured in consequence. Sooner than let their people die, they went in debt. From this dreadful year the ruin of two-thirds of the old aristocracy of Bengal dates; while the revenue farmers, "being unable to realise the land-tax, were stripped of their office, their persons imprisoned, and their lands, the sole dependence of their families, relet."[1] The Rajah of Nuddea survived the famine so much in default, that he was glad to surrender his estates to his son. The Rani of Rajshie, though previously esteemed as a woman of business, and as a lady who exercised justly much territorial influence, was threatened with eviction and the confiscation of her lands. The young Rajah of Beerbhoom was thrown into jail for arrears of land-tax; while the aged Rajah of Bishenpore was only let out of a debtor's prison when his end visibly drew nigh. Out of an assessment of £1,380,269 only £65,355 was remitted during the famine year. The ruin of the Hindu gentry excited little pity or forbearance. The clearing of great tracts of country by famine caused more concern; a third of the land was reported in the next two years to have gone out of tillage. This was a serious evil, and accordingly schemes were set on foot to tempt immigrants to take farms and settle. There was to be a new plantation by men of a hardier breed, and, as was said, of a superior race. But the work of home colonisation proved more slow than probably was expected. Sheep from the other folds did not come so quickly at the click of the shears: stupid creatures! that did not know what was good for them. Villages remained in ruins, field after field lay fallow, and rapidly returned to jungle. Beerbhoom and Bishenpore had been cultivated by six thousand rural com-

[1] Hunter's Annals of Rural Bengal, p. 56.

munes. Three years after the famine a fourth of these agricultural communities had disappeared. For fifteen years after the famine depopulation went on; and in 1789 a minute of the Viceroy in Council declared that one-third of the Company's territories in Bengal was "a jungle inhabited only by wild beasts."

Something more remains to be told. Shameful frauds appear to have been practised during the famine by persons in office. They were known to have dealt in grain, imported for the supply of the famishing multitude, to have made false returns of its distribution, and to have appropriated the exorbitant price it brought. The Council tried to throw the blame upon the subordinates who were natives. The Directors refused to be thus duped; said plainly that they believed the guilt lay at the door of their own countrymen high in office, and called for the disclosure of their names; but the names were never audibly disclosed. One who held an important place at the time, returned to his own country a wealthy man, founded a family, since ennobled, and amid "honour, love, obedience, troops of friends," lay down to spend the evening of his days in peace. But that best of blessings was denied him. His nights were haunted by images and sounds which would not let him sleep; and though a man of what is called iron frame and of ready courage, to his dying hour he never would allow the lights to be extinguished round his bed.

The next harvest was plenteous, but the labourers were so comparatively few that a great extent of land was left untilled, and it was many years before the population rose to their former numbers. All the computations made officially at the time, and afterwards, set down the extent of depopulation at from nine to ten millions. Nothing like this has been even asserted as having happened elsewhere in any part of the world for centuries. Nevertheless the land revenue was within two years brought up once more to the former average of a million and a half sterling, though not, as Warren Hastings owned, without the exercise of cruel severity. By the practice termed "naja," each district was throughout compelled to furnish its quota, regardless of depopulation and abandonment of farms. The practice which, in ordinary years, was hardly complained of by a people traditionally accustomed to a rude but regular solidarity of local interests and industries, became an instrument of inhuman rigour when there was famine in the land. The more utter the insolvency occasioned by dearth in one portion of a district, the more intolerably fell the weight of exaction upon the portion that still struggled for life. What frugality had saved from the sickle of dearth, the pitiless clutch of the tax-gatherer gleaned; but the coffers of the alien dewanny were kept full, and the remittances to the absentee owners afar off were not suffered to fail.

The tidings of the terrible disaster startled from the apathy of neglect the popular conscience at home; and in the following session, select committees of inquiry were moved for—the one by Mr Dundas, and the other by Colonel Burgoyne. In the voluminous evidence brought before them, the scandalous history of Clive's and Vansittart's administrations was laid bare. Clive was threatened with impeachment, but he boldly faced the accusations laid to his charge; and the House of Commons, after censuring many of the leading acts of his government, voted, by way of set-off, that he had rendered great services to his country. His haughty spirit was not appeased by this, or by the cheers with which he was subsequently received on entering the House. His solitude was haunted by thoughts to which he gave no utterance. At length the burthen of his unhallowed fame and fortune grew insupportable, and the public learned with a shudder that he had perished by his own hand.

In their anxiety to escape impending condemnation for past mismanagement, and to offer guarantees of something better for the time to come, the Directors professed themselves ready to send out a commission of three men of repute and standing, awaiting whose report Parliament might fairly be called on to abstain from permanent legislation. The Vice-Chairman, Sir George Colebrooke, suggested to his colleagues that they should invite Edmund Burke to preside over this Commission of Supervisors, as, in the counting-house language of the Board, they were to be called. Lord Rockingham, then leader of the Whigs in opposition, was consulted; but, from a feeling of delicacy, or from some other cause unexplained, he abstained from expressing any opinion. The over-sensitiveness of his friend and follower seems to have been hurt at the want of interest thus shown in a matter which he regarded as of importance not only to himself but to the nation. He took time to consider, and his family dissuading him, he declined the offer. How different might have been the subsequent course of events in India, had even a ground-plan whereon to build been laid down by the noble, just, generous, and far-sighted intellect of him who has been truly designated by Macaulay as beyond comparison the greatest man of his time!

Meanwhile another but very different man, daring as Clive, and of more comprehensive and persistent purpose, was climbing fast and climbing high the rounds of ambition in the East. Failing to obtain the services of the eloquent statesman, the Directors bethought them of their most astute and versatile official. He had no friends of consequence to push his interest with them, and no resources wherewith to purchase favour. But he had the faculty of impressing all with whom he came into personal contact that, though diminutive in form and delicate in feature, he possessed indomitable energy, profound sagacity, and an iron will. They thought he was the sort of man they wanted; and the next decade in the annals of annexation is identified with the name of Warren Hastings.

CHAPTER VII.

WARREN HASTINGS.

1771—1773.

"In such a state of affairs, what influence can exist except that of fear? Can those who have been deprived of their power and their wealth like the Government who have been the instruments of their ruin? Is it possible that their relations, friends, and former dependants, should not sympathise with them? And will not the people, who are taxed with much greater severity than they ever were before, be ready to concur in their complaints? The ruin of the upper classes (like the exclusion of the people from a share in the government) was a necessary consequence of the establishment of the British power; but had we acted on a more liberal plan, we should have fixed our authority on a much more solid foundation."

—F. J. SHORE.[1]

UNTIL the year 1773, the English possessions in India were governed by the three separate Councils of Bombay, Madras, and Calcutta, each of them presided over by one of their number specially designated by the Directors at home for the performance of that duty. Between these independent and co-equal Governments, no little jealousy prevailed. Their local interests were often different, and they were separated from each other, not only by distance and diversity of circumstances, but by mutual jealousy and distrust. As their respective relations with the native states grew more complex, their need of one another's aid in time of peril grew more plain. Concerted action and unity of policy was every year more obviously desir-

[1] Notes on Indian Affairs, vol. i. p. 162.

able; and to secure this unity, the Minister of the day recommended Parliament to create a supreme executive at Calcutta, which should in all great affairs control the two remaining Presidencies, and to erect at the same time in the future metropolis of British India, a High Court of Judicature, invested with unlimited jurisdiction, civil as well as criminal, over all English settlers in the East, and over all matters wherein they might in any way be concerned.

By an Act passed in 1773, Government for the first time explicitly assumed paramount authority over the English possessions in Asia. George III. and his Ministers had long coveted this increase of patronage and power; but it was not until the Board of Directors came for a loan of £1,500,000 to the Treasury, to meet their excess of expenditure, that the opportunity arose for effecting so great a change. For five years the heavy quit-rent to the State and the dividend of 10 per cent. to the proprietary had been punctually paid; but the price of stock steadily went down, and at length, in the autumn of '72, Leadenhall Street found itself on the brink of insolvency. Lord North readily agreed to a loan from the Exchequer, adequate to meet all pressing wants. He intimated at the same time, however, that the executive should henceforth be regarded as supreme in all questions of acquired territory, and that a provincial administration, political, military, and judicial, must be nominated by the Home Government, though paid for out of the revenues of the Company. Its internal constitution, moreover, would be modified so as to restrict the constituent votes by whom the Directors were to be chosen, to persons registered for twelve months as holders of £1000 of stock. This sweeping measure of disfranchisement and of centralisation raised a storm of opposition in the City. Corporate privileges were said to be endangered, and both Houses were prayed to hear counsel at the bar. The prayer was granted, and some eight-and-twenty Whig commoners, and about as many peers, divided against the principal clauses of the bill. Their resistance eventually availed nothing. A Governor-General with four colleagues, to hold office for five years, were named in the Act, and a supreme tribunal of justice, to sit at Calcutta, as a court of appeal from all inferior jurisdictions, whether native or English, was in the same manner established. General Clavering, Mr Philip Francis, Colonel Monson, and Mr Barwell, were named in the Act as the colleagues of Warren Hastings, the new Proconsul of Hindustan.

When it had served its turn, this first imperial statute for India was superseded, and most of its provisions were swept away among the dead leaves of legislation. But one clause remains to be ever memorable in the history of modern society—more pregnant with consequences than all the statutes taken together enacted in the longest reign of English kings. To eke out the help they needed in their plight of financial embarrassment, the Company asked and obtained a remission of the duty on tea imported in their vessels. For clearness' sake, the additional port-dues of 3d. in the pound chargeable in the colonies was declared to be repealed. Parliament took upon itself to confer this fiscal boon on the Transatlantic as well as home provinces of the Empire, by declaring that the drawback should be allowed in both upon all tea borne in the East India Company's bottoms. The King was fooled with a device which Lord Hillsborough assured him would entrap the colonists, by the bait of a remitted duty, into acknowledging the right of taxation in Parliament, which they had in the case of the Stamp Act so stoutly denied. Speakers in opposition warned Ministers that the people of Pennsylvania and New England were not likely to be thus beguiled; and the event soon verified their prognostics. Upon acquiescence in that arrogant assumption to remit imposts, the converse right to impose them manifestly hung. The colonists would admit neither, and, to show that they were in earnest, they flung the cargoes of tea free of duty into Boston harbour. We all know what followed.

Meanwhile, the ablest man in the Company's service, Warren Hastings, was, apparently without opposition, nominated Governor-General of India. He had filled the chair of President in Bengal for the two preceding years, to the satisfaction of the Company. Several of his acts had indeed drawn down on him the censure of the Opposition in Parliament; but the merits of the questions at issue were ill understood, and no audible objection was heard when he was named for the newly-created dignity. Why was he chosen? and what had he done to earn this high distinction? What was the character of the man, that the responsible advisers of the Crown should confide to him so great a trust? In their early instructions the Board of Directors positively forbade the assumption of a military position, and enjoined a peaceful adherence to strictly commercial objects. But Hastings had no mind to obey these suggestions further than in name. There was neither rapid fortune nor the reputation of a conqueror to be made thereby. Clive's example had, in fact, debauched all the adventurous and unscrupulous class who were at this time, and for many years after, in the East. The affairs of the Company at home were in great embarrassment; Hastings took advantage of this on the one hand, and the Ministers of the Crown took advantage of it on the other.

The new President wrote to the Secret Committee—

"The truth is, that the affairs of the Company stand at present on a footing which can neither last as it is now, or be maintained on the rigid principles of private justice. You must establish your own power, or you must hold it dependent on a superior, which I deem to be impossible." The reply [1] of the Secret Committee expresses their "entire approval" of his conduct. The vigour he displayed at the same time in curbing subordinate abuses, and the retrenchments he effected in many quarters, rendered them unwilling to supersede him; and Ministers at home, who wanted to obtain a larger share of patronage, not only left him undisturbed, but by the Act of 1773 raised him to a position of unprecedented power. Thus it was that this singularly able, fearless, and unscrupulous man came to be the first individual who ever filled the post of English Viceroy of the East.

The family of Hastings was of ancient and honourable name, but at the beginning of the century its fortunes had fallen into decay. The last portion of its heritable possessions seems to have been the manor of Daylesford, in Worcestershire. The vicarage was held for many years by the grandfather of Warren Hastings, and under the old man's roof his earlier days were passed. Of his father, who was a runagate, we only know that he married, at fifteen, a lady of the neighbourhood, who died in the infancy of her only son; and that from his birth the portionless boy was virtually left in the condition of an orphan. Of his father, who survived many years, he was never known to speak. The poor old vicar treated the child with tenderness. He was sent to the village school, and in his playhours, as he used afterwards to tell, he would stroll through Daylesford Wood, or lie beside the margin of the stream that rippled through the meadows, pondering in his boyish

[1] Despatch, 16th April 1773.

heart how his grandfather had been driven from the pleasantest-looking place in all that country-side, and wondering if he ever should be rich enough to buy it back again. Throughout a long and chequered life, the thought, nurtured in his speculative and romantic brain by the family talk he had overheard in winter nights while sitting in the chimney-corner—that thought exercised an inexorable mastery over his whole fate, spurring his ambition and goading his avarice, reining his fierce passion, and stimulating him in hours of despondency to endurance, enterprise, and crime. By his uncle, a clerk in the Customs, he was put to school at Newington, where he learned little, and was half starved. He used to ascribe his stunted and delicate frame to the treatment he experienced there. Subsequently sent to Westminster, he soon distinguished himself as a scholar, and won the good-will alike of his playfellows and his teachers. There he became known to Lord Shelborne and other men, eminent in after life; there too began his intimacy with Elijah Impey, that fatal friend, whose life-thread was destined so disastrously to be interwoven with his own. At his uncle's death he was offered a cadetship by his guardian, who was a Director of the East India Company. The head-master said—No; India was very far off. Hastings was a very good Grecian, and he was sure to make a distinguished figure at the University: if expense alone was the consideration, he would pay for a couple of years the necessary charge himself, sooner than allow such a pupil to be sent for life beyond the seas. There must have been something really likeable about the boy, to have opened the heart and the purse of the old school-master—something more than his mere proficiency in classics.

Uncle Chiswick, however, had no faith in Sophocles

or Aristotle; so it ended in the youth's acceptance of a writership at Calcutta. In a brief summary of his early days, found amongst his papers, he mentions how he was the junior of eight young men of respectable middle-class parentage, who went out at the same time. The prospects of such adventure were then held in moderate estimation. They were soon to brighten marvellously, and soon to multiply, so as to form items of household calculation in the contingent resources of a too numerous family. Any one might buy India Stock; the Directors were chosen by the stockholders; and nominations for the Company's service became widely diffused through various sections of the community.

Hastings could never be induced to talk much of his earlier days. Peering, as one tries to do, through the glare of his subsequent career, the circumstances and incidents of that portion of it which was, perhaps, the purest and the best, look indistinct and dim, like objects seen through a telescope turned the wrong way. It is the saddest of sad things, and one of the worst of bad signs, of a man that has fought his own way to greatness, that he should endeavour to ignore the earlier reminiscences of the struggle. There certainly was no lack of courage or persistency in the young cadet. He worked hard at the Factory, as it was called—that is, the place where the few English in Bengal resided, and where they had built storehouses for carrying on the export trade of the Company.

When Clive, in 1756, was sent from Madras to retrieve the disaster on the Hooghly, he was looked upon by the outnumbered and desponding English at Calcutta as a Heaven-sent deliverer. Hastings gazed on the passionate features of Clive with wonder, and was fascinated by the energy and self-reliant daring of the man. On his part, Clive, who was ever quick in discerning special aptitude for the work he wanted done, saw that there were things of difficulty and moment which the pale and pensive little cadet could do much better than mounting guard, or heading a party of sepoy skirmishers. He was sent to Moorshedabad to keep his eyes about him at the Nawab's court, to insinuate himself into the confidence of his Ministers and followers, to make them believe from time to time whatever Clive thought necessary, and to report all faithfully to him. He drew forty rupees a month at this period, and the only recorded duty he performed was every day to read prayers,—to whom, does not appear. What minor share of the booty fell to Hastings, none now can tell. In 1764 he returned to England a widower, and soon after prematurely lost his only child. The bulk of whatever fortune he had brought home was lost about the same time by the failure of the house in which he had invested it. How he occupied himself during his residence in London must be left to conjecture. Could the periodical literature of the day be thoroughly discriminated, according to its authors, it would probably appear that Hastings was ambitious of literary fame. He had a project for the establishment of a professorship of Oriental languages at Oxford, and he sought the acquaintanceship of Dr Johnson, whose approval he wished to engage on its behalf. The Doctor, a man not easily propitiated, was pleased with his deferential manner towards him, and liked his talk about Persian poetry. But there is little evidence in the mountainous piles of the public and private correspondence of Hastings that he had any original gift of composition; and Burke, when his antipathy grew hot, and he was looking round for missiles of all kinds to fling at him, did not omit, amongst other taunts, to upbraid him with not knowing how to write intelligible English. This was just the sort of stab, in a tender spot, that was more likely to make the imperturbable culprit wince, uttered as it was in presence of the beauty, fashion, and genius of England assembled in Westminster Hall, than all the fierce political invectives levelled at him.

He had been examined as a witness before the Select Committee of 1766, and the clearness and vigour of the views expounded in his evidence produced a great impression. He continued, nevertheless, some time longer chafing at the want of adequate employment, and wasting his hours in pleasure or literary obscurity. Meanwhile, under the infirm rule of Clive's successors, the affairs of the Company in Bengal went ill, and in the Presidency of Madras they fared little better. Men of greater capacity and nerve were wanted for their retrieval, and Hastings was invited by the Court of Directors to take the place of a Member of Council at Fort St George. He accepted without hesitation. In point of fact, the offer did not come a day too soon. The gains of his former residence in India were well-nigh spent, and he was obliged to borrow a considerable sum of money to provide his new outfit. It deserves to be remembered that during the season of his embarrassment he continued to pay some small annuities which he had granted to straitened relatives and others who he felt had some claims upon him; and in going to the East a second time, he endeavoured to provide to the utmost of his power for their unabridged continuance. Like many other men of a similar cast of mind, he was at once greedy of money, and munificent in its expenditure; he had as little objection as any feudal freebooter to rifle or overreach in a public way; and he was equally ready to lavish what he thus obtained in acts of hospitality and kindness. In the ship that bore him to Madras was Baron Imhoff, who, with his wife, was proceeding to India in the hope of making a subsistence there as a portrait-painter. The lady was very fascinating and very fair; and her great mistake in life, she thought, was having thrown herself away upon the Baron ere she was old enough to really know her own mind. Her husband did not appreciate her as she deserved. Hastings did, as he tenderly assured her, and her confidence and affection were speedily transferred from the unprosperous father of her children to the plausible and accomplished politician. During the voyage he fell ill, and Madame nursed him with assiduous care. The Baron looked on and said nothing. On arriving at Madras, Hastings suggested that it would be better for all parties if proceedings were initiated in Franconia for the dissolution of the marriage; that until then the emigrant household should not be broken up; but that after that he should marry Madame, provide for the children, and settle a handsome allowance on the Baron. The terms were accepted, the legal proceedings were taken, the Baroness eventually became Mrs Hastings, and the painter of portraits, with the price of his conjugal emancipation, returned to his own country to be heard of no more.

The plague of personal rapine was at its height. The razzias made with impunity in Bengal and elsewhere had fired the cupidity of adventure in every station, high and low. The counting-house was deserted continually for marauding expeditions, undertaken on one pretence or another, generally under native leadership, but generally devised and prepared within the precincts of the Company's settlements. Commerce was forsaken for soldiership, and soldiership was but another name for freebooting. During this period the business of a servant of the Company was simply to wring out of the natives a hundred or two hundred thousand pounds as speedily as possible, that he might return home before his constitution had suffered from the heat to marry a peer's daughter, to buy rotten boroughs in Cornwall, and to give balls in May Fair.[1] Atkinson and Benfield were types of this class, of whom more by and by. Hastings was not blind to opportunities, or deaf to the promptings of personal ambition. As he remembered Daylesford, and looked at the showy and accomplished Marion, he doubtless dreamt many a dream of gain and glory to come; and what perilous jungles and quagmires he was ready to tramp through on his way to opulence and honour, he was soon to prove. In the meantime, however, he had the shrewdness to discern that what the Company wanted most at Madras was somebody to look after their investments, for upon these depended the dividends which formed the jewels of the joint-stock crown. While his comrades and colleagues at Madras were filling their private chests, drinking hard, and preparing to ship off their spoils to England on the first alarm, he set about overhauling the ledgers of the Presidency, pulling up the brokers for overcharge, and endeavouring to resuscitate the profitable trade with the native merchants by greater punctuality in dealing, and by giving more remunerative prices than they had for some time been able to obtain. Leadenhall Street was delighted. What a man this Mr Hastings! a man in a thousand! a man who had the Company's interest at heart; eminently deserving of promotion. And promotion quickly came. Next year Hastings was promoted to be second in Council at Calcutta, with the reversion of the President's chair on the next vacancy.

Clive had burst open the gilded gates of power in Bengal, rifled the treasure, and kept the key. He made himself and

[1] Warren Hastings, by Lord Macaulay—Essays, vol. iii. p. 229.

his successors the irresponsible finance Ministers of the province, with unlimited powers of taxation, collection, and expenditure. But the native Government still in name subsisted. A liberal civil list was guaranteed to the Nawab. He kept his court with hardly diminished splendour. Justice was still administered in his name; and it was through a native official of high rank, resident at Moorshedabad, that the produce of the taxes was received by the Company.

The forms of local administration remained as Clive had shaped them. In semblance, the imperial authority still subsisted, the titles of the Mogul being still emblazoned on all public documents, and money being still coined only in his name. The Feringhees had contracted to be responsible for the produce of the Dewanny and of all imports in native hands. Instructions from England[1] were precise that the old forms should be kept up, because the Directors deemed it essential that the local dignity and state of the Nawab-Nazim should be upheld. This organised hypocrisy of deputed rule was, nevertheless, too complicated for efficient working; and even though it had had time to be amended and improved, it would hardly have lasted long. It was but a compromise hastily framed and rudely imposed upon the weaker party at the end of a struggle which had its origin in the worst of motives, and the scars inflicted in which had not been healed. The Naib of Dacca, Mahomed Reza Khan, was at once the chief Minister of the Nawab and chief collector of the Dewanny. There is no reason for doubting his integrity in the discharge of both functions. But he would have been more than man if he could have infused into a multitude of native subordinates, sentiments of sudden fidelity and zeal for the

[1] Letter of Court of Directors.

interests of the new-comers. He owed to them his appointment as Naib or Vice-Treasurer of Bengal, for which he received one lac of rupees. His first duty was to pay the civil list, which, in the lifetime of Nudjum-ul-Dowla, had been fixed at fifty-three lacs, but which, on the accession of his brother, Syef, was reduced to forty-one lacs.

Mobaruck-ul-Dowla, a minor, had been recognised as heir to the Nizamut, and thirty-two lacs of rupees, guaranteed to him by treaty,[1] continued to be paid for the maintenance of his court and dignity. In 1768,[2] the Directors had forbidden any further reduction of the Soubahdar's civil list, fixed by the treaty of 1766 at forty-one lacs; but their pecuniary needs growing more urgent, they wrote in 1771[3] to Mr Cartier, the acting Governor-General—"We mean not to disapprove the preserving the succession in the family of Mir Jaffir; on the contrary, both justice and policy recommend a measure which at once corresponds with the customs and inclinations of the people of Bengal." But they reproved the want of thrift, shown in squandering on the "parasites and sycophants" of a minor so large a sum, and peremptorily required that it should be cut down one half, until he should come of age. By what right and on what plea they thus varied the specific terms of a treaty which gave them no semblance of discretion, and which concludes with a solemn guarantee that, "with the blessing of God, this treaty shall be inviolably observed for ever," has never, during the century which has since elapsed, been explained. If, however, there was fraud in this frugality, there was likewise frugality evinced in working out the fraud; for the Directors wrote—"As the reduction of the Nawab's stipend is adventitious and temporary, we by no means intend that the

---

[1] 21st March 1770. [2] Despatch, 16th March 1768.
[3] Despatch, 10th April 1771.

commission of 2½ per cent. granted to our servants on our net territorial revenues should be increased by this alteration; and, therefore, the former stipend of thirty-six lacs must still be deducted from the gross amount of those revenues. In like manner, no commission must be drawn on the sums which may be retrenched from the appointments to the Nawab's Ministers."

These abatements were successively exacted upon the plea that reductions had been made in the native troops previously maintained to enforce the payment of the revenue; and these reductions were rendered possible from time to time, as the powers and duties of the Dewanny, despite the inhibitions from home, were absorbed by the Company's officials. As the native forces of Moorshedabad diminished, those in the pay of Fort William increased in number. It was a period and a policy of transition; and when Mr Verelst retired from the Presidency in 1772, his more daring and unscrupulous successor resolved that it should cease.

Before quitting England, Hastings had told the Directors that the relations which Clive had established between the native court at Moorshedabad and the English settlement at Calcutta could not long be maintained. They must either relinquish the anomalous powers of interference with the entire concerns of the province, or take its whole administration into their own hands. This was the political side of the question, but there was another which touched them more nearly. The extravagant expectations raised by the spectacle of the first few years of spoliation were speedily disappointed. Even Indian palaces can be plundered but once. Every year after Clive's departure the remittances fell off, and the Company were led to believe that they were defrauded of their due.

Hastings was desired to remove the Minister of the Nawab and appoint another, or take the collection of the revenue into his own hands. He resolved upon the latter, but thought it necessary to dissemble. He took counsel with Nuncomar, a Hindu of high rank, great wealth, and an intriguing spirit. He suffered him to believe that he was to succeed Mahomed Reza Khan as Minister. They plotted together for his overthrow; and when all was ready, Hastings ordered a body of British troops to surround the palace of the unsuspecting Minister, and bring him a prisoner to Calcutta. His friend, Sitab Roy, the Naib of Behar, was at the same time arrested and confined. Many months elapsed before they were brought to trial—the only excuse for which alleged by Hastings being that the influence of the deposed Minister was so great, that it was necessary to show the people it was broken ere he could be brought to judgment. At length the day arrived, too long postponed. Nuncomar's proofs entirely failed, and both of the accused were honourably acquitted. A small pension for life was given to Mahomed Reza Khan; but, regardless of the stipulation he had made with Clive, that in any event he should have the reversion of the office he had held previously at Dacca, he was not allowed again to hold any post of consequence. Sitab Roy had for years been the cordial and fearless partisan of the English. He had rendered them many signal services; and when their factory at Patna was beleaguered, he had contributed to repel the assailants, extorting from his European comrades enthusiastic acknowledgments and praise. Too late he learned that his best days had been devoted to the humiliation of his race and creed; that no fidelity could insure him against bad faith, and no truthfulness against treachery. He was sent back to his province with a profusion of blandishments and gifts, but his spirit was broken, and he survived only a few months.

Goodias, the son of Nuncomar, was appointed treasurer at Moorshedabad; and instead of the young Nawab's mother, Munny Begum, formerly a dancing-girl, and afterwards an inmate of the late Soubahdar's harem, was appointed guardian. The insulting nature of these appointments under the circumstances admitted of no dispute. They were justly characterised afterwards as savouring of the very wantonness of oppression, unless they were to be ascribed to the more cruel purpose of deliberately humbling in the eyes of a Mohammedan community what still remained of the semblance of native rule. "It was on Nuncomar's abilities, and on the activity of his hatred to Mahomed Reza Khan," that Hastings owns he had relied "for investigating the conduct of the latter, and by eradicating his influence, for confirming the authority which we had assumed in the administration of affairs."[1] The work done, the tool was contemptuously thrown by. Nuncomar and Hastings had known each other years before as rivals in intrigue at Moorshedabad, and their distrust was mutual. The Brahmin found that he had been thoroughly duped, and his rage, though mute, was bitter and implacable. He had seen Mahomed Reza Khan preferred to him by Clive in the appointment he desired, and he had ever since plotted his overthrow. That accomplished, he had been taught to reckon on the reversion of the lucrative post; instead of which, it was abolished, and its profits swept into the stranger's lap. The nomination of his son to titular dignity, at a small salary, and without power, was not calculated to soothe him. He vowed unsleeping vengeance, and resolved to bide his time.

[1] Despatch to Secret Committee, September 1772.

Following quickly on these changes others came, chiefly of internal administration. Under the Act of 1773, a Board of Revenue was established at Calcutta, with provincial inspectors under them, whereby the entire management of the Dewanny was withdrawn from native hands. About the same time two new courts of justice, the Sudder Adawlut and the Nizamut Adawlut, were erected, for the trial respectively of criminal causes and civil suits. The local tribunals in Bengal were said to have fallen into decay, and justice between man and man, it was averred, was bought and sold. It is probably true that where servants or dependants of the new and encroaching power had disputes with natives, the latter should resort to means of corruption in self-defence; and instances of this kind becoming known, it was natural that unscrupulous and overbearing intruders should denounce the whole system to superiors so covetous of extended patronage and power. But what were young officials newly imported from England likely to know of the ordinary administration of law between man and man throughout the country?

G

CHAPTER VIII.

PUNCHAYET AND ADAWLUT.

1772.

"An intelligent native is better qualified to preside at a trial than we can ever be. A native of common capacity will, after a little experience, examine witnesses, and investigate the most intricate case, with more temper and perseverance, with more ability and effect, than almost any European. The Munsif (magistrate) is in the society of the parties, and they cannot easily deceive him. But if the cause comes before the Zillah Judge, besides the inevitable delay and expense at the outset, the conditions of the case are probably entirely changed, intrigue and counter complaints occur, the most impudent falsehoods are advanced with impunity, and, in the end, perhaps an erroneous decision is passed. But who shall distinguish between mistake and imposture? What English Judge can distinguish the exact truth among the numerous inconsistencies of the natives he examines? How often do these inconsistencies proceed from causes very different from those suspected by us? how often from simplicity, fear, embarrassment in the witness? how often from our own ignorance and impatience?"

—H. STRACHEY, 1802.[1]

THE spirit of conquest paused not at the palace gate. We have already heard it there, and marked its tone of scornful menace and imperious boasting. We must now observe its gait and mien in the Adawlut, in the Cutchery, in the Dewannee. How fared it with the rajahs, the talookdars, and the ryots?

It will have been seen how the great lieutenants who were intrusted by the Court of Delhi with the rule of large provinces, succeeded in establishing for themselves

---

[1] Circuit Judge—Fifth Report of Select Committee, p. 541, *et seq.*

almost independent governments. In a different sphere, the local chiefs in many instances had played successfully a similar game. Availing themselves of the embarrassment of their suzerains, they tried to emancipate their particular domains from those tributes that pressed most heavily upon them; though, in a majority of instances, a real as well as nominal fealty was kept up to the Soubadhar or the Mogul. The continual recurrence of war made this a matter of self-defensive necessity. A rajah desired to be independent within his own territories, and to administer the laws without the intervention of a distant and necessarily ignorant Court. But he knew how little he could stand alone against external enemies; and he willingly rendered for the protection afforded to his little principality, as an integral portion of some powerful state, that contributive aid which it in return demanded. The terms, indeed, of these mutual obligations were various, and depended much upon the strength of the rajahs and the position of their territories. Sometimes these chieftains were united among themselves by the ties of blood or friendship, and sometimes by the ties of neighbourhood and common interest. We may conceive how jealously such associations were regarded by the superior princes; we may also conceive how powerful and how beneficial they were capable of being made to those included in them. It was the confederacy of local power against centralised ambition, the strengthening of an authority which, though not theoretically responsible to the opinion of its subjects, was at least always present to receive information, generally identified with the interests of the people, and seldom strong enough to defy with long impunity their prejudices or remonstrances. The peasant cultivator, when he tilled his farm, might grumble at the share that went as rent to the zemindar or the rajah; but he had, at least, the protection of a native local judge, if not a jury, against undue exaction; and he had the satisfaction of seeing what was taken from his industry spent among the community of which he was a member. Many of the native Governments, from the times of the Arab conquest, adhered to the social and political precepts of the Prophet, and in many respects the civilisation they enjoyed was superior to that of the Hindus. Their laws, their arts, their manners, above all, the simplicity of their worship, vindicated their claim of race to pre-eminence, and imparted to their Government a character and tone less unlike that of Europeans.

But there never was an error more groundless than that which represented the ancient systems of Indian rule as decrepid or degrading despotisms, untempered by public opinion. It accords too well with the arrogance of national self-love, and serves too easily to lull the conscience of aggression, to pretend that those whom it has wronged were superstitious slaves, and that they must have so remained but for the disinterested violence of foreign civilisation, introduced by it sword in hand. This pretentious theory is confuted by the admissions of men whose knowledge cannot be disputed, and whose authority cannot be denied. Malcolm and Elphinstone, Munro and Mill, are witnesses whose testimony it cannot withstand, and from them we learn not all perhaps we would wish to know, but far too much to leave one stone upon another of this poor refuge of lies. If we would really know what a people have lost and gained by foreign subjugation, it is requisite to view them as they originally were under their indigenous institutions.

In religion, the communities of Southern Asia were divided, the aboriginal majority being followers of Brahma;

while a powerful minority professed the faith of Islam. This minority, though severed by opinions and by victorious arms from the mass of the community, and differing from them irreconcilably in many usages and ideas, had nevertheless begun to blend their sympathies and associations with those of their fellow-countrymen; and except when the fanaticism of foolish men, or the craft of worthless men, rekindled now and then old jealousies, the Hindu and the Mohammedan lived happily together, and, at the approach of an enemy, went forth cheerfully to fight side by side for one another's homes.

They believed dissimilarly of human destiny in the world to come, and of the things which they supposed would influence their individual lot therein; but in the duty they owed their country and their children, they found many points of common obligation, for Mahomet and Brahma had alike ordained that no behest is more imperative upon faithful votaries than that of guarding intact the family hearth, of seeing justice done among neighbours, and of faithfully defending the head of the state as the fountain of order and law. No exception was specified in their holy books wherein they should be justified in compromising the integrity of their native soil, or in bartering their material rights and immunities for foreign gifts or favours. A few rich bankers in their cities, and a few abandoned characters, might lend themselves to earn the wages of intrigue or espionage; but the bulk of the population, high born or of low degree, worldly or devout, viewed with instinctive aversion the intrusion of strangers whose language they did not understand, whose morality they could not square with any rule of right and wrong, and whose professed belief in the worth of a gospel of peace, and in forbearance, righteousness, and judgment to come, they could not but set down to mere dissembling. It was not that they any more than other men were exempt from evils in their social and political condition. Oppression in its varied forms had from time to time lived its predatory life in many portions of their golden land. Government in the hands of bold and bad men, like Sivajee and Hyder Ali, assumed the form of capricious tyranny, and was for the time grievous to be borne. But these were usurpations, exceptional, violent, and unpopular, like those of Borgia, Louis XI., Philip II., Richard III., Mary Tudor, and the last of the Stuarts. In every country, evil deeds, however exceptional, are most talked of and best remembered, and "blessed is the land whose annals are vacant." It is no more true of Southern Asia than of Western Europe to say, that the everyday habits of either supreme or subordinate rule were semi-barbarous, venal, sanguinary, or rapacious. When a Rajah, Maharajah, or Peishwa, Naib, Nazim, or Padishah, contrived for a season to make himself strong enough to clutch and keep more than his share of the goods of the community, he was sure to defend his ill-gotten gains by acts of cruelty or corruption; for he had become for the time, or thought he had become, irresponsible; and in that one word is briefly told the otherwise innumerable oscillations of popular fate, from good to evil and from happiness to misery, of which every country that we know of has at some time or other been the scene.

Nor have we any reason to suppose that Indian despots were any better than such characters have proved to be in every other part of God's fair world. Wherever they have been suffered to pervert a country or a province, intended for the secure dwelling-place of the people, into a princely hunting-ground, we are told of periodical alternations in the pursuit of the game, caused by the variety of personal disposition. Occasionally we find intervals of different length, when the objects of the chase got breathing time; and again we hear how this intermission gave a higher zest to the renewed sport. But in general these incidents of mercy and forbearance occur pretty much as often in one quarter of the globe as in another. In both, marked and noteworthy respites from oppression have, we know, taken place. It may, however, be doubted whether, under the monarchies of the East, the people have not as frequently found justice and protection, as under those of feudal or over-centralised Europe. Looking back through the family pictures of misrule, from Catherine de' Medicis to Louis le Grand, from Philip the Cruel to Ferdinand the Fool, and from John the Faithless to Charles the False, not forgetting parricide Peter of Muscovy, and the Neapolitan Bourbons, it will appear somewhat difficult, and rather uncharitable, to imagine how any worse than these could have ruled over Hindustan. Into the comparative merits of the dynasties that, during the eighteenth century, governed Southern Asia, we cannot at present enter. That many of them used their too great prerogatives for evil may be naturally supposed. Every analogy tends to confirm such a surmise, and we are not without records which sufficiently attest its justice. But if the dark side of the picture admits of little scepticism, neither does its opposite. We have both analogy and proof abundant for the assertion, that better princes never lived than many of those whose memories are still affectionately cherished among the descendants of their people. Perhaps the most striking proof that is anywhere recorded of the triumph of a pure and noble nature over the corrupting influences of irresponsible power, is that of Ahalya, who for thirty peaceful years reigned over the rich and populous kingdom of Malwa, honoured and respected by surrounding princes, and an object almost of adoration among the people blessed by her rule. In 1765 the male heirs of the house of Holkar became extinct, and the sovereignty devolved upon Ahalya Baee, the mother of the last monarch, and wife of his predecessor. From the moment that the onerous duties of government fell into her hands she evinced a superior capacity to discharge them. Her foreign policy was as successful as that of Catherine of Russia, but her pillow was not drenched with a husband's blood. In personal courage and address she was not inferior to Elizabeth of England, but she did not slay her captive competitor in a prison. The circumstances of her elevation resembled those which raised Margaret of Denmark to the throne; but she neither trampled on the rich nor oppressed the poor, nor caused the breath of suspicion to assail her virtue.[1] The leading object, we are told, she sought to achieve, was by justice and moderation to improve the condition of her country, and to increase the happiness of her people. She kept on foot but a small force, "yet her troops were sufficient, aided by the equity of her administration, to preserve internal tranquillity." Ahalya was a pagan, but she was accustomed to say "that she deemed herself answerable to God for every exercise of power;" and when her officers would urge her to measures of severity against the misguided or the guilty, she used to say, "Let us mortals beware how we destroy the works of the Almighty." Intolerance is not a defect of Hinduism; but Ahalya, though devotedly attached to the opinions in which she had been reared, was, we are told, "peculiarly kind and considerate to such of her subjects as differed from her in faith." Ahalya was not a Christian, but she was merciful, self-denying, assiduous in performing the duties

[1] Vertot's Revolutions of Sweden.

of her station, faithful in dealing out justice to all; and through the course of a long and public life, she lived blameless and unimpeachable. The premature decease of those she loved tinged her heart with the pale hue of sorrow; and humble amid splendour, unambitious on a throne, she retained unaltered her unforgetting garb, and died as she had lived, the childless and widowed Queen. Whether it lies in the mouth of those who, twenty years after her death, entered the territories she had ruled over, and reduced them, after infinite bloodshed and ruin, to that state of subjection in which, to use the compunctious phrase of the invading general, the people, as compared with other conquered nations, were treated " with unexampled scorn " —each of us must answer to his own heart.

During the reigns of the earlier Emperors of Delhi, to the middle of the seventeenth century, complete tolerance was shown to all religions. Shall they who build the tombs of those who, at that very time, were busily employed in making Europe one mighty charnel-house of persecution, and in colonising America with fugitives for conscience-sake, rise up in judgment against India, or load the breath of history with the insolent pretence of having then enjoyed a truer civilisation? What if they were taken at their word, and called forth with the Covenanters' blood, and the Catholics' blood, and the Puritans' blood dripping quick from the orthodox hands that all that time were building scaffolds, riveting chains, and penning penal " Acts of Uniformity ? "

Neither Moslem nor Hindu was incapacitated for public employment on account of the belief in which he had been brought up. Mohammedan princes gladly confided to learned and astute Brahmins civil trusts of importance; and many a Mussulman rose to honour and won fortune in a Maharajah's camp. The Ministers of Hyder Ali, who concealed for a time the event of his death, were Hindus of the highest caste; and when a Chancellor of the Exchequer was to be appointed at Moorshedabad, the Nawab-Nazim tried to have Nuncomar appointed instead of Mahomed Reza Khan. Sivajee was a bigot, and Tippoo a fanatic. But the Governments of Southern Asia, when we began to meddle in their affairs, were strangers to the system of penal laws, which were then among the cherished institutions of our own and nearly every other European state. While no Catholic in Ireland could inherit freehold, command a regiment, or sit on the judicial bench; while in France the Huguenot weaver was driven into exile beyond sea; and while in Sweden none but Lutherans could sit as jurors; and in Spain no heretic was permitted Christian burial;—Sunis and Sheahs, Mahrattas and Sikhs, competed freely for distinction and profit in almost every city and camp of Hindustan. The tide of war ebbed and flowed as in Christian lands, leaving its desolating traces more or less deeply marked upon village homesteads or dilapidated towers. But mosque and temple stood unscathed where they had stood before, monuments of architectural taste and piety, unsurpassed for beauty and richness of decoration in any country of the world. The wise and humane institutions consolidated by Akbar were not shaken until Aurungzebe, by his real or pretended zeal for proselytism, alienated the confidence of the Hindu majority of his subjects; and the Mahrattas, when they invaded his dominions, were hailed as religious deliverers, notwithstanding all the miseries they caused.[1] From that event the Mogul Empire declined, and the Mahratta leaders succeeded in establishing themselves as sovereigns of the fair provinces of the central plain, while the enfeebled dynasty of Delhi was forced to

[1] Malcolm, chap. ii.

be content with its suzerainty over the eastern and southern regions. It would require volumes to recount the incidents by which alterations were effected, and to tell how each princely or viceregal house flourished or faded as compared with its contemporaries. The general features that characterised them, and their general influence on the communities they governed, are matters of more interest in our eyes, and it is only in this point of view that the condition of the people then can be fairly contrasted with that which it since has been. Though the supreme Governments were nominally absolute, there existed in the chieftains, priesthood, courts of justice, the municipal system, and, above all, in the tenant-right to land, numerous and powerful barriers in the way of its abuse. "Property was as carefully protected by laws as in Europe," and their infringement sometimes cost a prince his throne or life.[1]

When the Mohammedans overran all the kingdoms of the East, the laws they introduced, though undoubtedly defective, were, if compared with the Roman or the Norman code, not so remarkably "inferior as they who are only familiar with those systems, and are led by the sound of vulgar applause, are in the habit of believing."[2] It formed no part of their policy to crush the spirit of the Rajpoots or armed nobles, whom they found in every province. "The yoke was made light to them; they were treated as the first princes of the Empire, and their adherents were raised to honour and wealth." In a word, the dynasty was changed, but not the Government. The Omrahs and the Rajahs mingled in the same festivities, enjoyed the same privileges, and, after a single generation had passed away, felt

---

[1] The Land-Tax of India Considered, by General Briggs.
[2] Such at least was the judgment of the ablest English writer upon Indian History, James Mill. See Hist., vol. i.

equally proud of what was equally their country. Next to them in rank were the landed gentry, the Talookdars of Oude, and Zemindars of the Deccan and Bengal, who held their lands by customary tenures, varying in incidents and conditions; and under whom were the Putneedars or farmers, holding at a rent from year to year, or sometimes at a quit-rent in fee; and lastly, there were the Ryots or cultivators, whose condition resembled in many districts that of the cottiers of Ireland, and in other places more nearly that of the tenants of the smaller udal holdings in Norway. To an agricultural people, the dearest and the best of privileges is that which gives them a sense of property in the soil they till. Liberty of conscience is dear, but it is in some respects a matter of degree. Municipal liberty is dear, but it is essentially a political benefit. Liberty of land is far more; it is the one thing without which all other things are unenjoyable. Tenancy, determinable at the will of a superior, is but the legal definition of serfhood.

Among the oldest and most revered of their social usages was that whereby every peasant had a tenant-right to the land he cultivated. Military tenures never touched the ryot, compulsory service in war never prevailed, and armies were raised only by personal influence or the promise of pay. The soil belonged to the farmer, not to the noble, and this right was never questioned. "Even when violence or revolution either extirpated or expelled the original inhabitants, the mere fact of occupation for two or three generations regenerated the rights of the cultivator, who claimed, so long as he could pay the Government share (or land-tax), the field that his father had tilled as his own, as the inheritance of his children, and the claim was admitted by the worst of oppressors."[1]

[1] Malcolm, vol. ii. chap. i.

The natural fruit of such a system was an ardent attachment to the family roof-tree, to the village, to the pergunnah, and the chuckla, within whose inner or outer confines dwelt all whom the peasant knew or loved. Few nations have retained, under every heart-break of hope, a deeper love of native land than the people of Southern Asia. Amid all their misery, humiliation, and disfranchisement, those who know them best, believe that they have never wholly given up the hope of better days again to come. The families of each village, though remote from each other, maintained a constant communication, and the links that bound them together were only strengthened by adversity. When tranquillity was restored, they flocked to their roofless homes. "Every wall of a house, every field, was taken possession of by the owner or cultivator without dispute or litigation."[1] They seem to have been governed by strong national prejudices and social affections. One of their conquerors, who knew them well, declares that he found them "simple, harmless, honest, and having as much truth in them as any people in the world."[2] It is further noted of them, that if they can earn a competence in the neighbourhood where they have been brought up, they prefer remaining there to migrating into other lands holding out a more lucrative prospect. "Nothing but the extreme of hardship could drive the native cultivator from the fields of his fathers."[3] They preferred enough at home to wandering far in quest of gold.

In most parts of India the village community was, as it is still, the unit of social, industrial, and political existence. In each family the father or head of the household exercises an absolute authority. The dwelling is inviolable, and may

[1] Malcolm, vol. ii. chap. i. [2] Munro, vol. i. p. 280.
[3] Malcolm, vol. ii. chap. i.

never be entered by a neighbour, save with his consent. Time out of mind, the village and its common interests and affairs have been ruled over by a council of elders, anciently five in number, now frequently more numerous, but always representative in character, who, when any dispute arises, declare what is the customary law, and who, when any new or unprecedented case occurs, "occasionally legislate. If strict language be employed, legislation is the only term properly expressing the *invention* of customary rules to meet cases which are really new."[1] For the best Indian authorities concur in saying, that, when not actually the fact, the reverent fiction is resorted to that the village council is but declaring what is the customary law. "The municipal and village institutions of India," says Sir John Malcolm, "were competent, from the power given them by the common assent of all ranks, to maintain order and peace within their respective circles. In Central India, their rights and privileges never were contested even by tyrants, while all just princes founded their chief reputation and claim to popularity on attention to them."[2] Sir Thomas Munro, who was intimately acquainted with other districts, says—"In all Indian villages there was a regularly constituted municipality, by which its affairs, both of revenue and police, were administered, and which exercised, to a very great extent, magisterial and judicial authority." He describes minutely the division of duties and gradations of office in these corporate systems; how the public treasurer was a distinct functionary from the magistrate, and how they had at their command a body of tahars or constables to guard the security of individuals.

The most remarkable of all the native institutions was the universally acknowledged jury system. The manner

[1] Professor Maine, p. 116. [2] Malcolm, vol. i. chap. xii.

in which the members of the punchayet were chosen depended upon the nature of the cause at issue. But in every case they were named by popular suffrage. The presidents of these traditional courts "were always men whom the voice of the people had raised into consequence as their defenders against misrule; and who looked to a reward in an augmentation of personal influence and reputation. This they frequently gained, and the applause and attachment of their fellow-citizens was always greatest when they were successful aids to good rule, or courageous opponents of bad." [1] The panel out of which the members of this tribunal were selected was unlimited as to rank and creed. Either party might challenge such persons as he deemed unfavourably disposed to him, and this right extended under certain restrictions even to the *mookh* or president. To be frequently chosen president of the local court was considered the highest compliment which any one could be paid, and to be selected a member was held to be a distinction among both rich and poor. [2]

This was equally true regarding civil and criminal issues, and its essentiality in the moral and social life of the people is plain. Subordination to authority, the security of property, the maintenance of local order, the vindication of character, and safety of life, all primarily depended upon the action of these nerves and sinews of the judiciary system. To maim or paralyse such a system, reticulated minutely throughout the whole frame of society, and acting silently and habitually, without question or friction, to the remotest extremities, may well be deemed a policy which nothing but the arrogance of conquest could have dictated, and the blindness of irresponsible domination could have persisted in. Yet these municipal institutions, which con-

[1] Malcolm, vol. ii. chap. xvi. [2] Malcolm, vol. i. chap. xii.

fessedly had been scrupulously respected in all former changes of dynasty, whether Mohammedan or Mahratta, were henceforth to be disregarded, and many of them to be rudely uprooted by the new system of a foreign administration. Instead of the native punchayet, there was established an arbitrary judge; instead of men being tried when accused, or appealing when wronged, to an elective jury of their fellow-citizens, they must go before a stranger, who could not, if he would, know half what every judge should know of the men and things to be dealt with. Instead of confidence, there was organised distrust; instead of calm, popular, unquestioned justice, there was substituted necessarily imperfect inquiry, hopelessly puzzled intelligence, all the temptations to indolent inattention, and all the liabilities to unconscious mistake; the mute despair of injustice suffered, or the gnashing of teeth at irreparable wrong,— not the less wrong when inadvertently and unintentionally done. A settled purpose was disclosed of substituting rudely the arbitrament of foreign officials, guessing at the facts through interpreters, and stumbling over habits and usages it must take a lifetime to learn, but which every native juryman or elder could recall without effort, and apply to the facts before him without hesitation. No wise or just historian will note these things without expressions of wonder and condemnation.

Hastings himself was fully conscious of the lawlessness of the newly-imposed laws. He admitted that the taking of the whole criminal jurisdiction of the country into their own hands " was a usurpation, but they could not avoid it," he said; " they would have had clashing powers," and so " that justice might have a footing, by hook or by crook, in Bengal, we took it under our own protection."[1]

[1] Letter to Mr Dupre, January 1773.

The substitution of an exotic system of jurisprudence for that which was indigenous, and had its roots in the ideas, traditions, and manners of the people, had ever since the transfer of the Dewanny been steadily going on. Under the advice of Hastings it was completed by the Regulation Act in 1773, the third clause of which constituted the High Court of judicature at Calcutta, with a Chief-Justice and three puisne Judges, clothed with plenary powers, both of first instance and of appeal in all cases, whether civil or criminal. Four English lawyers took their places the following year on the new judgment-seat, their chief being the early friend of Hastings, Sir Elijah Impey.

CHAPTER IX.

THE ROHILLAS.

1773—1776.

"The object of Hastings' diplomacy was at this time simply to get money. His finances were in an embarrassed state, and this he was determined to relieve by some means, fair or foul. He laid it down as a maxim that when he had not as many lacs of rupees as the public service required, he was to take them from anybody who had. The Directors never enjoined or applauded any crime. Whoever examines their letters will find an admirable code of political ethics. But every exhortation is nullified by a demand for money. 'Govern leniently, and send more money;' 'Practise strict justice and moderation towards neighbouring powers, and send more money.' Being interpreted, these instructions simply mean, ' Be the father and the oppressor of the people ; be just and unjust, moderate and rapacious.' He correctly judged that the safest course would be to neglect the sermons and to find the rupees."

—Lord Macaulay.[1]

WHEN Lord North and his colleagues determined to confer the chief place in the remodelled system on Mr Hastings, they secured, as they believed, the services of the ablest man on the spot, and the benefits of the greatest administrative experience ; but they chose along with him three men of a wholly different stamp, who might, it was hoped, curb his ambition, and temper his exercise of power. General Clavering, Colonel Monson, and Mr Philip Francis were named in the Act as members of Council. They were all persons of high political character, and Francis, though still unrecognised as the author of the work which has become identified with his name, was confessedly

[1] Critical and Historical Essays, vol. iii. p. 244.

possessed of rare intellectual endowments. Even those who deny him the credit of being the author of the "Letters of Junius," must admit that he showed in his acknowledged productions a grasp of thought and vigour of conception, a power of illustration and striking idiosyncrasy of style, rarely to be met with either in politics or literature. The new Governor-General, elated with past success and new promotion, could ill brook the shackles Parliament had imposed on him. He regarded his new associates from the outset as men whose ignorance he was fitted to instruct, but who could teach him nothing he did not already know. He understood the purpose for which they had been chosen, and from the first resolved to baffle it, while they distrusted him too deeply to throw over it a veil. Nor were they long in discovering ample grounds for their distrust. The exchequer was low, the Company's debt was increasing, and the demands from home were more importunate than ever. Hastings was a man full of expedients, and not particular as to their nature. The Vizier of Oude was rich and covetous, and might be tempted by the loan of British troops to pay handsomely for territory to be filched from a weaker neighbour. The project was kept a profound secret from the new members of Council, and its execution was prepared before they were made aware of its scope and aim.

Upon the confines of Oude, where the deep waters of the Caramnassa wind their way through many valleys, dwelt the freest race in all that land. They were girded in on almost every side by rocky hills, and, unambitious of augmenting their wealth by injury of their neighbours, they lived on the fruit of their own toil, and Heaven blessed them. Like the people of other districts, the Rohillas were locally ruled by their own chiefs and magistrates, but they enjoyed more than ordinary freedom, and consequently more prosperity than many other communities. "They are never to be feared," said Governor Verelst in 1768, "from the nature of their government. When attacked, their natural affection will unite, the common cause will animate them; but it is not practicable to engage their voice on any other motive than their general safety."[1] And of the result of their steady adherence to this traditional policy we are thus informed: "Their territory was one of the best governed in Asia; the people were protected, their industry encouraged, and the country flourished steadily. By these cares, and by cultivating diligently the arts of neutrality, and not by conquering from their neighbours, they provided for their independence."[2] The Vizier of Oude had never been able either to subdue their military spirit, nor yet to seduce it into schemes of suicidal aggression. While so many of the Governments of Hindustan were perpetually encroaching on each other's territories, in much the same wise and useful manner that the monarchs of Europe amused themselves in times past, the Rohillas, like the Swiss, sedulously cultivated the arts of peace, and such a spirit of self-defensive war as could alone secure them its enjoyment.

During the war of 1772, they had faithfully adhered to their alliance with the Vizier. Their territory lay between Oude and the recent conquests of the Mahrattas; and when that restless people in the following year menaced the dominions of the Vizier, and offered advantageous terms to the brave mountain clans, if they would allow them a passage through their country, the offer was steadily and repeatedly refused.[3] By this they exposed themselves to the whole tempest of the Mahratta inroads—a danger whose greatness the haughtiest sovereigns in Hindustan were not ashamed

[1] Verelst's account.   [2] Mill, book V. chap. i.   [3] Mill, book V. chap. i.

to avert by great concessions. The treaty of mutual alliance by which these noble people deemed it their duty thus to abide had been entered into at the express instance of the English, and under their solemn guarantee;[1] and when the forfeit of their fidelity had been incurred, and Rohillcund was ravaged by the Mahrattas, in 1773, the allied forces of the English and of Oude were employed to co-operate in opposing the common enemy. No sooner however, were the western invaders repelled, than the Vizier secretly devised with the Governor-General a plan for annexing their territory. This project, says Hastings, writing confidentially to the Directors on 3d December 1774, "I encouraged as I had done before."[2]

For we are come to the period when a so-called Viceroy, with more by far than kingly power, was to wield at will the stolen sceptre of the East,—a man trained in the school of Clive, and who, if inferior to his master in personal daring and military genius, was perhaps more than his equal in political craft and far-sighted rapacity. His account of the transaction in question is too instructive to be given in any other words than his own. "As this had been a favourite object of the Vizier, the Board judged with me that it might afford a fair occasion to urge the improvement of our alliance by obtaining his assent to an equitable compensation for the aid he had occasionally received from our forces."[3] The meaning of this sleek villany was this:—Hastings had induced the Vizier to employ a subsidiary force within his dominions, on the plan afterwards prescribed for the acceptance of other princes. This force was professedly to defend the Soubahdar against foreign enemies, but it was officered and com-

---

[1] Mill, book V. chap. i.
[2] Fifth Parliamentary Report, written by Edmund Burke.
[3] Fifth Parliamentary Report.

manded exclusively by the Company. Once introduced, there were always reasons why it could not be withdrawn; but as yet this part of the design was not perceived by the cunning but outwitted Soubahdar. Meanwhile the sums stipulated for its support were such as to yield an overplus, and to be systematically relied on as a source of profit and revenue; and it was with a view to the increase of this profit, and to supply deficiencies in other departments, that the sale of Rohilcund was agreed to. All advices represented the distress of the Company at home as extreme. For a long time the income of the year had been found inadequate to its expenditure, to defray which a heavy bond debt had been gradually accumulating.[1] A secret treaty was therefore entered into between the Soubahdar and the Governor-General, whereby the Company engaged, whenever a suitable pretence should be found or made, in consideration of a sum of forty lacs of rupees, and payment of all expenses to be incurred in the business, in concert with the troops of Oude to crush the Rohillas, and to add their country to the dominions of the Vizier. The impolicy of this seems manifest enough. The Rohillas were, as they proved themselves to be, the best soldiers in the East, and they formed a permanent outguard and defence against the Mahrattas. But the insane desire of territorial acquisition blinded the Vizier to his interest as well as to his honour; and the ambition of duping him into pecuniary and military relations with the Company, from which it was clearly foreseen he would never be able to get free, seared the conscience of Hastings to all remorse or shame. By him was the precedent set of hiring out to the princes of Hindustan, permanent bodies of British troops under the designation of subsidiary forces, and thereby was a means established of sapping the authority

[1] Fifth Report.

and independence of every one of them. Hastings avows that in establishing such a force in Oude, he designed to weaken the native Government, and reduce it to dependency; and how soon his accomplice found that he had sold himself with his prey, subsequent events clearly set forth.

The treaty of Benares was signed in September 1773; but the article for the destruction of the Rohillas was not disclosed till January 1774. Various pretences of claims unsatisfied had been duly made in the interval; and if any one is curious on the matter, he may on inquiry satisfy himself that they were not even colourably true; such, at least, was the verdict of Parliament and of the Directors at home some years afterwards. Why waste words upon them here? On the 17th April the allies in iniquity entered Rohilcund. In vain the brave but outnumbered people sued for mercy; in vain they proffered bitter and miserable submissions. The Vizier feared that they might live for vengeance, and insisted that nothing but their entire dispossession from their homes could give him security. Sooner than submit to this, they chose rather to abide the fate of battle. Ranged on the steep sides of the Babul Nulla, they awaited the murderous onslaught. "It were impossible," said the English commander, Colonel Champion, "to describe a more obstinate firmness of resolution than they displayed. Numerous were the gallant men who advanced, and pitched their colours between the two armies to encourage their men to follow them. Two thousand fell upon the field, among them many Sirdars and Hafiz Rahmet, their commander, who was killed whilst bravely rallying his people."[1] The memorable battle of Rampûr took place on 23d April, and may be said to have determined the issue of the war.

[1] Fifth Parliamentary Report.

Fyzoola Khan retired to the mountains with the broken remnant of the gallant host, but the country was left bare to the knife of rapine. Seldom, if ever, have what are called the rights of victory been more inhumanly abused. "Every man who bore the name of Rohilla was either put to death or forced to seek safety in exile." But this did not exceed the stipulations of the treaty; for by Hastings' own letters it appears that in its provisions there was the specific agreement that, if necessary, "the Rohillas should be exterminated,"—the language is his own.[1] By the time the work of confiscation was complete, and the red gleam of burning homesteads no longer lit by night the once happy vales of Rohilcund, the allies found the season spent, the country utterly exhausted, and Fyzoola Khan intrenched so strongly in the mountains that no immediate hope could be entertained of his reduction. To him and his followers they granted, therefore, terms of amnesty; and thus ended the war.

We had not the slightest pretence of quarrel with the Rohillas. We had not even a colourable complaint against them. Rohillcund was rather a defence to our newly-acquired provinces, and its commerce and agriculture nourished ours. But money was wanted to meet exorbitant salaries and charges, and the Governor-General made up his mind to pay the usury of blood. He accepted the money from Oude, and hired the Company's troops to the Vizier, to seize and expropriate Rohillcund. The liberties and lives of a friendly race were the price of the subsidy. He well knew the bravery of the people he was engaging to hunt down, and the misery, violence, and desolation to which he was devoting them. He was remonstrated with by Champion, who offered to throw up

[1] Fifth Parliamentary Report.

his command, and deprecations the most touching came from the unfortunate Rohilla chiefs. But the Viceroy was inexorable. Not a single stipulation was made as to the use to which the British troops were to be put, or the severities they might be called upon to execute. They were placed unconditionally at the disposal of the Vizier; the word was given and the doom of a gallant race was sealed. Hastings pocketed £20,000 as a private present for signing the treaty, and the public treasury was replenished to the extent of £400,000.

Disagreements and divisions in the Council at Calcutta, at first whispered only among the English there, gradually became noised about. Native resentment, long repressed, at length found utterance. A majority of the Council were ready, for the first time, to listen with impartiality, if not with sympathy and pity, to the plaints of an injured people. Recent grievance and long-cherished grudge welled up on every side like the surging waters of an inundation. The danger of Hastings grew imminent, but his courage did not fail. He continued to occupy the chair of state regardless of sarcasms, inuendoes, and protests. Clavering, Monson, and Francis recorded their strong disapproval of the bargain with the Vizier, recalled the troops from Rohilcund, and refused to ratify the Treaty of Benares. But the Viceroy was not to be turned from his purpose. He understood what his employers wanted better than his antagonists did. The protests of the triumvirate appealed to the conscience of the Company, whatever that might be; his congratulations touched their heart. Exemplary regrets and admonitions not to do it again were, after due deliberation, despatched to India; but, as we shall presently see, the Ministers of the Crown thought it would be absurd to call Hastings to account for the triumphs he had achieved; and both they and the Directors acquiesced in the profitable wrong.

Specific accusations were publicly made against the Governor-General of vast sums exacted from natives, under the name of presents, for promotion to office and for other considerations. Hastings steadily refused to hear, far less to meet, these accusations. To entertain them at the Council Board, he said, was to disparage his authority, and lower the Government in the estimation of the natives; he would not condescend to answer any of them, and whenever the majority attempted to pursue their investigations, he made a point of rising and quitting the room. They persevered without him, and placed on record the complaints of Munnee Begum, the Ranee of Burdwan, and her adopted son Ram Kaeheen, Roda Shurn Roy, a vakeel of the Nawab of Bengal, Casmul, the farmer of a large district, and three English gentlemen—Mr Grant, accountant to the Council of Moorshedabad, and the two Messrs Fowke—all of whom charged him specifically with acts of gross venality and extortion. A minute of the Council, adopted by Clavering, Francis, and Monson, in March 1775, summed up his offences thus—" There is no species of peculation from which the Governor-General has thought it reasonable to abstain. We believe the proofs of his having appropriated four parts of the salary of the Phousdar of Hooghly are such as will not leave a shadow of a doubt concerning his guilt in the mind of any unprejudiced person." These accusations subsequently became the subject of inquiry by Parliament, and testimony the most conflicting was adduced to sustain and rebut them. There was in existence then, however, a piece of evidence of which neither Lords or Commons were aware, and which weighs more heavily than a score of vindictive affidavits or unwrappings of finance accounts. In a letter to Lord North, dated 27th March 1775, while the charges were still fresh, Hastings elaborately inveighs against the mischief of the course taken by Clavering, Monson, and Francis, and reasons most ingeniously on the irrelevancy of the questions raised by them to the ultimate interests of the State. He assigns, moreover, many plausible grounds for assuming the improbability of much that they alleged against him; but there is not from beginning to end the simple assertion on the word of a gentleman that the allegations with regard to taking bribes were false, or any statement that can be stretched into a denial. Lord North was the Minister who had made him Vice-King of Hindustan. There was not living the man with whom it was so important for him to stand well. He was little likely to hesitate about any amount of varnish or colouring of facts, if that would have done ; yet, writing confidentially on the spur of the moment, he does not venture on one manly or straightforward expression of denial, such as honest men wrongfully impugned are wont to utter. But this is not all. We have the damning fact that when impeachment at home was subsequently impending, Hastings thought it prudent to lodge in the treasury of Calcutta £200,000, which he could only account for as having been from time to time received by him in his public capacity, and having been inadvertently omitted until then to be placed to the credit of the State.

At the head of his accusers stood Nuncomar. His pride as the ablest man of his race had been wounded by Hastings, his ambition as a skilful financier and diplomatist had been baffled by him, his self-love as the wiliest of intriguers had been stung; for he had been outwitted partly by the craft of Hastings, when Resident at Moorshedabad, in the affair of

Mahomed Reza Khan. He had waited for revenge, and the opportunity at last had come. Between these two men there existed that antagonism, intense, profound, and inextinguishable, of which perfect sympathy alone is capable. They had looked into each other's soul, and recognised in each the image of himself reflected there. Of all his race none probably but Nuncomar knew all Hastings had done; for none but he had the same purpose to gain in watching the windings of his dark and devious course, or possessed the means of obtaining so much information with respect to all his secret doings. On the other hand, there was no Englishman in India who had motives so strong as the Viceroy for observing closely and scrutinising thoroughly the acts and aims of the subtle and specious Hindu. Their resemblance morally and intellectually was complete. Fair-spoken, impassive, fearless, and unfathomable, they were alike insensible to the sufferings of others, and devoted to self-worship. Insatiable of money, yet munificent in its outlay; admired by those who came not too close to them, and distrusted most by those who knew them best; gentle in prosperity and superbly self-possessed in danger; unwearied in business, inexhaustible in resources, imperturbable alike in the gloom of adversity and the glare of triumph, at the bar of judgment and in the face of death.

Nuncomar placed in the hands of Francis a petition to be heard in person by the Council, before whom he undertook to prove that Hastings had sold appointments to office for large sums of money, and that Mahomed Reza Khan had been exonerated from vast peculations for a bribe of unusual magnitude. The Governor-General refused with contempt to be confronted with his accuser, and denied the right of his colleagues to constitute themselves his judges. They might, if they would, refer the question home, but he would not lower the dignity of his office by sitting there to have his word weighed in the balance against that of a corrupt and mendacious Brahmin. The majority resolved notwithstanding to proceed with the investigation of the charge. Hastings with Barwell thereupon withdrew, and Nuncomar was called in. He had long sat patiently by the well of vengeance, and at length had found wherewith to draw. Hastings was informed by his colleagues of all that was sworn against him. More than one of the English servants of the Company came forward to sustain the charges. The accused inflexibly refused to answer; and the Council, in his absence, recorded their conviction of his guilt. Nuncomar's revelations were declared by them to have shed "a clear light upon the Governor-General's conduct, and the means he had taken of making the large fortune he was said to possess—upwards of forty lacs of rupees—which he must have amassed in the course of three years." [1]

Driven to bay, Hastings clutched at a weapon which lay at his feet, but which no one else had thought of using. The newly-created Supreme Court set up by Parliament to administer English law in English fashion among the people of Bengal, had been given unlimited jurisdiction, and the power of life and death. The Judges had sided with him throughout the schism which had brought society in Calcutta to the verge of anarchy, and the Chief-Justice was his confidant and friend. Suddenly an indictment for the forgery of a bond six years before was preferred in the name of an obscure native, as was generally understood, at the instance of Hastings, and under a warrant of the court Nuncomar was thrown into prison. Indignant reclamations were made by the triumvirate, and they ordered the prisoner's release; but the troops obeyed the commands of Hastings, and no sense

[1] Minute of Council, 11th April 1775.

of decorum or of generosity restrained him. The arraignment was indeed a hideous mockery. Technically and substantially the indictment could not have been sustained had an appeal lain to Westminster. The statute of 1773, which was said to give jurisdiction in the case, could not have had a retrospective effect; and it was not promulgated or even passed until after the alleged crime had been committed; for the crime itself had been made capital even in England only by a modern Act, and in no part of Asia had such a law been ever known. Time out of mind, the falsification of a private contract had been regarded, as it was in this country before Walpole's time, as a grave misdemeanour and no more. Nuncomar may or may not have been guilty of the offence; but if anything is certain, it is that he was innocent of breaking the law under which he was accused of a capital crime. The claim to take away life for the breach of an English criminal statute had indeed been made before. In February 1765, one Radachurn Mittre was indicted for forgery at the General Quarter-Sessions of the town of Calcutta, convicted and sentenced to be hanged. The Bench of Justices having subsequently made a proclamation that English laws were to be extended to the natives, the latter issued a protest against this in a petition to the President and Council.[1] The petitioners set forth the general "consternation, astonishment, and even panic with which the natives in all parts under the dominion of the English were seized by the example of Radachurn Mittre. They found themselves subject to the pains and penalties of laws to which they were utter strangers, and were liable through ignorance unwittingly to incur them. As they were in no way instructed in those laws, they could not tell when they transgressed them, many things it seemed being capital by English laws which were

[1] Long's Records, vol. i. p. 67.

only fineable by the laws of the petitioners' forefathers, subject to which they had hitherto been bred, lived, and been governed, and that (till very lately) even under the English flag."[1] The petition concluded with a prayer for a "rehearsal, or respite of execution till an appeal had been made to the King of Great Britain, and further, that the English law might be translated into the Bengalee tongue." Mr Verelst in council approved the petition, and characterised the proceedings of the Justices as an "act unjustifiable in itself, and in its nature and consequences cruel and oppressive." Hastings and Impey could not have been ignorant of these circumstances, though, strange to say, they have been overlooked by one who, in our own time, filled the office of legal member of the Supreme Council, and to whom was specially confided the task of framing a criminal code.[2] A jury, on which there was not a single native, found that the fact of the false signature was proved; and the Chief-Justice condemned Nuncomar to die. Clavering, Monson, and Francis remonstrated against the execution of the sentence, and earnestly demanded a respite until the pleasure of the Crown could be known. But they expostulated in vain, and in presence of a multitude such as never before had been gathered together within range of the guns of Fort William, the aged chief of the Brahmins was put to death.[3] A wail of horror rose as the drop fell, and the echoes of that cry did not cease until, long years after, in Westminster Hall, Burke denounced Hastings for having "murdered Nuncomar by the hands of Sir Elijah Impey."[4]

---

[1] Long's Records, vol. i. p. 430.
[2] Lord Macaulay, in his Essay on Warren Hastings, has fallen into error in asserting that no attempt had been made to enforce the law of forgery among the natives of the East. In Long's "Unpublished Records," there is a succinct account of the case above cited.
[3] 5th August 1776.
[4] Speech of Mr Burke on sixth count of the impeachment, 25th April 1789.

Led by Mr Pitt, a majority of the House of Commons subsequently voted, on the motion of the Marquis of Graham, that these words ought not to have been spoken; but Fox, Windham, and Sheridan defiantly adopted them, and declared that the Managers would make them good. The resolution of censure remains to this day unexpunged; but history has reversed the vote, and the memory of the great international Tribune needs no vindication.

CHAPTER X.

BENARES AND OUDE.

1777—1780.

"It had been said of the Company that there was something in their operations which combined the meanness of a pedlar with the profligacy of a pirate. Alike in the military and the political line could be observed auctioneering ambassadors and trading generals; and thus we saw a revolution brought about by affidavits, an army employed in executing an arrest, a town besieged on a note of hand, a prince dethroned for the balance of an account. Thus it was they united the mock majesty of a bloody sceptre and the little traffic of a merchant's counting-house, wielding a truncheon with one hand, and picking a pocket with the other."

—R. B. SHERIDAN.[1]

FROM the reports sent home by the baffled triumvirate, Ministers learned enough to justify them in desiring the recall of Hastings. The Regulating Act enabled the Crown to supersede him only on an address to that effect from the Company; and that body was so nearly balanced in opinion that he only escaped a resolution for his dismissal by a few votes.

Lord North, though the most good-natured of men, was much incensed, and threatened to summon Parliament earlier than usual in order to put an end to a state of things that had become scandalous, and to reduce the privileges of the Company to those which gave them a monopoly of trade in the Indian Seas. Colonel Macleane, alarmed at

---

[1] Speech on the Begums of Oude, 7th February 1787—Parliamentary History, vol. xxv. col. 287.

what might happen, acted on a discretion given him, and tendered the Viceroy's resignation. Wheler was at once appointed in his stead, and Clavering named to act as *locum tenens* until he should arrive. But ere the news could reach Calcutta, Colonel Monson died. By virtue of his casting vote, Hastings regained his ascendancy in the Council, and at once resumed the exercise of unlimited authority with respect both to measures and to men. Clavering vainly attempted to assert the temporary power assigned to him. He sent for the keys of office, and they were refused; he issued orders to the troops, but they were disobeyed. The question of who should govern was referred to the Supreme Court. Hastings repudiated his resignation; declared he had kept no copy, or that, if he had, he could not find it. Not having resigned, there was no vacancy in point of law, and all the proceedings founded on the supposition were consequently null and void. The Judges ruled in his favour; and when Wheler arrived, he had to content himself with taking a subordinate seat in the Council. The ascendancy of superior intellect and audacity combined was shown in a personal incident about this time. Baron Imhoff, under Viceregal patronage, had continued to practise his art at Calcutta; but after long delay the decree of divorce arrived from Germany, and the superseded husband thereupon departed with his share of Indian riches. The Church at last bestowed its benediction on Mrs Hastings, and the exculpatory rite was solemnised with courtly splendour. Clavering excused his absence on the ground of illness, but the cup of triumph would not have been full without his presence, and the Viceroy, to ensure it, paid him a visit, and carried him to the wedding-feast.

Francis was a man made of different stuff. When he hated he hated with his whole heart; and he hated nobody

so much as Hastings. He had, by the help of Clavering and
Monson, succeeded in deposing him for a time; and with the
help of Fowke and Bristowe as witnesses to his corruption,
he had branded him with administrative reproach. The
tide of fortune had turned, and Hastings, once more in the
ascendancy, was all but absolute lord of the East. There
were few things probably Francis would not have done to
redress the balance of power thus overset. While he
brooded in bitterness and discontent, overtures of peace
came from the enemy. The Governor-General had learned
to respect, if not to fear, the tenacity of his rival's purpose
and the inveteracy of his aversion. The day must come
when, returning to England, Francis, unappeased and un-
forgiving, might be a serious impediment in the way of his
ambition. Better win him over, and commit him if possible
to concurrence in the general policy of Indian administration while there was time, than run the risk of having to
defend the measures of to-day and to-morrow, as well as
those of yesterday, in a Court of Proprietors, in the press,
and in Parliament. Might not Francis be tempted, by one
or two triumphs in hand, to relinquish the hope of half a
dozen in the bush fifteen thousand miles away? The result
justified the experiment of reconciliation. Francis, over-
reached and over-matched, chafing with disappointment,
half-forgotten in England, and conscious that he was regarded by his countrymen in Calcutta as one who, with all
his talents, had been baffled, might well apply to himself
the terrible words of Swift, that after all his fame his fate
seemed to be—" To die of rage, like a poisoned rat in a hole."
Unexpectedly the door of his chamber opened, and an
emissary charged with offers of accommodation entered. If
his own pen has not depicted his amazement and delight,
how should another's. It was one of those exquisite moments

that compensate ambitious men for years of embitterment and chagrin. He agreed to the general basis of arrangement, and promised not to thwart certain measures then about to be taken against the Mahrattas. He insisted for the public restoration to all their dignities and emoluments of Fowke and Bristowe, whom he felt bound in honour to see righted for the part they had taken, and for the sacrifices they had endured. This was a bitter dose, but *Junius* was inexorable, and with a shrug Hastings gulped it. It was an ineffaceable admission that these men were not perjurers, as they had been called; if not, their testimony remained; and Hastings, by the fact of their reappointment to the Residencies of Lucknow and Benares, confessed himself to have been corrupt, calumnious, and cruel.

For two years peace was maintained in Fort William, but at length the old antagonism broke out afresh. In dealing with the Mahrattas, incidents arose which drew forth differences of opinion. Francis was on the side of nonintervention, Hastings was for taking the high-handed line. Unable to persuade, he tried to silence his opponent by alleging that acquiescence in his views of external policy was one of the terms of the accommodation between them. This Francis stoutly denied; he said it had been proposed, but refused by him, and that in an unlimited sense it would manifestly be incompatible with his sworn duty as a member of the Executive. A minute of Hastings pronouncing him incapable of candour and unworthy of credit provoked him to send a challenge, which the Viceroy did not hesitate to accept. A duel took place next day; Francis was wounded, but not dangerously, and he soon recovered. Two years before, Lord Townshend, then Viceroy of Ireland, was challenged by Lord Bellamont for having turned his back upon him at levée. They fought with swords, and the challenger was wounded. Such were the manners of a time not yet a century past.

The last efforts of Francis in India had been directed chiefly to limit the scope of aggressive hostilities against the Mahratta States, with whom he and his late colleagues had always advised that we should seek to live in amity. Clavering had placed on record his opinion on the subject. When the Government of Bombay had seized Salsette, invaded Broach, and rashly committed themselves in disputes as to the successor to the musnud of Poona, the General, who disapproved of these proceedings, would have had the Government at Calcutta exercise its overruling authority, and vindicate its character for good faith with its neighbours. He hoped " that the Mahrattas thus seeing our justice and moderation, and that our intentions were finally to put a stop to that spirit of conquest, encroachment, and injustice, which seemed hitherto to have prevailed too much in India, would listen to the proposals we had made to conclude a firm and everlasting peace with them."[1] But these were not the intentions of Hastings; and when Monson and Clavering were dead, he was no longer restrained from aiding and abetting the schemes of aggression which had been immaturely and improvidently commenced at Bombay. Expeditions under Popham, Goddart, and Carnac were launched against Scindia, Holkar, and Berar. Fresh feats of valour added greatly to the reputation of the English for enterprise and endurance; and so far contributed to create that belief in their invincibility which rendered subsequent conquests possible. After four sanguinary campaigns, peace was made in 1780, restoring all the acquisitions which had been made on either side. At the close of the year Francis returned to England, and thus

[1] Thornton's History of British India, 3d edit. p. 145.

expired the attempt, never again renewed, to temper by constitutional checks in Council viceregal despotism in the East. For the purposes of advice, and with powers of suggestion, what is termed a Supreme Council still remains. But it is a consultative body of précis writers, not a Cabinet.

Left once more to himself (for the new members of Council were not men of the sort that could have effectually curbed him), he entered upon various enterprises of expansion and expropriation. Among the chiefs of secondary rank friendly to the English, when friends were few and aid invaluable, was the Rajah of Benares. He was one of the wealthy feudatories from whom the Viziers of Oude had been satisfied with fealty and a payment of certain contributions in peace and war. Bulwunt Singh was an excellent ruler; the local administration was never interfered with; his people were happy, and the country prosperous. The description by Holwell of the condition of Burdwan applied equally to the holy city of Siva and the districts around it. Hindu pilgrims from far and near brought rich and varied gifts to the famous shrine; and the peasantry, fearless of unjust exaction or personal wrong, cultivated their fields like gardens, and throve on the fruits of their unwearied industry. Their numbers were estimated at more than half a million, and their chief had but one fault in the eyes of his neighbours—that of being suspected of opulence greater than their own. By the partition treaty of 1775, the Vizier had transferred his suzerainty over Benares to the Company, who issued sunnuds confirming Cheyte Singh in all the rights he had inherited from his father. On the outbreak of war with France, they called on him to raise and equip three battalions of sepoys, at a yearly charge of five lacs of rupees. After some parleying and grumbling, he submitted. But when, in the third year, he was told he must likewise raise a body of cavalry, he ventured to refuse; whereupon the Governor-General undertook to overcome his reluctance, and intimated his intention to visit Benares with a numerous train. The Rajah met him at Buxar with all due honour, deprecated his anger respectfully, and by way of homage placed his turban on the Viceroy's knees. Resentment long concealed burned in the breast of Hastings, and though polite and imperturbable, he pursued his pitiless ends. Three years before, when his dispute with Clavering in the Council was at its height, Cheyte Singh, not knowing who had proved the stronger, had sent an agent to propitiate the General, on whose favour he might one day have to rely. Before his envoy reached Calcutta, the tidings spread that Clavering and his friends had been worsted in the struggle, and the message never was delivered. But Hastings learned the fact, and could not forget or forgive it. Arrived at Benares, he demanded satisfaction in peremptory terms for the alleged remissness shown in meeting the military requisitions, and the reply being deemed to savour of insubordination, the Resident was ordered to proceed with two companies of sepoys to the palace and to take the Rajah into custody. The populace, indignant at such an outrage, fell upon the troops, who had been hastily summoned without ammunition, and who were speedily put to the sword. Another company was sent to avenge them, and a sanguinary conflict ensued. During the night the Prince was let down from a window of his palace by a rope formed of the turbans of his attendants, and crossing the Ganges, fled to Ramnaghur, a fort some miles distant on the opposite bank, which contained the chief portion of his treasure. Thither his wife and mother followed him. The place was forced to surrender, but not until its coveted contents had been removed, and the Rajah himself escaped to Bidgeghur, whence he was finally driven to spend his days as a refugee in Gwalior. Meanwhile the Viceroy proclaimed his deposition, and set up as Rajah a youth of nineteen, who was not allowed to take on himself any of the more important duties of his station. The tribute payable by the district was raised to £200,000 a year, and its collection placed in hands deemed hard enough to be depended on. Turbulence, not always stifled, alternated with passive resistance among the people, much incensed by what they had beheld. All sense of security was at an end. Capital fled, and was followed by labour of such descriptions as were not dependent on the soil. Misery and distraction took the place which had recently been occupied by comfort and content. The new exactions, though rigorously pressed, did not yield what was expected; and two years later, when Hastings revisited the scene of his personal vengeance, he found it one of desolation. The number of inhabitants steadily declined, and in 1822 it was estimated at no more than 200,000.[1]

The want of money was still urgent, and what the spoliation of Benares failed to meet, fresh exactions from Oude must supply. Asaph-ul-Dowla pleaded poverty, and named, with some truth, that amongst its causes was the annual contribution he was obliged to pay for the maintenance of the subsidiary force. Dreading a visit from the Viceroy, he went to meet him; and at the fortress of Chunar the negotiations took place which resulted in the memorable device for replenishing the exchequer of Calcutta without exhausting that of Lucknow. "It was," says Lord Macaulay, "simply this, that the Governor-General and the Nawab-Vizier should join to rob a third party, and the third party

[1] Malte-Brun's Geography.

whom they determined to rob was the parent of one of the robbers."[1] The mother and widow of the late Vizier were supposed to have derived, under his will, vast treasures. They dwelt with a numerous retinue at the favourite palace of Fyzabad, which he had bequeathed to them. Asaph-ul-Dowla shrank in shame from the villany suggested by his Right Honourable accomplice. But he was only a Mussulman, and his scruples were overborne. The confederates, having ratified the bargain, parted, and each went his way to prepare the formalities of fraud. A conspiracy to aid Cheyte Singh in his resistance to intolerable exaction was to be imputed to the withered women who dwelt at Fyzabad. If such a breach of friendship could be proved, it would justify any penalty or forfeiture; therefore it must be proved, and proved in a regular respectable way. When it was known what was wanted, false witnesses rose up, as they are apt to do when they are wanted, and when there is an imperial treasury to pay them. But the worth of their testimony against the undefended Princesses of Oude, there was no tribunal to test, no advocate to tell. Still there was a difficulty: a silken cord of conventional decency had to be snapped before the palace gates of the Begums could be forced open by English troops. The dying Vizier had placed these members of his family under the special protection of the British Government, and for reasons apparently good at the time, but good no longer, that Government had accepted the trust. It might be a quirm, a punctilio, what is sometimes called a sting of conscience, no matter what. But there it was, a thing to be silenced somehow: and the question was how? Not for the first time Sir Elijah Impey proved himself to be a friend in need. There had been a grievous quarrel between

[1] Historical and Critical Essays—Warren Hastings.

the Chief Governor and the Chief-Justice, arising from a conflict of jurisdictions; and both had indulged in vows of wrath and fury. But the Chief Governor had mollified the Chief-Justice with the gift of a place worth £6000 a year, terminable at his pleasure; and from that day Herod and Pilate had been reconciled together. So now, at a pinch, Sir Elijah got into his palanquin, and posted to Lucknow, by relays of pagan bearers;—for were not pagans made to bear Christian Chief-Justices on their shoulders, when at full speed to aid in the commission of robbery at a command of a Right Honourable Viceroy? What could more clearly prove to a soul-darkened population the superiority of European manners and morals? Arrived in the capital of Oude, the Chief-Justice took a number of affidavits which accused the Begums of complicity with Cheyte Singh, in his supposed conspiracy against his lawful masters, the Company. Sir Elijah did not read the affidavits, or hear them read. They were in a dialect he did not understand, and he had not time to wait for an interpreter. So he took them as chief magistrate of England in the East; and this "scandalous prostitution of his high authority"[1] being completed, he got into his palanquin again, and returned to Calcutta. In the memorable words of Sheridan, "With a generous oblivion of duty and of honour, with a proud sense of having authorised all future rapacity, and sanctioned all past oppression, this friendly judge proceeded on his circuit of health and ease."[2] The farce concluded, tragic scenes began. The palace of Fyzabad was surrounded by English troops, the Princesses were told that they were captives, and required to deliver up their

---

[1] Speech of Sir G. Elliot (afterwards Lord Minto and Governor-General), on impeachment of Impey, 12th December 1787—Parliamentary History, vol. xxvi. col. 1339.   [2] Speech on the Begum's Charge, 7th February 1787.

gold and jewels. On their refusal, their ladies were subjected to semi-starvation and their servants to torture. Unable to endure their groans and tears, the Begums gave up casket after casket, and store after store, until the sum of spoil was reckoned at £1,200,000. Then, and not till then, their wretched menials were let go. Such are the bare outlines of the dreadful tale. Over all that could furnish forth the true colouring of the picture, the veil of oblivion has fallen, and it cannot now be raised. What the people of Oude thought of these things we know not. We only know that Asaph-ul-Dowla did not find his account after all in agreeing to the shameful ransom. His Government henceforth appears to have lost influence and power. When Lord Cornwallis, a few years later, visited Oude, he was received with every mark of deference and respect; but nothing could hide from him the desolation that overspread the country, the spectacle of which shocked his very soul. He asked the Vizier why he was not able to do something to improve the popular condition, and amend this state of misery. The Nawab told him in reply, that "as long as the demands of the English Government upon the revenue should remain unlimited, he could have no interest in economy, and that while they continued to interfere in the internal administration of his country, it would be in vain for him to attempt any salutary reform, for his subjects knew he was but a cypher in his own dominions, and therefore despised his authority, and that of his Ministers."[1]

[1] Letter of Lord Cornwallis, quoted by Mr Sheridan in his speech on Oude, 31 June 1788.

CHAPTER XI.

HYDER ALI—MYSORE.

1781—1782.

> When at length Hyder Ali found that he had to do with men whom no treaty or no signature could bind, and who were the enemies of human intercourse itself, he determined to make the country possessed of these incorrigible criminals a memorable example to mankind, to put a barrier of desolation between him and those against whom the faith which holds the moral elements of the world together was no protection."
>
> —Edmund Burke.

THE other Presidencies had long been emulous of the fame in successful aggression achieved by that of Bengal; but they were compassed round by native states more warlike and intractable, with whom their intermeddling as often brought discomfiture and loss as gain and victory. The Dutch, Portuguese, and French, as well as they, were incessantly intriguing with the Hindu and Moslem courts for privilege or pre-eminence; and the struggle, intermittently carried on, was quite as much with other European colonists as with suspicious Nawabs and Rajahs.

The war between the French and English, which was terminated by the treaty of Paris, left the former scarce a remnant of their once great possessions on the Coromandel coast. The feeble and corrupt Government of Louis XV. took little trouble to devise means for recovering what had been lost, and the flag of their ancient rivals now floated peaceably over many a fort and field that had long and bloodily been contended for. Nor seemed there any power remaining all along that shore whom the conquerors need henceforth fear. Masulipatam, and other maritime provinces of the Nizam, were already theirs; Chingleput lying around Madras had been taken from the Nawab of the Carnatic; Surat and Salsette had recently been wrested from the Mahrattas; and the Dutch began to fear for their possessions in Ceylon. In 1766 three brothers were contending for the Musnud of the Deccan; and each of them was ready to purchase English aid by the offer of half the revenues of the seaboard provinces called the Five Circars. Nizam Ali prevailed, but being sore pressed by the Mahrattas, he agreed that the coveted districts should be committed to the charge of Hoossein Ali, half their revenues to be paid to the Company on condition of their affording help in collecting them. Sunnuds from Delhi were then secretly obtained by Clive, conferring the Circars on the English in absolute sovereignty. But these, when published, the Soubahdar refused to recognise. Force and negotiation were by turns employed, and at length a treaty of compromise was made, by which the fiscal possession of the Circars was yielded to the Presidency of Madras, subject to the payment of a considerable tribute, and an undertaking that the Company would in every event support the Nizam against his enemies. The tenure of these additional estates was thus confessedly one of occupancy at a quit-rent defeasible for breach of covenant. But from that day to the present it has been treated as one of absolute sovereignty.[1]

One native power alone had the presumption to retain a seaboard territory. Mysore was indeed without a navy worthy of the name, and without any apparent means of

[1] Thornton's History of British India, 3d edit. p. 111.

creating one; but to the jealous eye of political and commercial monopoly all things are possible, probable, impending, when it is desirable to find them so. Disputes had sometimes arisen with the rulers of Mysore, but it was not until 1767 that an English corps, commanded by Colonel Smith, suddenly crossed the southern frontiers of the Carnatic, and took possession of the rich and important province of Baramahal. Why then, and not sooner, the latest apologist of English acquisition avows his inability to explain. The appropriation of a volume to the subject would not, he says, afford a satisfactory or lucid exposition of the events, or of the motives of the actors engaged in them. "It may be doubted," adds the historian, "whether the persons then forming the British Government of Madras understood their own policy; and it is quite certain that to all others it must ever remain inexplicable."[1]

Baramahal was one of the most fruitful provinces of Mysore, and from its position served to give that inland realm access to the Indian Sea. A long series of domestic troubles had unnerved the vigour of the Mysorean Government, and opened the way for the elevation of a Mohammedan soldier of fortune to more than a participation in the power and dignity of the ancient Hindu throne. The Rajah was still permitted to enjoy the pomp and luxuries of regal captivity, but Hyder was sole Minister and General, and virtually head of the State. Imperfect as the materials are for enabling us to estimate the genius and character of this singular man, enough remains to testify that, as a leader and a ruler, he was of that stamp which seldom breaks the level of ordinary capacity. The power of creating internal organisation where he found decrepid custom and incipient anarchy; the vigour he imparted to

[1] Thornton's History of British India, 3d edit. p. 111.

the outworn mechanism of the administration both in peace and war; the aptitude he evinced for applying to the external defence of his country, and to the internal development of its resources, the arts and inventions of a foreign civilisation; his activity, his perseverance, his self-reliance, his personal daring, and, above all, the instinctive faculty he possessed of attaching men to him, have sufficiently been attested by those who, having bearded him in an hour of weakness, learned to tremble at his very name. Rapacious, false, and cruel, no epithet of obloquy was probably unjust, as applied to his long and chequered career; but his power, by the steady course of a system of policy which his untaught genius had created, had reached a height in 1767 which the surrounding Governments could no longer afford to disregard. The Mahrattas and the Nizam had their own quarrels with this formidable chief; but the Company had not as yet been brought into collision with him. On the contrary, throughout his long reign they had always hitherto kept up with him friendly if not intimate relations; and if their expressions of esteem in latter days grew less sincere, care was taken that they should be at least as loud, or perhaps a little louder even than before. It is said to be a habit to which diplomatists are prone, to render their mutual salutations more impressive as their schemes for each others' ruin approach maturity. Of this we shall not fail to meet with some edifying examples by and by.

Grievance against Hyder the Company had none, but part of the price promised for the Circars was a defensive alliance with the Nizam, and this was now conveniently interpreted to mean an offensive pact against Mysore. Seringapatam and Hyderabad happening to be at feud, the occasion might be improved by seizing Baramahal.

Hyder's usual fortune appeared to have deserted him in his wars with the combined forces of the Mahrattas and the Nizam. The frontiers of Mysore were threatened on the north and east at one and the same time. His resources were still great, but it took them all to meet the opposite dangers that were converging upon his unaided kingdom. This was the moment chosen by the Council of Madras for suddenly invading his dominions. It is true that they were, up to the day when the invading corps began their march, not only at peace with Mysore, but bound by terms of friendship and alliance with its formidable ruler. But what of that? Though ruler still, he seemed formidable no longer; and was mere faith to stand in the way of the clear and manifest opportunity of helping themselves out of the exposed possessions of their friend? Were they to allow him to recover from the stunning blows already dealt upon him by his enemies? or to wait till the Mahrattas had appropriated perchance the whole of the spoil? The Governor of Madras and his colleagues were too wakeful to let such an opportunity slip. They determined, accordingly, to avail themselves of the defenceless situation of the Mysorean territory nearest to their own, and which, moreover, happened to be one of the best worth appropriating. Baramahal, they said, should henceforth be numbered with their possessions. By one of those sudden changes that in oriental war are of frequent occurrence, Hyder found himself relieved within a few weeks from both his native enemies, and at full liberty to devote his entire attention to his foreign friends. With stern promptitude he abandoned all other cares until he should not only satisfy them that they had seen quite as much of his territories as such visitors usually desire to become acquainted with, but, with a more than ordinary ceremony, he resolved never to quit them till he had seen them home. And scrupulously did he keep his word. With the speed of the whirlwind fell the whole wrath of the still mighty chief upon the new occupants of Baramahal. From point to point, breathless and panic-stricken, the invaders were hurled back across the borders, down, onwards, headlong, till they reached, with heavy loss and total discomfiture, the mound of St Thomas. Under the walls of Madras, Hyder dictated a new treaty with the Company; and among its provisions was a solemn stipulation that, "in case his dominions were attacked by any foreign enemy, they should furnish him with seven battalions of sepoys."[1] To the humbled and beleaguered garrison of Madras such a stipulation sounded almost like mockery. But it was destined to prove a memorable stipulation, not alone to him and them, but, in its eventual consequences, to the people of the entire Peninsula. By the time that Hyder found himself free to set about restoring the somewhat exhausted resources of his kingdom, the year 1769 had closed, and ere his more peaceable occupations were well begun, the Mahrattas were once more upon the border. His natural endeavour, under these circumstances, was to present, if possible, so imposing an aspect to the enemy as to deter them from entering on a renewal of their devastating warfare. To effect this purpose, he desired to show that the English were his allies in reality as well as in name; and in right of the treaty he had so recently made, he demanded a moderate force from the Company. In reply they alleged that their troops were few, their resources spent, and that they could not spare any which would be of use to him. This, or some like excuse, was always ready when no scheme of acquisition was in view; but whenever a prospect of annexation or mediatising, however perilous, was opened to them, then heaven and earth were moved to raise

[1] Memoirs of Sir Thomas Munro, vol. i. chap. ii.

supplies of men and arms. Hyder was not the man, however, to be outwitted thus. He resolved to put their sincerity to the test. If they could not send a large force, he would be content with a small one; if they had not money available, he would find it himself. But they persisted in refusing every requisition, and kept their troops shut up in garrison.

Meanwhile, the Mahratta tide poured down through the rich valleys of Mysore; province after province was overrun by the irregular horsemen of the hills. The aged chief in vain out-generalled and defeated them in a hundred fights and marches; they wasted his territory as much in retreat as in advance, and, by dint of their locust numbers, wrought all the ruin he had striven to avert. Month after month the harassing conflict lasted, and every month Hyder appealed to his "allies" at Madras for aid; but they doggedly adhered to their purpose, and "did not send a man to his assistance."[1] One party among them even desired to espouse openly the side of the Mahrattas, and proposed a partition of Mysore; the President and Council preferred to behold their ally's kingdom wrecked by other hands, and the sight of a Mysorean camp under the walls of Fort George was still too recent in their memories.[2] At length, in July 1771, Hyder was fain to purchase peace by extensive cessions of territory, and the payment of heavy contributions to the Mahrattas. Slowly did Mysore recover from the effects of this fatal war. Not all his wounded pride nor thirst of vengeance could tempt him into hostilities for many years afterwards. He saw that his country could not be recruited by a brief repose, and he resolutely maintained a strict neutrality for several years. His old antagonists in 1777 ventured once more to assail him;

[1] Munro, vol. i. chap. ii.   [2] Mill, book V. chap. iv.

and, "though deeply exasperated against the English by their evasion of the treaty, he was now induced to make a fresh proposal, requiring only a supply of arms and stores, for which he would pay, and a body of troops for whose cost he would provide."[1] This, as before, was refused. The veteran bridled his resentment and went to seek his assailants. He found their main army encamped near Adoni; in a pitched battle he routed their imposing force, the scattered remnant of which retreated hastily to their own land, and the Mahrattas from that day troubled him no more.

While these events were taking place in India, the recognition of the independence of the American Colonies by France had rekindled war between that power and Great Britain. In the course of 1778 Pondicherry and other towns, where the French still retained their factories, were besieged, and after some resistance taken. An expedition was likewise organised against Mahé, a place of no importance in itself, but, as the last relic of the conquests of Dupleix, worth seizing, and worth crossing an ally's territory to seize. Mahé was situated in one of the provinces of Mysore, and consequently was under the protection of its ruler. The Company well knew, however, that his consent to their investing it was not likely to be obtained; and they alleged, not without some truth, that Hyder had lately shown an inclination to cultivate a greater intercourse with the French than he formerly had done. "They acknowledged that had not the treaty of 1769 been evaded, he never would have sought other allies than themselves,"[2] and it is now unquestionable that up to the year 1779 he had no treaty with the French. When, however, the beleaguerment of Mahé commenced, Hyder loudly protested; and finding his expostulations disregarded, he declared that

[1] Mill, book V. chap. v.   [2] Ibid.

if Mahē should fall, he would invade the Carnatic. The siege was persisted in, and on the 19th March 1779, Mahē surrendered.

Terrible is the record left by eye-witnesses of the long-delayed retribution taken by Hyder on the possessions of the English,—imperishable is the eloquence which devoted its best efforts to the commemoration of that fearful scene. On every point the Carnatic frontier was assailed; towns and villages were occupied and laid under contribution; the cities were besieged, the crops everywhere consumed or fired. They who had taken the guardianship of the country from its native princes, and who had now provoked this fearful inroad, had taken no precautions adequate to resist it. They said, in extenuation of their neglect, that they were unable;—a poor excuse! They had wrested the direction and the means of public defence from those who, if not the best fitted to govern, had at least an incomparably better right to rule than they; and now, in the midst of dangers their own cupidity and incapacity had drawn down, they left their involuntary subjects to the mercy of a ruthless foe. They had usurped the sovereignty of the Carnatic,—what a commentary was their confession that they were wholly unable to defend it! They affected to bewail the sad condition of the people, and in their letters home implored the sympathy, and strove to kindle the indignation, of the Government and the public in England against Hyder Ali. But the disposition of the people, who had now had experience of the comparative benefits of indigenous and exotic rule, has been written for our learning. The great historian of Anglo-India tells us that, amid all the devastations committed by his troops, Hyder was less detested as a destroyer than hailed as a deliverer. While Colonel Cosby, the English commander, found himself in great distress for intelligence, which by no exertion was he able to procure, every motion of his was promptly communicated to Hyder by the people of the country. In an official letter he says, "There is no doubt that Hyder has greatly attached the inhabitants to him."[1]

The sincerity of their preference was signally illustrated by an incident mentioned by Munro. When the main army was endeavouring to re-unite with Baillie's corps, three men were found near the road, who were told by the General, that if they would conduct him to Baillie, he would reward them, but if they should misguide him, he would instantly put them to death. They walked at the head of the army, with halters round their necks, and conducted them to the side of a lake, where the road terminated.[2] They were suffered to escape, though Munro does not conceal his indignation at the lenity manifested towards men who, without the expectation even of one farewell cheer from their countrymen, thus deliberately prepared to sacrifice themselves. Such is the perverting spirit of conquest, and such, too, is the instinctive love of country! The self-devotion of these men determined probably the fate of Baillie. His corps had been unwisely separated from the main body, and on the 8th and 9th of September, it was pursued and nearly surrounded by the hosts of Hyder. Anxiously he wrote to the British General apprising him of his situation, and proposing by irregular night-marches to endeavour to elude the vigilance of the enemy until relief could be afforded him. The entire force under Sir Hector Munro was at once put in motion. On the second day they heard distinctly the sound of continued firing; and had they known the country, there is now no doubt that they would have come up in time, if not to avert a conflict, at least to

[1] Mill, book V. chap. v.   [2] Munro, vol. i. chap. ii.

cover a retreat. But the precious hours were spent in wearisome and ineffectual attempts to find the road; and the very night they returned in despair to their quarters at Conjeveram, the doom of Baillie's corps was sealed. At sunrise on the 10th September, they beheld themselves hemmed in on all sides by the Mysorean army under the command of Tippoo Saib. Hour after hour they withstood unbroken the terrible onslaughts of the enemy. The hope of aid sustained them long; after that—despair. At length, outworn, they sank down man by man on the ground where they had defied their myriad foes throughout the murderous day, overwhelmed but unconquered.[1]

No further attempt was made to oppose the invasion, and the main army forthwith retreated to Madras. So rapid was their march, that two hundred men belonging to a Highland regiment dropped down from absolute exhaustion, having been compelled to march thirty miles during a sultry day.[2] Amongst the baggage taken during this retreat were the military papers belonging to Lord M'Leod, the second in command, and these contained a plan for the reduction and appropriation of Hyder's dominions.[3] How far the perusal of such a document was calculated to appease the triumphant chief's resentment, it is unnecessary to speculate. On the 3d November, Arcot fell. The Pettah was taken by storm, and the town was compelled to surrender. The inhabitants were treated with humanity; no plundering or license was allowed; "every one was continued in the enjoyment of his fortune, and all who had held places under the Nawab retained them;" to the English officers who were taken prisoners, Hyder gave money to provide for

---

[1] Wilk's Historical Sketches; and Munro.
[2] Munro, vol. i. chap. ii.
[3] Ibid.

their necessities.[1] The minor cities now opened their gates, and the general disaffection was no longer hidden. At the close of 1780 the authority of the Company extended little beyond the precincts of Madras. Early in the ensuing spring, however, reinforcements arrived from Bengal, and a squadron appeared off the coast. Sir Eyre Coote succeeded to the command, and ventured to advance against Hyder. He was twice severely worsted by the veteran chief, and the English were at the end of the season beaten back once more to St Thomas' Mound. They soon began to suffer from disease, and to the horrors of disease were added those of famine. Hundreds died daily in the streets; no means of relief existed, and those who survived were hourly doomed to see the dead-carts trail their piles of unshrouded corpses outside the ramparts, where huge trenches for promiscuous burial had been made. But death, while busy with the enemies of Hyder, found time to seek him also. At the moment when his vengeance had been sated to the full, and the renown of his genius had reached its zenith, the strength of his constitution, though singularly great, gave way, and the greatest spirit whose presence India has in latter times confessed was summoned from its earthly wanderings.

The death of Hyder Ali in the winter of 1782 did not terminate the war. The event was concealed by Purnia and Kishna Rao, two Brahmin Ministers in whom he had placed special confidence, until his son, then at a distance of 400 miles, could reach the camp. Tippoo found himself at the head of an army of 100,000 men, with three crores of rupees in the treasury, besides wealth in jewels to a vast amount. Early in the spring General Matthews invaded Mysore

---

[1] Munro, vol. i. chap. ii. How this demeanour was requited will be seen in the narrative, gathered chiefly from the same witnesses, of the taking of Seringapatam.

from the side of Malabar, and ere the season closed Onore, Mangalore, and Ananpore were in his hands. Excessive cruelties were perpetrated in the reduction of these places, orders being given to put to the sword every man found within the walls with arms in his hands.[1] The inhabitants were likewise subjected to unlimited extortion, not, we may be sure, to gratify any vulgar lust of rapine, but just that they might be taught an early and impressive lesson of the superior benefits of European rule. In the course of the campaign, Bednor was captured, and recaptured by Tippoo, as well as Mangalore. General Matthews was taken prisoner, and was supposed to have been put to death in prison. His successor, General Stuart, failed to redeem the prestige he had lost; and Lord Macartney, sick of the suffering and slaughter around him, and deaf to the incentives of Hastings, who was all for continuing the conflict, offered to make peace.

In March 1784 peace was signed, the basis of its terms being a mutual restoration of all conquests made during the war. For some years the Peninsula, which was now governed by four great powers—the Mahrattas, the Nizam, Tippoo, and the Company—enjoyed comparative repose. A few minor states were suffered to maintain a nominal independence, under the exacting friendship of one or other of the greater powers; and from this circumstance arose the pretext for the second war with Mysore.

[1] Mill, book V. chap. v.

CHAPTER XII.

RIVAL INDIA BILLS.

1782—1786.

"There is a tribunal for individuals; is there none for nations? Is there no law by which bodies of men acting in a social and political capacity are bound to act with fidelity and confidence in their mutual intercourse? The obligations of justice are fundamental, and are not to be violated by any subsequent or adventitious system whatsoever."

—J. ANSTRUTHER.[1]

AT the beginning of 1782, America was lost, and Parliament once more grew anxious about India. Misled by a voluble and accomplished Minister, who for years had contrived to retain the favour of the Court and of large majorities in both Houses, vast establishments by sea and land had been kept up, at extravagant cost, to preserve our empire in the West; yet it had not been preserved. On the 19th October 1781, the last army sent to reduce the colonies had, under Lord Cornwallis, surrendered at Yorktown, and all hope of retrieving the disaster had been abandoned. Mortified ambition turned its eyes towards the East. Another empire was growing there, or, if duly fostered and nurtured, it might grow. But strange tales were continually told of errors and misdeeds; and the in-

---

[1] Debate on the Rohilla Charge—Impeachment of Warren Hastings, 2d June 1786.

quiries that had slumbered since 1772 were renewed at the instance of the same men who had then endeavoured to invite Parliament to take into its own hands direct responsibility and control. Dundas moved for a Select Committee, the report of which strongly condemned the conduct of Sir Thomas Rumbold and of Warren Hastings. Burke at the same time moved for a Select Committee to inquire into financial and judicial abuses. Its report censured in no measured terms Sullivan, the Chairman of the Court of Directors, and Sir Elijah Impey. A bill of pains and penalties was introduced against Sir Thomas Rumbold for his abuse of power as Governor of Madras; and an address to the Crown was voted to recall Sir Elijah Impey, for the corruption and oppression of which he had been guilty as Chief-Justice of the Supreme Court. The last of a string of forty-four resolutions adopted by the House declared it to be the duty of the Directors to recall Hastings; but this the Board declined to do, as they were not bound to take directions from one branch only of the Legislature. When Lord North's Administration fell, that by which it was succeeded undertook to frame a comprehensive and permanent measure for the government of India. Lord Rockingham's demise drove Fox and Burke for a time into opposition; and Lord Shelburne, looking round for allies wherever they might be found, thought of resorting to Hastings, as one whose talents might materially aid the Administration both in the Cabinet and in Parliament. On receipt of fresh tidings regarding Cheyte Singh, Dundas brought up a second report from the Secret Committee renewing the question of recall. A Court of Proprietors forthwith assembled, in which this proceeding was denounced, and the Directors were warned not to supersede the Governor-General without their previous assent. To this defiance of the House of Commons they were no doubt emboldened by the tone of Lord Shelburne and Colonel Barré, who warmly defended the policy of Hastings. In a letter to Lord Shelburne,[1] when First Minister, the Viceroy disclaimed the authorship of the Mahratta war. It originated, he said, with the Board of Directors and the Presidency of Bombay. It was begun without his knowledge, and upon grounds which he disapproved; but finding the Bombay Government committed to its perils and consequences, he supported them heartily; and he asserted that it was he who saved the Carnatic. "Forgive me then the boast, when I add that I have been the instrument of rescuing one Presidency from infamy, and both from annihilation."

In 1783 the Coalition Cabinet devolved once more on Burke the task of preparing an India Bill. It was introduced by Fox on the 18th November, and pressed through all its stages in the Lower House before the Christmas holidays. A Board of seven persons, to hold office for four years, were named in the Bill, and as vacancies fell they were to be filled up by the Crown. These were to constitute a new department to which the entire direction of Asiatic affairs was to be confided. A subordinate Board of eight for a like term was to superintend the commercial affairs of the Company, which thenceforth was to be relieved of all political functions. Supplementary provisions were designed settling once and for all the rights of the native princes and proprietors in relation to the paramount power; rendering highly penal the receipt under any form of bribes or presents by persons holding office, civil or military, fiscal or judicial; and putting an end to monopolies of all descriptions. It was indeed, as its eloquent authors declared, aimed against all those perversions of justice and political iniqui-

[1] Letter, 12th December 1782.

ties by which individuals had enriched themselves at the cost of the Indian people, and to the dishonour of the English name. Pitt, Grenville, and Wilberforce opposed the measure, as giving too much power to Ministers. Jenkinson, who was understood to speak the personal sentiments of the King, characterised it as an attempt on their part to render themselves too strong for the sovereign; and Scott (afterwards Lord Eldon) made a maiden speech in which he compared the Board of seven to the Apocalyptic Beast with seven heads arising out of the sea, an augury of human woes unspeakable. By decisive majorities, however, it passed through all its stages in the Lower House, and evoked no symptoms of unusual hostility when brought up to the Lords. The intention was not disguised of superseding Hastings, as a fitting preliminary to the inauguration of a new policy founded on new principles; and nothing more inflamed the anger of the Court and its antipathy. Lord Mansfield warned Ministers that if they attacked Hastings they would lose their India Bill and ruin themselves; and George III. declared his belief that if he were recalled, India would be in jeopardy.

The King resolved at any risk to be rid of Ministers whom he hated. A card in his handwriting authorised Lord Temple to tell the peers individually that his Majesty would regard as his personal enemy any man who voted for the Bill. The Upper House consisted at the time of 190 members, of whom the chiefs of the great Whig families were by far the richest and most influential. But the Court was powerful, the Anglo-Indian interest great, and the Coalition Cabinet unpopular out-of-doors; and on the 17th December the bill was rejected by a majority of nineteen. Next day Fox and North were dismissed, and Pitt called to power.

In the new Parliament, the youthful Minister had a majority, and in the session of 1784 was passed the rival India Bill which long bore his name. As originally framed, its defects were numerous. They were laid bare by Francis in a speech full of glittering sarcasm and incisive reasoning. The inexperienced Premier's first essay in legislation had failed; the machine of subtle contrivance would not work; it must be taken to pieces while still new, and put together again with fragments more or less numerous from the workshop of contemned rivals. Its boasted checks were so perfect that, instead of balancing one another, and easing further action, it was felt, upon reflection, that they could only bring all progress to a stand. It was clear that responsibility would be rendered illusory by the empirical separation of trusts, and by the complication of details. Parliament had discarded its wisest and truest counsellors in the matter, and followed the advice of clerks and changelings. Francis, who seldom carried with him so completely the attention of the House, paid just tribute to the years of unrequited toil and care Burke had devoted to unravelling the errors and misdeeds committed in India; and with a tenderness of sympathy and heartiness of homage of which he was not deemed capable, he uttered prophetically that consolation to the wounded and worn spirit of his friend which, sooner than he expected, public opinion confirmed. "I am not here to pronounce his panegyric; nor, if I were equal to the task, would I venture to undertake it: it would lead me to reflections that would utterly discompose me—to the recollection of virtues unrewarded, and of services growing grey under the neglect, if not ingratitude, of his country. If fame be a reward, he possesses it already; but I know he looks forward to a higher recompense. He considers and believes, as I do, that in some other existence the virtues of men will meet with retribution, where they who have faithfully and gratuitously served mankind 'shall find the generous labour was not lost.'"[1] The omission of the right of appeal to a jury drew forth the allusion to the memory of Chatham, the ambiguous drift of the concluding words of which were long remembered and resented. "Had such an attempt been made when a great man who is now no more had a seat in this House, he would have started from the bed of sickness, he would have solicited some friendly hand to deposit him on this floor, and from this station with a monarch's voice would have called the kingdom to arms." He paused, and looking steadily at the First Minister, he added, in a tone of ineffable regret, "but he is dead, and has left nothing in this world that in the least resembles him."[2] By the provisions of the amended Act, the Governor-General had been invested with the power of filling up vacancies in the Council, and of overruling its members whenever he should think fit. From the President of a Privy Council of five, he was elevated into an absolute ruler. The Opposition loudly but vainly protested against this creation of a viceregal despotism; but once created, an authority so precious in the eyes of Centralism was never destined to be relinquished. The instincts of executive power impel it to encroach, to absorb, and to monopolise ever more and more. Its aims are irrespective of party interests, its acts regardless of party traditions. In our own time its inroads on urban and provincial freedom have been continuous and uncompensated; and each new concentration of authority affords an analogy and constitutes an example for further aggression. The East India Company was still too

---

[1] Parliamentary Debates, vol. xxv.
[2] Debate on the Amended India Bill, 26th July 1784.

strong, and the military force at the disposal of the Crown in Asia still too weak to render it prudent or possible, as yet, to assume absolutely the whole patronage and revenue of our dependencies. For seventy years more the Company was permitted to enjoy the honours of titular sovereignty, and to appropriate the exclusive profits of Indian commerce, and of the subordinate posts in Indian administration. But henceforth the political direction of affairs in Asia was strictly held and exercised by the Imperial Government. Despatches and accounts in duplicate were regularly sent home, indeed, to the Board of Control and the Board of Directors, and each maintained a learned and efficient staff to assist them in the work of consultative comment and advice. But every year Cannon Row gained what Leadenhall Street lost in the power of influencing the general policy of the Anglo-Indian Government. The latter seldom failed to indite wise admonitions to its officers, high and low, as to the duty of forbearance towards its distant subjects, toleration of their prejudices, and the development of their productive capabilities by the maintenance of peace. Simultaneously the former wrote directing attention to whatever circumstances seemed propitious for further acquisition or absorption of territory. Every year the never-failing plea alleged was that of self-defence. Somebody was always said to be plotting our expulsion or caballing with foes beyond the frontier for our ruin. One President of the Board of Control after another, with a rare exception now and then, translated the old formula into new phraseology, full of disclaimers of territorial ambition, but having substantially no other meaning. In the scathing words of one who has himself been admitted to the secrets of power, "Whenever existing revenues showed symptoms of failing, or there was nothing else to engage popular attention, the best thing to be done was to take to the road." Every time the landmarks were pushed farther north or west, the permanent military charges of the establishment were increased, and the ways and means were found comparatively less adequate to defray them. The Directors, left to themselves, would doubtless have restrained the tendencies to expansion within narrower limits; and when occasionally a Governor-General proved himself to be sincerely averse from war, it is but due to them to say that they were content to let him alone. But from the passing of the Act of 1784, it was extremely difficult for them to curb the military spirit ever growing more intractable in the East, or to prevent instigation being given by the Board of Control, and acted on by the Governor-General, to an extent committing the whole force of the Indian Empire, and staking its security on the success of some fresh enterprise, before they had time, in the then course of post, to make their deprecation audible. When it was too late, regrets were said to be vain, and amid the exultations of victory, cold reasons of prudence or unwelcome qualms of conscience seldom found a voice. The assent of the Directors was still required in the choice of each new Viceroy, and they were suffered to retain the power of recall without the concurrence of the Crown. On two or three occasions they vetoed informally, but not ineffectually, the choice of Ministers, when the job attempted was felt to be "too bad:" and in one instance they exercised their power of recall. But generally speaking, Government found means of carrying their point in the city, and disagreements of a serious nature seldom arose between the two Boards which, according to law, formed the double government. The statute of 1784 established a system which balanced the authority of the Court of Directors by a Board of Control named by the

Crown, and removable with the Administration of the day, but which was practically invested with such privileges, and hedged round by such forms as effectually to be exempted from accountability to Parliament. It was the converse in every respect of the rejected plan. Fox would have made Parliament supreme in the affairs of India; Pitt would have the patronage divided between the Company and the Crown, understanding clearly what measureless influence this system must give the Minister.

Burke opposed the last Pitt's India Bill, which he foresaw would create an effectual screen for a policy of aggrandisement and oppression, like that already branded by Committees of the House of Commons. Despairing of legislative reform, he turned his thoughts to the duty of exposing, and if possible of bringing to punishment, past delinquencies. Late in the session he asked for papers regarding the partition of Oude. Major Scott, the acknowledged agent of Hastings, seconded the motion for their production, as certain to vindicate the conduct of the Viceroy. Government, more wary, made reservations, saying there might be some things that ought not to be inconsiderately disclosed. Burke waxed wroth. A long debate ensued; the hacks of Government ironically cheered the threats of the great accuser; and Pitt brought the altercation to an end by raising a point of form. Burke, laying his hand on one of the Select Committee's reports which lay upon the table, with grim deliberation said, "I swear by this book, that the wrongs done to humanity in the Eastern world shall be avenged on those who have inflicted them. They will find, when the measure of their iniquity is full, that Providence was not asleep. The wrath of Heaven will sooner or later fall upon a nation that suffers with impunity its rulers thus to oppress the weak and innocent." He then gave notice of his intention to move in the following session for a full inquiry into the alleged crimes of the Governor-General, and of his determination to seek from Parliament reparation for the wrongs of India.[1]

On the 28th of February, Fox moved for confidential papers which, if produced, would show, he said, the injustice of sequestrating certain provinces of the Carnatic, to pay the usurious debts claimed by civil servants of Madras from the Nawab of Arcot. These transactions were of a kind denounced by the Committee of Enquiry, and interdicted by the recent India Bill. Nevertheless they were now screened by the newly-constituted Board of Control of which Dundas was the head; and in spite of the irrefutable speech delivered by Burke, but sixty-nine members were found ready to divide in favour of the motion. This result was mainly attributable to the direct interest which two of the ministerial majority had in the retention of the mortgaged provinces for the liquidation of their unrighteous claims. Richard Atkinson, a Government contractor, had obtained a seat in the House, and had become a sort of extra whip for the Government. He was largely connected with Paul Benfield, who, having gone out early in life to Madras as an engineer, had turned money-lender there on an extensive scale, fleeced the Prince of Arcot and other natives, and returned home to buy an estate in Hertfordshire, a town house in Grosvenor Square, and no fewer than seven rotten boroughs, whose representatives at will were among the safe votes on which the new minister could rely. For the moment the allies in corruption carried their point, and the ill-fated districts of the Carnatic were assigned over to pay the debts contracted by the improvident Nawab. Atkinson did not long survive to enjoy his share of the

[1] Parliamentary History, vol. xxiv. p. 1272.

gain; and Benfield, like so many others who made haste to be rich, overstretched himself in speculation, became a bankrupt, and died in France in abject want.

Hastings by this time had had enough of pro-consular exile; and Hyder being dead, and the war with the Mahrattas at an end, he deemed the time propitious for returning home. Through a long continuance of toil and danger he had held his persistent way, and at length the obstructions that had hitherto barred his upward path to opulence, fame, power, and dignity, seemed to be overcome. Lord Shelburne in one Cabinet, and Lord Thurlow in another, had assured him of the favour of the Crown, and that the honours of the peerage awaited him. The Chancellor had even gone so far as to say, that to the sympathy of Warren Hastings, and the influence of his name, was in no small degree attributable the fall of the Coalition and the establishment of his friends in power, declaring that he knew no man who cut so great a figure on the stage of the world, and that his influence had been potently felt in the recent change of Administration. It would be ungrateful, therefore, in the new Cabinet if he were neglected. The faithful Major Scott suggested Daylesford as a suitable title; the Chancellor approved, and wished the affair to be left in his hands. Lords Weymouth, Gower, Sidney, and Carmarthen agreed in supporting his view, and nothing was wanted but the First Minister's consent. Pitt was specious in flattering acknowledgment of public services rendered; but he had a difficulty about the vote of censure carried by Dundas in 1773. He was not himself in Parliament at the time, and personally therefore he was not embarrassed by the vote. The charges, he said, on which it was founded were ridiculous and absurd, and were, as he really thought, fully refuted; yet until the sting of the resolutions was done away by a vote of thanks, he did not see how he could with propriety advise his Majesty to confer such an honour upon Hastings.[1] Thurlow continued to urge the point, and in an interview at Putney, pressed the Minister to say what were his real objections. Pitt replied that there were four. The Governor-General had sought to extend our territories in India, a policy of which he strongly disapproved; he had forfeited the confidence of the native princes; he had frequently disobeyed the orders of the Court of Directors; and he had created enormous salaries in Bengal to gratify those attached to him. The Chancellor pressed for instances, and when Pitt confessed himself at fault, he laughed at him for knowing as little about India as the rest of his colleagues.[2] About the same time Hastings wrote to his wife in England that he was not to be deceived by the fair words of the First Minister, some of whose expressions, when introducing his India Bill, had mortified him deeply, and whose purpose was to keep him from returning home until the new Administration should have had time to strengthen itself without his aid. Full of chagrin, he vowed that he would disappoint his enemies by resigning his post ere they wished him to do so; and this threat he carried into execution in January 1785. In laying down the office, he congratulated the Directors that at last they were rid of him; and applying to himself, in scornful irony, the words of Pitt, he wrote: "I am in this act the fortunate instrument of dissolving the frame of an inefficient Government, pernicious to your interests and disgraceful to the national character."[3] In reality, his exultation was great. As he looked back over the twelve years of his viceregal reign, and reviewed the opposition he had overcome, and the denunciations he had braved,

---

[1] Conversation with Major Scott, Gleig's Life of Hastings, vol. iii.
[2] Ibid.   [3] Letter to Directors, January 1785.

words of haughty triumph broke from him. He had found the treasury empty, and the Executive infirm; he restored the finances and invigorated every department. "I was a man unknown, unprotected, and unconnected at home, and possessed of no other influence abroad than that which I had acquired by my own knowledge and practice, in the credit which the success of my measures impressed on the people of Hindustan, and in the attachment of my fellow-servants and citizens. For six years I was thwarted and insulted openly by the rest of the Council. But even during that time they never tried to take the current of business out of my hands; while I was sustained by consciousness of greater ability and merit. I suffered in patience; I did my duty when I could; I waited for better and more lasting means; no act or word escaped me; no meanness of submission ever afforded my assailants the triumph of a moment over me; my antagonists sickened, died, and fled. I maintained my ground unchanged; neither the health of my body nor the vigour of my mind for a moment deserted me."[1] Well might Burke declare that this was no ordinary offender, but in every sense "a Captain-General of iniquity."

As President and Governor-General, Hastings had borne locally irresponsible rule in India for twelve years. Everywhere he had changed the ancient landmarks and added field to field. He had slain and taken possession, and he could point alike to the spoils of war, the triumphs of diplomacy, and the augmentation of revenue as the proofs of his vigour and success in administration. Beggared princes, impoverished towns, and a starving peasantry might curse his name, but the Board of Directors and the Board of Control found no fault at all in him; and if he had enriched himself, had he not added tenfold to the riches of

[1] Letter to Anderson, 13th September 1786.

his masters? Great merchants in the city and high Ministers of State applauded him, and he had smiles of approval from the Woolsack, York Minster, and the Throne. All hailed his return as that of a conqueror who had won for his country a new empire to compensate for the old one lately lost. Who should gainsay such testimony?

Nevertheless, the clerks in the finance department of Leadenhall Street were much exercised in spirit by the question—Did conquest pay? The financial results of his administration are thus summed up by one who had the privilege of access to every detail of the accounts. In 1772 the Government receipts were £2,373,650, and the expenditure £1,705,279, leaving £668,371 to be divided between shareholders, bondholders, and holders of office at home. In 1785 the income was £5,315,197, and the expenditure £4,312,519, leaving a balance of £1,002,678. On the other hand, the debt in India was augmented from £1,850,866 to £10,464,955, while a large increase of liabilities to the Home Government and to private creditors had accumulated. "The administration of Hastings added £12,500,000 to the total debt of the Company; and the interest, at 5 per cent., of this additional debt was more than the amount of the increased revenue."[1]

These nett results were not indeed disclosed at the time in such a form as that the public at large might understand them. According to the established custom in such matters, they were permitted only to see the light piecemeal, and then enveloped in so many disguises and swathed in so many deceptive folds of extenuation, that no one could feel sure that he knew what they were. It would never have done to let the naked truth be seen. Othello's occupation had been gone. Hundreds and thousands who

[1] Mill's History of British India, vol. iv. p. 442.

had benefited largely by the process of absorption and exaction were ready to testify how profitable was the work. It was not the field or the owners of the field that were benefited, but those who drove the ploughshare through its bosom, and made away with such gleanings as each could secure of its fruit.

Mrs Hastings was sent home to prepare good society for her husband's appearance in its circles. Whig duchesses refused to know her as a *divorcé*, but Queen Charlotte received her at court with every mark of distinction, and great ladies without number crowded her salons and boasted of the curious and precious gifts which she bestowed. Royalty itself did not refuse to accept the unique present of an ivory bedstead, elaborately carved; and the wits of Brooke's had no end of stories about the gems and pearls which fell from Marion's hair, or dropped from her gorgeous train. This indiscreet ostentation, and the still more unwise audacity of Scott, was not without its effect, perhaps, in rekindling the embers of Burke's indignation, and fanning into flame the resentment of Francis.

On the 30th of June, Hastings returned to England, and he was received by King, Ministers, and nobles with every demonstration of respect. Burke lost no time in giving notice that, as the session was then so far advanced, he would, when the House re-assembled, redeem his pledge of demanding that strict inquisition be made into recent viceregal acts. He spent the autumn at Beaconsfield in further study and contemplation of his task, exchanging confidences by letter with Fox and Francis, the first of whom would gladly have dissuaded him from an undertaking of success in which he himself had little hope, but the duty of which Junius concurred with him in thinking imperative. In the dark chambers of his imagery, the scenes of daring spoliation, and harrowing injustice which had been sketched by Francis were filled in with every detail of oriental life, and coloured with all its glow. In the solitude of his study, and of his rambles in the woods, he began to paint those marvellous historic pictures, the like of which has never been seen in our day, and the effect of which upon the mind of Parliament and the nation he did not at the time venture to estimate. He knew that the Whig party was utterly broken by the late general election; that of those who had retained their seats, very few cared a jot for India; and only recalled with bitterness the fact that it was to the India Bill the ruin of their party was ostensibly if not altogether due. On the eve of the session, at a meeting of the opposition chiefs at Burlington House, the preponderant feeling unmistakably was against risking further battle on this ill-fated ground. But Burke was inflexible. It was the great occasion of his life; and though all the men of fashion and fortune around the Duke of Portland should desert the cause, he told them plainly that he had made up his mind to go on. Seeing him thus firm, Fox remained faithful; and a young countryman of his own, who had already made his mark in debate as a man of surpassing eloquence and wit, volunteered his service as a subaltern, as little dreaming as his leader that by him, in the great struggle, the highest honours of the fight would be borne away. This was Richard Brinsley Sheridan.

CHAPTER XIII.

TYRANNY ON ITS KNEES.

1787—1788.

" The business of this day is not the business of this man. It is not solely whether the prisoner at the bar be found innocent or guilty, but whether millions of mankind shall be made miserable or happy. Exiled and undone princes, extensive tribes, suffering nations, differing in language, manners, and in rites, by the providence of God are blended in one common cause, and are now become suppliants at your bar."
—EDMUND BURKE.[1]

ON the 4th April 1787, Burke brought forward eleven accusations against Hastings.

The first count of the indictment charged him with injustice, cruelty, and treachery in hiring British soldiers to extirpate the Rohillas:

2. With cruelty to the Emperor Shah Alum, in withholding his tribute:

3. With extortion and oppression in the case of the Rajah of Benares:

4. With ill-treatment of the family of the Vizier of Oude:

5. With improvidence and injustice in his policy towards Faruckabad:

6. With reducing Oude from a garden to a desert:

7. With sanctioning extravagant contracts and inordinate salaries:

8. With receiving money against the orders of the Com-

[1] Speech on the Impeachment, 23d February 1788.

pany and the Act of Parliament, under secret engagements, and using the same unwarrantably :

9. With resigning by proxy with a view to resume his office :

10. With treachery to Murzaffir Jung, his ward :

11. With enormous extravagance in bribery to enrich favourites and dependants :

Five other charges were subsequently laid upon the table. The great offender petitioned to be heard in his defence at the bar. "Everybody," he wrote, "came to ask me why I had done so imprudent a thing; everybody condemned it, all except my great friend the Chancellor. I had but five days granted me to defend myself against eleven historical libels, to which five more were added before the second day of my appearance." Great was the curiosity to hear him, and all parts of the House were crowded. Every ear was strained, and every eye fixed to catch the expected accents of eloquent indignation. But eloquence there was none. Hastings, in the opinion of every one but himself, had no skill in composition. His egotism was too profound to stoop to the common arts of controversy; and he was thoroughly convinced that a cold and somewhat contemptuous narrative of the facts, as he thought fit to give them, was alone needful for his vindication. The House thought otherwise. They had come full of hopes of a chase, and found nothing but a slow march. After an hour or two, the unusual effort of reading aloud compelled him to delegate the continuance of his task to one of the clerks at the table. This was too much for parliamentary patience, and by degrees the legislative crowd melted away. But his equanimity was imperturbable, and he continued his recital during three successive days. "I was heard," he said, "with an attention unusual in that assembly, and with the most desirable effect, for it instantly turned all minds to my own way, and the ground which I then gained I still retain possession of." In this he was strangely mistaken. He had but committed the error of telling his accusers beforehand on what he relied for his exculpation. He told Parliament that, having been the servant of the East India Company, he was accountable to them alone in his administrative conduct. Ministers took no exception to the matter or the manner of his apology, and rather showed a friendly disposition throughout. Copies were ordered to be printed and circulated for the benefit of the great majority of both sides, who had heard but a small portion of it.[1]

When a month had been allowed for consideration, Burke moved, on the 1st June, that Hastings be impeached for his cruelty to the Rohillas. His conduct in the affair had been censured by the House in a resolution moved by Dundas, founded on the evidence of the Select Committee of 1773; but Dundas was now a member of the Board of Control, and he refused to confirm his own language of thirteen years before. The debate lasted two long nights. As the first gleams of sunrise grew visible, Pitt rose, and warily avoiding the substance of the charge, pleaded in abatement, that the sin had been condoned long since by the retention of Hastings in his post of Governor-General, and that the precedent would be fraught with inconvenience, if not injustice, if deeds remote in place and time, though known the while to all men, were made the subject of criminal proceeding. The motion thus encountered, was defeated by a majority of two to one.

On the reassembling of the House after Whitsuntide, Fox brought forward the second charge, regarding the extortion practised upon Cheyte Singh. Pitt, who had hitherto

[1] Memoirs of Hastings, vol. i.

frowned on every attack, and shielded the culprit from every blow, to the surprise of all but Hastings, suddenly gave way. Better than subservient colleagues and imprudent friends, he discerned the signs of the times, and, for his own sake, he felt it necessary to abandon the position of an accessory after the fact. Did he really foresee the issue of the impending trial, or believe that the best chance of escape for the ex-Viceroy, whom till now he had striven to exonerate, lay in the uncertainties of what must inevitably be indefinitely protracted proceedings? We know not, and can never know. Hastings, who always distrusted him, ascribed so sharp a turn to jealousy, and fear of a possible rival in the esteem of the Court, or a possible competitor for parliamentary sway. Probably such an idea never crossed the mind of the haughty Statesman; and few who had heard Hastings toil through his folios of vindication, when pleading on his own behalf, would have heard the suggestion without a smile. Another explanation was whispered at the time, and subsequently gained credence. Dundas had for years been conspicuous in demanding that the "great public offender," as the Governor-General was called by Fox, should be brought to justice. Few men have ever been more accommodating in office; but he felt, no doubt, that his individuality would be wholly compromised if, on this count of the indictment as well as all others, the accused should escape by the protection of the Administration. Early in the morning he had roused the First Minister from sleep, and had remained closeted with him for an unusual time. The subject of their conference was inferred from the unlooked-for incident of the evening.

Upon Sheridan fell the task of bringing forward the charge of cruelty towards the Begums of Oude. An audience, consisting of placemen, peers' sons, squires of old family, East India proprietors, and lawyers on the lookout for promotion, was not likely to be led away by a penniless playwright, on a great question of national policy and criminal justice. But nature had given Sheridan odds in the race which enabled him to distance all competitors, whether envious friends or party foes. His speech on this occasion having been, like most of his other works, composed in scraps, and owing its great effect at last to adaptations on the spot, and unpremeditated additions, was dependent for preservation on the reporter's pen; and, from some cause never explained, the pen on that memorable night lamentably failed. The House, fairly carried away by the versatility, eloquence, wit, and passion of the man, forgot itself, and mingled with its cheers the expressions of applause which have always been forbidden as disorderly. Pitt was riveted with admiration, Fox was loud in praise, Burke shed tears in the agony of his delight, and the fastidious Windham declared long afterwards that it was the finest speech which had been delivered within the memory of man. Poor Sheridan was offered the next morning a thousand guineas for the copyright, but he was too happy in his new condition of celebrity and congratulation to sit down alone to work up over again what he had spoken. He promised, and perhaps at times he meant to do it. But the delicious hours rolled on, and he had not resolution to forego their enjoyment for the sake of future fame. The matchless invective is lost, and we can only guess at its colour, texture, and strength by the influence it exercised on those who heard it, nearly three to one of whom voted as Sheridan bade them. He stigmatised Hastings as "a great delinquent, and the greatest of all those who by their rapacity and oppression had brought ruin upon the natives of India and disgrace upon the inhabitants of Great Britain."

Some days later Mr Frederick Montague moved that the author of the impeachment should proceed forthwith to the other House, and at the bar of that high court should lay the plaint of the Commons. Accompanied by many members, Burke appeared at their Lordship's bar requesting audience, and in set terms there preferred his weighty accusation. Hastings was taken into custody by Black Rod, and bound over in sureties to appear before the Lord High Steward in Westminster Hall when called upon.

Nobody at the time appears to have regarded with apprehension the issue of the impending trial. The friends of the great culprit went about railing against the malignity of party, and the injustice of ruining a distinguished man who had spent his best years in the service of the country, by compelling him to bring witnesses from the other side of the globe, and to employ lawyers to compile unreadable and unintelligible volumes of documentary proof. His successor Lord Cornwallis, when the tidings reached him, treated the matter as a vexatious practical joke. "I am very sorry that things have gone so much against poor Hastings, for he certainly has many amiable qualities. If you are in the hanging mood, you may tuck up Sir Elijah Impey without giving anybody the smallest concern."[1] It is the old story: those who allow themselves to be made use of as tools, when they are done with are flung aside with a scoff. The ensuing autumn and winter were spent by both sides in preparation. The name of Francis had been struck out of the list of managers by the Commons, on the ground that he was the personal enemy of the accused, and that he had engaged with him in mortal combat. Fox and Windham wrestled stoutly for their friend's inclusion. "A judge,"

---

[1] Letter to Lord Sydney, President of the Board of Control, dated Calcutta, January 7, 1788.

exclaimed the latter, "ought indeed to be impartial; but it is new to question the zeal of a prosecutor." Burke, feminine in his affections and aversions, condescended to entreaty, and wrote to Dundas asking as a favour to himself that he should not be mutilated of his right hand. But the renegade was reckless, and Pitt was obdurate; there was nothing for it, therefore, but to stifle the glowing rage of Francis with splendid flattery. Burke in the name of the managers wrote him a letter—such a letter! It was dated from the committee-room of the House of Commons; it declared in the name of the managers that he was indispensable to the achievement of national justice; and it adjured him not to forsake in their last resort the afflicted people of Asia, over whom he had so long "exercised paternal care." Junius could not refuse; and in his capacity of assessor, throughout the protracted and arduous proceedings, he was never wanting by the side of his illustrious friend. Among the managers were Fox, Sheridan, Grey, Erskine, Windham, Anstruther, Elliott, and Burgoyne.

After many postponements, the day at length arrived. It was sixty-three years since the Peers had assembled as a court of justice for the trial of Lord Macclesfield. They were then much more limited in number. To the roll-call of the Lord High Steward upwards of two hundred peers now answered to their names, and proceeded from their own House to Westminster Hall, which had been furnished as a court for the occasion. The Heir-apparent and other princes of the blood, many of the chief dignitaries of the realm, and its most brilliant lights of literature and art, were there assembled. The Duchess of Devonshire was surrounded by the great Whig ladies, who glanced encouragement on Fox and Grey and Windham in the managers' box. The ladies whose sympathy was Ministerial occupied

seats near the Duchess of Rutland; and every nook and
cranny of the Hall was early filled by some more or less
distinguished listener to the unusual and almost unbe-
lievable arraignment. Of all the notabilities of the day,
Pitt alone was absent; not even once did he afterwards
condescend to show himself during the trial. The great
Proconsul was conducted to the bar, and in compliance
with old usage, was told to drop upon his knees. The
indignity sent a sharper pang to his proud heart than
the enumeration of all the crimes laid to his charge. It was
but momentary. The Lord High Steward bade him rise
and be seated; and there throughout the day, and for days
to come that seemed innumerable, the tiny, pallid, plainly
attired, but dignified and intrepid culprit, sat observing
calmly the features of his judges, watching keenly every
movement of his pursuers, and now and then conferring
with Plumer, Law, and others of his counsel. It was a
strange sight; and to us, looking back at it historically, it
seems as strange as it did then. It was a signal experiment
in the way of exacting accountability, made with consum-
mate skill, earnestness, and persistency, in a case where
there was unprecedented need. Fitness in the tribunal
only was wanting; but that want was irremediable. A court
of peers had aforetime sat as judges and as jurors to try the
guilt or innocence of one accused of native treason, domestic
violence, or breach of municipal law, the incidents of which
were recent, and the proofs capable of being fairly weighed
during the sunlight of an ordinary day. But here was an
appeal from mediæval Asia to modern Europe, from unintelligible Paganism to so-called Christianity, from the help-
lessness of the conquered to the privileges of constitutional
freedom, from unnumbered millions of sufferers to two
hundred listless men of fashion—some old and gouty,

others giddy and gambling, a few painstaking and conscientious, and a few more benevolent and well meaning, but phlegmatic, hypochondriacal, and too easily bored. Estimated by the capacity derived from experience, there never was an Areopagus more helpless; for precedent to guide them there was literally none. Estimated by any theoretical standard, the constitution of such a court was simply absurd. Of the Lords Spiritual and Temporal who actually heard Hastings arraigned, but twenty-nine voted him, seven years afterwards, innocent or guilty. The power of impeachment had been a valuable power, and had done good work in its time; but work like this it was never meant to do, and work like this it was wholly incapable of doing as it ought to be done. Through the grey winter-fog of February 1788, these truths, clear to us now, were not, however, discernible; and, upon the whole, it may be doubted whether men would ever have been brought unanimously or even generally to accept them, had not the great experiment been elaborately tried under circumstances so favourable to success, as that which characterised the case of Warren Hastings. The delusive belief in a phantom can only be dispelled by affording every one repeated and continuous opportunities of seeing that the resuscitated form cannot be grasped, or held, or made to speak coherently and accountably. Until the faith in phantoms be exploded, we cannot hope to get to realities. A learned, wise, exalted, and catholic-hearted court of appeal for those who suffer wrong within the confines of the empire is indispensable to the maintenance of the empire in equity and honour; indispensable, indeed, to its permanent existence; but the Lord High Steward's court, convened to try a colonial Viceroy on a writ of impeachment, is utterly unlike what such a court should be. It was necessary, therefore, that the obsolete pageant should be once more reproduced, were it only to prove how ill adapted it was for the modern purpose required. And in this historical point of view it may not be waste of time to note some of the particulars wherein it egregiously failed.

The arbitrament of political controversies between equal and independent nations is sufficiently difficult under the most favourable circumstances, for the obvious reason that it is of necessity extremely hard to constitute a court capable at once of appreciating the just claims of both sides, and of rising superior to the passionate and partial importunities of either. But immeasurably more difficult is the task of arbitrating between suzerain and vassal, the aggressor and the aggrieved, the lord paramount of conquest and his brow-beaten if not beggared subjects. Whether the dispute lie between a distant and comparatively diminutive community on the one hand, and the contumelious power of centralism on the other, or whether the question be one raised on the part of deposed or mediatised princes and the exchequer of an imperial dynasty, there is need of the greatest care in selecting the judges, and of the greatest precaution against the law's delay, the insolence of office, and the conscious or unconscious interposition of personal, party, and national predilections. It is a matter of daily observation how men, who, as jurors in a common lawsuit, would stare contemptuously at any attempt to tamper with their independence, betray no conscientious scruple, and affect no sting of shame, at being importuned, threatened, and talked over, when they have votes to give as peers or commoners, electors or elect, on questions involving quite as certainly and clearly the character of individuals or the interests of the public. This is so even when the controversies are between fellow-subjects or neighbours; how much more when the complainants are strangers, aliens, it may be recent foes, or doubtful allies, whose reputation has been hardly dealt with, and whose means of correcting misimpression are practically *nil;* while the respondent in the political suit stands upon the presumption of national honour, and appeals to all the interests and feelings interwoven with national pride. It is hard even for a moment to set the balances fair, but it is useless and hopeless to try and do so, if there be no staid, learned, responsible, and, above all, jealously limited number of arbiters, in whose hands the scales are to be held. From the days of the Ecclesia of Athens and the Senate of Rome, to those of the Convention Parliament and the National Assembly of France, there has never been a *practically* indeterminate assembly, elective or hereditary, which has not signally failed whenever it undertook to perform judicial duties. It would seem as if there were in the very nature of the thing a fault ineradicable. Apart from the multiplied chances which a multitudinous jury presents, that part of the case may be heard by one set of men and part by another, neither of whom, therefore, can properly join in giving judgment, though both are empowered to do so;—there is the still more fatal characteristic of all such assemblies, that they are necessarily constituted of materials egregiously unequal in their intellectual abilities, that they are palpably for the most part untrained for such work, and that they are invariably prone to evade or repudiate openly the individual responsibility of forming and expressing a decision, because that decision may not be decisive. It is idle to answer that logically this is unreasonable and unsound. The fact that in such cases men are not governed by logic is too plain; and equally plain is the fact that a supreme court of appeal, whether it be composed of priests or laymen, delegates or citizens, soldiers or civilians, is capricious, inconsequential, impulsive, and morally impotent,—just in proportion as it resembles a popular assembly instead of a strictly limited and specially chosen bench of justice. It is the instinctive sense of this truth that has made the hereditary peers, in the exercise of their ordinary jurisdiction, habitually abstain from taking part in the appeals between man and man that are brought before them. Every one knows and understands that not one in a hundred of the Lords feels himself justified in meddling with these appeals, even to the extent of putting a question to a witness, or asking for the explanation of a phrase. How much more, then, does it behove the members of such an assembly to abstain where the power of the Crown or of the nation at large is on one side, and the equities invoked by a conquered prince or people are upon the other? What was wanted in 1788, and what is wanted still, was a high court of federal jurisdiction, consisting of the best men to be found in the legislature, the administration, and the law, on whom the great responsibility might safely be devolved of trying a complicated issue, and of putting on record the reasons of their decision. By some such method as this, the proceedings might have been brought to within decent limits as to cost and time, and the ineffable mockery of justice avoided which the prolongation of the impeachment for seven years, and the unassessed mulct of the defendant in £100,000 of costs, entailed.

When Hastings was at last summoned by the Chancellor to appear before the Lords on the 23d April 1795, to receive judgment, but twenty-nine peers in their robes were in attendance. A good many more, who shrank from sharing the judicial responsibility, appeared in their ordinary costume near the steps of the throne, curiously observing the forms of procedure, as though it concerned them not. The members of the Upper House had been considerably augmented in the interval, and numbered now two hundred and sixty-two. Of these, forty-nine had acceded by inheritance, and forty-four had been created, or elected as Scotch peers. Pending the suit, eighty-seven who sat in the previous Parliament had died, or had not been re-elected. Looking worn and aged by the anxieties of his seven years' trial, Hastings advanced to the bar, and once more knelt in submission. In turn the peers were called upon to say on their honour whether he were guilty or not. Six answered in the affirmative; in the negative twenty-three. The six who were for condemnation were the Duke of Norfolk, the Earls of Carnarvon, Radnor, Fitzwilliam, and Suffolk, and the Chancellor, Lord Loughborough. Those who voted for acquittal were Markham, Lord Archbishop of York, the Dukes of Bridgewater and Leeds, the Marquis of Townshend, the Earls of Beverley, Warwick, Coventry, Mansfield, Morton, and Dorchester, Viscount Falmouth, the Bishops of Rochester and Bangor, and Lords Fife, Somers, Rawdon, Walsingham, Thurlow, Hawke, Boston, Sandys, and Middleton. Lord Loughborough then pronounced the judgment of acquittal, and ordered the prisoner to be discharged. What a moment was that of supreme excitement and exultation! Surrounded by nobles, prelates, courtiers, soldiers, India directors, agents, dependants, flatterers, and friends of all sorts, the phlegmatic little man was almost overpowered with gratulations. When they had ceased, ambitious hope once more stirred within him; and for a season he had cause to fancy that fortune might return. His costs during the trial amounted to £76,528, and other expenses which it entailed had exhausted nearly all the accumulations of his guilty reign.

A meeting of East India proprietors voted him, by way of compensation, £4000 a year for twenty-eight years; and capitalising the sum to meet his known exigencies, they advanced him £42,000, together with a loan of £50,000, vested in trustees for the purchase of Daylesford, that darling object of his boyish dreams, for which he had gone so far afield, and waded so deep in sin and shame. Daylesford was won at last. The reaction in his favour spread; and by the advice of many influential friends, he resolved to petition the Crown for the reimbursement of his legal expenses. Ministers, notwithstanding, held aloof, and no persuasions could prevail on Pitt to present his petition to the King.

Sir Elijah Impey likewise escaped punishment. On December 12, 1787, Sir Gilbert Elliot brought forward a motion for his impeachment in a speech of great ability. He charged him with "gross corruption, positive injustice, direct disobedience, intentional violation of the Acts under which he held his powers, and with having suborned evidence and given to falsehood the sanctity of an affidavit." The ex-Chief-Justice had, he said, been guilty of the most "scandalous enormities; he had perverted law to the purposes of tyranny; and thus he had alienated the hearts of the people of India, and had stained the name of Britain. . . . Next to the duty of bestowing honours on great and distinguished men who, being intrusted with the custody of the lives and properties of their fellow creatures, had preserved them against outrage and oppression, was the necessary, though painful, task of drawing down the vengeance of Parliament on the head of a servant whose pride had stretched his power into tyranny, and whose avarice had perverted his trust into plunder;—more than any other species of delinquency did the crimes of a judge call for the vengeance of a nation."[1] The crimes, indeed, did call, and Parliament for a season seemed attentively to listen, but the vengeance of the nation did not come. Government, while professing only to perform the duties of umpirage, contrived to let it be understood that they thought exposure was sufficient, and that they would rather not have the matter pressed to a conviction. So it fell through; and the name of Impey has come to pass as synonymous with judicial impunity. While the proceedings against his illustrious accomplice were still pending, the ex-Chief-Justice found a borough sufficiently ripe in decay to recognise in him a fitting representative. In mercy to the little town, now disfranchised, and long since, let us hope, repentant, let us omit its name.

[1] Parliamentary History, vol. xxvi. p. 1338.

CHAPTER XIV.

TIPPOO SAIB.

1786—1793.

"The unity of our Government and our great military force give us such a superiority over the native princes, that we might, by watching opportunities, extend our dominion without much danger or expense, and at no very distant period, over a great part of the Peninsula. Our first care ought to be directed to the total subversion of Tippoo. After becoming masters of Seringapatam, we should find no great difficulty in advancing to the Kistna, when favoured by wars or revolutions in the neighbouring States. But we ought to have some preconcerted general scheme to follow upon such occasions."

—SIR T. MUNRO.[1]

FOR the vacant place of Viceroy there were many competitors; yet the fitting man was not so easily found. If long experience, great ability, dauntless courage, marvellous success, powerful friends, and court favour, could not insure a Governor-General on his return home from being arraigned as a culprit, what safety could there be for his successor. The example of Hastings was calculated to deter cautious and punctilious men, and to disenchant reckless and avaricious men. There remained, however, a crowd of restless, needy, and adventurous waiters upon fortune, any of whom would have grasped with delight at £25,000 a year, and the jobbing of India for five or six

---

[1] Letter to his father, 21st September 1798—Memoirs by the Rev. G. R. Gleig, vol. i. p. 203.

years. Mr Pitt had no mind indeed to throw away so great an appointment upon any of the class in question. In common with Lord Shelbourne, he thought of Lord Cornwallis at first for the command in chief, and afterwards for the chief direction of civil affairs likewise. Without any of the political talents of his grandfather, who had been First Minister of George I., or the energy of character that gave promise of his retrieving the disaster which had virtually brought the American war to an end, Lord Cornwallis occupied a position in public life which no Minister was likely to overlook. With good manners, good connections, and good fortune, his friendship was sought by men of all parties; and enemies he had none. Left to himself, he would probably have sauntered happily and unnoticeably along the down-hill steep of life, grumbling occasionally in the House of Lords at what he did not approve, but never engaging deeply in party plots, or aspiring to lead a parliamentary campaign. What he wanted was to be made Constable of the Tower, and he betrayed some vexation at being passed over for that sinecure post; but it was certainly not with any view to get rid of him as a troublesome critic or a dangerous opponent that the Ministry in 1786 pressed upon him the government of India. He was thought eligible, as an amiable and respectable man, who might be relied on to keep peculation in check, and to curb the violent courses which had brought the administration of his predecessor into question. Not without hesitation he agreed at length to go; little foreseeing probably how lastingly his name would be written on the financial and territorial records of Hindustan.

He sailed for the East in the latter end of April 1786, and arrived in Madras the following August. His first letters home express his strong dissatisfaction at the part already taken by the Madras Government in aiding the Mahrattas to violate the treaty with Tippoo Sultan. He denounced also the incapacity and peculation of the Company's servants in no measured terms. In one letter he writes: "You will see in the letters from the Board previous to my arrival, a plan for obtaining Allahabad from the Vizier, to which he had spirit enough to make a successful resistance. Unless I see some new lights, I shall not revive it. I at present think the advantages of our possessing that post very doubtful, and I am sure it was intended as a scene of gross peculation, at the expense of the Vizier and his Government."[1] Complaints of interference and maladministration poured in from all sides. Among the most prominent were those of Mobaruck-ul-Dowla, the Nawab of Bengal, who, having succeeded to the musnud during his minority in 1770, was now come of age: and who repudiated alike the control of his former guardians, and the retention by the Company of the greater part of the income guaranteed to him by treaty on his accession. It was then fixed at thirty-two lacs a year; but in 1772, Warren Hastings, acting on instructions from Leadenhall Street, reduced the amount one-half, on the plea that sixteen lacs was sufficient during the Prince's minority. The rightful sum, however, was not restored, as was expected, while he had still to pay the whole staff of Company's officers, as part of the establishment originally imposed upon him. In a letter to the Court of Directors soon after his arrival, the new Viceroy wrote, that "from all he had already heard, he thought it highly probable that it would appear to be decent in the Government to abstain from much of the interference that had hitherto been used in the detail of the business of that household, and which had been

[1] Confidential letter to Right Hon. Henry Dundas, Nov. 15, 1786.

attended with great expense to the Nawab.[1] Through his agent in London, the Soubahdar had formally complained to the Directors of the injustice with which he was treated, and they instructed the Governor-General in a secret despatch to "take care to provide for his support and dignity, by securing to him the clear and undiminished receipt of the real stipend allotted to him, or even by its immediate augmentation;" adding, "You will always keep in view the claims he has upon us by treaty, and necessity will dictate to you a due consideration for the present state of our affairs."[2] On the plea, however, that dependants on the native Court would be chiefly benefited, were the whole of his income restored to him, Lord Cornwallis advised that the Company should still retain half of it for themselves. In his judgment, it was only a question between whether so many lacs a year should be spent in luxury in London or in luxury at Moorshedabad. His sympathies were with the former.[3]

The peace concluded at Mangalore lasted six years. Tippoo in that interval reduced to subjection several of the minor states in his neighbourhood, and built or purchased several armed vessels, which helped to spread the terror of his name along the coast of Malabar. Fanaticism was with him an impulse even stronger than ambition, and his assumption of the title of Sultan was supposed to be preparatory to that of Prophet. He persuaded himself that he had a mission to clear the land of idolatry; he compelled multitudes to conform to his faith, and to behold their temples levelled with the dust. He boasted that he had destroyed 8000 shrines, and distributed 100,000 unwilling converts among his

---

[1] The Cornwallis Correspondence, edited by Charles Ross, vol. i. p. 235.
[2] Despatch from Court of Directors, 21st July 1786.
[3] See despatch, 4th March 1787.

garrisons. He bore, in fact, a strong resemblance to Philip II. of Spain. They had both been educated for empire, and both possessed considerable talents, natural or acquired. Both were brave, industrious, and sagacious, and both sustained with signal constancy the ills of fortune. But both also were, perhaps from the very fact of their having been bred in the expectancy of vast dominion, far inferior to their predecessors. With less experience and original resources, they were equally despotic and exacting, more self-willed and obstinate, less fit to turn victory to account, and less versatile in retrieving the losses of defeat. Both were cruel from suspicion and resentment, both were bigoted to the faith in which they had been reared, and both sacrificed to their superstitious zeal the affection of their subjects and the security of their dominions. While history, therefore, dwells upon the memory of neither with respect or pity, fidelity to truth requires that their misdeeds should be weighed in the same balance of justice as that wherein the faults of their adversaries are measured; and if circumstances are to be allowed to aggravate or mitigate reproach, history's duty is to mete out carefully the blame which is due. It is necessary to remind those who really desire to know the truth how distrustfully we are bound to read all that is written in apology or eulogy of triumphant aggression? The beaten are always worthless, the victors always great and good; a thousand influences of selfishness or sympathy, consciously or unconsciously, combine to tinge the narrative of victory; but where are the annals of the conquered? who shall bring garlands to the nameless grave? Of Tippoo Saib we may not err widely if we content ourselves with saying, that from all we have been enabled to glean from out the unfruitful stubble-field of military memoir, we infer that he was not much worse than other men who have been placed in similar situations elsewhere. His indifference to human life was probably about the same as that of Louis le Grand or Nicholas I., of Alba, Strafford, or Radetzky. His reluctance to employ any one holding religious opinions different from his own was probably as intolerant and oppressive as that of the most Christian Ferdinand VII., or the most religious and gracious George III.[1]

Towards the close of 1789 an incident occurred which led to what is called the third war with Mysore. Two forts belonging to the Dutch stood at the mouth of an estuary near the frontier lines of Travancore, and being threatened by Tippoo, their commandant, under the terms of a subsisting treaty, called on the Rajah to aid in defending them, or, if he would not, to become their purchaser. Against this Tippoo protested. The Dutch had no right, as he averred, to alienate a possession for which they paid tribute to the Rajah of Cochin, who in turn owed him fealty. The facts were disputed, and he proceeded to force the lines, whence he was repulsed with serious loss. Mr Holland, then acting President of Madras, proposed to send commissioners to inquire and negotiate. The Sultan did not forbid their coming, but said he had investigated the matter already, and he was confident as to the ground of his pretensions. Not long afterwards General Meadows became Governor, and instead of negotiating, prepared to interpose by arms. Tippoo wrote congratulating the General on his accession to the Government, and deprecating a rupture. "Notwithstanding the bonds of friendship were firmly established, in consequence of the representations, contrary to the fact, of certain shortsighted persons to the Governor, they

---

[1] Munro sneers at the bigotry of Tippoo in not employing any but Mohammedans in posts of confidence; somewhat absurd this from an officer in an army where none but those of the orthodox sects of Christians were then eligible to hold command.

had caused an army to be assembled on each side." As such an event was improper among those mutually in friendship, in order to clear it up Tippoo sent a person of dignity to explain the whole circumstances, that "the dust which had obscured the upright mind of the Governor might be removed."[1] Meadows replied that he regarded as an insult the attack upon the Rajah of Travancore, who was under English protection; and they must now abide the issue of war. The Sultan, being wholly unprepared, fell back with his army towards Seringapatam. Autumn was spent in the capture and recapture of places of secondary importance, and in strategic movements without decisive result.

It is clear, that to repel the aggression, or, at most, to obtain for Travancore compensation for any loss it might have sustained, did not of necessity imply operations on a great scale, or the formation of a general league for the subjugation of Mysore. But the humiliation supposed to have been incurred by the treaty of Mangalore rankled in the minds of not a few of the military class, and the accounts of what had been achieved by the more daring and adventurous policy of Hastings in the eastern Presidency, stimulated the wish to try issues once more with the aspiring and pretentious Sultan. To vindicate the insulted majesty of Travancore, possession was taken of Baramahal in 1790, and from that hour to the present it has remained a revenue district of the Madras Presidency. We are not left to supposition or conjecture as to the designs with which the war was recommenced. Munro, one of the best and ablest officers engaged during this and the following period in the service, in his confidential letters, written in 1790, argues against the unsatisfactory nature of the attempt to hold a balance of power between the

[1] Thornton's British India, p. 191.

native kingdoms. He says plainly, conquest is the true policy; and argues that the British revenue in the East might thereby with ease be trebled. "I do not mean that we should *all at once* attempt to extend ourselves so far, for it is at present beyond our power, but that we should keep the object in view, though the accomplishment of it should require a long series of years. The dissensions and revolutions of the native Governments will point out the time when it is proper for us to become actors. But it can never arrive while Tippoo exists."[1] Why not remove so formidable an enemy?

Accordingly, for this purpose, Lord Cornwallis concluded a league with the Mahrattas and the Nizam, identical in substance, and with some curious points of coincidence in phraseology, with that which was signed in 1795 by the sovereigns of Russia, Austria, and Prussia, for the dismemberment of Poland. By the terms of this holy alliance, Nana Farnavis on the part of the Pagans, Nizam Ali on the part of the Mussulmans, and the Viceroy as representative of Christian England, undertook to bring into the field proportionate contingents of troops and guns, and not to make peace until half its provinces should have been reft from Mysore and parcelled out amongst them. Baramahal, won and lost in the former war, was again overrun, and this time retained securely. The Viceroy proceeded to Madras, and early in the spring assumed command of the army in person. The whole of 1791 was spent in the reduction of strong places and in conflicts, the most sanguinary of which was that of Arikera, about six miles from the capital, which was not, however, invested until the following year. The outworks were stormed on the night of 6th February, and after losing in killed, wounded, and deserters 20,000 men, Tippoo sub-

---

[1] Memoirs of Munro, vol. i. p. 123.

mitted to the terms imposed by Lord Cornwallis; one half his dominions to be ceded to the allies adjacent to their respective boundaries and agreeably to their selection, while three crores were to be paid for the expenses of the war. Two of Tippoo's sons were to be detained as hostages for the fulfilment within a year of the pecuniary conditions.

When the preliminaries were signed, and the youthful hostages had been, with great state, conveyed into the camp, they were confided to the care of the Viceroy, who embraced them and gave them the assurance of his paternal solicitude while in captivity. The dramatic incidents of the scene have been preserved by the pencil of Singleton; and Lord Cornwallis for a few days felt that he was playing successfully the part of Scipio.

But the fine gold of magnanimity soon grew dim. In utter disregard of the terms of the preliminaries, Coorg, on the Malabar coast, containing 2165 square miles, was demanded among the cessions to the Company, in addition to Dindigul and Baramahal. Tippoo inquired in vain to the territories of which of his conquerors it lay near, and scornfully asked why no hint had been dropped of this further humiliation until his children had been parted from him, and a large portion of the war-mulct paid. In his anger he threatened to resume the offensive; and had he known accurately how much sickness and want of stores had weakened his assailants, he might with difficulty have been dissuaded from putting his threat into execution. Coorg had been subdued by his father, and ruled with such rigour by him, that the Rajah, Vira Rajendra, invoked English aid to recover his independence. Lord Cornwallis was obliged to own that the principality did not fall within the scope of the preliminaries; but he set up in extenuation of the breach of faith proposed that it would be ungenerous to leave the Rajah to the resentment of Tippoo. The controversy ended in Coorg being given up.

"Our acquisitions on the Malabar coast," wrote the Viceroy, "are inaccessible to any enemy that does not come by sea, except on the north frontier. The possession of Coorg and Palghatchery effectually secure the two passes by which only Tippoo could possibly disturb us. The Rajahs on that coast are not independent, but are now become our subjects, and if we can put them in some degree on the footing of the Bengal Zemindars, and prevent their oppressing the people, the commerce of that country may become extremely advantageous to the Company. The nett revenue amounts to about twenty-five lacs of rupees, which will be a great help at present to Bombay."[1] The court of Markara, which had been the centre of an independent state for three hundred years, was suffered to exist, with certain local jurisdictions, till 1834, when, on the pretence of failure of heirs in the house of Rejendra, the Raj was incorporated with the rest of the Empire.

Tippoo's resources had proved to be greater than were anticipated, and it took two years of war to induce his haughty spirit to sue for peace. Munro declares the terms granted him to have been far too moderate, although it gave the Company increased revenues, amounting to thirty-nine and a half lacs of rupees (£395,000).[2] The extent of territory acquired was not less than 24,000 square miles; in addition to this, a portion equally great was given to the Nizam, as a reward for his services in the campaign. For how short a space he was permitted to enjoy these acquisitions we shall presently see. The Mahrattas absolutely refused to

---

[1] Despatch to Mr Dundas, camp before Seringapatam, 18th March 1792—Correspondence, vol. ii. p. 158.

[2] Munro, vol. i. p. 129.

take any part of the spoil, influenced, we may suppose, less by any regard for him whose power they had helped to prostrate, than from the too late conviction how much their own safety must be endangered by the removal of such a barrier to European aggression as the Mysorean kingdom formed.

The humiliating treaty was signed, and the conquerors, laden with their booty, disappeared from before Seringapatam. With what emotions Tippoo saw them depart we may easily conceive. The empire which his father's genius had cemented and bequeathed to him was riven into fragments and partitioned among his foes. His pride was humbled in the dust, his treasury was emptied, the fear of his enemies and the confidence of his subjects were alike undermined. But, as the last troop of his foes defiled through the frontier hills, he breathed freely again; and hope—the hope of yet recovering all he had lost, and of avenging his dishonour—rose within him. For this alone he henceforth seemed to live. Every department of his internal administration underwent a rigorous and searching reform. He anxiously sought every means of introducing into his army the tactics and discipline of Europe, believing that these afforded him the likeliest chance of successfully coping with his adversaries. But the exhaustion and depression of national defeat is a perilous time to attempt the introduction of arbitrary innovations; and the impetuous energy of Tippoo made him forget that the unprepared changes which his superior intellect and knowledge suggested could only cause bewilderment and distrust among his dispirited people. The severe economy he was forced to use alienated many of his powerful dependants. Symptoms of general discontent became apparent, and drew forth the worst dispositions of a temper naturally harsh, and now embittered by ill-fortune. A dark and superstitious gloom deepened the shades of cruelty over his remaining days; and long before the diadem of Mysore finally perished, its lustre had faded in the eyes of men.

Thus was the honour of our ally vindicated. We can nowhere find that his Highness of Travancore was benefited in any way by the sanguinary conflict or the partition treaty. Like the Prince of Hohenzollern, his name was wholly forgotten from the moment the first gun was fired. The Nizam was humoured by the show of new provinces, while in reality he was to be treated as a mere trustee for those who gave and who could also take away. But if the manufacturers of the treaty forgot their allies, they did not forget themselves. "Thirty lacs of rupees (£300,000) were demanded and given as durbar khurutch, or expenses, avowedly to be distributed amongst the officers concerned in settling the treaty."[1] The Viceroy returned to Calcutta. The reproach of York Town was effaced, and Lord Cornwallis was made a Marquis.

Soon after the news of these brilliant achievements reached England, the public became partially aware of the means whereby they had been accomplished; and certain folk asked querulously whether wars of annexation were not administrative jobs, got up by powerful individuals for the sake of realising fortunes after the Clive fashion? The following year, when the Company sought a renewal of their charter, a storm of political virtue broke out, with all the violence by which the epidemic has, at capricious intervals, been characterised amongst us. A show of penitence for past misdeeds was deemed expedient on the part of the Company to appease the outcry; and ere Parliament granted the renewed charter, it solemnly declared " that

[1] Malcolm, vol. i. chap. vi. note.

the pursuit of schemes of conquest and extension of dominion in India is repugnant to the wish, the honour, and the policy of the nation."[1] This declaration was said to have the validity of a command; and upon the assumption of its being obeyed, the fate of Hindustan was once more intrusted to those whom Chatham used to call "the lofty Asiatic plunderers of Leadenhall Street." For a season the injunction was observed, at least in appearance. The states which had been cajoled into admitting subsidiary forces within their confines fell daily more abjectly under the control of their protectors. As the pay of their garrisons fell into arrear, they were required to mortgage the revenue of additional provinces to the Company; for the honour of British protection was no longer optional, and the last step in each case usually was the complete and formal cession of the mortgaged lands. Before Hyder's invasion in 1780, a large portion of the revenues of the Carnatic had been thus assigned by the Nawab. The expenses of the war were declared a sufficient pretext for demanding the entire, a sixth part being reserved in the nature of a pension to Mohamed Ali. Mill, like a true utilitarian, argues that this arrangement was quite a boon to the pensioned Prince, inasmuch as he was punctually paid; that he was relieved from all anxiety and risk, and that the annual stipend allotted him was, in money, rather more than he had been in the habit of appropriating to his own use.

[1] East India Act of 1793.

CHAPTER XV.

THE LAND SETTLEMENT.

1793.

"Bengal is one of the most fertile countries on the face of the globe, with a population of mild and industrious inhabitants, perhaps equal to, if not exceeding in number, that of all British possessions put together. Its real value to us depends upon the continuance of its ability to furnish a large annual investment to Europe, to give considerable assistance to the treasury at Calcutta, and to supply the pressing and extensive wants of the other Presidencies. The consequences of the heavy drains of wealth from the above causes, with the addition of that which has been occasioned by the remittance of private fortunes, have been for many years past, and are now, severely felt by the great diminution of the current specie, and by the languor which has thereby been thrown upon the cultivation and the general commerce of the country. A very material alteration in the principles of our system of management has therefore become indispensably necessary, in order to restore the country to a state of prosperity, and to enable it to continue to be a solid support to British interests and power in this part of the world."

—CORNWALLIS.[1]

THE conditions of land tenure, and the methods of assessment throughout India, were as various as the features of the country itself; the customs prevailing in one region being often wholly unknown in another. When by the treaty of 1765 the Company became Dewan of Bengal, Behar, and Orissa, they continued the system of land taxation then existing. This was principally a produce assessment. The fruits of the land were equally divided between the Government and the actual occupier, the Zemindar receiving about one-tenth of the Government share.

[1] Minute on Land Settlement, 10th February 1790.

An account of the land under cultivation, the produce, rent, and other details, was kept by native officials in each village, who were paid fixed salaries by the cultivators, or received allotments of land for their services. A collection of villages was called a Pergunna, a combination of these again formed a Circar, and the union of two or more Circars constituted a Soubah. The holders of large areas, who became directly responsible to the Government for the revenue therefrom, were called Zemindars, under whom were the Talookdars, or owners of smaller estates, and the Ryots, who were the actual cultivators of the soil. A few Zemindaries, as Burdwan, Barrackpoor, and Berbhom in Bengal, were nearly four thousand square miles in extent, and their occupiers were Rajahs, or native princes of high rank; but the greater number were of much smaller proportions, held by men of less influence and authority. On the acquisition of the Dewanny, the Directors had instructed their officers to confine themselves to the simple duty of receiving the revenue, the details of collection being left to the ordinary native hands. But the corruption which attended the arbitrary substitution of foreign for native local rule bore the usual fruit of weeds in the fiscal field. The Court of Directors, alarmed for the state of their balance-sheet, in 1769 appointed English supervisors over the native collectors. In the following year, Boards of Inquiry and Control were established at Moorshedabad and Patna, but they did nothing but expose abuses which they lacked the power to remedy. In 1772, Warren Hastings revolutionised the entire fiscal department. European were substituted for Indian collectors. The Calcutta Council were constituted a Board of Revenue; several new officers were created; the treasury was removed from Moorshedabad to Calcutta, and four members of Council were sent on a tour of inspection through the country to collect the materials on which to base a re-assessment. A purely Feringhee executive however did no better for Leadenhall Street than its half-blood predecessor. A number of native clerks were turned adrift, and a few more adventurers were benefited, but the earth brought forth no greater increase, and the India House dispensed no greater blessing in the shape of an improved percentage. In 1774, the newly-appointed Viceroy reverted to the employment of black collectors, as they were termed, and set up six district councils of superintendence. An experimental assessment had been made for five years, but the results were not sufficiently satisfactory to warrant a renewal; and on its expiration in 1777, annual settlements were decreed for the four years ensuing. In these the Zemindars were encouraged to become responsible for the land revenue, Government retaining power over lands in their own occupation as a guarantee for the faithful performance of their duty. In 1781 another scheme was tried. The district councils were superseded, and a central committee of revenue was formed, and the collectors were encouraged to replenish the exchequer by the grant of a percentage on their collections, in addition to their salaries. How this bribe succeeded may be estimated from a fact mentioned by Lord Cornwallis, that one collector, with a salary of 1000 rupees a month (£1200 a year) had an income of at least £40,000 a year.

By Mr Pitt's Act of 1784, the Company were empowered and directed to "inquire into the alleged grievances of the landholders, and if founded in truth, to afford them redress, as well as to establish fixed rules for the settlement and collection of the revenue, and for the administration of justice according to the ancient laws and usages of the country." The first official duty of Lord Cornwallis, therefore, and the one with which his name will always be associated, was, the settlement of land revenue on a definite basis. We have had a good many personal confessions of blundering and mismanagement up to this time, but here we have an admission comprehensive and candid, by Parliament itself, solemnly uttered when giving legislative judgment in appeal, that thirty years of domineering power had been spent in doing the things that ought not to have been done, and in not doing the things that ought to have been done. After turning the country upside down, rack-renting Ryots, beggaring Rajahs, goading Tehsildars into rigour, and alternately bribing and threatening collectors, some of a white, and some of an olive skin, into higher exaction, Parliament was compelled to admit that the system worked ill, and that it had become necessary to reform it altogether. Bengal was going back to jungle, and the Chairman of the Company was asking loans from the Exchequer to square the dividend account.

Early in 1787 the Board of Revenue at Calcutta was directed to collect information for a new assessment; but an undertaking so vast as a survey of the extent and boundaries of the several estates, together with the interests, rights, and titles of their owners and occupiers, could not be completed in a few months; and it was not till 1789 that any action could be practically taken on the results, such as they were, which had been thus obtained. The basis said to be laid was soon found to be imperfect and untrustworthy. "It was evident," says one writer, "on consideration of the answers made to official inquiries, that although when the Company succeeded to the Dewanny gross abuses prevailed, yet in the best times of the Mogul Government, the rights and privileges of the people were secured by institutions mainly derived from the original

Hindu possessors of the country." By some it was thought advisable to continue and develop that system; but the Viceroy, with Mr Shore, Mr Duncan, and Mr Barlow, deemed it better to establish the Zemindar as the landowner, whether he had previously occupied such a position or not. Lord Cornwallis was mainly actuated by a desire to place this most important source of the Company's income on a sure footing, as well as by a laudable wish to relieve the actual cultivators of the soil from the evils inseparable from the habit of farming the land-tax which then prevailed. The settlements from year to year, and for other short periods, had not answered expectation. "Desperate adventurers," said the Governor-General,[1] "without fortune or character, would undoubtedly be found, as has already been too often experienced, to rent the different districts of the country at the highest rates that could be put upon them; but the delusion would be of short duration, and the impolicy and inhumanity of the plan would perhaps, when too late for effectual remedy, become apparent by the complaints of the people and the disappointment at the treasury in the payments of revenue, and would probably terminate in the ruin and depopulation of the unfortunate country." Again he wrote, "Experience has fully shown that the farming system is ill-calculated to improve a country, and it is contrary to principles which we wish to establish, of availing ourselves as much as possible of the service of the proprietors of the lands."

Though there was a concurrence of opinion among the majority of the Council as to making settlements only with the Zemindars, there was greater divergence as to the term and amount of taxation to be levied. Mr Shore objected to the permanent assessment, on the ground that "we had

[1] Letter to Court of Directors, 3d November 1788.

not a sufficient knowledge of the actual collections made from the several districts to enable us to distribute the assessment upon them with the requisite equality; that the demands of the Zemindars upon the Talookdars and Ryots were undefined; and that even if we possessed a competent knowledge of these points, there were peculiar circumstances attending the country, which must render it bad policy in the Government to fix their demands upon the land." [1] He had no good opinion of the Zemindars, whom he accused of "ignorance of their own interests, irregularity and confusion in the details of business, and collecting their rents by rules which were numerous, arbitrary, and indefinite;" [2] that we had not sufficient information to enable us to decide all cases with justice and policy; and that erroneous decisions would be followed either by "a diminution of the revenues, or a confirmation of oppressive exaction." For these and a variety of collateral reasons which he embodied in an able minute on the subject, he deprecated a perpetual and unalterable assessment, and recommended a decennial settlement, when the experience acquired in the interval would suggest improvements and correct mistakes. On the other hand, the Viceroy argued that many years had already been spent in collecting information, and that the various tentative and experimental measures tried during that period had not benefited either the people or the Government. "I am clearly of opinion," he said, "that this Government will never be better qualified, at any given period whatever, to make an equitable settlement of the land revenue of these provinces," and that further delay would compromise the happiness of the people and the prosperity of the country. The idea uppermost in the mind of Lord Cornwallis was indeed the formation of a powerful body of landowners with perpetual tenure. He

[1] Minute of the Governor-General, 10th February 1790.   [2] Ibid.

sought in the re-establishment of such a class a guarantee for stability, founded on the sense of interest which its members would naturally feel in the perpetuation of a system that might insure them for ever against fitful and periodical enhancements of taxation. "In case of a foreign invasion," he said, "it is a matter of the last importance, considering the means by which we keep possession of this country, that the proprietors of the lands should be attached to us from motives of self-interest. A landholder who is secured in the quiet enjoyment of a profitable estate can have no motive in wishing for a change. On the contrary, if the rents of his lands are raised in proportion to their improvement, if he is liable to be dispossessed, or if threatened with imprisonment or confiscation of his property on account of balance due to Government, he will readily listen to any offers which are likely to bring about a change that cannot place him in a worse situation, but which hold out to him hopes of a better."[1]

The Board of Control and the Ministry at home concurred in these views; and in March 1793 final regulations were issued, declaring that all lands held by Zemindars, independent Talookdars, and others, the actual proprietors of land, and their heirs and lawful successors, were to be thenceforth subject to a perpetual and unalterable amount of tax therein stated. Land not then under cultivation, and consequently not assessable, if afterwards brought in, was to be the subject of special arrangement, as the estate escheated by failure of issue was to revert to the Government, who would become owners on the same terms as the last possessor. The proportion which the tax should bear to the rateable value of the land was to be moderate; but there were differences of opinion as to the rateable value itself.

[1] Minute of Governor-General, 10th February 1790.

Mr James Grant, who was at the head of the Khalsa or Exchequer, and who had had great experience in the financial department, was of opinion that Government had been defrauded to a very great extent in the previous temporary assessments, and the estates were capable of sustaining a much larger impost. This view was successfully combated by Mr Shore, and the assessment was finally decided on an average of the receipts from land-tax during several preceding years. These had amounted in 1790–91 to £3,109,000 for Bengal, Behar, and Orissa; and to £400,000 for the district of Benares, equal to nine-tenths of the nominal productive value. The views of those who favoured a large augmentation of revenue from this source were partially met by fixing the perpetual rate at ten-elevenths of the rateable value; though, from the complication and confusion that prevailed, it was, or was thought, impossible to define that amount with precision.

But the operation of the permanent settlement in Bengal ultimately justified the protests of Mr Shore. Its chief fault was found to be, as he had foretold, that, in its hasty promulgation, the interests of the subordinate ranks of the community had been overlooked, or left to be dealt with only when injury had accrued, and hardships had accumulated.

The provisions of the land settlement were deficient, and its execution was defective. If we are to trust the evidence of one who has had the fullest opportunities of accurately estimating its nature and effects, the assessments for the purpose of fixing the land revenue in 1789 were made carelessly and recklessly, and even, in some cases, corruptly. In many cases, persons were confirmed in proprietary rights who had been merely farmers or collectors of revenue under the native Government, and who had not a shadow of legal title to the land; only the person who paid the revenue for a whole estate into the treasury was taken to be the owner; the definition of the village unit was neglected in the arrangement with the larger proprietors, some of whose estates were afterwards found to comprise districts widely separated from each other. Numerous varieties of sub-tenure then existed in Bengal, but of these the Government took no account; and while they exhausted language to limit their own demands on the Zemindars, they enacted no rules to protect and encourage the Ryots or sub-tenants in their holdings. They reserved, however, a right of interference in the relations between cultivator and owner, when, as they deemed it not improbable, that interference might become necessary. Lord Cornwallis considered many supplementary arrangements would be requisite to render the principles of the plan applicable to the various rights and customs that existed in different parts of the country, and they must be made by Government, as the propriety of them might appear. "It is impossible," observes Mr R. D. Mangles,[1] "to exaggerate the recklessness and carelessness with which the permanent settlement in Bengal was made;"[2] and he confirms the remarks of Mr Holt Mackenzie on the subject, who says, "Our settlements were made in haste, on general surmises; on accounts never believed to be accurate, and never brought to any clear test of accuracy; on the offers of speculators and the bidding of rivals; on the suggestions of enemies; on the statements of candidates for employment, seeking credit with the Government by discoveries against the people; of information of all kinds, generally worthless; the collector and community playing a game of "brag," in

[1] Evidence before Parliamentary Committees on Indian Finance.
[2] Report of Committee, par. 638.

which all knowledge was on one side and all power on the other."

While the Viceroy congratulated the Court of Directors on the inauguration of a fiscal policy which he assured them would be "of the utmost importance for promoting the solid interests of the Company," he was fain to admit the decline of internal commerce and agriculture under British rule. "Excepting the Shroffs and Banians," he wrote,[1] "who reside almost entirely in great towns, the inhabitants of these provinces were advancing hastily to a general state of poverty and wretchedness. In this description I must include almost every Zemindar in the Company's territories, which, though it may have been partly occasioned by their own indolence and extravagance, I am afraid must also be in a great measure attributed to the defects of our former system of government." In a country recently desolated by famine, and impoverished by rack-rents and short leases, the one-sided legislation of 1789 soon entailed the supplementary arrangements of which its well-meaning but mistaken author had himself anticipated the probable necessity. The permanent land assessment of the Bengal provinces was ten-elevenths of the assumed rental, a calculation only based on a mere rough and ready valuation, that was presumed to fall considerably short of the actual rental and value, though how far, no care was taken to ascertain. Such a charge upon a *bona fide* value would have been indeed ruinous and preposterous; but the real value of the land was two or three times greater than the nominal one for assessment. It is in evidence that a farmer, during the minority of the proprietor, paid a rental of thirty-three times the assessment value, and made his own profit besides. Where no limit was fixed upon the de-

[1] Letter to Directors, 2d August 1789.

mands which the immediate holder from the State could impose on the cultivators of the soil, the door was left open for agrarian oppression, and it became necessary to enact laws for the protection of the Ryots and sub-tenants. The Putneedars of the Rajah of Burdwan were thus protected by a special law, and a later enactment ordained that an uninterrupted holding for twelve years confirmed a Ryot in his tenancy during punctual payment. This remedial legislation, consequent on the hastily framed measure of 1793, was various and fluctuating, at one time favouring the Ryot, at another time the Zemindar. One of the chief recommendations of the new system was the punctuality of payment it promised, and the undertaking was rigidly enforced. The Zemindars, accustomed to the loose and capricious methods of dealing under the former system, were not at first prepared for such exactitude, and a few of them paid the penalty of default in the sale of their estates by auction. In the first years after the settlement, some estates changed hands in this way, the buyer succeeding to the first holder's rights in perpetuity, without any increase or diminution of assessment. This proceeding involved the lapse of all leases granted by the outgoing proprietor; but it was found to bear hardly on the sub-tenants, and a measure of relief was subsequently passed, giving under-tenants, under certain conditions, a right to hold their tenures against Government sales. It was found, also, that while the Government rigorously exacted prompt payment of the revenue from the Zemindars, the latter had no means of enforcing the like punctuality in payment by the Ryots. A law was therefore passed enabling them to collect their rents with certainty; but this power being abused, fresh laws gave to the Ryots the right of replevying, a privilege of which they were not slow to avail themselves. It is recorded that three thousand suits of replevin were instituted against a Zemindar at one time.

Such were the general characteristics of a measure which forms a distinctive landmark in Anglo-Indian story. That it would be of unmixed benefit to the revenue, or to the agricultural community, was doubted by far-seeing men at the time, and has been denied by competent authorities since then. The land settlement of Bengal by Lord Cornwallis, and other agrarian enactments more or less closely modelled thereon, have, in the opinion of Sir Henry Maine, passed into a proverb of maladroit management. They all rested on the outlandish assumption, imported from Westminster, that the soil of the country belonged to the King, and reverted to him by lapse or forfeiture. This was morally, socially, and politically irreconcileable with the oldest, the strongest, and the best ideas of Indian civilisation. It never struck root in the convictions or consciences of the people, and wherever it was planted by overwhelming force, it failed to bear any fruit of good, and speedily withered where it grew. That the primary sentiment which influenced the framing of the Bengal settlement was not the prosperity of the country, is clearly indicated by the passage quoted at the head of this chapter from the elaborate minute drawn up by the Governor-General. Bengal, Behar, and Orissa, the first of which provinces had, under native rule, been designated as " the paradise of nations," were only valuable as they were able to supply the holders of India stock with large dividends, to support an expensive government, backed by an army of occupation, and to recoup a treasury exhausted by wanton and wasteful wars elsewhere. Maladministration by encroaching power had sapped the financial resources of the country, and damaged the whole machinery of revenue.

With hostility without, and reluctant submission within, the Indian Government saw the necessity of an effective stroke of policy, and bethought them of a way to gain a hold on one class of the people, and to induce a show of order in the finances, even if this was gained at the expense of the suffering millions. That this important act of State was not framed or put in operation without a certain amiable regard for the preservation of ancient customary rights, was probably due to the high-minded and humane disposition of Mr Shore, who placed upon record his opinion that "the demands of a foreign dominion like ours ought certainly to be more moderate than the impositions of the native rulers; and that, to render the value of what we possess permanent, our demands ought to be fixed; that, removed from the control of our own Government the distance of half the globe, every possible restriction should be imposed upon the administration of India without circumscribing its necessary power, and the property of the inhabitants be secured against the fluctuations of caprice, or the license of unrestrained control."[1]

[1] Minute by Mr Shore on the Land Settlement.

CHAPTER XVI.

LORD WELLESLEY.

1797—1801.

"The recent extension of our territory has added to the number and description of our enemies. Wherever we spread ourselves, particularly if we should aggrandise ourselves at the expense of the Mahrattas, we increase this evil. We throw out of employment and means of subsistence all who have hitherto managed the revenue or served in the armies. Upon all questions of increase of territory these considerations have much weight with me, and I am, in general, inclined to decide that we have enough."
—WELLINGTON.[1]

EUROPE had been convulsed for more than five years by the struggles of the French Revolutionary war. The conflict, which had begun for principles, was already become one for empire. The league of despots which had striven to overthrow the immature liberties of France, had been exemplarily punished by Pichegru, Moreau, and Bonaparte; and the Peace of Campo-Formio might have been lasting had other powers been content to forego what they had lost in the war. But France, intoxicated with her single-handed victory over the coalesced legitimists of the time, was too easily led into the race of empire—first by the necessity of resisting, and then by the ambition of eclipsing her implacable foes. Napoleon, the incarnation of the national will, rose with the occasion, and because he best knew how to satisfy the popular enthusiasm, he became as by witchery the idol of his country.

[1] Letter to Munro, August 20, 1800—Gleig's Life, vol. i. p. 266.

It was a time of universal fermentation. The old ideas of what was possible and what was right were shaken from their hold of men. Events of such magnitude and novelty had crowded on each other with rapidity from 1789 to 1797, that no scheme was any longer regarded as incredible, no project as unrealisable or vain. Had right principles prevailed in the councils of Great Britain, the frenzy of men's minds might have had time to cool ere the entire world was wrapt in flame ; Italy would have been allowed to recover her strength, and to naturalise her alien-born liberties ; Germany had been spared the loss and woe of sixteen further years of bloodshed ; the final partition of Poland, and the dispersion of her best and bravest sons, might not have been attempted, and would certainly not have been recognised and sanctioned by Western Europe; France might not have been driven from one step to another of military fury, at the sacrifice of constitutional freedom ; unhappy Ireland might not have been goaded into rebellion in order to precipitate an incomplete and unassimilating scheme of incorporation ; and Great Britain would have had the benefits of internal reform and religious liberty thirty years earlier, and she would to-day have been burthened with less than half her debt. But the policy of Pitt was one of selfish isolation, until every ally and neighbour that could serve us, or was worth serving by us, had been brought to the verge of ruin ; and then, in desperation, of indiscriminate and unlimited interference. It was a policy of peace at any price, until it suddenly became one of war at any cost. We shrunk from defending the maritime States, whose freedom was older than our own, on the old plea of not being our brothers' keeper, and on the beggarly calculation that we could not afford to interpose ; and it ended in our having to fight for our life, leagued with every despot who would accept our subsidies, and whose oppressions and annexations we would condone.

In 1798 the Republican armies had been victorious almost everywhere. The dreams of Louis XIV. had been more than realised. Belgium and Savoy had been annexed; Holland and Italy reduced to dependency; Austria, after four disastrous campaigns, was well-nigh exhausted; and Prussia feared to stir. Bonaparte, full of invention and daring, had become the idol of the French soldiery and the terror of French politicians. To find him employment at a safe distance from Paris, he was sent to conquer Egypt, and no enterprise seemed more fitted to dazzle and perplex his enemies than that which was spoken of sanguinely as the first step to the conquest of the East. In the autumn of 1797, the English Government had information of intrigues carrying on with various Asiatic Courts and the French Directory. Tippoo Saib, ten years before, had sent envoys to Paris in quest of aid to drive us from Bengal. He had frequently renewed proposals of this kind, and it was imagined that at length his solicitations were about to be successful. France had still several possessions in the Indian Seas. The Nizam as well as Scindia had considerable bodies of troops organised and officered by Frenchmen permanently in their pay. Mr Pitt and his colleagues were convinced that a vast plot was thickening around us in Asia, and that it would require vigilance, courage, circumspection, energy, insight, and aptitude of no common order to anticipate the impending blow, and paralyse the arm already raised for our undoing. The exigency was a rare and perilous one. The Ministers looked round among men of civil and military reputation for a man adequate to the occasion. The first intention was to send out Lord Cornwallis a second time, and his reappointment was actually announced. After the lapse of a few weeks, however, the veteran was induced to relinquish the viceroyalty of India for that of Ireland; and the onerous charge was conferred on Lord Mornington, who, for the four preceding years, had been a member of the Board of Control, under the presidency of Mr Dundas. His father was a man of fine taste and considerable talent for musical composition; but he died while his sons were all still young; and Richard had more of his mother than his father in his intellectual nature. Lady Mornington was, in many respects, a very remarkable person,—full of sagacity and resolution to meet and to surmount difficulties; proud of her children, and full of ambition for them. She lived to see the gratification of her heart's desire,—to see four of them in succession created British peers,—to hear her first-born designated as the rescuer of the Empire of the East; and a younger son thanked by the assembled monarchs of Christendom as the deliverer of their realms and restorer of their thrones. The youth of the future statesman was chiefly distinguished by a mutiny, of which he was the principal ringleader, at Harrow, and for the facility he subsequently showed at Eton in writing Greek and Latin verse. The latter accomplishment he continued to cultivate at Oxford, where he became the intimate friend of Mr, afterwards Lord Grenville, by whom he was early made known to Mr Pitt, and to whose friendship he was indebted for his introduction to official life. Not content with the opportunities afforded him as a peer of Ireland, he sought and obtained a seat in the English House of Commons; and such was his thirst for distinction, that we find him, in the course of the same session, taking part in the debates of the Upper House at

Dublin, and in those of the Lower House at Westminster. His early oratorical displays were open to the charge of being too ambitious. His elocution was overdone, and his tone too dramatic to escape the raillery of opponents. Lord Mountmorris bantered him on the excellence of his imitations of Garrick; and Sheridan quizzed him on his premature solemnity of air, and the studied gracefulness with which he leaned upon the table as he spoke. He must have been very unlike in temper the man he was in later life if *badinage* of this sort was unfelt by him. But he could afford to be upbraided with slight faults. If his cause was not always good, he was always sure to make the best of it. He never, in those days, spoke without preparation. Though given to pleasure, he grudged no toil necessary to master a subject on which he was to speak; and there are traces in more than one of his speeches, at the period in question, of great care and no ordinary amount of research. In 1786 he was made a Lord of the Treasury, an appointment which he held for seven years. To take part in debate without being bidden was a thing impossible; and the occurrence of his name more than once in important discussions of the time, proves that the Minister did not disdain the assistance which his young adherent could render him. Some eminent critics have fancied they discerned in these early speeches, made to order, the foreshadowings of the dignified and masculine eloquence of maturer years, and that they can recognise the lineaments of the masterly style of subsequent despatches and state papers in the classic verses of the *Musæ Etonenses* or other early writings. It has even been supposed that his performances in this way influenced the judgment of the refined and accomplished Minister in promoting him to a trust so high and enviable. But it was more probably the vigour of unpremeditated thought, and the brilliancy of unset expression, drawn forth in conversation, that made an impression on the mind of Mr Pitt.

Before Lord Mornington reached India, he had fathomed the difficulty of the position. At the Cape of Good Hope he opened and read the last despatches of his predecessor on their way to England. They confirmed all he had before surmised, all that had been suggested by his younger brother Arthur in his private letters to him from India, and all that he had hypothetically discussed with Mr Pitt before leaving home. By England the shabby and short-sighted system in foreign policy had been at length abandoned, and the reckless expenditure of panic had begun. Armies on an unaccustomed scale were organising, and an unusual number of ships of war were afloat or making ready for sea. When occasions near home could not always be found for employing them, they were sought for in distant latitudes. Trinidad and Ceylon had recently been captured, and it was part of the new Viceroy's instructions that he should surprise and seize Batavia. All acts of further aggression had been forbidden by Parliament in 1793. But the Earl knew the governing spirit of the Court and Cabinet of England far too well to hesitate on account of these inhibitions. He well understood the value of the solemn interdict against new encroachments and further appropriation of jewels, lands, and revenues. Failure or success was, in truth, the only question. Failure would indeed expose him to a real storm of abuse; virtuous indignation, or even to more serious inconveniences. But he was content to take the risk of ill-success, confident that if triumph crowned his projects, the censure he might incur would be accompanied with generous indemnity—the formal prelude to unbounded praise.

But more dazzling projects soon suggested themselves.

The new Governor-General found himself invested with vague but vast authority. Large bodies of troops were at his disposal, officered by Europeans, and disciplined in recent campaigns. A few months put him in adequate possession of the weakness and disunion of the still independent Courts of Hyderabad, Poona, and Seringapatam. It was impossible not to see that the means of wide acquisitions were thus placed within his grasp; and in the existing condition of Hindustan, pretexts for encroachment could not long be wanting.

That all things, however, should be done decently and in order, a case of necessity for self-defence against some enemy of some sort, was felt to be requisite. This indispensable danger was not long in being discovered. French designs were traced, and magnified to the necessary size, in the summer of 1798. The native princes, ever since the wars of the Carnatic, had been anxious to teach their troops the use of European arms and tactics; and that vague ideas may not have been kept alive in France that her former position in the East might be regained, it were hard to question. That the hatred and jealousy wherewith the two nations regarded each other would suggest the desire, or even dictate open menace on the subject, was highly probable. But neither Hyder or Tippoo succeeded in forming a French alliance until 1798. The Sultan was at peace with the Company, but how long they would suffer him to retain what he still held of his inheritance, he could not tell; and his experience of their disposition towards him, both before and since the partition treaty, was ill-suited to disarm apprehension.

The official despatches of the Governor-General are the most authentic materials for the narrative of the memorable events that took place during his administration. They also contain irrefutable proof of the preconcerted designs out of which those events subsequently sprung. The first communications between Tippoo Saib and Lord Mornington related to Wynaad, a province which the former alleged was not included in the cessions under the treaty of 1792; but which had been kept by the Company, along with their acquisitions of that date. His repeated remonstrances had been treated with studied disregard; and at length he resolved to assert his rights by sending a small detachment of troops to occupy a portion of the frontier. The Viceroy proposed to name an envoy to meet one from the Sultan for the settlement of the dispute. To this Tippoo immediately assented; upon investigation Wynaad was found to belong rightfully to Mysore, and was consequently declared to have been held wrongfully by the English. The Governor-General thereupon wrote, on the 7th August, to the Sultan formally restoring Wynaad, and felicitating him on the cause of any interruption to their amity being removed. Nevertheless, at that very moment every resource of the Government in India was actively devoted to preparing an armament for the invasion of his dominions.

About the close of 1797, envoys had been sent from Mysore to M. Malartic, the Governor of the Isle of France, soliciting his friendship, and asking recruits for a small corps of European troops which the Sultan was desirous to employ. This was no breach of amity with us on his part. French officers and soldiers had for some time been engaged in the service of the Nizam, without calling forth any protest or objection from his neighbours; and the Mahratta Princes, with whom no quarrel then existed, had likewise succeeded in establishing auxiliary corps of the same kind. Malartic, being unable to spare any of the garrison under his command in the Mauritius, issued a proclamation to all French citizens who happened to be then in the East, authorising them to enlist in the service of the Sultan. Expressions of antipathy to Great Britain were gratuitously introduced into this document; and if France had had a squadron off the coast, or fortified possessions on the mainland, where an invading expedition might have been in waiting, or had the injured chief of Mysore been at war with the Company, such an appeal would have warranted strong words of protest, if not measures for self-protection. But the reverse of all this was true. Not half-a-dozen vessels bearing the tricolor had been seen beyond the Cape for the last four years, and Tippoo was utterly destitute of even the materials for creating a navy. His anxiety for war could not have been very great, when he consented to expostulate in vain for years about Wynaad, and when he forbore any violence which might provoke retaliation. The entire number of recruits who landed in April at Mangalore from the Isle of France did not amount to two hundred men. Yet this was the force, and these the circumstances, against which Lord Mornington felt it imperatively necessary to prepare a vast army at enormous cost, lest the English should "be expelled from India."

While the preparations were going forward, not a syllable of remonstrance was breathed. The dispute concerning Wynaad was arranged with a specious show of fairness and urbanity. Not a sentence do we find in all the letters which that affair called forth of virtuous indignation or honest apprehension at the gasconade of M. Malartic's proclamation. While matters stood in this position, towards the end of October news arrived of Bonaparte's expedition to Egypt. The alarm which this excited was partly allayed by the tidings, which soon followed, of Nelson's victory of the Nile; and the Governor-General wrote to Tippoo acquainting him of the reverse with which Providence had thus visited the enemies of Great Britain. The invasion of Egypt, he said, was but "another excess of that unjustifiable ambition and insatiable rapacity which had so long characterised the French nation, and nothing could more clearly expose their total disregard of every principle of public faith and honour than this unprovoked aggression." These are harsh words, and in other lips they had not been unjust; but with what feelings must they have been read by Tippoo? Even he, however, could not feel all the depth of their mockery, for as yet he had had no intimation of the long-preparing wrath that was about to burst upon him. The fear of Bonaparte's pushing forward from the coast of the Red Sea towards India still paralysed all active resolution against Mysore. Whether the impetuosity of the Governor, or the impossibility of any longer concealing warlike preparations, was the incentive, we find him at last, on the 8th November, addressing an elaborate complaint to the Sultan on the score of his alliance with France. The style and tone of this extraordinary epistle are too curious to be passed over without notice. "It is impossible that you should suppose me to be ignorant of the intercourse which subsists between you and the French. You cannot imagine me indifferent to the transactions which have passed between you and the enemies of my country; nor does it appear necessary or proper that I should any longer conceal from you the surprise and concern with which I perceive you disposed to involve yourself in all the ruinous consequences of a connection which threatens not only to subvert the foundations of friendship between you and the Company, but to introduce into the heart of your kingdom the principles of anarchy and confusion, to shake your own authority, to weaken the obedience of your subjects, and to destroy the religion which you revere."

The pious solicitude here expressed for the stability of faith and morals in the Sultan's realm is quite touching. Oh, that Lucian could arise from the dead, that he might confess himself outdone in serious irony by the official despatches of modern times! Half the prey is already gorged; the knife is loudly whetting for the remainder, and by way of grace before meat, we have a pious exhortation against irreligion, subversion of legitimate authority, and, above all, entreaties to beware of aught that may interrupt the affection and respect that subsists between the jaws and the meat that is next destined to fill them. What is the plain English of this exquisite appeal? Your Highness and we are excellent friends, therefore we are jealous of your love. The French are unreliable republicans; we know them better than you do. They will teach your Mussulmans democracy if you let them near you; in friendship we cannot allow this. They will undermine your throne; surely it were better suffer us to pull it down, than that we should witness your dishonour. They will preach infidelity; think of your poor soul,—or if you will not think of it, we must, and remit it from a wicked world, ere its faith is staggered by the jests of Voltaire or the sophistries of Rousseau. And when you are gone before your time to your account, we will look after the bodies and souls of your people. We may possibly establish a diocese, or at least appoint a Bishop of Mysore; that is our way. But fear no compulsion for conscience' sake from us. It is only fellow-Christians we persecute; temples and mosques may remain for us to the end of time, provided we get the temporalities into our hands. Nay, sooner than behold the scandal of French principles being introduced among your people, we are ready to turn tax-gatherers to Mahomet or Brahma, or both; and willing to beat idols' drums and fire salutes in honour of Vishnu or Juggernaut, if you will only let us into Seringapatam. This edifying document proceeds to say, that the arming, which could no longer be entirely concealed on the part of the Company, was merely "for self-defence;" and it concludes with an elaborate profession that "the British Government, wishing to live in peace and friendship with all their neighbours, entertaining no objects of ambition, and looking to no other objects than the permanent security and tranquillity of their own dominions, would always be ready, as they then were, to afford every demonstration of their pacific intentions."[1]

On the 20th November Tippoo replied, complaining of warlike preparations going forward, and praying that peace might be preserved.[2] On the the 9th of January 1799, the Governor-General wrote to the Sultan, setting forth for the first time the grievous offence which His Britannic Majesty had received by reason of M. Malartic's proclamation, and plaintively representing the ingratitude of Tippoo in having sanctioned such a document, when, immediately before its reaching India from the Mauritius, he had received, in the restoration of Wynaad, a conclusive proof of the friendly dispositions of the Company. "I had hardly formed the decision on your Highness's claim to Wynaad, by which I had afforded an unquestionable testimony of my disposition to render impartial and ample justice to your rights, and to cultivate and improve the relations of amity and peace with your Highness, when I received from the Isle of France an authentic copy of the proclamation," &c.[3] It is rather unfortunate that, in the same volume which contains this letter, there are reiterated and copious proofs that the Vice-

[1] Marquis Wellesley's Despatches, vol. i. No. xcvi.
[2] Ibid., vol. i. No. cii. [3] Ibid., vol. i. No. ciii.

roy had in his possession this terrible manifesto fully two months before his vaunted generosity touching Wynaad. It had been received and made "the subject of general ridicule"[1] as a serious threat, and chuckled over as a God-sent and timely pretext for hostilities. General Harris had been written to on the subject, and secretly apprised of the advantage that would be taken of it.[2] The expedition for invading Mysore had been planned, and directions given to the Governors of Madras and Bombay to organise all the military resources of their respective Presidencies; and they had remonstrated against "plunging Tippoo into war; for whatever might be the object of his embassy to the Mauritius, the late intelligence from the islands left no room to doubt that no rupture was to be apprehended but by our own provocation."[3] Lord Mornington himself had written to Mr Dundas, telling him, that from want of money and the impossibility of completing their preparations in time, he was reluctantly forced to suspend his immediate design of "seizing the whole maritime territory remaining in Tippoo's possession, and then marching upon his capital to compel him to purchase peace by a formal cession of the territory seized, and compelling him to pay all the expenses of the war—objects which appeared most desirable, and which every motive of justice and policy demanded;" and he had resolved that "a temperate remonstrance would be sufficient to satisfy their honour, and convince the native powers that their moderation alone induced them to abstain from a more rigorous course."[4] All this was prior to the

---

[1] Letter from Governor-General to Mr Dundas, 6th July 1798, No. xxii.

[2] Letters of 9th and 20th June, Nos. xiii. and xvii.

[3] Letter from Mr Webbe, Secretary of Madras, to Governor-General, 6th July 1798, No. xxii.

[4] Letter to Mr Dundas, then Secretary to the Board of Control, 6th July 1798, No. xxii.

magnanimous restoration of Wynaad, which Tippoo was asked to take as a convincing proof of our sincerity. In reality, the surrender of that district was but a solemn farce, tending to lull the Moslem Prince into security until the measures against him should be ripe for execution. Till every engine of muffled power was in readiness, wounded honour felt no pain—could even take credit to itself for confiding generosity, and levy, under false pretences, the repute of moderation. Within nine months from this virtuous act of restitution, Wynaad was again taken possession of by this just and self-denying Power, together with the residue of Tippoo Saib's dominions.

By the end of January 1799, the preparations for war were complete, and the threats of M. Malartic, which were by that time about twelve months old (having been published in January 1798), were no longer to be endured. Orders were given for the invading army to begin its march; a letter came from Tippoo accepting an offer to negotiate, which, as a portion of the farce of decency, had been sent to him. The time named in the offer had elapsed by eight days, and it was solemnly declared that the season was then too far advanced to arrest the march of the troops;[1] but Tippoo was informed that General Harris would receive any propositions at the head of the army.[2] Even this was rendered illusory by secret instructions to Harris, ordering him to advance "without an hour's delay," and not to forward the letter to Tippoo till within a day's march of the frontier,[3] thus rendering it absolutely impossible for the doomed Prince to propose any terms until the invaders were in occupation of part of his territory. There were other secret instructions. No conditions of peace under any circumstances

---

[1] Declaration of War, 22d February 1799, No. cxl.
[2] Letter from Governor-General to Tippoo, No. cxli.
[3] Letter from Governor-General to General Harris, ibid. cxlii.

were to be proposed or accepted until the siege of Seringapatam should have been formed, or some equally advantageous position secured. Tippoo was then to be informed that he must cede Canara, a valuable maritime province, to the English, and two others equally valuable to the native powers in alliance with them, besides paying one crore and a half of rupees (£1,500,000) for the expenses of the campaign. If these terms were not agreed to before the siege was actually begun, not less than one half of his remaining possessions were to be exacted;[1] and letter after letter was despatched to Harris, lest "he should suffer any attempt at negotiation to retard the march towards Seringapatam."[2] The tragical event is well known. Tippoo, finding that nothing but his destruction could appease his pursuers, resolved to maintain a desperate fight to the last. Gathering his best troops around him, he shut the gates of his capital, and prepared to defend it so long as he was able. But the odds against him were too heavy for any courage or skill he could oppose; his troops had lost the confidence in him and in themselves they once possessed; and he sunk without disguise beneath the weight of his adversity in mute and sullen gloom. On the 4th of May, as he sat in his palace in the heat of noon, he was roused from his dreamy gaze into the pit of fate by the shout of the besiegers. The breach was stormed; and Tippoo, vainly endeavouring to rally his broken troops, was slain and trampled under foot in the streets of his plundered city.

Thus fell the kingdom of Mysore. Of those whose laurels were gathered from its broken bough, we have nought here to say; of those who grabbed a fortune from its ruin, we have no desire to chronicle the names. 'Tis no part of the duty of the political annalist to challenge the pro-

---

[1] Letters, No. cxlii. [2] Id. No. cxlvii.

fessional merit of the soldier, even when he is compelled to fight in an unrighteous cause. It is the system, not the men —the secretly planned and oft repudiated purpose, not the frank and gallant instruments by whom it is worked out, that calls for blame. Mysore was declared to be a conquered country. The infant heir of the Hindu dynasty which had been deposed by Hyder was sought out and placed upon the Musnud. His family and friends were required to guarantee the observance of two treaties; the one was that of the second partition whereby Canara, Coimbatore, Wynaad, and Seringapatam were annexed to the English possessions, while the districts of Gurramcotta, Gûti, and others near Hyderabad, were made over to the Nizam, and another province was reserved for the Peishwa. The other treaty provided for the permanent maintenance of a powerful subsidiary force by which the state, reduced within secondary limits, was to be garrisoned. It bound the Rajah and his heirs in political subordination to the paramount power, and authorised the direct interposition of the Governor-General, whenever he thought fit, in any and every detail of financial administration. In return it bound the Company in ties of specific guarantee to protect and defend the rights of the restored Prince in his circumscribed inheritance. "The mass of the people," wrote Colonel Wellesley (afterwards Duke of Wellington), "seemed to be passive spectators of the change, and looked on with philosophic indifference." Recovering after a little from the stunning effect of Tippoo's fall, several of the Polygars in various provinces tried to rally around them the means of desultory warfare. Powerful columns were sent to suppress these futile efforts at resistance; and, to save time, they appear to have made short work of it. Hear Munro's account of his share in the consolidation of conquest:—

P

"I have got Vettel Hegada and his heir-apparent and principal agents hanged; and I have no doubt that I shall be able to get the better of any other vagabond Rajah that may venture to rebel."[1]

Lord Wellesley's administration marks an important epoch in Anglo-Indian story. The want of a comprehensive scheme of policy, which had been so often felt, was now for the first time supplied. Conquest had hitherto proceeded at an irregular pace, and had been directed with little political foresight. Whatever could be clutched at the moment, was indeed laid hold of as opportunity served; and the Company had by one means or other managed in forty years to get possession of about 220,000 square miles of territory—a dominion which many wise and patriotic men in England thought quite large enough to be kept safely or profitably. In England, and in India also, provident guardians of the Company's interests, as a trading corporation, believed that they would do better to keep near the coast; and, by living peaceably with their neighbours and punctually paying their way, drawing to their *entrepôt* the fabrics and the wares of the inland realms, with whose institutions they could not meddle without incurring the distrust and hatred that invariably besets the pathway of invasion. Conscientious men who had seen or heard the doings of Clive at Moorshedabad, of Hastings in Rohilcund, of Matthews in Baramahal, or Cornwallis in Coorg, shrank from the repetition of similar scenes elsewhere. And, finally, men, endued with that instinct of forethought and foresight which more than all else constitutes statesmanship, and which no training can teach or other gifts supply, began to mutter to themselves, and whisper to one another, that we had already quite as many dependencies as we could

[1] Gleig's Life of Munro, vol. i. p. 270.

permanently afford to keep, and that the vanity of adding indefinitely to their number might one day cost us dear. There was in garrison a young officer who had been promoted by family interest somewhat faster than his fellows, who occasionally ruminated on the subject, and wrote in confidence to certain friends the result of his reflections. He had been through the campaign of 1799, and was named, as of favour rather than for any special service he had rendered in the field, to be one of the Commissioners at Seringapatam for the dismemberment and dissection of Mysore. Thomas Munro was one of the Secretaries to the Commission, and to him, in confidence, Arthur Wellesley, arguing against plans of further conquest, already talked of freely in viceregal councils, thus wrote—" I agree with you that we ought to settle the Mahratta business, and the Malabar Rajahs, but I am afraid that to extend ourselves will rather tend to delay the settlement, and that we shall thereby increase rather than diminish the number of our enemies. But," he adds, characteristically, in conclusion, "as for the wishes of the people, I put them out of the question."[1]

But the notion that the people were indifferent to the subjugation of their country is refuted in every page of these gallant correspondents. Mysore, under the Government of Tippoo, "was the best cultivated, and its population the most flourishing in India; while under the English and their dependants the population of the Carnatic and Oude, hastening to the state of deserts, was the most wretched upon the face of the earth; and even Bengal, under the operation of laws ill-adapted to the circumstances of the case, was suffering all the evils which the worst of Governments could inflict."[2]

[1] Gleig's Life of Munro, vol. i. p. 266.
[2] Mill, book VI. chap. viii.

Munro was sent from Canara to the ceded districts, which, by the former partition treaty, had been taken from Tippoo, and for a time given nominally to the Nizam, but which now without disguise were taken possession of by their real owners, the Company. Munro was desired to raise the public taxes in the provinces placed under his authority. They had been described as unable to yield more than the tribute which they paid formerly to Tippoo, by reason of their great sufferings in the war, and during the famine which was its consequence. To see whether they had suffered as much as they were reported to have done, Munro tells how he made a circuit of inspection, and says—"There was no doubt some exaggeration, but not a great deal. Most of the houses were in ruins, scarce one-fourth of them were inhabited. But he had little doubt that in seven years the full amount of the schedule" (or proposed standard of English taxation) "might be realised. The principal obstacle was that the desire men at the head of affairs usually had, of seeing the public income flourishing under their auspices, would probably compel him to proceed too rapidly. He had no thought of precipitating matters for the present, though he should, for the sake of the public want of money, press the ryots rather more than he ought to do."[1] The Polygars, or armed nobles, offered considerable resistance to the fiscal designs of their new masters. Munro calls them robbers and banditti opposed to the establishment of order, whom it was necessary to get rid of without delay. Notwithstanding all his enlightened efforts to win them over to increased taxation, two of these chieftains still held out in 1802, so that it became advisable to move large bodies of troops into the neighbourhood. "It might also be necessary,"

[1] Munro, vol. i. p. 334.

he thought, "to proceed against the Zemindar of Panganore, because he was not sure that he would submit to an addition to his peshcush or tribute, which must be laid on in order to reduce his power."[1] Not much philosophical indifference on the part of the conquered here.

Far other thoughts and dreams filled the brain of the egotistic Governor-General. A step in the peerage had been granted him in acknowledgment of his services above narrated. The desire to accomplish something more notable is betrayed by the newly-made Marquis in every act of his memorable career, and in every line of his ambitious correspondence. He was in the highest sense of the term an actor. He always took care to look the character. His attention to the state toilet was minute as that of a woman of fashion. He had a deep belief in the doctrine that the world is governed to a great degree by the shows and semblances of power; and loving the reality of power as he did, he would have thought it mere quixotism to discard any means so harmless for maintaining the personal consideration which is one ingredient of it. In the East, the display of magnificence was, in his day, considered a maxim of state policy. The sovereigns we had supplanted had never been seen but in gorgeous array, and surrounded with glitter and pomp. The transition to simplicity of costume and equipage would have been, it was supposed, a needless and injudicious violence to popular habits; and accordingly we find successive Governors-General sorely puzzled how to be grand enough without being too grand, and how to be high and mighty looking without being lost in the clouds of impalpability. Lord Wellesley had an instinct for this kind of thing. No man was ever more beloved by those about him; and yet there was not one of them who ever

[1] Munro, vol. i. p. 337.

thought of asking him an impertinent question. Although constitutionally irritable and impatient, his nature was so full of courtesy and generosity, that those who thought him oftenest unreasonable and wilful could not but love and honour him. When the prize-money came to be divided after the campaign of 1799, £100,000 would, according to rule, have fallen to his share; but though his patrimony was small and his habits expensive, he waived his right in favour of the troops, preferring to purchase praise rather than landed property. His talents, which were not inconsiderable, hardly equalled his aspirations; and had he been placed in other circumstances, they might have met with as mortifying results in India as they were subsequently doomed to undergo elsewhere. But owing to a rare coincidence of fortune, the civil and military establishments, at the period in question, contained a combination of talents apt for the purposes of the Governor-General such as they had never known before. Beside Malcolm, Close, Harris, and Munro, there were Edmonstone and Stewart, and above all, that younger brother, whose views of Indian as of Home policy throughout life differed from his so widely. The times were singularly favourable from other circumstances for the gratification of that thirst of distinction, which was the leading trait in his character.

The century opened in peace. The Viceroy's policy had proved successful in all respects but one, and was everywhere extolled for its vigour in contending with difficulties, and its magnanimity when they were overcome. His personal friends rejoiced; his flatterers applauded; his baffled enemies silently succumbed. Mr Pitt was well satisfied with his choice; and his choice was intensely proud of himself. But he had not paid his way, and his merchant-masters qualified their compliments and thanks with regrets and grumblings at the augmented debt occasioned by the war. They could not be made to understand at the outset why it was necessary at all, or why at its conclusion it had not been made to recoup its cost.

In Leadenhall Street, aggression and absorption were viewed but as means to one great end; viz., the increase of the dividend upon East India stock. Glory might be all very well for a venturous peer riding the Company's white elephant; but the keep of the voracious and unmanageable creature was the paramount thought of the Board of Directors. If he could be guided into fresh pastures, and set to browse there with impunity at any neighbour's expense, well and good; but grand marches up the hill of distant conquest and then down again, no matter with what amount of flags flying, tom-toms beating, and salvos of artillery stunning the amazed multitude, did not seem to the prudent rulers of the Company to be a game worth the candle. The Board of Control might be delighted at the check given to French influence in the East, and the disciples of Mr Burke in Parliament might commend the picturesque air of generosity which was thrown over the re-settlement of Mysore; but the Directors persistently continued to press the viceregal victor to explain how he proposed to pay the bill.

Disgusted with their want of appreciation of his genius, and their parsimony as partners in the lordship of the East, he replied haughtily that he knew best what the necessities of the case required; and then, in his grand manner, he proceeded to expound all the advantages which were certain to come as the fruits of his policy at some future time. These promises of profit to come did not content them or still their fears lest he should go on as he had begun. The King had made their enterprising Earl a

Marquis, as a reward for the annexation of Mysore—who could tell what he might be tempted to do next? News came that he had availed himself of a disputed succession to the Musnud of Surat, to exact terms from the competitor he favoured, which virtually annexed that principality to the other provinces subject to the Presidency of Bombay. The Nawab was to retain the title and income his predecessors had enjoyed; but the responsibilities of governing and defending the country were henceforth to be borne by its new masters. Then followed similar intelligence regarding Tanjore, where a subsidiary force was permanently stationed at the cost of the Rajah, and the British Resident invested not only with an absolute veto, but the right of initiation in all matters of revenue and expenditure, the same liabilities being undertaken on the part of the Company. The Nawab of Arcot had long been mediatised, but henceforth even the semblance of local jurisdiction was to be taken away, and the Carnatic treated in form and in fact as an incorporated portion of the English dominions. Leadenhall Street grew still more uneasy, and much more querulous with the Viceroy; but, supported by the Cabinet, and delighted with a sense of supreme power, he was not to be weaned from his purpose, or worried into relinquishing his post by treatises on the duty of forbearance, or financial interrogatories, which he believed were contrived only to perplex and annoy him. As he looked in the glass of his fame, he saw reflected there the builder of England's empire in the East. The ground plan had been traced by Clive, the elevations and the estimates had been left by Warren Hastings. He would execute them.

The state of Oude was reported to be especially propitious for interference. By the modifications of the subsidiary treaty, made with Sir John Shore in 1797, the Vizier bound himself to pay a tribute of seventy-six lacs a year, and a further sum when the British force exceeded 13,000 men. He was not to be allowed intercourse with other sovereign states, or to permit any foreigner to dwell within his borders without leave from Calcutta. How far these humiliating conditions helped to worsen the state of affairs by weakening what remained of respect for the native Government, we cannot tell. But in 1801, the tribute was in arrear, the country was described as disorganised and wretched, and the unfortunate Nawab was driven to desperation by the sense of his weakness and the difficulties wherein he was entangled. Lord Wellesley's gaze was steadily fixed upon him. He indited a series of epistles, which are models of composition in their way, to persuade him to relinquish the cares of State, and to be content solely with its pomps and vanities. The Company would do all the rest. Or, if he would not, the cession of Allahabad and nine other districts might suffice to provide for the support of the garrison. The Vizier chose the latter, and by this partition territories were acquired worth more than a million and a quarter sterling.

Lord Wellesley's purpose in persuading the native Governments to maintain within their confines bodies of British troops, organised on our model instead of native corps officered by Frenchmen, was too obvious to be misconceived. It was a substantial pledge exacted from jealous neighbours, that they finally renounced the hope of any other European alliance, and all privity in designs which led that way. It was obviously meant and felt, if not in public words declared, to be a guarantee against the development of schemes hostile to English interests, and the growth of English ascendency. Under the direction of an intelligent Resident at the native Court, a compact force, well-armed, well-paid, and well-in-hand, would render sudden tumult abortive, and cause secret intrigue to waver continually, and to look back ere committing itself too far; and in the last event of open secession (or, as it soon came to be termed, revolt), it would form a rallying point for any friends it had, and an outpost capable of defence till succour should arrive. There was about the subsidiary force, at the same time, a specious affectation of regard for the severalty and nominal independence of the State to which it belonged, which soothed the outward vanity, if it stung the inward pride of the durbar and the bazaar. Scrupulous care was taken to keep up the distinction between native service and the service of the Company. A subsidiary force in time of peace was never moved out of the State to which it belonged, and even in time of war only with the assent of the Prince at whose expense it was equipped and maintained. It was the glove of mail courteously but undisguisedly laid upon the shoulder of native rule, with an irresistible but patronising air, felt to be a little heavy and a little hard at first, but soon destined to become habitual. Slowly but steadily it begot that sense of security and irresponsibility in the Prince and his advisers which has ever proved to be the gangrene of authority, for which there is no cure.

Its financial scope and tendency were conceived and executed with the same pitiless and inexorable purpose. The permanent appropriation of revenue for the maintenance of the subsidiary force was calculated mainly with reference to the inability of the State to bear it. Large or small, it was a tree whose seed was in itself, and was therefore chosen, that it might bear fruit after its kind. The cases were rare in which the districts ceded for the maintenance of the subsidiary force yielded within the year the sum that was needed for their food and pay. This was exactly what was anticipated, the opening of a running account of deficiencies, arrears, balances cleared off from time to time by new concessions, and complaints of remissness, neglect, and evasion, all which, in the nature of things, became inevitable. Arriving at ultimate supremacy, the means taken were by the subject race called perfidiously wicked, by the conquering race profoundly wise. The historian will probably compare them to the chronic injection of poison into the veins which allays fever and spasmodic pain, and produces a sensation of relief and quiet at the risk, and, when prolonged, with the certainty, of causing paralysis and death.

Lord Wellesley applied the power gained by the destruction of Tippoo, and the partition of Mysore, to lay the foundations of that edifice of empire which, in the space of sixty years, was so rapidly piled in Asia. Clive had made treaties for a subsidiary force at Moorshedabad and Delhi, Hastings at Benares and in the Deccan. But neither of them had ever been in a position to attempt the application of the system on a wider scale, still less to couple with it covenants and conditions which permanently bound the Company to protect, at any cost or sacrifice, their native allies from all enemies whatsoever, and virtually constituted the Company, in return, suzerain over them. In every case, the daring ambition of the Governor-General sought to obtain concessions of territory in lieu of money for the payment of the subsidiary force to be permanently kept by the protected State. He compelled the Vizier of Oude to subscribe a treaty ceding large portions of his dominions to pay for British troops to be maintained in those provinces he still governed. This was in 1801. He proceeded to carry the system further, and thereby to enthral those States of Central India which, since the days of Sivajî, had successfully defied their more civilised and luxurious neighbours.

CHAPTER XVII.

THE MAHRATTAS.

1802—1805.

"From factories to forts, from forts to fortifications, from fortifications to garrisons, from garrisons to armies, and from armies to conquests, the gradations were natural, and the result inevitable; where we could not find a danger, we were determined to find a quarrel."
—PHILIP FRANCIS.[1]

AT the beginning of 1802, Lord Wellesley tendered his resignation. His services had not been estimated by the Directors as his staff at Fort William and the Cabinet of Mr Addington thought they deserved. He aspired to the proconsular fame, both of conqueror and reformer; and Leadenhall Street was in no humour to acknowledge or encourage him in either capacity. When the bills came in of the Mysore War, they took away the very breath of financial prudence, and the diplomatic engagements subsequently formed with a view to territorial aggrandisement in Tanjore, Surat, and Oude, only lengthened the perspective of indefinite liability, and deepened the jungle of costly entanglement in various directions. Nor did Lord Wellesley's exercise of patronage, or his projects of reconstituting the Civil Service on a high educational basis, commend him any better to his frugal masters. Without consulting them, he had planned and published an elaborate and ex-

[1] Speech on Indian Affairs, 1787.

pensive design for the foundation of a college of governing functionaries at Calcutta, in which every cadet sent out from England should pass at least two years in acquiring a knowledge of Oriental tongues, habits, traditions, beliefs, and chronicles. The scheme was on a splendid scale, but it pointed specially and specifically to the creation of a school for the constant supply of political Sappers and Miners, whose every boyish hope and adolescent thought should be concentrated upon the extension and consolidation of the empire. The Directors loathed the very notion, and sickened at the pecuniary prospects it involved. *Point de zéle* was their invariable admonition to young men suspected of possessing dangerous ability. They wanted larger returns, not a greater number of rebel subjects; higher dividends, not more dominions. They thought of Lord Wellesley as a restless Satrap, whose vanity was like to ruin them; and he thought of himself as a sovereign in all but the name, of whom an ungrateful world was not worthy. The projected college was peremptorily forbidden, and instead of it, an institution of another kind was decided on. They grumbled at his choice of soldiers for political appointments, as indicating a settled purpose of encroachment and aggression. They would have him cancel Colonel Kirkpatrick's nomination as Secretary in the political department; they desired him to recall Colonel Scott from the Residency at Lucknow; and they forwarded to him a minute, which roundly declared the extra allowances to Colonel Wellesley, who had been appointed to the command in the Carnatic, as a job. This was the crowning affront, which he would not endure. He told them that he felt intensely disgusted at the notion that he could be capable of yielding, or his brother of receiving, any emolument or advantage that was not fairly due. If they believed such a rebuke to be deserved, the offenders should at once be recalled, either one or both. For himself, he was weary of such treatment, and he begged that they would seek a successor, who should relieve him at furthest in the course of the autumn from a charge he no longer wished to retain. He was not, however, taken at his word. Lord Castlereagh became President of the Board of Control; and sympathising with him in most of his designs and aspirations, accorded him more effective support. Meanwhile new vistas of aggrandisement opened in a quarter where he had not ventured to anticipate them; and, in the hope of fresh acquisitions, he resolved to remain another year in India. In December 1802, he wrote to the Directors that a crisis was imminent, fraught with consequences of the greatest importance.

In 1801 the Mahratta chiefs were quarrelling among themselves. Scindia, the greatest in territorial strength, and Holkar, the most restless and warlike in spirit, distrustful of each other, alternately menaced the Peishwa, of whose traditional pre-eminence both were jealous, and whose enfeebled authority they sought to overthrow. Lord Wellesley, bent on turning their enmities to account, and bringing them all into gradual dependence upon English aid, negotiated separately with each in turn, and, by the adroit use of subtlety and daring, he succeeded ere long in drawing or driving them all into a state of dependency. His instructions to Colonel Close recite how " the Peishwa in 1798 preferred danger and independence to a more intimate connection with the British power, which could not secure him the protection of our arms without at the same time establishing our ascendency in the Mahratta empire;" how the Peishwa had reluctantly been forced into the war against Tippoo; how, when it was over, a proposition for a subsidiary force was made to him, which he refused;—how hostile a disposition this manifested; how "the inference to be deduced from these considerations was, that until irresistibly compelled by the exigency of his affairs to have recourse to the assistance of the Company, Baji Rao would never be induced to enter into any engagements which, in his apprehension, would afford to the British Government the means of acquiring an ascendency in the Mahratta empire;" and how it was "his object to avoid that degree of control and ascendency which it was our interest to establish."[1] Their increased distractions constituted a crisis of affairs favourable to the success of negotiations at Poona, and for the complete establishment of the interests of the British power in the Mahratta empire. The continuation of the contest between Scindia and Holkar would weaken the power and impair the resources of both, and would afford the British Government an opportunity of interposing its influence and mediation. No reasonable apprehension existed that the progress of this insidious scheme would be obstructed either by the union of the contending parties or the decisive success of either chieftain.[2] So long as the Durbar of Poona contained a Minister capable of penetrating the esoteric meaning of vice-regal policy, and of holding up the hands of his feeble chief, the independence of his country, though frequently imperilled, was preserved. Nana Farnavis had for many years been the real ruler of the State, contriving generally to keep on good terms with the Company without becoming entangled in obligations, the effects of which he looked upon with dread. He avowed his respect and admiration for the English, but shrunk from their political embrace; and whatever dangers might impend, he steadily refused to accept

---

[1] Letter from Secretary Edmonstone to the Resident at Poonah.
[2] Lord Wellesley, Despatches to Secret Department—Wellesley Correspondence.

their offers of permanent armed assistants. "With him has departed," said Colonel Palmer, the first English Resident, "all the wisdom and moderation of this Government." Baji Rao II. was the seventh of his family, the first of whom having been originally Mayors of the palace at Satara, had gradually taken the chief place in the Mahratta Confederation, leaving the Rajahs who claimed descent from Sivajî a nominal and pretentious semblance of supremacy, of which men had come to take little heed. The Hindu Durbar of Satara exercised in 1802 as little influence over Scindia, Holkar, and Berar, as that of Delhi over Oude and the Deccan. Scindia professed his readiness to help the Peishwa against Holkar; but from jealousy or some other cause left him unbefriended till too late. As this position grew more critical, the English Resident grew more urgent in his expressions of solicitude, and warm in his proffers of auxiliary aid. He was instructed to tender a subsidiary treaty, whereby a force of 6000 men, organised and officered like that already imposed upon the neighbouring Mohammedan states, was to be permanently maintained, ostensibly as a contingent for the protection of the Peishwa's dominions against his envious and troublesome neighbours, but really, as above noted, for securing his permanent adherence to English interests. Their pay was to be provided out of the revenues of certain districts in Guzerat, which, yielding twenty-six lacs of rupees, were to be mortgaged for the purpose. Such a force would be an effectual guarantee against the ever-threatening aggressions of Holkar and Scindia. This was the danger that was imminent. A greater danger loomed visibly in the future, and pride and policy revolted against the price demanded for immediate safety. The Ministers of the Peishwa were not insensible to the perils of the proffered aid, and month after month the lure was held out in vain. An outlying province, comparatively small, and whose revenues it was difficult to collect, might be ceded if the subsidiary force were kept there ready to be called in upon emergency, and then withdrawn to their quarters. This would imperceptibly, if at all, humble the independence of native rule. Every stratagem of argument was employed to make this the condition of the bargain. In the eyes of the Governor-General this, however, was the point unexpressed which was not to be yielded. While the negotiation lingered, the storm burst; Poona was compassed round about by the Arab cavalry of Holkar; the Peishwa fled, and was only restored to his capital by British arms, after he had subscribed the covenant of vassalage. It was not easy even in exile to bring him to this.

At length he yielded, and on the last day of the year at Bassein he signed away his independence. It was not, indeed, so written in the bond. On the contrary, this memorable pact set forth with more than usual ostentation every guarantee and pledge of mutual respect. It expressly declared that the friends and enemies of one of the contracting parties should be friends and enemies of the other; and it confirmed all former treaties and agreements between the two states, not contrary to the tenor of the new one. It provided for the joint exertions of both, to defend the rights or redress the wrongs of either of their respective dependants or allies—the British Government undertaking not to suffer any power or state whatever to commit with impunity any act of unprovoked hostility and aggression against the rights and territories of his Highness, and at all times to maintain and defend them in the same manner as the rights and territories of the Company. The imposed guard of six thousand infantry, with the usual proportion of guns and

European artillerymen, was to be permanently stationed within the Peishwa's dominions. The ceded districts were named in a schedule annexed. All forts with their equipments of ordnance and stores were to be surrendered without injury or damage. The force was to be at all times ready to execute services of importance, such as the protection of the Peishwa's person, the overawing and chastisement of rebels, the suppression of disturbances within the realm, and the due correction of such subjects and dependants as might withhold payment of the just claims of the State; "but they were not to be employed on trifling occasions, nor in a variety of ways which were enumerated." The Peishwa was bound to keep the peace towards his Mahratta neighbours, while he was guaranteed in turn against molestation by them. Should differences with them arise, he was pledged to abide by the Governor-General's award. When called upon, the Prince undertook to bring into the field the whole of his troops against the foes of his ally, whoever they might be. This condition was to be reciprocal; and Baji Rao renounced the right of negotiating with any native state save with the privity and consent of his inalienable protectors. The latter solemnly disclaimed all right of interference with the Prince's children, relatives, or subjects, regarding whom his authority was acknowledged to be absolute; but should disturbance or revolt arise, the Company's troops might be called in for its suppression. Finally, the treaty was to last "while sun and moon endureth." The day was soon to come when these eternal vows were to be pooh-poohed as mere dead flowers of Oriental rhetoric. But the original of the treaty from first to last stands in the handwriting of the Governor-General. Peishwa and Satara have passed away, but these words of his will not pass away.

The other Mahratta chiefs were naturally alarmed, and

refused to recognise the Treaty of Bassein. The Peishwa, they said, ought not, as head of the Confederacy, to have contracted obligations so unprecedented without consulting them. Scindia had undertaken to deliver and restore him, and too late repented the remissness he had shown. He had a powerful army in point of numbers, a *corps d'elite* well supplied with artillery, and a few French officers under Colonel Perron, who had long been in his service. Holkar, likewise, at the head of a multitudinous array, chiefly of horse, and the Rajah of Berar, were able to bring into the field no inconsiderable army. None of them, however, desired war; for all were conscious of the vast augmentation of military strength they would have to encounter. It is, indeed, admitted that Lord Wellesley almost despaired of the provocation he longed for.

The Court of Gwalior was at once jealous and wary. At the dismemberment of Mysore a tempting slice of territory had been offered to Dowlat Rao, by whom it had been "explicitly rejected;"[1] which proved convincingly an evil disposition, the more to be reprehended and in due time punished, as the Peishwa followed his example. Under any circumstances, Lord Wellesley "considered the reduction of Scindia's power to be an important object."[2] During the spring of 1803, Scindia diplomatised with characteristic subtlety, evading carefully every acknowledgment of the Peishwa's recent acts, and preparing, as he said, to effect his restoration. Not without difficulty was an understanding come to between the three native powers, and not even then was any overt act of hostility committed on either side. A small body of the Company's troops, which had formed the Resident's guard at Poona, had re-

---

[1] Gurwood—Wellington Despatches.
[2] Letter to Colonel Collins, July 1803.

mained unmolested there, and now received with royal honour at the gate of the palace so long his own the Prince who, as he entered it, must have felt that it was his no more, but was henceforth to be occupied by him only as tenant at will. Thus native rule was relieved of its moral accountability to domestic opinion, while it was made safe from outward fear. The device was perfect for its purpose—modelled on the great first precedent of temptation. "Life it promised, death it devised, and corruption it entailed from generation to generation."

Without ascribing to the Mahratta chiefs or their Ministers any profound sagacity, it is easy to understand how the spectacle at Poona must have irritated and troubled them. Whose turn might it be next? War with a power which was already gathering four armies on different points of their frontiers, it might not be prudent to precipitate; but one thing seemed clear, and by that Berar, Holkar, and Scindia determined to abide, namely, that they would not ratify the Treaty of Bassein. If peace had been the object of the Governor-General, he would have let their irritation cool and have taken the chances of persuasion at a future day. But, then, the glorious opportunity he panted for would have been lost, at least for him. Anxiously and vehemently he therefore pressed for the recognition they were mutually pledged to refuse; and when they reasonably asked further time to consider and to confer with the Peishwa, General Wellesley was ordered to demand that Scindia's army should fall back from the advantageous position it occupied without delay; while demands, equally difficult to concede, were simultaneously made at Nagpore.

Mill states that, "on the 14th July, General Wellesley addressed a letter, couched in respectful terms, to Dowlat Rao Scindia, setting before him the reasons which the

British Government had to consider his present menacing position an indication of designs which would render it necessary to act against him as an enemy, unless he withdrew his army across the Nerbudda; but making, at the same time, the corresponding offer, that as soon as the Mahratta chiefs should lead back their armies to their usual stations, he would also withdraw the British army."[1]

The Mahratta chiefs replied that, "By the blessing of God both armies were still on their own territory, and no aggression or excesses had been committed;" and if the English commander, therefore, would name a day when both should withdraw an equal distance, they would engage to do so. But such terms might have averted war, and they were therefore spurned. "As for the Peishwa," wrote Lord Wellesley, "I have no idea that he will attempt to fly from Poona, or that, if he should be so inclined, he could carry his plan into execution without the knowledge of his Ministers. I have urged Colonel Close to pay the Ministers, in order to have accurate information of what passes."[2] The tops of the replanted hedge around the throne were limed accordingly. If Scindia had been the greatest lover of peace and justice upon the face of the earth, he would still have had the greatest reason to resent the Treaty of Bassein, and to resist to the utmost its execution. What is that on the strength of which we have already seen the Governor-General boasting of the prodigious value of the treaty? Not the circumstance of its having made a dependant merely of the Peishwa. This in itself was of little importance. The treaty for receiving British troops by one of the chief Mahratta States was declared to be valuable because it afforded a controlling power

[1] Mill, book VI. chap. ii.
[2] Gurwood—Wellesley Correspondence.

over all the other governments of the Mahratta nation—the power of preventing them from doing whatever the Viceroy should dislike. If the loss of independence is a loss sufficient to summon the most pacific sovereigns to arms, Dowlat Rao Scindia and the Rajah of Berar had that motive for offering resistance to the Treaty of Bassein.[1]

The scene at Fort William when the news arrived that negotiations were broken off, is described as one of exultation and delight.

So much for the *casus belli*—what were the real objects of the war? They are stated with characteristic candour and perspicuity in the confidential letter of instructions addressed to the Commander-in-Chief several weeks before a blow was struck. They were, first, the destruction of a French State on the banks of the Jumna, with all its military resources; secondly, the extension of the Company's frontier to that river, with the possession of Agra, Delhi, and a sufficient chain of forts on its banks; thirdly, the transfer of the supreme authority of the Mogul; fourthly, alliances with petty chiefs southward and westward of the Jumna; fifthly, the annexation of Bundelcund. All the objects here set forth were destined to be accomplished except the first, and that for the best of reasons, viz., that a French State existed only in phantasy and make-believe. As a justification in the eyes of English critics, it sounded well; but as a matter of Indian fact, a French State on the banks of the Jumna had no more existence than the enchanted castle in Aladdin's dream. When the matter came to be discussed, Francis and others showed that there were but twelve French officers in the Mahratta service in 1803; that the foreign rank and file were hardly distinguishable from others, and that Perron their commander was an object of aversion to

[1] Mill, book VI. chap. ii. p. 370.

the Maharajah whom he served.[1] He was actually preparing to renounce the service of Scindia, and was ready to negotiate, as soon afterwards appeared, with the English. Yet Lord Lake was instructed that the first object of the campaign was to overthrow an independent French State on the banks of the Jumna.

From the borders of Mysore Arthur Wellesley led 8900 men to the siege of Ahmednagar. Ten thousand men under Lord Lake entered the Mahratta country from the side of Cawnpore. General Stevenson with 7900 held the bank of the Godivari; General Stewart held a large force in reserve on the Kistna. In Guzerat, 7300 under General Murray occupied the fortified places. Colonel Powell had 3500 in Bundelcund, and 5000 were held in readiness to invade Raghuji's territory. A circle of fire girt the Mahrattas round. Lord Wellesley boasted that he would be his own War Minister. He would show the Board of Directors why he had refused to reduce the army, and what he could do with it. We all know the brilliant feats of arms that followed. Enormously outnumbered, the assailing forces everywhere prevailed. A third of the victors were left dead on the field of Assaye; but the blow there inflicted on Scindia, followed up as it was by that of Laswari, was never recovered. Agra was stormed, and a large amount of booty distributed among the troops. Lord Wellesley's share of prize-money at the end of the war would, in the ordinary course of things, have been large. Though poor and in debt, he refused to take any part of it, and ordered its division among the troops. The fall of Delhi liberated Shah Alum II., who for some years had been the regal captive of Scindia. His deliverance was trumpeted as a great event to the Mohammedan world, indicative of

[1] Mill, book VI. chap. ii. p. 384. All this was known at Fort William.

the beneficence of our interposition. Several of the minor princes of Rajpootana were also declared to be set free from Mahratta thraldom. Selfish aims, personal or political, might be insinuated by the envious; but the world would judge. At length peace was made. Because they would not approve the cession of Guzerat by the Peishwa, from the Rajah of Berar was taken Kuttack, Balasore, and the rich cotton district of the Warda; from Scindia the whole of the vast country lying between the Jumna and the Ganges, including Agra, Delhi, and Bundelcund. This unfortunate Prince, who, by their own account, "when he wound up his affairs at the end of the war, would not have a disposable clear revenue" adequate to his defence in future, was forced to cede the "valuable territory of Baroach and Ahmednagar, where the jaghires of his family were situate, whose revenue it was computed would yield the Company a clear revenue of ten lacs of rupees annually" (*i.e.* £100,000).[1]

By a provision in the Treaty of Sirji Anjengaom, Scindia was offered the support of six battalions of infantry, with their complements of ordnance and artillery whenever he might stand in need of them, without any condition as to permanency or pay. The reason assigned by General Wellesley is not unworthy of note. In the course of this war, Scindia's power, reputation, and military resources had been greatly diminished, while his rival, Holkar, after having recovered the possessions of his family, remained with undiminished power and increased reputation. Compared with those of Scindia, his power and his military resources were much greater than they were previous to the war, and there was little doubt that the contest between

[1] Gurwood, 568, 569—Letter to Governor-General from Arthur Wellesley. He apologises for the smallness of the exactions from Scindia on the score of policy.

those chiefs would be revived. This would be a matter of little consequence if the parties were so equal in point of strength, resources, and abilities, as to render the event of the contest doubtful. But leaving the latter to his own means, he must fall an easy prey to Holkar, or his Government would become dependent upon that of his rival. Under these circumstances, it was thought expedient to hold forth to Scindia an option of becoming a party to the general defensive alliance, and to engage that it should occasion no further diminution of his revenue. He was induced to offer this last condition, by the conviction that Scindia would not agree to the treaty of general defensive alliance, although his Ministers proposed that he should unite himself more closely with the Company, if he were to be obliged to pay for the assistance which he should receive. The treaty further stipulated that in no case was this force to interfere in disputes between Government and subjects, but that it should at all times, and under all circumstances, be ready at Scindia's orders to punish and suppress resistance, no matter how provoked. And this is European civilisation, freedom, and morality![1] A British force are hired by treaty as janissaries to a despotic, and, as the authors of that treaty over and over again called him, a cruel and perfidious Prince, for an unlimited time. Holkar still held out, and prolonged a desultory warfare until 1805, when another Viceroy, who was bent on peace, agreed to a termination of hostilities without stipulating for any territorial cession.

The financial results of this era of subjugation are worthy of attention. In 1794 the revenues of British India were £8,276,770, and the total charges, including interest on debt, £6,633,951, leaving a surplus of £1,642,819. There was a

[1] Mill, book VI. chap xii.

diminution in the following year, though peaceful, and at the commencement of the Marquis Wellesley's administration there was a deficit of £118,746 on the year 1797-98. At the close of his extravagant rule in 1805, the revenue was £15,403,409, but the charges and interest were £17,672,017, showing a deficit of £2,268,608. The debt in 1793, was £16,962,743; in 1797, £17,059,192; in 1805, £31,638,827; in 1810, £41,233,876. So embarrassed were the finances of the Company, that on the 11th March 1808, they applied to the Government to repay the sum of £1,200,000, and to advance as much more to them by way of loan to meet the deficit caused by the profuse expenditure on unproductive objects of territorial aggrandisement. The Directors, in an elaborate despatch, condemned the course of Lord Wellesley in provoking and carrying on the war against the Mahrattas. The despatch was suspended by the Board of Control, but at a Court of Proprietors, numerously attended, a resolution was carried by 928 to 195 warmly commending the vigilant zeal of the Directors in seeking to assert their authority in the government of India, "to restrain a profuse expenditure of the public money, and to prevent all schemes of conquest and extension of dominion, which the Legislature had declared to be repugnant to the wish, the honour, and the policy of the nation."[1]

[1] Wilson's Continuation of Mill, vol. i. p. 167.

CHAPTER XVIII.

THE SWORD IN THE SCABBARD.

1805—1813.

"I deprecate the effects of the almost universal frenzy which has seized even some of the heads which I thought the soundest in the country for conquest and victory, as opposed to the interests as to the laws of our country. I shall come to the army with a determination not to submit to insult or aggression, but with an anxious desire to have an opportunity of showing my generosity."

—LORD CORNWALLIS.[1]

ALTHOUGH Mr Pitt had approved and applauded the aggressive policy of Lord Wellesley, he was not insensible to the opposition it had excited among men of all parties in the country; and in the winter of 1804 he felt that he had no popularity to spare for its defence or continuance. His second administration had failed to rally the enthusiasm he anticipated. His personal energies were beginning to fail, and there was great distress throughout the country; debt and taxation were steadily increasing, and the power of France, which they had been incurred to check, appeared to be greater than ever. He silently resolved, therefore, to acquiesce in a change of system in the East, and agreed that Lord Cornwallis should be once more sent out as Viceroy, with instructions to make peace, and to keep it for the future.

In resuming the Government, the aged Marquis found "that we were still at war with Holkar, and hardly at

[1] Letter to Malcolm, 14th August 1805.

peace with Scindia;" and that unless he himself at once proceeded to the Upper Provinces, he could not hope to bring speedily to an end "a contest in which the most brilliant success could afford no solid benefit, and which, if it should continue, must involve pecuniary difficulties which we should hardly be able to surmount."[1] To Lord Castlereagh he disclosed his dismay at finding himself with an empty treasury, the credit of the Government tried to the utmost at Benares and other places, where temporary loans had been lately raised by his spendthrift predecessor, and further entanglements recently created by a guarantee given to Rana Keerut Sing of the fortress of Gwalior, which Scindia protested he had never meant to give up. The statements of embarrassment were by no means overcharged, notwithstanding the recent violent transactions in Oude.[2] On learning that the Rajah of Jeypore (Juggett Sing) had by his conduct forfeited any claim to protection, the Viceroy observed, "Would to God that we could as easily get rid of the Rana of Gohud, and many more of our burthensome allies or dependants."[3] The pay of the army was at this time five months in arrear, and many of the civil departments had still greater cause of complaint. He had no choice but to stop *in transitu* the specie sent from England to pay for shipments in China, for "we had by our recent victories obtained a great acquisition of very unprofitable territory, and of useless and burthensome allies and dependants."[4] He knew that the opinions that prevailed at headquarters were unfavourable to the restoration of peace; that "all the gentlemen in the political line were of opinion that a system of power was preferable to one of conciliation;"[5]

[1] Letter to Secret Committee, 1st August 1805—Correspondence, vol. iii. p. 532.
[2] Ibid., p. 533.   [3] Ibid., p. 534.   [4] Ibid., pp. 536, 538, 539.
[5] Letter to Lord Lake, 1st September 1805—Cornwallis Correspondence, vol. ii. p. 545.

and that even Malcolm was full of schemes of military colonisation, not only as presenting a resource to meet existing difficulties, but as supplying a base for further operations in future. Lord Cornwallis told him plainly that in his judgment "no success could indemnify us for continuing this ruinous war" with the Mahrattas a moment longer than we could bring it to a termination without dishonour.[1] He also considered the possession of the person of Shah Alum, and of the city of Delhi, as "events truly unfortunate." Far from desiring to strengthen or expand the network of subsidiary engagements, the wise and humane Viceroy did not hesitate to make known his strong disapproval of the system. It had been imagined that after the third Mysore war he had proposed its extension to the Mahrattas, by whom the offer had been declined.[2] In disproof of this, he recalled a curious conversation he had had at the time with the General-in-Chief of their forces. When the victorious allies were about to separate, with mutual assurances of satisfaction and good-will, Hurry Punt asked him why he did not offer a subsidiary force to the Peishwa as well as to the Nizam. He replied that "he disapproved very much of all subsidiary treaties, as they tended to involve the British Government in quarrels in which they had no concern; that the treaty with the Nizam had been made many years before, and he was determined not to enter into any more engagements of that kind."[3] And to this determination, after the experience of the opposite policy under Lord Wellesley, he was resolved to adhere. He does not say, but we may

---

[1] Letter to Malcolm, 14th August 1805, p. 540.

[2] See a curious paper by General Wellesley, entitled, "Observations on the Treaty of Bassein," handed by Lord Wellesley, ere quitting Calcutta, to his successor, and quoted by him in Letter, 16th August 1805—Cornwallis Correspondence, vol. iii. p. 541.

[3] Letter to Sir Arthur Wellesley, 16th August 1805.

be very sure, that he clearly understood the real drift of the astute Mahratta's question. All that subsequently passed during the negotiations for the Treaty of Bassein, prove incontestably the aversion, amounting to loathing, with which the Court of Poona regarded the conditions on which alone a subsidiary force would be established within the Peishwa's dominions. The manifest purpose of the interrogatory was to fathom the thoughts of the Governor-General at a moment when, flushed with triumph, he might possibly be off his guard. Hurry Punt could have had no authority to treat just then on such a subject, but if he could have artfully extracted a design, theretofore unexpressed, of pushing further an intermeddling policy among the States that still preserved their independence, he would have chuckled at the success of his diplomatic artifice, and obtained for his court a warning betimes, which would have been no doubt regarded as valuable and worth bearing in remembrance. The reply of Lord Cornwallis, uttered in perfect sincerity, tended to allay distrust at Poona, and for another decade no more was said about the matter. The Mahrattas were thereby led to believe that whatever might be designed for others, the harness-makers of Fort William did not contemplate throwing the lasso over their wild heads, far less the notion of breaking them in and collaring them to the pole of viceregal rule. Under Lord Cornwallis and Sir John Shore the policy of abstention was faithfully adhered to, but under Lord Wellesley it was discarded; and we cannot wonder if the native princes, unable to comprehend the inconstancy of principles on which the administration of Indian affairs was conducted, should have believed that the yoke had been prepared for them much earlier than was actually avowed, when, after being repudiated in 1792, it was, in 1802, infrangibly imposed upon them. In 1805, it was, perhaps, too late to revert to the pre-existing state of things. It is one of the penalties of misrule that it cannot be safely or easily undone, and that very often we know not how to undo it at all. Confidence plucked up rudely will not grow again, though carefully planted, and watered with regretful tears. Lord Cornwallis was no sentimentalist, but he was a temperate, just, and sagacious man, and his last days were clouded with sincere regrets at finding that in the interval between his first and second administration, trust in our political moderation and forbearance had been eradicated in the native mind.

Colonel Close called attention to the disorganisation that prevailed in various branches of the administration at Poona. He counselled, admonished, tried to persuade, and tried to frighten the worthless purveyors of waste and jobbers at the public cost, but all to no purpose. The ear of the humiliated Peishwa was continually filled with suspicions too plausible to be disbelieved. Was not the Resident the impersonation of the power that had compelled him to sign away his independence, to forswear the traditions of his race, and to contract obligations which no economy would probably have enabled him to fulfil? On the other hand, what had sycophancy and malversation to gain, even by affecting self-denial and patriotism when dying? and why should it spare the resources of a Government plainly smitten with death, or the credit of a State about to die? Gudi and Durbar were daily growing more and more deaf to good counsel, as the benumbing sense of irresponsibility for evil acts became more and more habitual. The poison had begun to work, and its effects were what had been anticipated, similar to those, if not the same, which had been found elsewhere. The venerable Viceroy grieved over them, and, while resting from the fatigues of his journey into the interior, unburthened his mind to the Secret Committee. He lamented "the weak and wretched state of the Peishwa's internal government," and he had reason to believe that the authority of the Soubahdar of the Deccan over his dominions was approaching fast to the same state. The evils were sufficiently obvious; the remedy, unhappily, not so apparent. The positive obligations of treaties provided, in the most express terms, for the uncontrolled exercise of the internal government of both States being left in the hands of their respective Chiefs. He had called their attention to the articles in the treaties which so much concerned themselves; and had impressed on the minds of the Residents the necessity of encouraging the most active exertion of that authority and control on which the prosperity of their dominions and the security of their subjects so greatly depended. "In the hope that by degrees we might withdraw ourselves from the disgraceful participation in which we should be involved, by mixing ourselves in all the intrigue, oppression, and chicanery of the native management of distracted and desolated provinces," he had addressed instructions to the British representatives at Poona and Hyderabad,[1] to disentangle themselves gradually but steadily from duties which he would never have cast upon them. To Lord Lake, who was still at the head of the army in the newly-conquered country, he intimated plainly "that it was not the opinion of Ministers only, or of a party, but of all reflecting men, that it was impracticable for Great Britain to maintain so vast and unwieldy an Empire in India, which annually called for reinforcements of men, and remittances of money, and which yielded little other profit than brilliant gazettes."[2]

[1] Despatch, 28th August 1805—Cornwallis Correspondence, vol. iii. p. 543.
[2] Letter to Lord Lake, August 30, 1805—Cornwallis Correspondence, vol. iii. pp. 544, 545.

The Rajah of Berar and other Chiefs who had suffered great deprivation, could certainly entertain no friendly disposition; and unless a very great change could be effected in the minds of the natives of India, and in the ideas they must harbour of our views, he could not look forward with sanguine hope to the establishment of permanent peace. He expressed his regret in the same letter that he could not define, "in the multiplicity of cessions and conquests, what ought to be considered actually or virtually our territories;" but he did not conceal his anxiety to be rid of as many as could be relinquished with any show of honour.

The pacific policy foreshadowed by Lord Cornwallis filled Lord Lake and his staff with disappointment, and something more. What had been accomplished in the field by a brilliant combination of strategy, persistence, and valour, in their view promised, with certainty, further and greater conquests; without which they easily persuaded themselves that those already made could not be preserved. Every remission and restoration suggested, seemed to them confirmatory of their fears. Faint-heartedness and parsimony had fallen, just at the wrong time, upon the Councils of Empire; the daring and decision of Lord Wellesley had been overruled just at the moment when it was about to be crowned with triumph; the half-subjugated Mahrattas would only despise us for our forbearance, scoff at our irresolution, and take fresh courage to protract war for the recovery of all they had lost. "It would be melancholy to see the work of our brave armies undone and left to be done over again."[1] Had the "glorious little man" remained but another year at Calcutta, all would have gone well; but he had been worried into resigning, and a successor had been

[1] Confidential Letter from C. Metcalfe, in Camp at Muttra, to Mr Sherer, 31st August 1805.

chosen, who was past work, feeble in body and decrepit in mind. They knew that the ways and means of Government had long been straitened; for the pay of the troops every month fell more and more into arrear. But victorious troops seldom doubt that there is an easy way of squaring the accounts of a campaign, viz., by taking the balance wanting out of the coffers of obstinate foes, who have not the sense to see that they are beaten. The political inexpediency or injustice of this mode of getting rid of the difficulty, is not nicely weighed in camp scales; and there can be no doubt that the Commander-in-Chief, and his officers, felt fully persuaded that they understood the position much better than any old gentleman lately come out from England; and that they were much more competent to advise him what ought to be done than he was to direct them. One all-important fact they did not know, namely, that before quitting India, Lord Wellesley had conferred freely with his successor on the existing state of affairs, and on the policy which ought to be pursued; that an elaborate paper, regarding the North Western States, had been drawn up by Sir George Barlow, and agreed to by both the distinguished personages present. In truth, the retiring Viceroy had become fully convinced of the necessity of making peace, even at a considerable sacrifice of possible acquisitions; and that no other course, under the circumstances, was practicable.[1]

The previous campaign had been fruitful of victories, but barren of solid results. One after another the Mahratta armies had been vanquished and dispersed, but only to reassemble again. Scindia had even ventured to detain for a time, in qualified captivity, the English Resident at his Court, on the plea that Gwalior was retained in breach

[1] Kaye's Life of Metcalfe, vol. i. p. 171.

of the terms of the last treaty made with him. On receipt of peremptory instructions not to move, except in self-defence, lest anything should provoke an open rupture with Scindia, Lord Lake threw up his command. The last official letter of the aged Marquis was in reply deprecating this resolve, recalling their early friendship, testifying his sense of the General's services, and urging him to wait until they could meet and interchange frankly their respective views. But death was already at the door; and on the 5th October, Lord Cornwallis breathed his last at Ghazepore, in the Province of Benares.

The duties of Governor-General, *ad interim*, devolved upon Sir George Barlow, as senior Member of Council. He trod in the footsteps of the late Viceroy, which had had his entire approval, preparing to withdraw, as fast as it was prudent to do so, the British troops from their menacing positions, and concluding arrangements with various minor princes as preliminary to a general pacification. He disclaimed altogether the function of self-constituted arbitrator among the frontier tribes, and declared it to be our duty to leave them at their own peril to fight out their quarrels among themselves. This abstention was of course regarded as "shocking" by all the young diplomatists who had been brought to prematurity in what was called Lord Wellesley's political forcing-house. A still more shocking system in their view was founded upon it, which they regarded as inevitably tending to revive in every quarter of the frontier all those quarrels, wars, disturbances, and depredations which they would fain believe had been nearly extinguished by armed intervention. "Two objects," they said, "were necessary for permanent tranquillity and safety. The reduction of Holkar to a state of impotence, from which he should not be able to raise himself (his destruction would be most desirable), and the maintenance of our alliances and paramount influences with the petty States of Hindustan."[1] In after years, when better acquainted with the real circumstances of the case, Metcalfe, who was then among the most eager zealots for further aggression, confessed that his judgment underwent no little modification; and though he still disapproved of the forbearance shown to Holkar, he admitted that at the time there was no help for it.[2]

Before the year closed, Runjît Singh offered his mediation, and preliminaries of peace were concluded with Holkar on terms which the officers of the army pronounced to be disgraceful, but which the Governor-General and Council were glad to accept under the circumstances. Holkar asked that an envoy should be sent to him in order to satisfy his people, who were weary of war, and sighing for its termination. Metcalfe found "Ek-Chushm-ul-Dowla"[3] grave and polite, not in the least resembling the savage he believed him to be. His Durbar in camp was devoid of show, having nothing of opulence in it but the jewels of rare value worn by the chief. Not long before, he had declared in reckless mood that all he had as a prince he carried on his saddle-bow. Most of his possessions were now left to him, and Scindia, glad enough to take advantage of the moderate tone of the new Governor-General, entered soon after into negotiations which ended in an accommodation of all existing differences.[4]

Lord Lake used every argument against the peace, and finding his advice disregarded, withdrew from further participation in political matters. He was especially opposed to the restoration of Tonk Rampoora, which had been offered

---

[1] Letter from Colonel Metcalfe to J. W. Sherer, December 18, 1805.
[2] Kaye's Life of Metcalfe, vol. v. p. 208.
[3] The one-eyed ruler, a nickname given to Jeswunt Rao Holkar.
[4] Letter from Metcalfe to Sherer, 26th January 1806.

to Scindia and declined, and which, after all other provisions of the treaty had been ratified, was spontaneously given up to Holkar by a declaratory article appended thereto.

In a paper written in 1806, entitled "The Policy of Sir George Barlow," Metcalfe imputes to him the "design of directly fomenting discord" among the neighbouring States, with a view to our own safety. This Metcalfe brands as barbarous, unwarrantable, and monstrous. He would, in preference, have had us assume the sovereignty over all. There then remained, he said, but two great Powers in India, the English and the Mahrattas; and where we failed to exercise paramount sway, we left the inhabitants to be harassed and ill-used by them.[1] But the fixed principle of the Government at that period was to relinquish all possessions and protectorates west of the Jumna, and the treaties of 1806 embodied this rule.

A treaty of friendship and alliance, made between the British Government and the State of Lahore, on 25th April 1809, stipulated that the former should have no concern with the territory and subjects of the Maharajah north of the Sutlej; that Runjît Singh should never maintain on the left bank of that river more troops than were necessary for the internal duties of his Government; nor commit or suffer any encroachment on the possessions or rights of the chiefs in his vicinity. All the region between the Sutlej and the Jumna was thereby declared to be subject to our suzerainty. The vague relations theretofore subsisting with the local Rajahs gave place to the formal assumption of the protectorate by the Paramount Power. A declaration to this effect announced that Sirhind and Malwa were taken under British protection; that no tribute would be demanded

---

[1] Papers and Correspondence of Lord Metcalfe, p. 7.

from the chiefs; but that they would be expected to furnish all facilities for the movement of our troops through their districts, and to join them with their followers whenever called on. "But the mutual relation of supremacy and subjection, appeals from the inferior to the superior in disputes amongst themselves, and the imperative necessity of ministering public order, speedily multiplied," we are assured, "occasions of interposition; and, after no long interval, compelled the British Government to proclaim the right and the resolution to interpose. The regulation of successions from the first demanded the intervention of the protecting Power; and political expediency has dictated the enforcement of a principle, recognised throughout the feudality of India—the appropriation of a subject territory on failure of lawful heirs, by the Paramount Sovereign."[1]

In the Whig Cabinet of 1806, the Indian department was assigned to the friend of Burke who, as Sir Gilbert Elliott, had been one of the managers in the impeachment of Warren Hastings. There still remain letters which attest how highly his friendship and ability were valued by the great Tribune of the East. The charge against Sir Elijah Impey was confided specially to him, and the report of his arguments against the delinquent Chief-Justice go far to sustain the language of encomium bestowed on them by a critic difficult to please. In 1793, he was sent to Corsica to negotiate its annexation, and he remained as Governor of the island until the predominance of the party attached to France compelled him to withdraw. He was subsequently Ambassador at Vienna; and he now entered upon the duties of President of the Board of Control, with all the advantages of former study of Indian questions in Parliament, and of diplomatic experience abroad. With the consent of his colleagues he named Lord

[1] Wilson, vol. i. p. 203.

Lauderdale Governor-General, but the Directors positively refused their assent, desiring in preference that Sir George Barlow should be retained. After some weeks spent in altercation, it was finally resolved that Lord Minto should himself accept the post, leaving Mr Dundas to succeed him at the India Board, and allowing the Viceroy *ad interim* to subside into the Governorship of Madras. The six years of Lord Minto's administration were peaceful and unaggressive. All his antecedents indisposed him to revert to the policy of encroachment, and with the exception of Lord Grenville, "All the Talents" concurred in his views. He understood that his mission was to restore, if possible, the finances of the Company to an equilibrium, by the encouragement of trade and industry, and by enforcing retrenchment in the civil and military departments. In 1808, Travancore became the scene of disturbances, accompanied by many acts of treachery and violence by the dupes of a fanatical and unprincipled man, who had been for some time Dewan, and to whom the Rajah had absolutely committed all executive authority. Intrigues with the Rajahs of Cochin and Malabar were set on foot to shake off the Company's yoke. After some loss of life the revolt was suppressed; the Rajah affected ignorance of his Minister's designs, and regret for the acts of his people. For three or four years he was not forgiven, but in 1813 he was permitted to resume, under certain restrictions, the rule of his territory, which thenceforth remained tranquil.

The influences by which the people had been for the time excited to insurrection were the fear of their ancient religion being undermined by missionaries, erroneously supposed to be acting under the direction of the Government; and on the other hand, by unfounded hopes of a rising among the Mahratta and other Hindu communities in a general league against their European masters. The prevalence of such feelings could not be hidden from the watchful and discerning eyes of men who, having helped to build up rapidly an empire with the most heterogeneous materials, knew how insecure were its foundations, and how ill cemented was its apparent strength. What they deemed most formidable, was a community of religious suspicion, or a community of new religious belief. Political unity in India there had never been, and they were sure there could never be ; but " if the leading natives should turn Christian, we should lose the country ;"[1] and the popular dread of proselytism was likely to prove equally embarrassing.

Throughout the war with France our mercantile marine had suffered severely from cruisers, well equipped and armed, which issued from the harbours of Mauritius and the Isle of Bourbon. It had long been an object to get rid of this source of danger to our trade, the transport service not being protected by convoy. In 1809 a daring attempt was made on the lesser island by Captain Rowley and Colonel Keating, who, with a small detachment, not only effected a landing, but succeeded in taking the town of St Paul. The scantiness of the numbers at their command rendered it impossible for them to establish themselves in the island at that time; but they had succeeded in ascertaining that the strength of its defensive works had been greatly exaggerated ; and the following year a powerful expedition was despatched for its reduction, as well as that of Mauritius, which has ever since remained a dependency of the British Crown. In 1811 Lord Minto conceived the idea of effecting a still more brilliant achievement. Holland was no longer an independent Power, and its greatest colony in the East lay too near our possessions to

[1] The words of one who held high office under Lord Minto.

render safe the use that might be made of them by an enterprising enemy. After due preparation, a squadron under Commodore Rowley, having on board a sufficient land force, sailed from Malacca, and, somewhat to the surprise of many who had regarded Lord Minto as too much a man of peace, he himself accompanied the expedition. A landing-place near Batavia had been left unguarded, and the debarkation was effected without molestation. The city having been occupied without resistance, a brief campaign in the hilly part of the island ended, without much bloodshed, in the surrender of the forts and harbours which had for many generations belonged to the Dutch, but which had recently been treated as colonial dependencies by Napoleon. There was no longer left in the Indian Ocean any place of strength over which the British flag did not wave. For three years Batavia had for its Governor Sir Stamford Raffles, and at the conclusion of the war it was honourably restored to Holland. On the mainland, Lord Minto adhered to his pacific policy, from which he could not be provoked into departing either by the occasional plundering of the Pindharries, or the exaggerated importance given by many about him to the swaggering demeanour of the Ghoorka Chiefs. He was not blind indeed to the real condition of the country under his charge, which he felt required repose. It was as much as he could do to maintain the credit of the Government, without adding to taxation which the people were unfit to bear, or withholding a comparatively moderate dividend, which the Company expected.

Economy was the order of the day. Conquest had had its fling; and having sown its wild oats, the time was said to have come when it must lead a more sober and frugal life, retrench wasteful expenditure, and if it did not clear off debt, contrive at least for the future to pay its way. It was not easy to cut down the cost of the army; it was not considered safe to seem even to do it. The ablest and most thoughtful men who had been engaged in the work of provincial administration did not dare to disguise the truth, that what had been won by force was held only by the influence that fear inspires. "Our situation in India," said Metcalfe, "has always been precarious. It is still precarious, not less so, perhaps, at the present moment, by the fault of the system prescribed by Government at home, than at any former period. We are still a handful of Europeans governing an immense Empire, without any firm hold on the country, having warlike and powerful enemies on all our frontiers, and the spirit of disaffection dormant, but rooted universally among our subjects."[1] To disband any important number of troops, or even to reduce the muster-roll in any perceptible degree, might jeopardise all. There was no other alternative but that of parsimony in the civil administration; and to this every one objected who had a voice in the matter at home, because it implied curtailment in the number of primary appointments; and everybody objected in India who had advancement to seek for himself or his friends. Still something was effected by Lord Minto; and, unlike most of those who had gone before him, he was able to say that, in his time, nothing had been added to the debt.

[1] Lord Metcalfe, Selections from Papers, Edited by J. W. Kaye.

CHAPTER XIX.

SCINDIA AND HOLKAR.

1814—1817.

"I think it well to sketch what appears to me the corrective for many existing embarrassments. Our object ought to be to render our Government paramount in effect, if not declaredly so. We should hold the other States as vassals, in substance, though not in name; not precisely as they stood in the Mogul Government, but possessed of perfect internal sovereignty, and only bound to repay the guarantee and protection of their possessions by the British Government with the pledge of the two great feudal duties. First, they should support it with all their forces on any call. Second, they should submit their mutual differences to the head of the Confederacy (our Government), without attacking each other's territories. A few subordinate stipulations on our part, with immunities secured in return to the other side (especially with regard to succession), would render the arrangement ample without complication or undue latitude."

—Lord Hastings.[1]

IN the stormy days of the Regency, Lord Moira was one of the conductors kept at Carlton House to save it from popular wrath. He was chiefly known for his fine manners and fine sentiments, parliamentary pliancy, and a measureless load of debt. By profession a soldier, by trade a courtier, and by occupation a spendthrift, one vainly seeks for any act worth remembering, or for any performance to account for the position of influence he held in the world of politics and fashion. More insensible to party ties than to personal considerations, he clung, like Sheridan, to the Prince, when nearly all his early friends felt that he had deceived

[1] Private Journal, vol. i. p. 54.

them. The Regent was said to be incapable of gratitude; but he understood the value of an instrument fit for his purpose when he had it. For him the Earl was thoroughly trustworthy, and accordingly, he trusted him in 1812 with the task of attempting to form a Coalition Cabinet, in which he only failed because, though there were many able Whigs and accomplished Pittites, there was only one Moira, and neither section shared the royal confidence in him. Next year witnessed his compensation and reward. Those who knew what manner of man was really needed sighed: the Directors shrugged their shoulders, and took care to explain privately that the selection was not theirs: but the creditors of the insolvent Earl were enthusiastic in their approval, and met to pass votes of congratulation on the propitious event. They did more. As a signal proof of the interest they took in the welfare of their fascinating debtor, they proceeded to appoint an official assignee to receive his splendid salary every quarter. This attaché-extraordinary was actually sent out to Calcutta, and there awaited his Excellency's arrival.

Lord Moira visited Madras on his way out, and reassured by kind and courtly words the Nawab of the Carnatic that he need not fear from him any further degradation " of his already abject condition;" observing that " he would always construe the terms of existing treaties in a way most considerate towards the party whose security was in reliance on the honour of the other." On returning his visit, the Viceroy was struck by the inanity and *ennui* to which the Nawab's life must be a prey, living amid great magnificence without pursuit or power of any kind. He adds expressions of pity at seeing one occupying his situation subjected to many vexatious restraints; such as being compelled to negotiate for leave to enjoy the pleasures of the chase, so strict was the surveillance held over him. Yet this was the descendant of Princes whose chief sin in the eyes of their countrymen had been their constant alliance with the Company. These expressions are taken from a private diary kept during the earlier years of a long viceroyalty, and from which many curious and suggestive admissions may be gleaned. Did we know nothing of his policy as an administrator but what might be inferred from this talk to himself, we should be led to anticipate a long epoch of tranquillity and conciliation. The first Bishop had been sent out at the same time, with an endowment, recently created, on the renewal of the Company's charter; and at the end of half a century, it was nearly time that the acts of the State should show some regard for the precepts of the Church. How little they corresponded with these, or with the opinions and designs expressed in the private journal, the military annals of India record. Lord Moira found the usual lack of money in the treasury of Calcutta, but remembering the pressure put upon him at home, he began by remitting £300,000 in pagodas. This left him very bare in resources, and led him to prolong negotiations pending with the warlike tribes of Nepaul. He succeeded in composing disputes with Scindia and the King of Ava, from neither of whom any serious mischief was to be apprehended, and with whom contentions on paltry subjects appeared to him to be sources of unmixed evil, as tending to keep alive "an inveterate spirit of animosity against us in the breasts of those whom we had overborne."

In the absence of all recognised occasions for the interchange of confidence, or for the performance of duties of political co-operation, the position of humbled, yet still proud Princes, could not but be one of perpetual oversusceptibility and tantalisation. No good reason could be assigned for the interchange of courtly amenities, not to speak of political views; and beyond the most mechanical contrivances to improve the physical condition of the people, there was little if anything for the Princes to do. How different would have been the case had they been gradually led to take counsel, and to make proposals at Calcutta, with a view to the development of the resources of their States, the better organisation of their internal forces, and the reciprocal development of all that goes to make up the strength of federal empire! Every Native Prince, on the contrary, whether he called himself independent or protected, believed—and believed with reason—that every act of his calculated, however remotely, to remind his nobles or his people of better days gone by, was certain to be regarded as covertly treacherous or threateningly hostile by the ill-advisers of the Paramount Power. Lord Moira had sagacity enough to discern the truth, and to himself he avowed it. "A rational jealousy of our power," he thought, "was not likely to excite half the intrigues against us, which must naturally be produced by the wanton provocations which we had been giving on trivial subjects to all the States around us."[1] Looking, for the first time, at the anomalous state of things everywhere prevailing, it seemed to be only too evident that a community of resentment for past wrongs, and a being held at arm's length by misgivings of the future, must perennially prepare the subject-chiefs for concerted resistance to our sway whenever opportunity should occur. He imagined Runjit Singh to be the likeliest source of trouble on the frontier, and prognosticated (erroneously as it proved) that his personal influence and activity would prove to be sources of probable danger. But though he erred in this respect, he evinced true discernment in his

[1] Private Journal, vol. i. p. 44.

general estimate of the situation, and of the perils that encompassed it. "We have not," he wrote, "simply to look at the irritation of those whom we have scourged with nettles. Each Sovereign must have brought the case home to himself, and must have secretly sympathised with the Durbars which he saw insulted and humiliated."

The Nawab-Vizier of Oude was at this time bitterly incensed against the Central Government. He had been promised complete immunity from its interference when he agreed to surrender the half of his dominions in 1801; nevertheless, he had been subjected to every species of petty and prying interference in the management of what remained of his affairs, until at length he declared, "in open Durbar, that we had driven him to desperation." The Rajah of Berar, though professing to be friendly, was not able to conceal his distrust of our intentions towards him —with what good cause he was soon to see. The Nizam, who had so early admitted a subsidiary force within his confines, "did not disguise his absolute hatred of us," although unable to make any attempt at disenthralment. Scindia found it difficult to keep his irregular forces together, and might fairly be credited with the hope of being able to quarter them in other territories than his own. Holkar was in similar case. If one day these ignitable elements should burst into flame, it would be owing, thought the Viceroy, to our own fault, in not "defining to ourselves, or making intelligible to the Native Princes, the quality of the relation which we had established with them. In our treaties we recognised them as independent Sovereigns. Then we sent Residents to their courts. Instead of acting in the character of ambassadors, they assumed the functions of dictators, interfered in all private concerns, countenanced refractory subjects against them, and made the most ostentatious exhibition of this exercise of authority."

The Nawab of Kurnool died, and his second son seized the capital and was proclaimed his successor. His elder brother happened to be in English territory at the time, and obtained the assistance of the Madras Government to place him upon the musnud. That done, his allies forthwith proposed to the Governor-General that, while their forces remained in occupation of the city, their *protegé* should be mediatised, and the province incorporated with the Madras Presidency. The Viceroy indignantly rejected the proposal. It did not seem to him a natural consequence of our military interposition that, without the surmise of any misconduct urged against the Nawab, he should be deprived of his authority and revenues, except as to such portion as we might munificently leave to him. This was a remnant of the old system, in which our convenience was the only influencing principle. It was evidently an unjust principle when no real necessity could be pleaded; but he was further convinced that it was a thoroughly impolitic view. "In nothing did we violate the feelings of the Native Princes so much as in the decisions in which we claimed the privilege of pronouncing with regard to the succession to the musnud." The ignorant assumption that the rule of primogeniture would be recognised among the Mussulman families as binding, if the British Government openly lent it their sanction and support, appeared to him thoroughly delusive. The eldest son would of course avail himself of our aid as far as he could; but the moment he had succeeded, he would begin to assert the same freedom of choice among his children as his father had done; and against such an impulse no sense of gratitude to us would weigh. Thus early do we find the question seriously engaging the minds occupied with Indian affairs, which, at a later period, was destined to exercise so great an influence over the whole course of opinion and action.

The quarrel with the Goorkhas was certainly not of the Governor-General's seeking, and in a certain sense it may be said to have been forced upon him. He evinced a desire to parley until his forbearance tried the temper of most of those around him; and it cannot be doubted that, relying on the remoteness of their country, the excellence of their irregular discipline, the number of their well-armed forts, and, above all, the indomitable spirit of their people, these sturdy highlanders mistook tardiness for weakness, and prudence for irresolution. A fiercer struggle, over a wider range of country, has never been maintained in India. Upwards of 100,000 combatants of all arms were brought into the field on our side; and the numbers on the other must have been much greater. Again and again detachments were beaten back, and columns compelled to retreat. At length we triumphed; but only at a cost of life and treasure such as had never been expended before. The territorial gains, though not large, were important, extending, as they did, our sway from the Jumna to the Sutlej. Lord Moira might well have been content with these successes; but he had caught the prevalent disease in camp. He could resist neither the promptings of military ambition, or the appetite for popularity and praise. Metcalfe early gained his ear, and whispered temptations, varied and splendid, in the shape of territorial acquisition. In a confidential paper on the conduct of the war with Nepaul, and its probable extension to other regions, he laid down as propositions incapable of dispute or doubt, that our Empire in India had arisen from the superiority of our military power; that its stability rested entirely on the same foundation; and that if this foundation were removed, the fabric must fall to the ground. Whatever delusions might prevail in England respecting the security to be derived from the affections of our Indian subjects, and a character for moderation and forbearance with foreign Native States, our power depended solely on our military superiority. Yet there was reason to apprehend that this comparative superiority had in some measure diminished. The signal repulses we had met with at Bhurtpore, Kalunga, Kumano, and elsewhere, showed that our military pre-eminence was no longer uncontested, as it once had been. Analysing each sanguinary check, and crediting our antagonists with augmented discipline and valour, he urged, that as "a great portion of our former military fame had been buried at Bhurtpore," it had not been retrieved by any successes since obtained. Our opponents were better able to hold their ground than formerly, and our troops had not the same confidence in themselves they used to have. The sight of a white face or a red coat was not sufficient on all occasions, as it once had been, to make our adversaries flee in dismay. Either the gradual circulation of knowledge had given them a better mode of defence, or the charm which insured our success was dissolved, or from some other change we were less invincible than we had been. "The numbers of our troops must be permanently augmented in proportion to the increase of our possessions;" again and again laying stress on the fundamental fact, that the existence of Empire in Asia must ever be dependent on the sword, and that it had no root in the affections of the people. It could derive no support from the good-will, or good faith, of our neighbours. That policy was best suited to our situation in India, which tended in the greatest degree to increase our military power by all means consistent with justice. Increased levies, well disciplined and equipped, would, as he elsewhere explained,[1] furnish the means of fresh conquests; and these in return would supply the resources requisite to drill, feed, and pay additional levies. In a word, Metcalfe's estimate of our position was, that we had gone too far in the way of acquisition to stop; that when we abandoned the attitude and aptitude of aggression, we could no longer hold down writhing discontent, or keep external enmity at bay; and that, so long as hardy and courageous races lay beyond the frontier, that frontier must continually expand, or, at least, be capable of expansion.

Lord Moira, who at Westminster, and even at Fort William, had been full of moderate and forbearing sentiments, speedily became acclimatised in camp, and learned to think and act in concert with the habits of thought and action that prevailed around him. The greater portion of his nine years' administration was consumed in wars, entailing vast sacrifices of life and treasure, and productive of comparatively small benefit of a lasting character. The Pindharries, the great robber clan of Central India, were indeed hunted down, after a long and sanguinary chase, and their chief was found in a jungle with his head cut off. But this was about the most useful of Lord Moira's costly wars. A harder fight was carried on with the Goorkhas, many of whose strongholds were razed to the ground, and a portion of whose territories was annexed; but after varied conflicts with these proud and gallant mountaineers, the Governor-General was fain to make peace, and to leave them for the future unmolested. The Goorkhas have well repaid in later times the immunity they have been permitted to enjoy from further interference.

[1] Metcalfe's Papers, from pp. 82-90.

The States of Central India in 1816 were disturbed and disorganised in a degree which temptingly suggested a policy of intervention. Each of the Mahratta Chiefs who still maintained a substantive or independent existence was jealous of his neighbours, and each had his stifled grudge against the still expanding Power that ten years before had humbled him. In every Durbar the English Resident was feared and hated as the symbol of past humiliation, the espial of existing weakness, and the fugleman of future attack. It was the aim of every shrewd native official to mislead him—the purpose of every subtle and inventive politician to foil him. Any expedient or device seemed justifiable to baffle the designs imputed by all, and not without reason, to that encroaching State whose most sagacious advisers in their turn believed, and truly, that the Mahrattas desired our overthrow, and would not scruple to have recourse to any measures destructive to our provinces.[1]

It was clearly "our interest to annihilate them, or to reduce them to a state of weakness, subjection, and dependence." But with regard to weak and harmless petty States, it was a just and proper object of a wise and liberal Government to support them. Scindia, Holkar, and Berar, from whom alone we had anything to fear, had confessedly committed no overt act of hostility; nor was there any decent pretext for attacking them. But all of them in turn harboured the Pindharries, and paid them black mail, if they did not occasionally hire them as auxiliaries. These it was now declared to be an imperative duty to crush; their existence was a scandal, their impunity a discredit to imperialising rule. Their complete extirpation could hardly be effected without active co-operation on the part of the Mahratta powers; and the scheme was formed of

[1] Metcalfe in Kaye's Life, p. 432.

a crusade against the freebooters, with a clear prevision of the more important consequences that might or might be made to ensue. Once engaged in hunting down predatory tribes on the border, who should say what constituted hindrance of pursuit, or help to escape? Every day and every movement would bring new cause of quarrel; every mosstrooper sheltered would be an occasion of complaint; every presumed accessary would be the subject of altercation; the multiplication of such sparks would be sure to generate flame, with mutual distrust, resentment, and aversion fostering and fanning it on every side. In pursuit of Pindharries a free passage through the territories of the Mahratta States might be demanded, and if refused, there would be at once a cause of war. "If Scindia, Holkar, and the Rajah of Berar, should neither co-operate nor remain neutral—if all or any of these Powers should oppose or obstruct our operations, we had no choice but to consider them as enemies, and attack them accordingly. Their territories would afford a recompense for the expenses of the war, and an increase of resources for the payment of additional force."[1] Here then we have avowed, in terms incapable of being mistaken, the anticipations with which a fresh campaign on a great scale was prepared, together with a frank confession of the objects of the war.

Events did not fall out precisely as was expected; but in the main the ends sought were accomplished in the wide region which is especially designated Hindustan. The formation of alliances with the minor States which lay on every side around the greater and more formidable ones, was at the same time pressed on the attention of Lord Moira by his confidential counsellors. These must be offered the guarantee of Imperial protection, in exchange

[1] Kaye's Life of Metcalfe, p. 437.

for tribute to be expended in the organisation and maintenance of additional corps. Scindia and Holkar would naturally object to be gradually encircled thus with dependencies; but if they did, so much the better: there would thus be another obvious cause of quarrel, and a manifestly good excuse for their destruction. "We ought to be strong enough," wrote Metcalfe, "to conquer them all, and annex the whole of their territories to the British dominions: or they might reluctantly submit, and then they must either devour one another or waste away."

One voice, indeed, was eloquently raised against these courses. It was the voice of one who, as we have seen, had in earlier days entered eagerly into the spirit of conquest for conquest's sake; but who had learned wisdom, justice, and mercy, in the administrative school whence others had drawn the opposite lessons. The words of Munro at this memorable juncture are too pregnant with meaning to be forgotten. Writing to Lord Moira in 1817, he says, "When I consider the weakness of the Native States, and the character of the Chiefs under whose sway they are, I see little chance of war, and none of a protracted resistance. There is so little subordination in Native Governments, that much more energy is required under them than under the more regular Governments of Europe. Scindia was never formidable, even in the height of his power. The exertions of Holkar against Lord Lake were still weaker. The power of Scindia's as well as of Holkar's Government has so much declined since that period, that it is scarcely credible that either they or Ameer Khan would venture to oppose by force any measure for the suppression of the Pindharries. But there is sometimes a kind of infatuation about Indian Chiefs who have lost a part of their dominions, which tempts them to risk the rest in a contest which they know to be hopeless. The situation of the British Government with regard to the Native Powers is entirely changed within the last twenty years. It formerly brought very small armies into the field, with hardly any cavalry. It now brings armies into the field superior to the enemy, not only in infantry, but also in cavalry, both in quality and number. The superiority is so great, that the event of any struggle is no longer doubtful. It has only to bring forward its armies, and dictate what terms it pleases, either without war, or after a short and fruitless resistance."[1] He argues against extending the system of subsidiary forces, and recommends instead, "compelling Scindia to cede the districts restored to him in 1805-6." Whenever the subsidiary system is introduced, unless the reigning Prince be a man of great abilities, the country will soon bear the marks of it, in decaying villages and decreasing population. This has long been observed in the dominions of the Peishwa and the Nizam, and it is now beginning to be seen in Mysore. He states, however, that "its inevitable tendency is to bring every Native State, sooner or later, under the exclusive dominion of the British Government. It has already done this completely in the case of the Nawab of the Carnatic. It has made some progress in that of the Peishwa and the Nizam; and the whole of the territory of those Princes will unquestionably suffer the same fate as the Carnatic. The Peishwa will probably again commit a breach of the alliance. The Nizam will do the same. Even if the Prince himself were disposed to adhere rigidly to the alliance, there will always be some amongst his principal officers who will urge him to break it. As long as there remains in the country any high-minded independence, which seeks to throw off the control of strangers,

[1] Life of Sir T. Munro, pp. 461, 462.

such counsellors will be found. I have a better opinion of the Natives of India than to think this spirit will ever be completely extinguished, and I can have no doubt that the subsidiary system must everywhere run its course, and destroy every Government which it undertakes to protect. . . . Even if we could be secured against every internal convulsion, and could retain the country quietly in subjection, I doubt much if the condition of the people would be better than under their Native Princes. The consequence of the conquest of India by British arms would be, in place of raising, to debase the whole people. There is, perhaps, no example of any conquest in which the Natives have been so completely excluded from all share of the government of their country, as in British India. . . . Among all the disorders of the Native States, the field is open for every man to raise himself; and hence among them there is a spirit of emulation, of restless enterprise and independence, far preferable to the servility of our Indian subjects. . . . The power of the British Government is now (1817) so great that it has nothing to fear from any combination, and it is perfectly able to take satisfaction for any insult without any extension of the subsidiary system."[1] He concludes this letter to Lord Hastings, which was written on the eve of the war, by dissuading him from pushing the subsidiary system further. But his expostulations were disregarded, and the campaign began.

[1] Life of Sir T. Munro, p. 466.

CHAPTER XX.

THE PEISHWA.

1818—1823.

" The English join the most resolute courage to the most cautious prudence. If they showed as much concern for the circumstances of the farmers and landowners, and exerted as much solicitude in relieving and easing the people of God as they do in whatever concerns their military affairs, no nation would be worthier of command. But such is the little regard they show to the inhabitants of these kingdoms, and such their indifference to their welfare, that the people under their dominion groan everywhere, and are reduced to poverty and distress."

—Mutakheren.[1]

IT needed little sagacity on the part of the Mahrattas to divine what was contemplated, as we have seen, by the advisers of the Governor-General. So long as they submitted mutely or passively to be lectured for their indiscretions, and browbeaten whenever they betrayed any lingering pride or ambition, they might be suffered to escape further sacrifices. Under the fret and worry of incessant petty provocations, it was not in human nature that they should not sometimes forget the demeanour of prudence, and overstep the limits of deferential submission. In their camps and durbars, ill-educated and irritable men were ever ready to take umbrage at what they regarded, if it was not intended, as an overweening tone of dictation on the part of British Residents; and it would have been marvellous if the weak and irresolute Princes who overheard

[1] A Native chronicler of the English invasion.

malcontent mutterings, had not drifted into the dangerous condition of doubtful fidelity to existing engagements. At Poona especially, uneasiness at the threatening forces on the frontier early showed itself, the pacifying language of Mr Elphinstone having small effect. Trimbuckjee, an intriguing, reckless and cruel man, exercised unbounded influence over the Peishwa, and helped eventually to precipitate his ruin. As if such secrets could be kept, under the lynx-eyed vigilance of well-paid espionage, he had striven to negotiate, with Holkar, Bhonsla, and Scindia, the formation of an offensive and defensive alliance; and when charged with the fact, he denied it with an equanimity which in European diplomacy would be recognised as natural and legitimate, but which was stigmatised at the time as the climax of semi-barbarous mendacity.

Since Dowlat Rao Scindia had lost the custody of the Mogul, he ceased to believe, perhaps, in the prudence of asserting, against superior odds, the guardianship of the Peishwa; and he entered into engagements by which, in effect, he severed himself from the other Chiefs of his race, and agreed to help in hunting down the Pindharries. Baji Rao wrote to him expostulating. "Your father, Madhajee Scindia, served us heart and soul. When you became his successor you entered into alliance with the English; thus you govern in Hindustan, and thus you show your gratitude. It is befitting you to put bangles on your arms and sit down like a woman. After my power is destroyed, is it possible that yours should stand?" He might have answered, that by the Treaty of Bassein, the Peishwa himself had first made separate terms with the conquerors; yet he was deeply moved by the reproachful appeal thus made to him, and might have yielded had he not already gone too far to hesitate. By the overpowering presence of the invading armies, "he was forced," says Malcolm, "to become, at the very moment he was recognised as its most powerful Chief, the marked deserter of the cause of his nation."[1] In truth, however, the struggle against foreign ascendancy could have been prolonged by him to little purpose, and he confided in the assurance that if he would enter into permanent engagements, he might combine local freedom with imperial union. Peace and safety would be the lot of his people, and all anxiety for the future of his dynasty and dominion would be at an end. He made the bargain, and he kept it. For half a century he and his successors have remained faithful to British connection, and in the worst of times they have proved true to their treaty obligations.

But what if the terms of these obligations should one day be eaten away by vermiculate questions as to their meaning in point of law? What if the vital spirit of the compact may be evaporated in the alembic of a capricious and unscrupulous experimentalist? What if public faith should one day be declared to be like a tenant's improvement, whereof the benefit is held to expire by the efflux of time? This, and nothing less, is the gist of the doctrine of lapse to the Crown, on default of heirs in tail male, recently set up and acted on, with regard to other governing families in India. Threatening notice has not yet, indeed, been served at Gwalior, and the instinct of self-preservation forbids the utterance of misgiving. But after what we have seen done and attempted elsewhere, it would be idle to affect disbelief in the existence of cankerous fears, in every Native State of sufficient importance to be coveted as food for annexation.

In 1817, Holkar's numerous and irregular forces, during the long minority of their Prince, had become mutinous,

[1] Memoirs of Central India, vol. i. p. 141.

and the Durbar presided over by Toolsah Bai, the favourite mistress of the deceased chief, and guardian of his son, was rent by personal feuds and enmities. A general disposition prevailed to side with the Peishwa; but no one possessed sufficient influence in council or in camp to bring about an accord, until the army of Sir Thomas Hislop approached Mahidpore. After a sanguinary struggle on the banks of the Seepra, in which the Mahrattas were defeated, a treaty of peace was made at Mundissore. The claim of ascendancy over the States of Rajpootana was renounced, as well as the lands of the Jeypore country, and the territories South of the Satpoorah hills were ceded to the British Government. The integrity of what remained was guaranteed to the boy Chief and his successors. To scenes of turbulence and violence there gradually succeeded the order and security of a settled government. The irregular horse, whose multitudinous array had long rendered the name of Holkar formidable, were dispersed and finally disbanded; and the Princes of Indore have never since appeared in arms against us. Bereft of the support of the two principal States of the confederacy, it seemed incredible even to Mr Elphinstone that the Peishwa should still seriously meditate repudiation of the engagements imposed on him by the treaty of Bassein; but the conduct of his chief Minister, early in 1817, had been such as to lead at last to a requisition that he should be banished, or surrendered as a hostage for their observance. Trimbuckjee fled, and his master first pretended not to know his hiding-place, and then refused to give him up, although he was believed to be actively engaged in organising plots for an armed insurrection. Communications with him from Baji Rao were discovered, whereupon the Resident insisted on the surrender of his family, who were still at Poona, and the occupation by the subsidiary troops of certain forts in the neighbourhood of the city. On the refusal of the Peishwa, he was warned that his conduct would be treated as equivalent to a cause of war. The parley being prolonged, instructions were forwarded to Mr Elphinstone to present as an ultimatum the draft of an amended treaty, whereby provinces yielding £340,000 a year were to be ceded for the maintenance of a more efficient subsidiary force; the right to send or receive envoys from other States was to be relinquished; the offending Minister was to be surrendered; and, finally, the Peishwa was required to renounce for ever all right to the headship of the Confederacy. To give emphasis to these requirements, the subsidiary troops were summoned to the gates of the city, and twenty-four hours were given for an answer. Baji Rao woke to a sense of his desperate position. His ministers appealed unreservedly to the forbearance and magnanimity of the Power they had, till lately, been counselling their master to defy. Some allowance ought to be made, they said, for the perplexities of his situation, which had to a great extent been created by previous concessions, and the attitude assumed by a foreign force so mortifying to the feelings of spirited Chiefs and a credulous people. The public opinion of the world, they said, would not justify treatment so pitiless, and the imposition of terms so degrading. Even if agreed to, they could not long be kept, for the Prince would lose all political respect and authority; and in either case they must be held to imply the extinction of their State. Their passionate logic was but too convincing. But Mr Elphinstone's orders were to yield nothing, and after a long but fruitless controversy the new treaty was signed. The poison of 1803 had done its work, and its latest symptoms were manifested in its effect upon the brain. Every subsequent act of the maimed and wounded

Government of the Peishwa was characterised by the craft and incoherency of madness. The treaty was no sooner signed than he repented; its publication alternately filled him with despair, or fired him with wild thoughts of revenge. He had fitted on the yoke with his own hands, but it was on that account none the more endurable; and after some feeble efforts to affect resignation, he entered recklessly into schemes of counter-revolution, and in the space of a few months drew down upon his throne and family utter and irretrievable ruin. The capital was occupied by the subsidiary corps. Two English armies entered the country from opposite sides, and on the 11th February 1818, a proclamation announced that it had been incorporated as a province of the British Empire. After two months' campaign Baji Rao gave himself up as a prisoner of war to Sir John Malcolm, and lived during the remainder of his days at Bitur, near Cawnpore, on a pension of eight lacs. Some years before his death, having no son, he adopted as his heir Nana Saib, to whom he bequeathed his jewels and resentments, cherishing to the last the hope that the house of Balaji Viswanath, which for more than a century had occupied an important place among the dynasties of Central Hindustan, should not utterly perish.

Appa Saib Bhonsla of Nagpore had from the first acted in secret concert with the infatuated Peishwa, and, like him, had attempted to escape from subsidiary thraldom, by attempting to surprise the Residency, and, failing that, to encounter superior discipline with greater numbers in the field. But he, too, signally failed, and was forced to seek refuge among the Sikhs. A grandson of Raghuji Bhonsla was elevated to the Gudi, under the guardianship of his mother, Banka Bai. The administration was virtually confided to the Resident, Mr Jenkins, by whom the resources of the country were carefully developed, and its productive capabilities much increased. The titular sovereignty of the State was respited during the minority of the new Rajah, who was allowed to reign, but not to govern. In the words of Metcalfe, "We took the government completely into our own hands, and the country was managed entirely by European officers posted, with full powers, in the several districts. There was not any Native administration, and the interference which we exercised was nothing less than absolute undivided government in the hands of the Resident."[1]

Sir John Malcolm, who, in 1818, took overruling charge of the whole of Central India, narrates with satisfaction the rapid progress to industrial recovery that took place after the war. Scindia's regular troops were reduced from 26,000 to 13,000 infantry, and his irregular forces were almost laid aside. The revenue rose 25 per cent., dilapidated villages were repeopled by the return of the fugitives, who rejoiced in the establishment of tranquillity. The recuperative energies of Holkar's country bore still more abundant fruit. Whole tracts had been laid desolate by the ravages of intestine broils, and the prolonged waste of military service, while every social tie, save that of allegiance to the head of the State, had been ruinously weakened. But here also the excessive levies were discarded, and peaceful production took the place of mutual plunder. The people, weary of warfare, rejoiced in the resumption of peaceful pursuits. Instead of four lacs a year, the Treasury received sixteen lacs as the year's revenue of 1820. Universally, the evidences of a reaction from disorder and insecurity displayed themselves: all of which proves, as far as it goes, that the protecting influence of suzerain power is not incom-

[1] Letters to Chief Secretary, August 14, 1826; Papers and Correspondence, p. 91.

patible with material prosperity and popular content, provided it is exercised forbearingly and considerately, and that the natural feeling of self-respect and of preference for customary laws and usages, and for Native rule, whether elective in the village or hereditary in the State, be not wantonly wounded or uptorn. The question, nevertheless, remains—how far does all this go? Of nations as of individuals, it has been written of old time, "Man shall not live by bread alone." Malwa prospered, as already noted, under Native rule, and was contented; Malwa prospered under alien rule, and was discontented. Safe roads, improving tillage, rising prices, diminution of the percentages of crime, an increase in the amount yearly netted for taxation, are undoubted signs of fat; and if the worth of a country, say to a vendor or purchaser, is to be appraised according to weight, fat tells for more than bone, and quiet is an antecedent and a consequent of fat. All which in policemanship is what is called highly satisfactory. But these things being admitted, history will ask, What then?

Metcalfe, the British Resident, arrived in camp from Delhi, to narrate the repeated efforts made by the Mogul to induce the Governor-General to visit him. He had been repeatedly assured that there was but one difficulty—namely, that no acknowledgment, direct or inferential, would be made of the dignity he claimed by inheritance as Suzerain of India. The Act of 1813, renewing the Company's charter, had specifically declared the sovereignty of all possessions held by the English in the East to be in the British Crown. It would be inconsistent, therefore, as well as impolitic, on the part of an English Viceroy to do any act that might be represented as acknowledging the ancient dynasty or dominion. The eldest son of the titular lord of the East, Jehangir, was a young man of spirit and energy, who might soon succeed his father. He was known to be inimical to the existence of European power, and he might one day take advantage of any admission of his hereditary title, to call the Mussulman Chiefs to arms. We should have difficulty in making out a good case, thought Lord Moira, consistently with our own theory; and the practical part of the business might be no less embarrassing. The hopes to which Shah Alum had for ten years clung, for ever passed away. His deliverance from the Mahrattas had been one of the excuses for the war of 1802; and that deliverance effected, he dreamt that he was free. Provinces might have been lost, and revenues lessened; the name of Delhi might have sunk in the estimation of the world, and the pomp of its Imperial parade might be impaired; but the throne of Akbar and of Aurungzebe remained; and he was its thirty-third occupant in the direct line of Kings. Faithless lieutenants might have forgotten to pay tribute; Chiefs whom he or his fathers had enfiefed might have abjured the ties of loyalty; but he was still the acknowledged and visible head of the Mussulmans in Southern Asia; and in the fluctuations of revolt and conquest, a day of restitution might come, when his descendants would reign again in splendour and in power. He had been held in captivity by Pagans, but Christians had delivered him; at least, they had gone to battle saying they would. Was he to believe them false? Had not his father given them, at the first, leave to live and trade in India; then grants of land and jurisdiction; afterwards the collectorate of three great provinces, and the lordship of many more? Had they not made solemn treaties with him, and ever until now recognised, with effusive protestations, his sovereign rank and dignity? And was not Mr Seaton their accredited Resident at his Court? How could he harbour a suspicion that all this was to go for nothing? They had unlatched the door of his gilded and jewelled cage; but told him, at first gently, then peremptorily, that he must not come forth. They would keep the door for him, and see that neither Goorkha nor Mahratta should again venture near. Why not be content to eat and drink, and smoke and doze, and issue daily mandates to a multitudinous train, and pray at eventide towards Mecca, and teach his son the philosophy of fickle fortune? Rich farms and pleasure-grounds and groves and gardens lay around the city, carefully kept for his support in the seclusion of voluptuous ease—their produce and rental being expressly guaranteed by his English deliverers for that purpose. They were once his allies: were they not so still? and if so, why would not the Governor-General, when not a long way off, pay him a visit? None had ever questioned his title, and he no longer questioned English dominion wherever it had been gained by the sword. Delhi had been the capital of the Empire; the Empire was gone, but Delhi remained; and it took ten years to make the aged monarch understand that in future it was to be simply his prison.

The Resident, a man of susceptibility and gentleness, shrank from the performance of his duties as a keeper. He thought he could not study too much the feelings of a Prince so situated; that the most obsequious attentions did not compromise our dignity; and that by yielding in small things we could with a better grace oppose his will when necessary. Metcalfe thought otherwise. In his view the helpless captive was but a "poor puppet," whose illusions it was false kindness to prolong by a show of deference that was wholly insincere. It served but to keep awake ideas in his mind "which ought to be put to sleep for ever." When Metcalfe became Resident, he lost no time in realising his theory of dis-illusion. The management of the lands round the city, and the direction of the police within it, as well as the administration of local justice, were successively assumed as part of the functions which the diplomatic representative of England, at what was still called the Court of Delhi, had to perform. In due time complaints arose of extravagance and waste, and the need of greater frugality in keeping up the pageant of superseded royalty. It took long to die; and those who witnessed its last agonies may have been tempted to regret that Metcalfe's summary way of deposition and dethronement was not taken.

To meet the military expenditure which four successive campaigns had entailed, the Governor-General was obliged to raise money on any terms that might be demanded from an insolvent treasury. He borrowed largely from the Vizier of Oude; and when other securities were not forthcoming, he sold him the provinces reft from the Goorkhas,— the foolish Saadut Ali forgetting that he who gave for a valuable consideration could take away without one. Provinces and their inhabitants were treated as chattels by this chivalrous statesman of the superfine Court of the Regency, who, being a man of sentiment and honour, and not as other men, might do, in short, anything he pleased. It pleased him to sanction a near relative becoming a partner in the financial house of W. Palmer & Co. at Hyderabad, whose usurious dealings with the Nizam were of a nature to call forth the denunciation of the Court of Directors, as being utterly regardless of the limits of decorum. The newly-made Marquis defended Palmer & Co. as injured and insulted individuals, and challenged the investigation of accounts which had been framed upon figure-proof principles. The friends of the Viceroy relied upon his character as a man notoriously indifferent as to money to show that he could not have been in any way to blame in the shameful business at Hyderabad. Had he not squandered his patrimony, nobody knew how, and then offered to govern India for the benefit of his creditors? Could anything be more gallant or unsordid? and was he not now "most noble?" The Nizam, it is true, was simply fleeced by a firm of whom the Viceroy's relative was one. But no one could believe that the Marquis knew anything of the transactions; and the tenderness of his domestic affections forbade him to think evil of his kinsfolk. So the Nizam was robbed; and Lord Hastings came home; and,—that was all. Lord Amherst, who succeeded to the government in 1823, was not a fine gentleman of the George IV. school, but was only an honest man; and one of his first acts, therefore, was to lend the Nizam money to liquidate his debts to Palmer & Co., which he did upon condition that the Court of Hyderabad should have no more dealings with the firm, soon afterwards compelled thereby to suspend their commercial enterprises. The conqueror of the Goorkhas and the Mahrattas reappeared in London society as badly off as ever, and after having seized and occupied for a season the throne of Tamerlane, he was glad to take the Governorship of Malta as a sinecure pension for his closing days.

CHAPTER XXI.

LORD WILLIAM BENTINCK.

1824—1835.

" The man who does most honour perhaps to Europe in Asia, is he who governs it. Lord William Bentinck, on the throne of the Great Mogul, thinks and acts like a Pennsylvanian Quaker. You may easily imagine that there are people who talk of the dissolution of the Empire, when they see the temporary ruler of Asia riding on horseback, plainly dressed, without escort, or on his way to the country with his umbrella under his arm. Like Washington, he mixed in scenes of bloodshed and tumult; and like him, he preserved pure and unsullied that flower of humanity which the habits of a military life so often withers. He has issued from the ordeal of diplomacy with the upright mind and the simple and sincere language of a Franklin, convinced that there is no cleverness in appearing worse than one really is."

—JACQUEMONT.[1]

A WAR undertaken with inadequate preparations, to revenge some affronts offered by the Burmese, lasted from 1823 to 1826, and was terminated then by a treaty, by which the King of Ava ceded eleven maritime provinces, and paid a crore of rupees. In England the war was highly unpopular, from the loss of life and treasure it entailed, and the unprofitable nature of the country sought to be partitioned. But Lord Amherst was made an Earl, millions were added to the consolidated debt, and the widows and orphans of the brave men who perished on the banks of the Irrawadi became permanently chargeable on the general estate of the Company.

[1] "The Travels of a French Gentleman in India," vol. i. pp. 87, 88.

The apologists for the conquests of 1826 admit that the provinces it was deemed advisable to exact from Ava were, at the time of their cession, of little value; and they particularly observe, that far from being hailed as deliverers, " our advent was followed by the disappearance of the whole of the population."[1] For many years districts lay wholly waste, contributing in no way to the cost of obtaining them. Partly to secure these doubtful gains, and partly to pay for previous wars, loans amounting to £19,000,000 were raised. Portions of these were employed in liquidating smaller incumbrances, but a permanent addition was made to the financial charge for the year, of over £1,000,000 sterling, in addition to two millions and a half paid in England in 1827–28, for what were termed territorial expenses.

Meanwhile, the weakening of garrisons everywhere throughout Central India, by the necessities of the Burmese war, created widely an impression that all the resources of the Imperial Government were taxed to carry on the contest. Disturbances broke out in many places, which, not without trouble were repressed; but the manifestation of general discontent on the part of both princes and people " showed how little sympathy united the subject and the sovereign, and the satisfaction with which the people were disposed to contemplate the downfall of their rulers."[2]

Mr Canning's friendship for Lord Wellesley, and his eloquent eulogy, when, as President of the Board of Control, he had moved the thanks of Parliament to Lord Hastings and the army which had vanquished the Mahrattas and the Nepaulese, have given colour to the notion that he too thirsted for territorial extension in Asia. His choice of a Governor-General in 1827 sufficiently confutes the

---

[1] Wilson's British India, vol. iii. chap. v.   [2] Ibid.

error. Beset with difficulties at Windsor and at Westminster, he might well have been tempted to use the greatest prize in the gift of Administration to silence or propitiate some of his influential adversaries. He preferred to give India security for peace, by nominating as its chief ruler, the man of all others who was known to cherish a deep repugnance to the policy of aggression, and who had actually risked and lost high office there, by the exceeding lenity he had shown to Native troops beguiled by oversusceptibility on account of their religion into mutiny at Vellore. The appointment of Lord William Bentinck was imputed at the time to favouritism, on account of family connection. But the sin of jobbing is the sin of selfishness: and had self-interest swayed the mind of the Minister, he would at least have hesitated long before bestowing the greatest place under the Crown upon one from whose disappointment he had nothing to fear, and by whose advancement he could not hope to gain a single vote on a division. Lord William Bentinck had not quitted England when the Ministry was changed, and he wrote at once offering to resign his new dignity. But the Duke of Wellington, who knew the real worth of the man, though differing widely from him in political sentiments, frankly assured him of his confidence, and confirmed his appointment. The truth is, that throughout his long and varied career, the Duke had but a very moderate appetite for conquest. We have seen his early objections to the system in India, and we know how patriotically abstinent was his tone, when the Kings of Christendom hung upon his words, and watched his every look, at the Conference of Paris and the Congress of Vienna. We shall yet find him giving other proof of the little store he set on territorial dominion in Asia.

Lord William was the second son of the Duke of Portland, who held in more than one Administration the nominal rank of Premier. Bred a soldier, he had witnessed the campaigns of Suwarrow in Italy, and he subsequently held a command during the war in Spain. As Governor of Madras, he differed with the military authorities, and was recalled. He subsequently held command in Spain and Sicily, where his name was long remembered with affection and respect. Lord William went forth as Governor-General full of good intentions, and with many advantages for their realisation which his predecessors had not enjoyed. The circumstances of the time were favourable. India was at peace. The Hindus were subdued, and the Mussulmans bowed to fate. Beyond the frontier no enemy stirred. No races, save the Sikhs and Affghans, could be said to be formidable; and there was no indication that their rulers meant to deviate from the policy they had long pursued. The new Governor-General had leisure, therefore, to apply himself uninterruptedly to the great business of peaceful improvement and administrative reform. One who served many years under him in India, has said, "He was nearer to the *beau idéal* of what a Governor-General ought to be, than any man that ever filled the office. There have been several good, and several great men in the same position; but there has been none like him. A paramount sense of duty to the inhabitants of India, and of desire to do them good, inspired all his words and actions." This is high praise; but it is just.

One of the earliest provisions of Lord William Bentinck, was that for the suppression of Suttee. Lord Cornwallis and Lord Wellesley had each desired to abolish the practice, but had shrunk from the popular resentment which might, it was feared, ensue. After much careful inquiry, which elicited considerable difference of opinion among both Natives and Europeans who were consulted as to the possible consequences of such an interference with superstitious usage, Lord William Bentinck, with the assent of the Council, issued a Regulation forbidding the immolation, whether voluntary or otherwise, of Hindu widows; and requiring the police to bring to justice all accessaries in such acts of suicide. In Bengal, where the cruel rite had chiefly prevailed, there were murmurs for a time, and attempts at evasion; but little or nothing that could be called resistance. In the other Presidencies one serious case occurred of the rite being performed in defiance of the police. In the Central and Northern Provinces, it had less extensively prevailed, and its abolition there excited, therefore, no observable emotion. In several of the Native States the example was followed, and decrees were issued putting an end to the inhuman custom. The interference of alien authority was ascribed by the people at large to its true motive, and recognised as being for once wholly disinterested. Even his enemies, and they were not few, gave the Viceroy credit for the cautious circumspection and courage shown by him in effecting this salutary change. Kindred in spirit, although wholly different in the subject of its operation, was a Regulation equivalent to law, made in 1832, exempting from forfeiture the property of Hindus abjuring their faith, as time out of mind had been the case under the system of jurisprudence founded on the enactments of Menu.

With regard to the condition of long misgoverned communities, it is sometimes forgotten that it is not so easy to do real or substantial good as those imagine who have never had the opportunity to try. Lord William's upright and benevolent intentions were not, indeed, wholly without fruit. They formed, if it were nothing else, a great and lasting protest against the policy of centralising absorption and excessive expenditure. They showed that the dignity and influence of the Paramount Power might be maintained without new aggressions upon neighbouring States, or further measures of absorption within the confines of our sovereignty. They proved that extravagance might be curbed, and the expenditure and income of the Government nominally balanced, without any worse effect than that of temporary anger among the classes who thrive upon corrupt and lavish outlay. They proved that justice might be done, in many essential particulars, to the Natives, without wrong to Europeans, or hazard to the stability of our empire. They showed that, without preaching a crusade, or troubling the waters of intolerance, some of the worst evils of heathenism might be lessened, and the protection of a humane and Christian-spirited law asserted in the dark places of cruelty. They showed that a man who despised the trappings and gauds of state, and disdained to defend his acts by stifling public criticism, could win respect and love as well as his more showy predecessors.

An insurrection at Mysore, in 1831, provoked by fiscal oppression, led the Government of Madras to interpose: at first in the hope of reconciling prince and people, and when that failed, with a view to obtain for the latter securities for enjoyment of their industry, and the tranquillity of the province. The Rajah, ill-advised and infirm of purpose, and who had at the time no son, was reported to be unpopular and undeserving of trust. He was persuaded to relinquish the performance of executive duties into the hands of a species of Commission, over which the Resident presided, a fifth of the net revenues of the State being allotted for his civil list. But the sovereignty of Mysore was in no way questioned under these arrangements; and all administrative functions, whether judicial, military, or financial, were continued in Native hands. Once, and once only, the Governor-General was induced to deviate from his maxim of non-interference with Native rule. Vira Rejendra was the last of a long line of Princes who governed Coorg. They had been subdued by Hyder Ali, and the country annexed to Mysore; but on its partition the local government was restored by English help, upon the usual terms of protection. Vira Rejendra enjoyed an unenviable notoriety, on account of his vices and his crimes, which were ascribed to confirmed lunacy. Yet even in his case the Governor-General showed great forbearance, after multiplied cause of offence; making repeated offers which any rational man in the position would have readily accepted, and refusing to believe to the last that the Rajah contemplated actual hostilities. Ten days sufficed to overpower his efforts at resistance, and when the capital was occupied without serious opposition, no male survivor of the Rajah's family was to be found. How Lord William Bentinck was persuaded to pass by the claims of the female line, does not appear; but it has been said that in after years he regarded his decision with regret, as tending to fortify the precedents in support of the doctrine of lapse. Coorg was annexed by proclamation, and the Rajah kept a state prisoner at Benares. The country has long since been reduced to the approved condition of dull and stagnant quietude. The Collector and Judge of the district is an artillery officer, of good attainments and intentions, but who, like his predecessors, lives apart, only known by the people when discharging his public duty. One Native gentleman only holds the commission of the peace; and in matters of any moment he does not interfere. A few enterprising Englishmen make money off coffee plantations in the hills, and when they are not content with decisions in law or equity by the gallant Judge and Collector, they appeal to the Supreme Court of Madras; but the Coorgis, when they are dissatisfied, have neither time, confidence, nor money enough to undertake a journey of 600 miles in search of justice; and nobody cares or knows how they like their lot.

Lord W. Bentinck found the Government heavily in debt, and frequently borrowing largely to make up the sum of its expenditure. He set resolutely about the reduction of salaries, perquisites, and sinecures; but his retrenchments made little impression upon the inveterate habits of waste and indebtedness. He was incessantly abused for his efforts at economy by all the jobbers of the civil and military establishments. They would have had him go on borrowing money, or adding to the taxation. He would do neither. He thought that, upon the whole, the pay of the functionaries of Bengal was too high. They shared amongst them no less than ninety-seven lacs of rupees, or nearly a million sterling. He reduced the total to ninety-one lacs, or somewhere about £900,000 a year, to be divided amongst 416 individuals; and this he did by curtailing the luxuries of the indolent, and cutting down the allowances of the overpaid. After all those distressing reductions, he still left each civilian, from the writer to the Member of Council, on an average, the sum of £2,200 a year.[1] These changes earned for him the execration of the lazy and worthless in the service. The tone in which he was spoken of by these much aggrieved characters is illustrated by an anecdote that is told of a pomp-loving old official, who was in the habit of having carpets spread upon

[1] *Calcutta Review.*

the ground whenever he alighted from his equipage; and who, though only a circuit judge, moved about attended by a showily-appointed retinue or guard. He was asked if he was not related to Lady William. "No," he replied; "unfortunately to the brute himself." The Viceroy was obdurate. He persevered; and not only abated the excess of expenditure, which Government could ill afford, but the sins of negligence, delay, and inefficiency in the administration, which the country could afford still less. His declaration at the outset was, that he had come to see what service he could render to the people of India, and that he was resolved to prove that he was open to suggestion and remonstrance from men of all ranks and races, and to show that he would not govern for the benefit of any particular class, or submit to be a puppet in the hands of others. These promises he faithfully redeemed. He spent some months of every year in visiting various districts of his vast vice-realm. The physical and social condition of remote regions thus became known to him in a way they could hardly have otherwise been. He invited, moreover, and, indeed, required, constant reports to be made to him confidentially, in addition to those forwarded in due routine to Calcutta, and thereby obtained acquaintance with personal and local circumstances frequently of great value in discriminating between competitors for promotion in the public service, and in estimating correctly the worth of official representations of all kinds. The labour of all this, superadded to the duties he had ostensibly to perform, was necessarily very great; great also was the odium it excited. Indolence, peculation, and incompetency of all sorts waxed wroth at the imposition of a yoke of surveillance to which they had not been accustomed. Old and tried servants of the Company complained that they were subjected for the first time in their lives to a system which they were pleased to term espionage, but which in reality had nothing in common with that worst artifice of police. The reception of complaints by the weak and timid against men clothed with absolute authority, is simply admission by those in supreme power of the only means by which oppression and delinquency can often be made known, and any species of redress secured. Public complaint is, in a free country, easy and natural; and none other need be there resorted to. But in a country governed arbitrarily like Hindustan, where no single tie of common feeling, origin, or creed exists between the disfranchised population and the dominant few, it was the impulse of a truly good and generous mind to open a door of appeal against hardship and oppression direct and immediate to the centre and seat of authority.

The great experiment about to be tried for the first time of a free press, was naturally viewed with the utmost apprehension by most of the officials of the old school. Lord William Bentinck did not deceive himself as to its effects. He believed that it would increase indefinitely the perilous position of the Paramount Power. Metcalfe thought otherwise; they agreed that the time was at hand when the hazard must be run. "If increase of danger," said Metcalfe; "be really to be apprehended from increase of knowledge, it is what we must cheerfully submit to. We must not try to avert it; and if we did we should fail." Nevertheless, Lord William Bentinck left to his successor the responsibility and credit of liberating the Indian press.

Metcalfe freely owned in 1830, that "were he asked whether the increased happiness of our subjects was proportionate to the heavier expense of our establishment, he should be obliged to answer according to his belief in the negative; for we were foreign conquerors, against whom the antipathy of our Native subjects naturally prevailed. We held the country solely by force, and by force alone could we maintain it."[1] Lord William Bentinck could not bring himself to realise the inevitability of this dismal and heart-hardening creed. It was an honest grief to him to think he was regarded as the greatest Jailor-General in the world. He longed to be respected and to be loved, and to make the name of his country loved and respected also. At least, he was determined to try. The most important of his many administrative reforms was the practical admission of Natives to various branches of the Civil Service. The system of Lord Cornwallis had been based upon their virtual exclusion from every object of legitimate ambition and every hope of reward; and the principle of administrative outlawry had been maintained inexorably by those who succeeded him. Lord William and his best advisers in Council were resolved to remove it. Experience had proved its impolicy; it needed, in their minds, no argument to demonstrate its injustice. One after another, natives were placed in minor situations of trust. The Governor-General was too wise a man to believe that such concessions could suddenly absorb the deep discontent prevailing everywhere among the subject population. Neither was he weak enough to believe that where perfidy or treason lay at the heart of an individual so trusted, the confidence reposed in him would work a miraculous change. He calculated upon many instances of political ingratitude, and was prepared to hear of disaffection in the mass, after he had done his best to disarm it. But he did not hesitate to do the right thing therefore. He had a faith in event-

[1] Metcalfe, vol. iii. p. 181.

ual good, and a sense of the duty those who bear rule owe to those whom they govern, that no miserable fear of ill-requital could disturb. And in this far-sighted view of policy, he clearly saw that through the path of gradual enlistment of the intellectual ability and ambition of the Natives in the permanent service of their own land, lay our only reasonable or definite prospect of retaining an ascendancy therein.

His seven years' administration did not indeed eradicate the greatest evils with which he tried to grapple, for that was beyond his power. He saw the unpopularity of the central Government, caused in a great degree by the pressure of excessive and unequal taxation; but he saw not how to cure it. He discerned the unreliability of the Native army, and left behind him a Minute, in which he sums up its characteristics in these words, "It is in my opinion the most expensive and the least efficient army in the world." Whether he felt sanguine, at the close of his career, that perseverance in a policy of peaceful and enlightened rule, would eventually reach the popular heart, and that we might hope to become trusted instead of feared in India, we know not, but there can be no doubt that he strove anxiously and patriotically to that end. He saw, as all the best men about him saw, that British rule in Asia was a stockade driven by sheer force into the ground, and impregnable so long as the garrison that manned it were numerous enough and loyal; but that it had no root in the convictions or feeling of the community. For the first time the amount of Anglo-Indian debt was palpably and substantially diminished. Swollen by the warlike administration of his predecessor to upwards of £30,000,000 sterling, it was reduced in the seven years of his peaceful sway to £26,947,000; and this was done notwithstanding the heavy blows to productive industry and general commercial credit, inflicted by the failure of the great English capitalists of Calcutta, consequent, as was believed, upon the sudden competition, which they do not seem to have anticipated, from the abolition of the Company's monopoly in 1833, and the complete emancipation of private trade. The revenue remained very nearly the same as it had been fifteen years before; the expenditure was reduced more than a million and a half; and thus at last, instead of a deficit, a surplus appeared in the accounts of the Indian Exchequer.

CHAPTER XXII.

AFGHANISTAN.

1835—1841.

"There is no expediency in the course which the Governor-General has pursued; there is no justice in the policy he has pursued; it is in complete dereliction of every ordinary rule of reason. I have not objected to the publication of the Simla Proclamation, but to the thing published; my objection is not to the manner of doing it, but to the thing done."
—Lord Brougham.[1]

AS senior Member of Council, Sir C. Metcalfe acceded to the musnud of Fort William, until the pleasure of his superiors in England should be known. Thoroughly informed on every subject of civil and military administration, and animated by a noble love of distinction, he could not deny himself the enjoyment of signalising his term of office, brief though it might be, by an act of State likely to preserve his memory in future years. Judging of the man only from his despatches, saturated with political despondency, and bitter with the belief that European ascendancy could only be maintained by military force, no one would probably have surmised what that measure would be. It was the emancipation of the Press, in which he was vigorously supported by Mr Macaulay, then Legal Member of Council; but for which they received the pointed reproof of Leadenhall Street. The Directors desired that Mount-

[1] Debate on Affairs in Afghanistan, 19th March 1839—Hansard, vol. xlvi. col. 869.

stuart Elphinstone should be placed at the head of the Indian Executive. He declined, on the ground of broken health. Lord Heytesbury was named by Sir Robert Peel, and was actually on his way, when, in April 1835, the Whigs returned to power, and recalled him. When questioned on the subject, Ministers defended their right to place, in a position of so much importance, one in whose political opinions and personal qualities they had entire confidence. Lord Grenville had laid this down as a constitutional maxim not admitting of dispute, and Mr Canning had always contended that, on each occasion of a vacancy, a representative of the Crown should be sent out from England, thus visibly and intelligibly asserting the unity of power throughout the Empire.

No final decision was made until Lord W. Bentinck's return to England, when, to the surprise of all, except the few who were aware of the influence whereby it was brought about, the public were informed of the unfit and unfortunate choice of Lord Auckland. Metcalfe was deeply mortified at being, as he said, pronounced less fit than an inexperienced stranger to fill the highest place in the profession to which he had devoted undividedly his youth and prime. But the ways of patronage are inscrutable; and as he knew nothing of the Western hemisphere, he was sent first to Jamaica, and then to Canada, as Governor.

A sense of uneasy languor lay heavily on Anglo-India. The romance of adventure slept. Occasionally a disputed succession in some Native State stirred a feeling of curiosity among listless collectors and dozing judges, or wakened hopes of something to do in barrack or in camp. But the drowsy monotony of unresisted domination was undisturbed. Conquest, though fat, had not grown fastidious, but it had nothing fresh to eat, and the expedient had not yet been suggested of grilling or boiling down the bones. Over every palisade it looked in vain for some hill tribe coming to molest it. The Goorkhas were quiet, the Sikhs affectionate, and the Burmese showed no disposition to budge. Was political invention dead; or could no ingenious young man, in want of a career, discover a danger, or invent a foe capable of being made to look formidable? Alexander Burnes did his best to find a new outlet for energy in want of employment; but he would, probably, have failed to rouse Lord Auckland from his poco-curantist dream of office, had not politicians in England, about this time, become haunted with a dread that the Czar Nicholas was bent upon aggrandisement at our expense in the East. Russian emissaries were everywhere to be traced throughout the border States of Central Asia. Persia was to be bribed or driven into making encroachments on Scinde and Candahar. Muscovite intrigues were suspected among the Afghans, and Runjit Singh, though he had never swerved from his alliance with us, was not to be trusted. The Indus had plainly been designed by Providence as the natural frontier of English Empire in Asia. How to get to it was the only question. In the sultry and still noon-tide of prevailing peace, it was so difficult to arouse people to a sense of belligerent duty. Burnes had astutely suggested that the matter should at first be put merely on a commercial footing. A harmless race, inspired about half-and-half with mercenary and missionary motives, ought not to be suspected of meaning any mischief by asking that the navigation of the Indus should be declared free from the sea to its mountain source. There was something noble and philanthropic in the demand. Suspicious and half-civilised tribes might not appreciate the worth of the disinterested idea; but they must be made to understand it. Once a footing gained on any pretence, all the rest was sure to follow.

Russia was stealthily, but steadily, advancing—or what was the same thing, making her political minions or stipendiaries advance—towards the Indus. We must cross the Indus and get firmly posted on the farther side, to prevent her reaching its shore. The siege of Herat, unwisely undertaken by the Government of Persia, and pressed for nearly a twelvemonth, threw a lurid light of reality on these speculations.

In 1837, a mission to the Courts of Hyderabad and Cabul, professedly for commercial objects only, for the most part failed. Dost Mahommed, who then ruled in Afghanistan, longed for Peshawar, which had been ceded to Runjît Singh by Shah Sujah, then deposed and in exile. Burnes could not promise him help; the envoy of Persia did, and to earn it he undertook to assist in the reduction of Herat. About the same time the English envoy, Mr M'Neile, complained of having been insulted at Teheran. Shah Sujah was ready to promise any terms as the price of assistance to regain his throne, and Runjît Singh was ready to enter into any compact that would secure him the possession of Peshawar. Fortune had dealt the cards, why hesitate to play them? On the 26th June 1838, a triple alliance was signed at Lahore, whereby Lord Auckland engaged to send a British army into Afghanistan, to replace his Majesty on the musnud of his ancestors, to secure the Lion Chief of the Sikhs the possession of certain territories named on the right bank of the Indus, and to bind in everlasting friendship the three Powers, for mutual defence against foreign intrigue and hostility.

Orders were forthwith given to prepare for war. Loud was the cry of joy that rose on all sides, that the lethargy of peace had been at length shaken off, and that the spirit of conquest was about to assert itself again. For, whatever illusions might be kept up in England about the scope and purpose of the movement, there was no misapprehension in India. In a proclamation issued at Simla, on the 1st October 1838, the Governor-General promised indeed, that an Afghan army would with our auxiliary aid conduct the legitimate King to the seat of his government at Cabul, and that done, that the auxiliaries would be withdrawn; but nobody, either then or afterwards, imagined that the raw levies assembled on the confines of Scinde, would be able to face the disciplined troops of Dost Mahommed, or that the fugitive Shah, in whose long-forgotten cause the Viceroy professed to take so deep an interest, had a lac of rupees to spare them for food or pay.

The Simla Proclamation was denounced in Parliament early in the session of 1839, by Lords Aberdeen, Ellenborough, and Brougham. In its vindication, papers were laid before both Houses, containing extracts from confidential despatches during 1837, from our diplomatic agents in the East, and especially from Captain Burnes, tending to show that a network of Russian intrigue had been stealthily spread over all the countries of the Indus. Being pressed upon the point, Lord Melbourne admitted that explanations had been sought through our Minister at St Petersburg, and that the reply "had been satisfactory."[1] But this explanation was not communicated to Parliament along with the accusations of Russia, and further time was thus permitted to elapse, during which the latter might have an effect upon the public mind, while tidings were awaited of the result of the campaign. Meanwhile the correspondence, thus presented piecemeal, was transmitted to Calcutta, where the chief informer against the Czar read with amazement information ascribed to him which he had never given, but which, through some unex-

[1] Debate, Lords, 11th April 1839—Hansard, vol. xlvi. col. 1305.

plained cause, had been published as accurate. Burnes told Lord Auckland that he meant publicly to correct these grave errors, but he was dissuaded by the representations of the Viceroy, who argued that now his country was committed to a momentous course of policy, it would be held unpatriotic in a confidential servant to cast doubt on its accuracy and good faith. He could not suppose that the misrepresentations had been intentional, and as all was well that ended well, he had much better resume diplomatic functions in Afghanistan, than worry himself and others about discrepancies of statement that had become historical. At the moment all looked bright with triumph, and Burnes felt that his name would for ever be associated with the notable changes that had been brought about by a combination of diplomacy and arms; and he contented himself with reprinting privately the more important of his original despatches, with the corrections needed, for circulation among his friends at home. And this is the way history is made. There were in those days no electric means of collation, correction, or confutation; and the people of England, without means official or unofficial of understanding what the quarrel was about, read only of conflicts worthy of their flag, and listened to the guns firing for victories gained, and lay down thankfully to sleep, unconscious of what manner of deeds were doing in their name.

A large Sikh force joined the British army under Sir Willoughby Cotton, at Ferozepore; and, proceeding through the Bolan pass, formed a junction with the main army under Sir John Keane at Quettah. Thence they moved on Candahar, where they proclaimed the restoration of the Afghan King early in May 1839. The fortress of Ghuzni was attacked soon afterwards, and taken; Dost Mahommed abandoned the capital, and on the 7th August, Shah Sujah was by British bayonets enthroned at Cabul. For months a desultory resistance to his authority was maintained; but after the battle of Purwan, Dost Mahommed, in a fit of despondency, surrendered and was sent to Calcutta, where he was treated with all the consideration due to his rank and reputation. The submission of the Afghans seemed to be complete. Sir John Keane was elevated to the peerage, and Sir William Macnaghten prepared to quit Cabul for Bombay, of which, as his reward, he had been appointed Governor. A portion of the British troops left the country, but 5000 men under General Elphinstone remained, to give confidence, as was said, to the partisans of the restored regime; while a corps under Nott still occupied Candahar, to insure the complete tranquillisation of the country. Sir Alexander Burnes was about to assume the duties of Resident in the outpost realm which he had contributed so much to bring within the ambit of the Paramount Power, when suddenly the ice of submission gave way, and he, with nearly all the best men of his race who had taken their stand on it, sunk to rise no more.

Bitter resentments had been thickly sown throughout Afghanistan during its two years' occupation, by the high-handed method of repression imported from beyond the Indus. Conspiracies were formed, discovered, and baffled; but only to be renewed again and again. Ominous warnings were confidentially given at head-quarters, by cool-headed observers of the scene, and listeners to the whispered talk of the people. But the lessons of eighty years of unchecked expansion were too deeply engraved on the minds of men like those in charge; and they could not be waked from their fatal security. To humour a whim of their regal puppet, the Bala Hissar, a citadel of great strength, was evacuated by the troops, and converted into a zenana. Little, if any care seems to have been taken to lay in stores on the approach of winter, or to arm the forts in the neighbourhood, which might have rendered the camp ordinarily safe from attack. On the 2d November, without any known provocation or notice, the Residency of Sir A. Burnes was beset by an armed mob, by whom, after vain expostulation, he and his staff were slain. A detachment ordered to occupy the quarter where the outrage had been committed, was hemmed in for hours in narrow streets, and after considerable loss was compelled to fall back. Incapacity and irresolution paralysed those in command. Macnaghten sent urgent appeals for relief to Nott at Candahar, and to Sale, who was still at Jellalabad; but some of his messages were never received, and the answer of Sale, when at length made acquainted with the exigency, was that he had neither commissariat or ammunition sufficient to justify his undertaking a winter march through a hostile country. Six weeks were wasted in fruitless negotiation. Food grew more scarce, and the severity of the weather more intense; while every day the compassing hosts grew more numerous and menacing, and the terms of accommodation demanded by their Chiefs grew more humiliating to yield. The situation had become desperate, when on the 23d December the Resident was beguiled into an interview by an invitation from Akbar Khan—now at the head of the insurgents—and on a signal given, seized and butchered in cold blood. No attempt was made to avenge his death; but some days later terms were agreed to by which fourteen lacs of rupees were paid as ransom, all the guns but six were surrendered, and six officers were given as hostages for the immediate retreat of the entire army from Afghanistan. Even this failed to secure the immunity so dearly bought. Hardly had the troops quitted their cantonments, when they were assailed by their implacable foes. On the third day, Akbar Khan appeared to deprecate the imputation of treachery, and to offer protection to the families of the officers if they were given up to him, declaring his inability to restrain the mountain clans through the midst of whom the retreating corps had to pass. Ten days later General Elphinstone, a few of his staff, and the ladies thus surrendered, alone survived. Four thousand troops, and eleven thousand camp followers, perished in the futile effort to reach Jellalabad; one officer only gained that fortress to tell the miserable tale. A disaster like this had never befallen the countrymen of Clive and Wellesley, and wherever the tidings were made known they spread mortification and dismay. Lord Auckland's term of office had already expired, and he was but too glad to leave to other hands the task of retrieving the results of his ill-fated policy.

Lord Ellenborough was sent out as Viceroy, with instructions from Sir Robert Peel to bring the Afghan business to an end as quickly as was compatible with honour; and, for the rest, to keep the peace towards all our neighbours. The first news that greeted him on his arrival was the repulse, with heavy loss, of General Wild's division in an attempt to relieve Jellalabad. This defeat was followed by the surrender of Ghuzni, and the repulse of General England while endeavouring to succour Nott at Candahar. Amid great difficulties Lord Ellenborough acted with energy and judgment. Fresh troops were concentrated under Pollock and Nott. Akbar Khan was defeated and driven from Cabul, which, having been re-occupied and dismantled, was finally abandoned. Shah Sujah had perished early in the struggle, and the claims of his dynasty were thought of no more. Dost Mahommed was set at liberty, and continued to reign over Afghanistan without molestation for more than twenty years. For all the blood and treasure wasted, and all the shame and grief endured, the Government of India had nothing to show but the gates of Somnath, which Lord Ellenborough boasted that our troops had reft from the tomb of Mahmud at Ghuzni, where they had stood for eight hundred years, as a trophy of Afghan spoil; but which it was afterwards discovered were not, as he supposed, the doors which belonged to the Guzerat shrine, but substitutes of modern workmanship made of the pine wood in which Cabul abounds.

CHAPTER XXIII.

THE AMÎRS OF SCINDE.

1843—1844.

" I have all along said, and ever shall say under all circumstances, and in all societies and places where I may hear it alluded to, that the case of the Amîrs is the most unprincipled and disgraceful that has ever stamped the annals of our Empire in India. No reasoning can, in my opinion, remove the foul stain it has left on our faith and honour; and as I know more than any other man living of previous events and measures connected with that devoted country, I feel that I have a full right to exercise my judgment and express my sentiments on the subject. I cannot use too strong language in expressing my disgust and sorrow."
—SIR HENRY POTTINGER.[1]

THE son of Runjît Singh feasted at Ferozepore the troops as they withdrew within the British confines; and amid mutual congratulations at peace restored, eternal vows were offered that nothing now should touch it further. Yet even then the sword was but half returned to the scabbard. A feeling intense and unrestrainable everywhere prevailed, that something must be done to efface the recollection of recent reverses, and to restore, at any risk and at any price, the prestige of irresistibility. Unavowedly preparations were already making for another conquest, to compensate for that which had been missed. Scinde and Cutch had been, in 1839, used without leave as places of rendezvous for the armies of Sir W. Cotton and Sir J. Keane. The military chiefs who, under the title of Amîrs, governed

[1] Letter to *Morning Chronicle*, 8th January 1844.

their secluded country in a rude and jealous way, had not disguised their reluctance to its being thus made a base of operations against the Afghans; not from any love for them, but from instinctive fear of consequences from us. From those who dwelt in the country previous to its invasion, we learn that the occupiers of the soil, and those who lived by handicraft and other kinds of peaceful industry, had no great cause to complain of their rulers. The Amîrs led their Beloochee followers in war, and administered justice among their people during peace, in a rough, irresponsible fashion, not very different from that which prevailed in most parts of Europe in feudal times. It was the absolutism of chieftainry, but it was absolutism tempered by a looking for sharp and swift vengeance for personal wrong. The spirit of equality, in the eye of the law, which has exercised so potent a spell over the minds of men wherever Islamism prevails, alleviated the weight of arbitrary power. It could not turn the edge of the sword when uplifted in passion, but it often sent it, half-drawn, back to the scabbard, and often snapped it in twain. The daughter of a Kazi of Khairpur, when visiting the Zenana, where she taught its inmates to read the Koran, attracted by her beauty the notice of Mohammed Khan Talpur, by whom she was seduced. Her father did not expostulate or plead, but entering the Amîr's hall, cut him down in the midst of his retainers: and instead of being sacrificed for what he had done, he was protected by the other Amîrs, who judged the provocation to have been intolerable, and the penalty no more than fair. In the administration of justice they "erred on the side of clemency." They were "most averse to the shedding of blood." Over the hill tribes they had no control: but their subjects generally were contented, and "their condition might have borne advantageous comparison with that of the people of many of our own provinces."[1] The Hindus stood in somewhat the same relation to the professors of the ruling faith as Dissenters in England and Catholics in Ireland did with reference to the Home Government fifty years ago. Plantations of sugarcane, and rich fields of grain, with innumerable waterwheels, attested the activity of labour and the sense of security. To the honour of the Amîrs it should also be remembered, that to political fugitives, whence soever they came, they fearlessly afforded the rights of asylum, which is more than can be said for certain Governments of the West, lofty in their pretensions to regard for the highest duties of civilisation.

Their mistrust of European intermeddling in their affairs had early been shown. A factory, planted at Tatta in 1775, had been abandoned in 1792, and an attempt to re-establish it in 1799 proved unsuccessful. In 1809, Lord Minto had with difficulty induced the Amîrs to make a general treaty of friendship, by which they engaged not to have any political or commercial dealings with the French. This was followed in 1820 by another, opening up, in a qualified manner, intercourse and trade. In 1831, when Sir Alexander Burnes explored the country on the right bank of the Indus, a Syud whom he encountered exclaimed, "Alas! Scinde is now gone, since the English have seen the river which is the high road to its conquest."[2] Next year Colonel Pottinger concluded a treaty of commerce, which gave English merchants access to ports and inland towns, but stipulated that they should not settle in the country; that having completed their business, they should depart; and that neither road nor river should be

---

[1] Mr E. B. Eastwick, M.P., Dry Leaves from Young Egypt, p. 69.
[2] The Conquest of Scinde, by General T. W. Napier, part i. p. 40.

used for military purposes at any time. There was also a supplementary convention regulating tolls and duties, which were to be abated if the British Government thought them too high. In 1838, the Amîrs admitted a permanent Resident at their capital. After the Tripartite treaty was signed, Lord Auckland volunteered to arbitrate between the Amîrs and Shah Sujah regarding arrears of tribute, said to be due from Scinde as an ancient province of Afghanistan. The Princes, who had never been consulted as to whether they would accept such arbitration, wholly denied the liability; and when pressed by Major Outram, produced a release in full of all demands, in consideration of a large sum paid in commutation to the ex-ruler of Cabul. Outram wrote to Calcutta, "How this is to be got over, I do not myself see." The reply was unhappily but too characteristic: "The Governor-General was of opinion that it is not incumbent on the British Government to enter into any formal investigation of the plea adduced by the Amîrs."[1]

One of the Chiefs was about the same time reported to be in correspondence with the Court of Teheran. This was denounced as duplicity and treachery; all the rest were held responsible for his acts whatever they might have been, and the Resident was instructed to demand the admission of a subsidiary force, and the engagement of the whole military strength of Scinde in the invasion of Afghanistan. When the armies had been collected at Shikarpore, a draft treaty was presented to the Amîrs, from which they learned with amazement that the Governor-General had directed a British force to be permanently kept in cantonments at Tatta, and that its numbers should from time to time be regulated by his pleasure. It was further provided that they should pay a fixed sum for its maintenance. One

[1] Thornton's History of British India, p. 589.

of the Amîrs drew forth the previous treaties, and asked significantly, "What is to become of all these? From the day that we made the first of them there has always been something new. We are anxious to live in friendship with you, but we cannot be thus continually persecuted. We have given your troops a road through our territories, and already you want them to remain." But in the face of overwhelming odds, they were unable to resist, and after many protests and objurgations, they succumbed. It was stipulated by them, that when no longer needed for the immediate objects then impending, the port of Kurrachee should be evacuated and restored. Outram consented, and forwarded the treaty, with this stipulation, and also with one that the camp of the subsidiary troops should be fixed at Tatta. Both stipulations were struck out, as it was not intended to give back Kurrachee to its owners, and it might be necessary to increase and remove the five thousand men. Though naturally mortified by these successive exactions, they took no hostile part against us in the season of disaster, and Outram reported that there was nothing dangerous to be apprehended from any ill-humour they might display. But that they talked and wrote as men civilised or uncivilised are wont to do under a sense of wanton humiliation and wrong, we may take for granted without proof, and their doing so was enough to draw down upon them the weight of viceregal indignation. "This," observes Sir William Napier, the historian of the subsequent war in Scinde, and eulogist of his brother's exploits there, " was the first open encroachment on the independence of the Amîrs. It is impossible to mistake or to deny the injustice. Was not this simply an impudent attempt to steal away the country? The proposal to mediate was not less immoral than subtle; the object was profit, covered with a sickening declamation about friendship, justice, and love of peace,—all of which recognised Scinde as an independent power."[1]

Lord Ellenborough, in October 1842, ordered Sir Charles Napier to take the command in Scinde, where he was to inquire and report whether any Amîr or Chief had evinced hostile designs against us during late events, which might have induced him to doubt the continuance of our power: "as it was the intention of the Governor-General to inflict upon the treachery of such ally or friend a punishment so signal, as should effectually deter others from similar conduct."[2] Outram's instructions peremptorily required him to lay before the General " the several acts whereby the Amîrs or Chiefs might have seemed to have departed from the terms or spirit of their engagements." He was, therefore, obliged to enumerate any acts, more or less frivolous and inconsequential, into which two or three of them had been provoked by the demeanour adopted towards them, but none of which, in his judgment as Political Resident, warranted a conviction or any actual punishment.[3] He added his testimony of the innocence of the majority, and reminded the Government at Calcutta of their collective fidelity to their engagements on the most critical occasions. He remonstrated, moreover, with Sir Charles Napier, who took a different view, and urged the expediency and duty of a policy of conciliation, and the wisdom of showing the chiefs a more excellent way of government than their own, by setting them a good administrative example. The grounds of complaint consisted chiefly of tolls levied, not upon the English, but upon the natives, which were said to have the construc-

[1] In despatch, Lieutenant Eastwick, 26th January 1839.
[2] Conquest of Scinde, by General W. F. Napier, p. 113.
[3] Outram's Conquest of Scinde, part I. p. 40.

tive effect of impeding trade. When the provisions of the treaty were pointed out to the Amîrs, which the levying of such duties was said to infringe, they exclaimed that they had not understood this to be the meaning of them, or they would not have signed them; and the Resident, when appealed to, owned that he took the same view. But Napier, now invested with supreme command, overruled him, and grimly warned the Chiefs that they must abate their pride or prepare for a day of wrath; unless, indeed, they would make a new treaty, and cede districts along the river in commutation of the three lacs they had bound themselves annually to pay. In any case, a certain province was to be expropriated to reward the fidelity of the Khan of Bhawalpore. Meer Roostum, the oldest and wealthiest of the confederate Princes, desired an interview with the General, but it was refused. He had been at all times an unswerving friend; and though far advanced in years, retained perfect intelligence and great personal influence. "Neither the venerable Prince, whose friendly advances were uncourteously repelled, nor any of his brethren, had ever injured the hair of a head of any British subject; but they had, in the hour of our greatest need, placed their country and its resources at our disposal."[1] They were now to have their reward. A new treaty was presented for signature on the 6th December, which, besides these terms, contained provisions that the Amîrs should supply fuel for all English steamers navigating the Indus, and in default, that it might be taken without leave from the neighbouring woods; that money should no longer be coined by the native Government, but by that of the Viceroy, and that the obverse should bear the effigy of England's Queen. If these provoking demands should fail in

[1] Outram's Conquest of Scinde, vol. i. p. 90.

their intended effect, the General wrote, he would forthwith take possession of the provinces enumerated; and, as if to shut out the remaining possibility that his letter might not be published by the Chiefs, a proclamation was issued announcing that no new tax or existing impost should be levied after the 1st day of the year, then at hand, in the territories which were to be alienated. Discussion was thus rendered a mockery, when every semblance of regard for the rights of negotiation was set at naught. Though disapproving of the policy pursued, Outram felt it to be his duty to dissuade the Amîrs from ineffectual resistance, and he actually induced several of them to affix their seals to the humiliating treaty. When doing so, they avowed that their wild and turbulent followers would not easily be reconciled to its conditions, and that it would be impossible to hold them within bounds if the English army continued to advance towards the capital. If half the tales were true of domineering violence and ruthless lust, set forth invidiously as illustrating the prevalent plight of the people under their Native Chiefs, some sect or section, minority or majority, of them would assuredly have shown gladness at their approaching deliverance, if not love for their deliverers. But no class or tribe affected to regard the invading army with joy, to put any faith in the sincerity of our professions, or to feel grateful for our interference.[1] The advance was not arrested, and the Beloochee soldiery, believing that Outram was the enemy who had insidiously beguiled their Chiefs into unworthy concessions, assailed the Residency, and compelled him to seek refuge in the General's camp. The victory of Meeanee, on the 17th February, virtually decided the fate of the campaign. In the murderous combat no quarter was given, and the havoc on both sides

[1] Eastwick, Dry Leaves, &c., p. 214.

was terrible. Many instances of heroism and of prowess are recorded, and at nightfall six thousand Beloochees lay dead upon the plain. "So heavy were the retreating masses, so doggedly did they move, without showing any sign of fear, that no attempt was made at pursuit."

The hopes of the General, deferred through long years of tantalisation, were fulfilled at last. At the head of gallant troops, pitted fairly against a numerous and well-appointed host, Napier had won a great battle. The hankering for fame which made him clutch with joy at Lord Hill's offer of command in India, and which breathed through all his communications with Lord Ellenborough, was satisfied. And yet he would fain have won the goal with less prodigal expenditure of blood. Before lying down to rest, he wandered forth through the midst of the dead, and involuntarily asked Heaven if he were responsible for all this misery and ruin piled in ghastly heaps around him. His conscience, as he tells us, answered no. The compunctious visitings of midnight passed away, and he slept so soundly that it was difficult to wake him. But who shall tell how often doubts may have recurred to the mind of one who plainly enough had had it in his power to avert the war, if not to mitigate its miseries? It is but justice to add, that when the struggle was over, no man could labour more diligently and devotedly to make civil reparation for the damage and detriment he had wrought. And if security and quiet could compensate a country for having its eyes put out, or if gravelled walks and carpetings of police could reconcile it to being forbidden never to get on horseback again, we might believe that Scinde was content at being nearly thrashed to death, and then bathed and fed and bade to slumber. How little the Beloochees thought of temporising with their assailants, is shown in two brief lines by the triumphant chronicler of the war. But three of the wounded were found still living after Meeanee.[1]

The next morning Napier sent to demand the surrender of the capital. When asked what terms he would give, he replied, "Only life." Not long afterwards six of the Amîrs rode into camp and surrendered. In the treasury of Hyderabad £400,000, besides a varied store of curious and precious booty, was found, the whole of which passed into the hands of the prize agents. In a few weeks Shere Mohammed had re-assembled an army of twenty-five thousand men; but he was attacked and defeated in a general engagement near the capital, and no further resistance of importance was made. Sheerpore and Omercote surrendered; Napier reported that the country was subdued; and its annexation having been formally proclaimed, he was rewarded with the appointment of Governor of Scinde.

Outram returned to England, where his narrative of events confirmed the impression on the minds of many that the invasion had been unprovoked, and that the annexation was unwarrantable. Thanks were voted by Parliament to the army, the Viceroy, and the General. Many who knew India well, and who appreciated keenly the difficulties of the situation, lamented Lord Ellenborough's policy, notwithstanding the success which apparently had crowned it. "Let it be remembered that all our treaties with the Amîrs were made after their warmest remonstrances against the intended honour of treating at all; that the mere circumstance of marching large bodies of troops through an independent country, contrary to the declared wish of its rulers, and cutting down timber, abolishing imposts, garrisoning forts, buying up grain and beasts of burthen therein, would

[1] The Conquest of Scinde, by General W. F. Napier, p. 390.

be in Europe considered a most flagrant breach of international law; and I think enough will be remembered to show that the Scinde case is one that justice (sweeten it however much you may) will find too nauseous to swallow."[1] Such is the verdict of one who was resident in the country during the years 1839 and 1841, and whose acquaintance with its language, and whose intimacy with its people and their customs, enabled him correctly to appreciate their character and conduct. Mountstuart Elphinstone, writing to Sir Charles Metcalfe, said, "Scinde was a sad scene of insolence and oppression. .Coming after Afghanistan, it put one in mind of a bully who had been kicked in the streets, and went home to beat his wife in revenge."[2]

Elated with his successes on the banks of the Indus, the Governor-General, ere the close of the year, sought fresh laurels in a less arduous and unaccustomed field. For five and twenty years the Mahratta princes of Gwalior had scrupulously observed the terms of the subsidiary alliance with the British Government; nor was there now any breach alleged of its obligations. The death of the Maharajah had necessitated the appointment of a Regent during the minority of his adoptive heir; but the internal administration of Mama Sahib was thwarted by a court faction, at whose nominal head was the Maharanee or widow of the deceased Prince. The unintelligible causes, details, and consequences of these disputes, are not worth recounting. The Resident endeavoured to interpose, but with little effect, and at length a battalion of native troops, when called on to overawe some disturbers of the peace, refused to obey orders; whereupon Colonel Spiers required that

[1] E. B. Eastwick, Dry Leaves from Young Egypt, p. 232.
[2] 14th March 1844. *Vide* Kaye's Lives of Indian Officers, p. 435.

the mutineers should be punished, and offered to lend the aid of the subsidiary troops for the purpose. The offer was declined by the Regent, on the very reasonable ground that such interference would inevitably awaken national suspicions and jealousies that had long slumbered. He undertook that discipline would be restored by other methods; but in this he unfortunately failed, through want of influence rather than inclination, and in the attempt he was compelled to withdraw from the seat of Government. One form of disorder followed another, and British troops, collected at Agra and elsewhere, were removed towards the disturbed districts. The Viceroy repaired to the headquarters of Sir Hugh Gough, then Commander-in-Chief, and from his camp issued a proclamation, which set forth that the tranquillity of neighbouring provinces was threatened by the turbulence and disorder in the State of Gwalior, and that he was about to interpose by arms for their suppression and the re-establishment of the authority of Scindia's Government. The Mahratta chiefs besought him to forbear, alleging that the disquietude would prove but temporary, and pointing to the uncontested fact that in no case had the evil overpassed their confines. The army notwithstanding received orders to advance, and when approaching Mahrajpore, the General unexpectedly found himself in presence of the main body of Scindia's forces. On the 29th December was fought a sanguinary battle, in which, though victorious, the loss on the side of the English was unusually severe. A new treaty dictated by the Viceroy was then imposed, in which the subsidiary force was increased, and certain districts ceded for its support. The minority of the Prince was to expire on his completing his eighteenth year, and in the interim the affairs of the State were to be conducted by a

Council of Regency, who not only in all affairs of moment, but generally, were to act upon the advice of the English Resident, who should be instructed from time to time by the Governor-General. The Maharanee was to be consoled for the extinction of her pretensions to any influence over the administration, by an annual allowance of three lacs. It is almost superfluous to note that for a period of ten years the whole executive authority was by these stipulations transferred from Gwalior to Calcutta. It was a tentative step towards annexation, and but for events then unforeseen, it might have been followed up to completion.

Lord Ellenborough's policy was so much disapproved by the Directors, that they resolved he should be recalled. The act was warmly disapproved by the Duke of Wellington, and the Board appeased his dissatisfaction by immediately proceeding to nominate Lord Hardinge Governor-General.

CHAPTER XXIV.

PUNJAB AND PEGU.

1845—1852.

"Many believe that a really Christian empire would obtain world-wide sovereignty by the voluntary and eager resort of all nations under the shadow of its wings. Whether by such means as these Great Britain shall accomplish the dominion of the East, remains to be seen. We have not, I fear, made an auspicious beginning. But if we are to gain no more by virtue, let us not lose what we have by injustice. Let us hasten to wipe out the awful rebuke passed by the natives on their Christian conquerors, as they were led away into captivity,—'Now, we perceive that there is no hope for us of judgment or justice until God Almighty shall sit in the last great Adawlut.'"

—Lord Shaftesbury.[1]

WHEN Lord Hardinge reached India the Sikhs were in commotion. The Maharajah had fallen by the hand of an assassin; and his brother, but ten years old, had been recognised as the lawful heir of Runjît Singh. As a child, he was full of excellent promise; and the Sirdars, though divided by internecine enmities, agreed to rally in defence of his endangered throne; for, reckless and illiterate though they were, they could not be unconscious of the imminency of danger. The spectacle of Afghanistan wantonly overrun, and only emancipated by the stern pertinacity of resistance on the part of its people, and the yet more recent spectacle of Scinde brow-beaten, overborne, and at length reduced to unqualified vassalage, warned them of

[1] Speech of Lord Ashley. Debate in the House of Commons on the Amîrs of Scinde, February 8, 1844.

what they had to expect so soon as their turn should come. How could the most trusting, credulous, or peaceful amongst them believe that they were safe? Already their subjugation had been publicly discussed in the British Parliament as a question only of time. Within two years from the annexation of Scinde, it had been openly foretold that the Country of the Five Rivers would be ours. The forecast had not been uttered by official lips, indeed, for such candour would have been without precedent; and Sir Robert Peel, above all men, trod faithfully in the way of Parliamentary usage. But the assertion made by Mr Roebuck[1] was not repudiated; and whatever may have been the confidential counsel given by his colleagues to Sir Henry Hardinge, it would be vain to pretend that his approval, as a soldier of experience and repute, for the post of Governor-General, was likely to tranquillise the misgivings of the Sikhs. The new Viceroy would gladly have deferred the apprehended collision, and those who knew him well will probably contend, with excellent reason, that he was of a nature too just and generous to incur the terrible responsibilities of a sanguinary conflict through any motive of military ambition or personal vainglory. Like the great master of strategy he had served so long, he had seen too much of the realities of war to wish to see any more of them. Had there been any man among the Sikhs of ascendant intellect and capacity for great affairs, he might have led them to restrain their fears, consolidate their resources, and wait for events; in which case, it is by no means clear that they would have been early molested or easily reduced. But it was not to be so; and the first duty of Sir H. Hardinge was to organise prepara-

[1] Debate on Lord Ashley's motion for liberation of the Amîrs of Scinde, February 1844.

tions to resist an irruption of the fierce and well-armed Khalsa army. The Ranee and her Minister Lall Singh could with difficulty control these restless bands, daily growing more distrustful, not without reason. Letters from the other side of the Sutlej described, day after day, the gathering of additional troops, and the strengthening of garrisons.[1] It was said that the next move in the game of aggression would be to sweep the Rajah of Bhawalpore and other weak powers off the board. A province of partitioned Scinde had been given him as the price of his aid; but the uninterrupted course of Anglo-Indian annals showed that what Saib Company had given, Saib Company could take away. The "devil's brother" also was still in Scinde. Had he not been thanked by Parliament for his doings there? and was he not believed to have said that his troops were ready for more work? All which did not, and could not justify indeed what followed, though it too clearly explains and accounts for it. Eighty thousand fighting men, attended by a multitude of camp followers, assembled at the tomb of Runjît Singh, where, according to the custom of their race, passages suitable to the occasion were read by the officiating Gooro or priest; after which, a sacrament of bread and wine, according to their rites, was publicly administered. Each chief, as he passed, touched the hem of the funeral canopy of the old Lion of Lahore, and swore aloud fidelity in life and death to the youthful Maharajah.[2] On the 4th December 1845 they crossed the Sutlej, and we were at war. Two days later Sir Henry Hardinge issued a proclamation calling on the protected states to assist him. An army of 32,000 men, comprising several European regiments, were already assembled at Meerut; and from

---

[1] Lord Dalhousie's Administration, by Edwin Arnold, p. 43.
[2] *Ibid.*, vol. i. p. 44.

other quarters contingents were ready to advance. In four general actions the Khalsa soldiery sustained their reputation for intrepid valour, and were not finally discomfited at Sobraon until they had inflicted fearful losses on their antagonists. Golab Singh, who throughout the campaign had avoided taking active part with his countrymen, whose blind impetuosity he disapproved, met Sir Hugh Gough at Kussoor, and, in the character of an envoy, offered terms of peace.

A treaty was made, which added to the Company's territory the Jullindhur Doab, a fine tract of country situated between the rivers Beas and Sutlej, which, together with the Cis-Sutlej States, previously under our protection, were now formally annexed. A war fine of a million and a half sterling was exacted, but the Lahore treasury being nearly empty, Cashmere was purchased back for two-thirds of this sum by Golab Singh. It was also stipulated that a British Resident should be accredited to the Court of Lahore, and that a force of 10,000 of the Company's troops should be maintained beyond the Sutlej, ostensibly to preserve order in the interest of the young Maharajah, Dhuleep Singh. By the Articles agreed on in a supplementary convention, the British Government acknowledged the severalty, and guaranteed the integrity, of the Sikh State, and undertook the political guardianship of the Maharajah during his minority. The engagement was to cease "and terminate on his Highness attaining the full age of sixteen years, or on the 4th September 1854." Sir H. Hardinge wished the stipulation respecting the trusteeship thus assumed, regarding the existing rights and future interests of the Prince, to be made as public as possible; for he was a soldier and a statesman, with a heart full of humanity, and an understanding true to honour. "It was determined," he wrote, "in communication with the Sirdars, that his Highness should come to my camp on this side of the Beas, and I proposed afterwards, when the agreement would be formally ratified, to pay his Highness a friendly return visit at Lahore."[1] In the proclamation subsequently issued, the Governor-General said that he felt "the interest of a father in the education and guardianship of the young Prince," and that "he had at heart the peace and security of the country, the firm establishment of the State, and the honour of the Maharajah and his Ministers."[2] During the period of Protectorate thus defined, the Queen's representative in India was to be empowered to occupy such outposts, and to keep such a garrison in the capital as he might deem necessary for securing the objects of the exceptional trust thus assumed. The Resident was, for the time, to be head of the Administration, and to preside over a Council of Regency, to whom was to be delegated all domestic and local control. This arrangement gave the British Minister at Lahore all the authority that could be desired. What Sir H. Hardinge meant by the conditions he made, we know from his own pen. Instructing the Resident how to act, he admonished him that it would in all cases be "politic to carry the native council with him." He might change them and appoint others, as they were "entirely under his control and guidance;" and in military affairs his power was as unlimited.[3] Sir H. Hardinge had sat in Cabinet where every Minister but one is removable at the pleasure of that one; but he remembered that such association, while it recognises pre-eminent responsibility in the head of the executive, neither involves or implies a mute or base subserviency on the part of his consultative fellows. And his own experience under the Duke of Wellington and Sir Robert Peel taught him, that this combination of the elements of ministerial rule is

[1] Punjab Papers, 1849.   [2] *Ibid.,* p. 53.   [3] *Ibid.,* p. 18.

not only not unworthy or unwise, but is indeed one of the best imaginable for securing the benefits of stable and efficient government. After some months' trial the experiment, far from proving chimerical, seemed likely to succeed. The "Durbar gave the Resident as much support as he could reasonably expect. There had been a quiet struggle for mastery; but though he was polite to all, he never allowed anything wrong to pass unnoticed, and the members of Council were gradually falling into the proper train."[1] It was, in short, a fair and honest attempt to adjust the claims of suzerainty with those of local rule, not indeed theoretically perfect; not perhaps capable, within less compass than that of a dissertation, of being analysed completely, as analysis is employed by political metaphysicians; but something much better—a practical expedient, which everybody who wanted to understand it could understand, and by means of which it would have been possible to preserve the self-respect, and to cultivate the confidence of a subordinated State with all the requisite guarantees of security for the peace and strength of empire. Unhappily there were those on both sides who would not be satisfied with this; and between them they succeeded ere long in overturning it, thereby furnishing despotism with another pretence for saying that nothing in India is possible, but the unquestioned sway of central whim. The undistorted facts speak otherwise. Constitutionalism in every form is a lesson that has never yet been learned without many blunderings and breakings down; nevertheless, it is better worth learning than most other lessons of life.

Ranee Chunda, the widow of Runjît Singh, belonged to a class of which India has furnished some notable examples, endowed with patriotism and an indomitable will, superior to

[1] Letter to the Governor-General, August 1847.

the reverses of fortune. The young Maharajah showed indications of teaching hostile to English domination, and it was easy to divine the source. Soon after, the disclosure of an alleged scheme to bring about a revolution was thought to furnish sufficient pretence for the separation of mother and son, and the detention of the Ranee in the fortress of Shikapoor. But though stripped of political power and guarded with the utmost caution, her spirit was not subdued, and, like the captive of Fotheringay, she became the centre of a thousand rash cabals and intrigues for her deliverance. Notwithstanding these petty rufflings of the stream, it seemed to flow on steadily and peacefully. On the eve of quitting India, Lord Hardinge complacently boasted of the "quiet" which prevailed in the Punjab, and he could write this with the more confidence, because he had permanently posted 50,000 men and 60 guns in strategic positions in the valley of the Sutlej, while the Sikh army, which four years previously had numbered 85,000 men and 350 guns, within two days' march of the British frontier, was reduced to 24,000 men and 50 guns, scattered in remote detachments.

Lord Dalhousie was received in Calcutta with congratulations by all classes. "He arrives at a time," said one journal, "when the last obstacle to the complete and final pacification of India has been removed, when the only remaining army which could create alarm has been dissolved, and when the peace of the country rests on the firmest and most permanent basis. The chiefs whose ambition or hostility have been the source of disquietude to his predecessors have one and all been disarmed. Not a shot is fired from the Indus to Cape Comorin against our will."[1] In the political atmosphere there was a great calm; but it was not the calmness of content—it was the lull before the

[1] *Friend of India*, January 20, 1848.

storm, the silent accumulation of elements for a violent effort to break the thrall of subjection in which the defeat of Sobraon had bound the high-spirited Sikhs. Ten thousand bayonets at Lahore, and thrice ten thousand within call, might indeed pinion native resentment against Feringhee domination, and the insults of its Moslem servants to Hindu caste and creed; but they could not extinguish it. Government was still exercised in the name of the young Maharajah, and the Sikh Council of Regency were the visible exponents of authority to native eyes. Foreign power was at least disguised under the mask of native forms, and the independence of native chieftains was not openly threatened. Pecuniary exactions, which, as we have seen, excited so much of the misfortunes of Bengal in the Company's earlier days, and the avowed intention to denude of his title and authority a popular chief, fanned the smouldering resentment of the nation into a flame of open resistance. Moolraj, the governor of the city and province of Mooltan, was indebted to the Court of Lahore in eighteen lacs of rupees, the reduced amount of a nuzzur he had agreed to pay on his confirmation in the Nizamut in 1844. Payment was demanded by the British Resident at Lahore, acting on behalf of the Council, and the amount was paid, a further engagement being extorted from Moolraj for a yearly payment of nineteen lacs. This sum he afterwards professed himself to be unable to pay; and failing to obtain any modification of the demand, and unwilling to resist the authority of the Durbar, he offered to resign if a suitable jaghire were given him for his future maintenance, and he were given a receipt in full for all past claims. But "the Resident was firm almost to harshness." Moolraj might resign if he liked, but no quittance or pension would be given him. On the contrary, ten years' accounts were demanded. "How can I produce my father's papers?" said the brow-beaten chief. "The ants have eaten them; or if the ants have left any, they are useless for your purpose." Then, conscious that he was in the power of those who were bent on his downfall, he added, "I am in your hands." This was construed into a resignation of office, and notice was quickly given him that he was superseded in command.

On the 14th April 1848, Sirdar Khan Singh, the new Governor, accompanied by Mr Vans Agnew and Lieutenant Anderson, in the character of Political Agent, arrived at Mooltan, and had an interview with the deposed Dewan outside the fortress. On the 19th, formal possession of the place was given, the keys were handed over to Khan Singh, and fresh sentries were posted. As the party, Moolraj among them, were returning to their encampment without the walls, the first signs of a Sikh outbreak betrayed themselves, in an attack on the English officers, who, severely wounded, barely contrived to escape to their quarters. A message from Vans Agnew to the native chiefs in Mooltan, to obey the mandate of the Maharajah, and accept the new ruler, only brought the reply that "Hindu and Sikh, they were all sworn on the Grunth and Koran to obey Moolraj as their leader, and to fight out his battle." Tidings of the outbreak were despatched to Lahore, as well as to other stations, and the two Englishmen, with Khan Singh, who remained faithful to his trust, prepared to defend themselves till aid should arrive. But the contagion of disaffection spread to their little escort of five hundred men, and before evening they were left with only their servants and half-a-dozen soldiers to repel the assault, which was not long delayed. The mob, fired with fanatical zeal, broke into the apartment where the wounded Englishmen lay, and despatching both, carried their heads to the palace in Mooltan.

There is not a tittle of evidence to connect Moolraj with the first assault, or the subsequent murder. On the contrary, the written testimony of the insurgent chieftains after the sad event, distinctly exculpates him from a share in the conspiracy which had been organised among the soldiery and priesthood. His dispossession enraged them, and the arrival of a successor, accompanied by, and known to be the subservient nominee of, the hated Feringhee, drove them to frenzy. The outbreak at Mooltan aroused further suspicion at Lahore. The imprisoned Ranee and almost every Sirdar of the Court, Moolraj himself excepted, were said to be engaged in a wide-spread conspiracy. He indeed drifted into a position which he would not willingly have chosen. It was eminently unsafe to provoke native patriotism by any formal proceedings against the Queen-mother; she was therefore suddenly and secretly spirited away to the less dangerous precincts of Benares; but an example was made of lesser delinquents, some of whom were executed as rebels at the gate of Lahore.

In the few hours intervening between the assault on the two Englishmen and their barbarous murder, they had found means to despatch information to the Resident at the capital, as well as to the detachment at Futteh Khan on the Indus. The officer in command there, Lieutenant Edwardes (afterwards Colonel Sir Herbert Edwardes), at once marched to the relief of his distressed countrymen, though too late to save them. Compelled by the superior numbers of the enemy to maintain a defensive warfare for some time, he held the Mooltan army at bay, and when joined by the friendly forces of the Nawab of Bhawalpore, he defeated Moolraj at Kineyru, and again at

Suddoosain a month after, forcing him to retire within the walls of Mooltan. The brilliant genius and energy of this young officer, indeed, saved the appearance of British influence in the Punjab. The Resident had sent earnest demands for aid to the Governor-General at the outbreak of the revolt. He deemed it dangerous to leave the British community at Lahore at native mercy by sending the European troops at his disposal to Mooltan, and to send Sikh soldiers for that purpose might only be to swell the ranks of the enemy. Assistance from Bengal was therefore urgently requested. If this insult were not punished, and speedily, we might expect the Afghans to establish themselves on the Indus; the Cis-Sutlej tribes would not remain quiet; and thousands of Sikhs would join Moolraj in the Manjha, giving him out as the restorer of Khalsa rule prophesied by their priests. Lord Gough, however, deemed it impossible to undertake operations at that season of the year, and the Governor-General coinciding with his military coadjutor, refused to consider events in the Punjab as immediately calling for the movement of an army to the north-west.

Executions, banishments, and the open manifestation of suspicion, only inflamed the passions of the discontented chiefs and soldiers, who saw in the disregard of treaties, engagements, and native forms, an intention to subvert the Sikh dynasty and dominion. The deportation of the Maharanee indeed decided the wavering opinions of some of the most powerful chiefs and their followers. "Greater indignation was felt than shown when the Maharanee was taken from her people and her child,"[1] and the manifesto of one of the malcontent chiefs " is a frank and straightforward state paper, as such things go." "It is known," wrote

[1] Arnold's Dalhousie's Administration.

Shere Singh in this document, "to all good Sikhs, in fact, to all the world at large, with what oppression, tyranny, and undue violence the Feringhees have treated the widow of the great Maharajah Runjît Singh, and what cruelty they have shown towards the people of this country. In the first place, they have broken the treaty, by imprisoning and sending away to Hindustan the Maharanee, the mother of her people. Secondly, the race of Sikhs have suffered so much from their tyranny, that our very religion has been taken away from us. Thirdly, the kingdom has lost its former repute." After the arbitrary deed was done, the Resident himself acknowledged its mischievous effects on the native mind in a despatch to Calcutta, wherein is reported the disturbance it caused among the Khalsa soldiery at Rajah Singh's camp, and their declaration that, the Maharanee being gone, and the young Maharajah in our hands, they had no longer an inducement to oppose Moolraj, and would seize their officers and go over to him. Dost Mahommed, the friendly ruler of Cabul, also warned the British Resident, Captain Abbott, that the Sikhs were "daily becoming more and more discontented," and he cited the treatment of the Maharanee as one of the chief causes of that discontent. The Sikhs were strongly possessed with the love of home and country; and banishment was regarded as a worse punishment for political offences than even death. "Such treatment," wrote the sovereign of Cabul, "is considered objectionable by all creeds, and both high and low prefer death." This incident affords another illustration of that want of equity in matters of State dealing with native powers, which is so often repeated in the pages of Indian history. It is not to be doubted or denied, that the widow of Runjît Singh was a steady opponent of British power in the Punjab; but, carefully guarded from collusion with more active plotters, her influence would have died out. "There was not a man who would shoulder a musket at her bidding," wrote one who had the best opportunities of gauging native inclinations at the time.[1] "Her memory survived, for she was not a woman to be forgotten," and the unjudicial and injudicious act of the Resident stamped that memory with the seal of martyrdom in the national cause. Though there was matter for grave suspicion, the Resident himself acknowledged that "legal proofs of the delinquency of the Maharanee would not, perhaps, be obtainable;" but he considered it was "not a time for us to hesitate about doing what might appear necessary to punish State offenders, and to vindicate the honour and position of the British Government."[2] That position, be it remarked, was, by the treaties of Kussoor and Byrowal, one of joint trusteeship with the native Sirdars. They had no right or title to act in any other capacity—Dhuleep Singh being the acknowledged sovereign prince, awaiting his majority. But the members of the Council of Regency affixed their names to the decree of banishment; one of whom was a known personal enemy of the Princess, the other two being separated from her by differences of creed. A show of numerical support was sought by the signature of a councillor's brother, but the native draughtsman of the document destroyed this flimsy disguise when he wrote the preamble that it was issued "according to the advice of Sir Frederick Currie, and Fakir Nur-ud-din," the first being the Resident himself, and the last a Mohammedan confidant. That there would have been considerable difficulty in obtaining "legal proofs" for con-

[1] Lieutenant Edwardes, A Year on the Punjab Frontier.
[2] Punjab Papers, 1849.

demning the Maharanee in a proper investigation, which she herself demanded, is clear from the fact that when, at the Resident's order, her papers and effects were seized, nothing of a compromising nature was found among them. True to the habit of confiscating the property of those whom they first forced to quarrel and then to fight, the invaders of the Punjab stripped the deposed Princess of all her jewels and valuables and her allowance, which had been fixed by the treaty of Byrowal at £15,000 a year, and on her imprisonment in Shikapoor reduced to £4800, was now cut down to £1200.

The feelings of resentment thus engendered were further intensified by fresh arbitrary acts on the part of the British political agents. The young Maharajah, Dhuleep Singh, was betrothed to the daughter of Sirdar Chuttur Singh, Governor of Hazara, and sister of Rajah Shere Singh, the commander of the Sikh royal army; and it was agreed between the two chiefs that the acquiescence or objection of the Prince's guardians should be regarded as a test of their intentions with regard to the future. Formal application was accordingly made to the Resident at Lahore to fix a date for the marriage ceremony. Major Edwardes, who united keen diplomatic instinct with military skill, supported the application by a letter, in which he reported the tenor of a conversation with Shere Singh on the subject; and added, " there can be no question that an opinion has gone very prevalently abroad, that the British meditate declaring the Punjab forfeited by the recent troubles and misconduct of the troops. It would, I think, be a wise and timely measure to give such public assurance of British good faith and intention to adhere to the treaty as would be involved in authoritative preparations for providing the young Maharajah with a queen. It would, no doubt, settle men's minds greatly." The answer of Sir F. Currie was just of the indefinite nature calculated to increase and not allay suspicion. He promised to consult the members of the Durbar, professed the desire of the British Government "to promote the honour and happiness of the Maharajah, the bride, and her family;" but he added this qualification, "I do not see how the proceeding with the ceremonies for the Maharajah's nuptials can be considered as indicative of any line of policy which the Government may consider it right to pursue now, or at any future time, in respect to the administration of the Punjab." The mischievous effects of this subtle rejoinder to a straightforward request were increased by the conduct of the Resident in the province of Hazara. Captain Abbott had the unfortunate distinction of disagreeing with every native of note with whom he came in contact, yet at this critical juncture he was suffered to remain at his post. Long before the events under consideration, Sir Henry Lawrence had written of him, that he was "too apt to take gloomy views of things," and that he had "unwittingly done Dewan Jowla Sahaee injustice," the chief referred to being, said the Resident, "a respectable, as he is assuredly an able man." On the outbreak at Mooltan he imagined that Chuttur Singh and other nobles were leagued with Moolraj for the extirpation of the English, and he became so offensive in his conduct towards them as to call forth remonstrances from his superior officer at Lahore. "The palpable distrust with which Captain Abbott regards Sirdar Chuttur Singh seems not unnaturally to have estranged that chief from him. He looks upon Chuttur Sing as a sort of incarnation of treason; and the Sirdar has been led to believe that Captain Abbott is bent on the annihilation of himself and the Khalsa army on the first opportunity." The suspected chief was old and infirm, and his connection with the royal family gave him a position in itself some guarantee for his being circumspect, if not cordial. Another British official had called him "a harmless old fool." Captain Abbott, however, refused all personal communication with him, and took up his residence at thirty-five miles' distance. A portion of the Churrunjeet regiment of horse having mutinied, the Resident charged their general, Chundah Singh, with wholesale conspiracy, and drew forth the rebuke from Sir F. Currie that such charges were "without foundation;" and that the Sikh commander "had closely and scrupulously obeyed his orders;" in a despatch to the Governor-General he also complains of the "ready disposition of Captain Abbott to believe in conspiracies, treasons, and plots; suspicion of everybody far and near, even of his own servants, and a conviction of the infallibility of his own conclusions, which was not shaken by finding, time after time, that they were not verified."[1] A small portion of the Pukli brigade of troops, stationed near the residence of Chuttur Singh, avowed an intention of joining the malcontents at Mooltan; but they were few in number, were wholly unsupported by their officers, who strove to quell the mutiny, and there was nothing to substantiate the idea that the Sirdar Governor approved or encouraged the movement. Captain Abbott, however, chose to regard it as a formal participation in the revolt at Mooltan, and appealing to fanatical instincts of men of a different race and creed, he called out the Mohammedan militia of the district in great numbers, surrounded the town of Horripore, where Chuttur Singh resided, and made such hostile demonstrations as forced that chief to dispose his troops, in order to repel the attack which

[1] Punjab Papers, p. 285.

seemed imminent. The commandant of artillery under the Sirdar,—an American,—when ordered to move his battery with the rest of the troops, refused to do so without permission of Captain Abbott. A second command, with an explanation that "Captain Abbott could not know that the guns were in peril of seizure by the armed population," failed to move the disobedient officer. Two companies of Sikh infantry were sent to enforce the Sirdar's commands; but Canora loaded his guns with grape in double charges, and when the native havildars or sergeants refused to fire, he cut one of them down, and applied the match himself. The gun missed fire, and Canora was shot down by the advancing files, not before he had pistolled two Sikh officers. That Canora met the due punishment of insubordination, there can be no doubt in the minds of impartial judges; yet Captain Abbott wrote a highly-coloured account, charging Chuttur Singh with "an atrocious deed," in the "determined" and "cold-blooded murder" of Colonel Canora. The Sirdar also sent a manly and consistent report of the transaction, and the unprejudiced mind of our representative at Lahore accurately estimated the value of each. Sharp, but just, was the remonstrance and reprimand which he addressed to his impetuous subordinate. He refuted the gratuitous assertion that Canora was basely murdered, affirming that he justly fell a victim to circumstances arising out of his disobedience of the lawful commands of his superior officer, the Sirdar Chuttur Singh. He deplored the injudicious excitement of civil war in Hazara. "I have given you no authority," he wrote, "to raise levies, and organise paid bands of soldiers, to meet an emergency of which I have always been sceptical. I cannot approve of your having abstained from communication with the Sirdar on the state of his administration, for the purpose of making his silence or otherwise on the subject a test whereby his guilt or innocence was to be determined by you. You had already withdrawn your office from the seat of Government, and had ceased all personal communication with him, and had told his Vakeel that you had no confidence in his master. It is not to be wondered at that, under the circumstances, a weak, proud chief should feel offended, and become sullen."[1] Nor is this a solitary illustration of the demeanour of subordinate officials. The correspondence of the time teems with proofs that the unjustifiable misgivings and domineering spirit of our agents goaded the Sikh chieftains at last into an open breach. In the words of Sir F. Currie, "the initiative was clearly taken by Captain Abbott," and that initiative was not openly repudiated at headquarters, but, on the contrary, being threatened with sequestration of estate and title, Chuttur Singh at last joined the ranks of his outraged and insulted countrymen. His son, Shere Singh, had striven by every means in his power to prove his own loyalty, and to preserve that of his troops. He showed his father's letters to Major Edwardes in the camp at Mooltan, discussed the matter, says the latter, "with great good sense," and, defending his father's resistance to Captain Abbott as perfectly natural and excusable, said, "No man will allow himself to be killed without a struggle." The same officer adds his testimony, "that up to the end of August, Rajah Shere Singh was still faithful, and determined to go any lengths to check disloyalty in his men." Early in September, however, he received letters from his father couched in terms of despair at the treatment to which he was subjected; and he wrote to his brother, Golab Singh, at Lahore, on the 14th, that he "resolved yesterday to join

[1] Punjab Papers, 1849, p. 316.

the Singh Saib (his father), and devote himself to the cause of their religion."

That which at first was nothing but an *emeute* of dissatisfied soldiery, was thus by perverse policy developed into a formidable outbreak. As late as July it had been recorded that, "the Sirdars were heart and soul on our side," and evidence is overwhelming as to their energy and sincerity in resisting the spread of military revolt. On the 18th August, Major Edwardes was reinforced by a contingent of British troops under General Whish, and the siege of Mooltan was commenced. The defection of Shere Singh in September left the besieging force too weak for safety, and the siege was accordingly raised on the 15th. The Rajah met with scant welcome in Mooltan. His previous fidelity to the Feringhees caused him to be regarded with distrust and suspicion, which a fictitious correspondence from the English camp helped to increase; and disgusted with the doubts cast on him, he left Moolraj to join the army of his father, Chuttur Singh. Reinforcements arrived from Bombay in December, and the siege of Mooltan was renewed on the 26th. The city was stormed and captured on the 2d January 1849, and siege operations were commenced against the fort, whither Moolraj had retired. After a gallant resistance he surrendered unconditionally on the 22d; and begged for instant execution by his conquerors rather than exile from his country or banishment over the Dark Sea. Partial engagements at Ramnuggur and Soodalapore, in which the British forces had suffered severely, showed that valour and skill were not alone on their side. Shere Singh's army now amounted to 30,000 men and 60 guns; Chuttur Singh was master of Peshawar, Attock, and other places in the north, and was moving to join his son; and Lord Gough was requested to "strike a blow at the enemy with the least possible delay." A drawn battle, which came very near becoming for us a defeat and rout, was fought at Chillianwalla on the 13th January. The Sikh commander eluding the vigilance of his foes, drew off his army unmolested, and effected a junction with his father's troops at Goojerat. Their united forces, 40,000 in number, occupied there a strong position, protected by 60 guns; but Lord Gough, strengthened by the contingent under General Whish, just relieved from Mooltan, gave battle on the 21st February with 25,000 men, and nearly 100 guns. From dawn to noon a terrible artillery duel went on; the superior numbers and heavier metal of the British guns gradually silencing and beating back those of the Sikh army; the infantry carried the Sikh positions at the point of the bayonet, and cavalry charges, in which Lord Gough himself took part, completed the discomfiture and rout of the Khalsa troops. Goojerat retrieved the disaster of Chillianwalla, and practically ended the second war. Flying columns were sent in pursuit of the broken squadrons, and especially to capture or extirpate a body of Afghan horse under Dost Mahommed, which had left the battle-field intact, but which was driven ignominiously through the Khyber Pass. On the 14th March, at Rawul Pindee, Lord Gough received the submission of the Rajahs Chuttur Singh and Shere Singh, who presented "nuzzurs" of fealty; thirty-five lesser chiefs laid down their swords, and their followers, passing through lines of British infantry, piled their arms and armour at the feet of the victors.

The submission of the army was speedily followed by the despatch of instructions to the Resident at Lahore, to inform the Council of Regency. It was Lord Dalhousie's first opportunity to grasp at territory, and he hastened to enjoy it by annexing the Punjab to the Queen's dominions. A brigade was sent to overawe any remonstrance or resistance that might be shown to the imperious edict, and Mr Elliot, the Governor-General's secretary, was charged to represent him at the Durbar. The time had arrived, it was said, when it was necessary to acquaint the Lahore Government with the determination formed regarding the future administration of the Punjab. If the Durbar acquiesced in that determination, the Resident was authorised to grant the terms contained in an enclosed paper, that on their relinquishing at once and for ever, on behalf of the Maharajah, the title and sovereignty of the Punjab, he and they should be secured in the enjoyment of an adequate state and income. In case of their refusal, the British Government would take its own course, and they would receive no such consideration. Six of the eight Sirdars of the Council had remained faithful to the treaty and to their trust all through the late outbreak. They well knew that it had been at first but an isolated effort of revenge on the part of a disbanded and disaffected soldiery, which prompt action in its earlier stages might have quelled; but which the supineness, suspicion, and wanton insolence of the British agents had spread through the Khalsa army, and which had entangled, much against their better judgment, two and only two of the higher nobles of the country. No wonder they told the Governor-General's envoy that they were unconvinced of the right and justice of the threatened proceeding, while they condemned the rashness of the war which had lent an excuse for it. Urgently and feelingly they pleaded against the expatriation of the Maharajah and the royal court. "When they have quitted the palace and its restraints," said the Dewan Deena Nath, "they will lead licentious lives, and bring scandal on the memory of Runjît Singh." It was answered that he would be sent to the Deccan, to which the Rajah Tej Singh replied, "He must not go there, God knows whether the people there are Hindus or Mohammedans. Let him go to Benares." It was finally promised that he should not be sent far from the sacred Ganges; and convinced that prayer and remonstrance were now alike useless, they reluctantly put their hands to the deed of abdication. No time was lost in publicly opening the new chapter in Indian history. On the following day (29th March 1849) the last Durbar was held in the palace of Lahore. Sir Henry Lawrence, who had reassumed the duties of Resident, and Mr Elliot, attended by a strong body of cavalry, were met at the gate of the citadel, and escorted by the young Maharajah and his suite to the hall of audience. There, with a callous disregard to the feelings of the Deena Dewan Nath, who made another effort to mitigate the harshness of the treatment of his sovereign, citing the treatment of France after the fall of Napoleon as a precedent for restoring the Punjab to native rule, the boy Prince was required to affix his initials to the conditions of abdication, and the ceremony was over. As the envoy left the palace the Union Jack was hoisted on the fort, and the thunder salute of artillery announced that the country of the Five Rivers had passed under British rule. Natives assembled in large numbers, and the farce of explaining the object of the meeting was gone through. A narrative of Sikh and British relations since the death of Runjît Singh from the British point of view was recited in English, Persian, and Hindustani. Its ingenious sophistries evoked no sign of anger or comment from the stupefied and overawed Sikhs.

The fruit of illegitimate conquest thus forced to ripening

was plucked without delay. On the 30th March a proclamation, dated from Ferozepore, was circulated throughout Anglo-India declaring the Punjab to be thenceforward a portion of the empire; and on the 5th April the Governor-General ratified the conditions of abdication which secured to Maharajah Dhuleep Singh a yearly allowance of five lacs, and the courtesies due to a deposed sovereign. Acquisition did not stop, indeed, at title and territory. It was stipulated that the splendid jewel known as the "Koh-i-noor," or Mountain of Light, the central gem in the state turbans of the Khalsa rulers, should be surrendered to the Queen of Great Britain, as a token of submission. The history of this wonderful diamond is remarkable and romantic. First heard of in the possession of Karna, King of Auga, invasion and conquest made it successively the property of Mohammedans, Hindus, Afghans, and Sikhs. Poison, bullet, or steel, captivity or defeat, had been the fate of most of its wearers, and native superstition ascribed to it baneful influences which its associations went far to justify.

The story of this transaction, when limited to the mere outlines of facts, or even when ingeniously coloured to give it a plausible excuse, must raise a doubt in the minds of reflective readers. But it is only after the perusal of official documents, despatches, and private letters, the minutiæ of intelligence and testimony which form the connecting links between prominent incidents of history, that we are able accurately to understand the true nature of such incidents, and to judge the character and policy of the individuals who figured in them. The full story of the Punjab annexation is only to be gathered from such sources. Measured by any known rule of public law, the deposition of Dhuleep Singh and the annexation of his country must be held to be unjustifiable. As a minor he was not personally accountable for political actions. At the head of the Regency sat the British Resident, who not for an hour during the insurrection was interrupted in the discharge of his duty. No tumult took place in the capital, and no proof, however faint, was even trumped up of any general outbreak among the people at large. The Ranee was a thousand miles off in captivity at Benares, and Golab Singh, the most powerful and opulent of the Sikhs, was confessedly unshaken in his devotion. Mooltan, the only strong place which had shut its gates against British troops, had been taken, and the crime committed by its wretched mob exemplarily avenged. If the proclamation for a time of martial law and the suspension of ordinary rights, with the disbanding of the insurgent Khalsa corps, had been decreed until punishment for acts of individual violence, and compensation for public and private losses had been exacted, rigorous justice would have been satisfied. Beyond this, impartial history will say that all was mere spoliation.

While Lord Dalhousie was laying out the Punjab like a Scotch estate, on the most approved principles of planting, road-making, culture, and general management, the chance of another conquest at the opposite extremity of his vice-kingdom summoned him to Calcutta. The master of a trading barque from Chittagong, who was charged unjustly with cruelty to a pilot, had been fined £100 by the authorities of Rangoon, and the captain of a brig had in like manner been amerced for alleged ill-treatment of his crew. To support a claim for restitution, two English ships of war had been sent to the mouth of the Irrawadi. The Burmese Governor had been removed, and his successor professed his willingness to treat. But misunderstandings arose on some inexplicable point of etiquette, which Commodore Lambert considered an opportunity "that he with sword would ope." The English residents in the town were warned to come on board the *Hermes* and the *Proserpine* without delay; whereupon at midnight on the 6th January, he proceeded to seize the Yellow Ship, a royal yacht which lay defenceless in the river. As might have been expected, this breach of the peace without any sort of notice proved too much for the discretion of the Burmese; the guns from whose forts commenced an attack in retaliation, which drew from the ships a damaging fire of shot and shell. With an unprecedented economy of time and trouble in the discovery or making of plausible pretexts, a second war with Burmah was thus begun.

A long catalogue of affronts, wrongs, and injuries, now for the first time poured in. When claims for compensation are receivable on national account, there are never wanting claimants. The subjects of the "Golden Foot" must be taught the consequences of their presumption, and must be reminded of their former lesson in the principles of civilisation. They must make an official apology for their misbehaviour, pay ten lacs compensation, and receive a permanent Resident at Rangoon. If these demands were not met within five weeks, further reparation would be exacted otherwise, and as there was no fear that they would, preparations were made for an expedition, troops being ordered from Madras and Bombay. The sepoys did not relish the notion of crossing the dark water. They had been enlisted, they said, only to serve on land, and when ordered to go on board they stood fast, and could not be induced to move. They were sent forthwith to Dacca to be decimated by cholera, then raging there; and the other battalions were quietly shipped to their destination. The Governor-General threw himself with enthusiasm into an undertaking which promised him another chance of gratifying, as his biographer says, his "passion for imperial symmetry." He resolved "to take in kingdoms wherever they made a gap in the red line running round his dominions or broke its internal continuity."[1] There was a gap in the ring-fence between Arracan and Moulmein, which Pegu would fill. The logical inference was clear, the duty of appropriation obvious. Let us have Pegu. Ten millions of silver happening just then to lie in the coffers of Fort William, how could they be better invested than in a jungle on the sea coast, inhabited by quadrupeds and bipeds after their various kinds, alike unworthy of being consulted as to their future destiny? More than countervailing damage had been done; and the king's ship was held in pledge for payment of compensation. Grievance, if any, lay the other way; but what did that signify? Ahab would have the vineyard: so the expedition sailed. In April, Martaban and Rangoon were taken with trifling loss. Operations being suspended during the rainy season, the city of Prome was not attacked till October, and after a few hours' struggle it fell, with the loss of a single sepoy on the side of the victors. There was in fact no serious danger to encounter, save from the climate; but that unfailing ally fought with terrible effect upon the side of Ava.

Lord Dalhousie was not blind to the financial consequences of this wanton and inglorious expedition. At the outset, he professed to regard further possession in Burmah as "second only to calamity in war," and on learning that Prome had capitulated, he confessed that the maintenance of 20,000 men at such a distance, and in such a country, would soon bring the Government of India to "exhausted cash balances and re-opened loans." Wherefore, then, had

[1] Dalhousie's administration of British India, by E. Arnold, vol. ii. p. 12.

he sent forth an army under General Godwin, at a huge expense and risk of life? or why, when vengeance had been sated for mere affronts, did he persist in the annexation of Pegu? Will history accept his answer to the question? "Let us fulfil our destiny, which there, as elsewhere, will have impelled us forward in spite of our wishes."[1]

Well might Richard Cobden say of this empty and thoughtless make-believe of a reason for doing what its author confessed to be wrong: "If we are to have credit for the sincerity of all this, what will be said of its statesmanship? I put aside the pretence of 'destiny,' which is not to be tolerated as a plea amongst Christians, however valid it may be in Mohammedan casuistry. But where lies the necessity for annexing any part of Burmah, if it be not our interest to do so? We are told that, if we do not seize a portion of the enemy's territory, we shall be disparaged in his eyes. In other words, unless the Government of India, with three hundred thousand troops, and backed by the whole power of the British Empire, pursues a policy injurious to its own interest, it will suffer in the estimation of the Burmese."[2] At first the Lieutenant of the Queen demands restitution of £990, and an apology, from the Governor of a Burmese town; without giving time for fair discussion, he raises the terms of his requisition to £100,000, and an apology from the Burmese Court; and while a temperate letter from the King, offering to negotiate, remains unanswered, he hurls an invading force against his realm, drops all mention of compensation or apology, and seizes an extensive province, with threats of further partition of his dominions if he will not pay the expenses of the

---

[1] Parliamentary Papers on Burmese Affairs, 1852, p. 93.
[2] "The Origin of the Burmese War," by Richard Cobden, Esq., M.P., p. 58.

war, the world being asked the while to believe that all has been done unwillingly, in self-defence.

On the 20th December 1852, a proclamation was issued, which, after reciting undisguisedly the ineffably inadequate pretext for the war, informed the inhabitants that the Governor in Council had resolved that the maritime province of Pegu should henceforth form a portion of the British territories in the East, and warning the King of Ava, "should he fail to renew his former relations of friendship with the British Government, and seek to dispute its quiet possession of the province, the Governor-General would again put forth the power he held, which would lead to the total subversion of the Burman State, and to the ruin and exile of the King and his race." But no depth of humiliation could bring the Sovereign or his Ministers to acknowledge the hopelessness of defeat or the permanency of dismemberment. Envoys came from Amarapoora offering to buy off the invaders, by payment of all the expenses of the war, if they would retire within the former landmarks; and subsequently Captain Phayre was sent on an embassage tendering a treaty couched in the threadbare phraseology of eternal friendship and peace, but it came to nothing. Twenty years have passed, and no treaty recognising the alienation of Pegu has yet been signed. Is there a Statute of Limitations barring the execution of predatory threats, or may the obduracy of Burmah be one day set up as a pretence for its further partition ?

CHAPTER XXV.

ZULM.[1]

1849—1853.

" The safety of our rule is increased, not diminished, by the maintenance of native chiefs well affected to us. Should the day come when India shall be threatened by an external enemy, or when the interests of England elsewhere may require that her Eastern Empire shall incur more than ordinary risk, one of our best mainstays will be found in these Native States. But to make them so we must treat their chiefs and influential families with consideration and generosity, teaching them that, in spite of all suspicion to the contrary, their independence is safe, that we are not waiting for plausible opportunities to convert their country into British territory."

—LORD CANNING.[2]

THE gilded frame of acquisition was complete : it remained only to paint out the forms and hues, yet unobliterated, which did not harmonise with the general tone, colouring, and perspective of empire. Two-thirds of Southern Asia owned our sway, and the rest no longer challenged it. Many Mohammedan and Hindu Princes still exercised the power of life and death, the right to levy local taxation, to enrol battalions of militia, to hold Durbars, to send Vakeels, and to enforce within their ancient limits the respect due to their dynastic dignity. But their territories lay like islands compassed round on every side by the encroaching waters of foreign rule. In every direction lay in ruins the moles and outworks of

---

[1] Oppression. [2] Adoption Minute, 30th April 1860.

native principalities and chieftainries, which but yesterday had been like their own. Of those that still retained nominal independence, none any longer struggled or, save in passing dreams, realised the possibility of secession from our Empire in Asia. Some acknowledged unreservedly their allegiance to the Suzerain whose sword had taken the place of the sceptres of Mahratta and Mohammedan dominion: others murmuringly bowed to *kismet*, but questioned no more the overruling authority of the Paramount Power. With all of them its relations were defined in treaties actually subsisting; and in each of these engagements one of the chief considerations named was the recognition of State severalty, and its permanent guarantee by the indefeasible inheritance acknowledged in the family of the reigning prince. On what principles the law of inheritance was based, to what exceptions, if any, it was liable, and according to what rule contingent remainderships were to be traced, was not set down in any of the pacts made in the name of England by successive Viceroys with the chiefs or rulers of Asia. Has any one ever heard of stipulations of the kind being embodied in similar documents by any other Government in the world, in any age or clime? Treaties have throughout all time been for the most part brief in language, general in the terms employed, and confessedly intended, not as exhaustive anticipations of all imaginable contingencies, but as laying down broadly, and in simple forms of speech, the outlines of peace and amity; upon the implied condition that the application of these terms to any and every case that might thereafter arise should be such as the common understanding of both communities would admit, or the judgment of an impartial arbiter declare. Tested by this obvious rule of international right, the guarantee of perpetual inheritance was undoubtedly intended, and undoubtedly understood, to imply the devolution of title, dignity, and power to whatever heirs could from time to time establish their respective claims,—not according to the *lex loci* of the foreign and alien party to the compact, but according to the *lex loci* of the State whose autonomy the treaty had been confessedly framed to assure. Until the circumambiency of conquest was complete, scarce the whisper of a doubt was ever overheard as to the simple honesty of this rule. The case of Coorg has indeed been sometimes relied on as furnishing an early precedent for lapse to the Paramount Power through want of male heirs. But it is enough to say, that no case resembling that of Coorg, either in point of fact or in point of principle, has arisen of recent years. Those which of late have engrossed unhappily the minds of men in India, have each and all of them turned upon the right of succession by collateral heirs, or heirs by adoption. About the traditional usages which recognised in native states such claims to succession, there is hardly, among unofficial men, standing room for doubt. The assumption by Lord Dalhousie, in the case of Sattara, that notwithstanding the treaties of 1818 and 1819, the Raj had lapsed to the British Crown, because the heir of Pratab Singh was not his son, was as blunt and bald an act of usurpation as though it had been made in the form of asserting that he was not of Pictish or Norman lineage. Time out of mind the rights and duties of adoption have been as notoriously part and parcel of Hindu law and religion, as the powers to dispose of fee-simple at the pleasure of the owner has been part and parcel of our own system of jurisprudence. The limitations as to property and privilege varied in different states, and when the Mussulmans began to interweave portions of Hindu law and custom with their own, one of the most prominent and important they appropriated was that of adoption. So long as the Nawab or Maharajah retained life and health, the hope of posterity remained, and he seldom bequeathed by anticipation his diadem, lest his grey hairs, like those of Lear, might prematurely be discrowned. But when his end palpably drew nigh, the childless prince was wont to nominate his successor, whose first duty after the decease was to perform his obsequies with pious care. If he were young, feeble, or depraved, a pretender sometimes started, bid high for popular support, and offered to abide the arbitrament of battle. Have we not heard of like questioning and conflict amongst kings and feudatories in Christendom, where the title by primogenitural right could not be disputed? But revolution is the converse of law, not a part of it; and the Paramount Power which would rely on the success of supplanters *vi et armis*, must prepare for the crop which proverbially springs from the teeth of the dragon. Death, which is no respecter of longitudes, any more than of conditions, sometimes stole upon the sick man in his sleep, so that he woke not on the morrow to fulfil his purpose of naming a successor; and then Muftis and Brahmins held that the Ranee or Begum should carry into effect the intention of the deceased, which she was naturally presumed to be most likely to know. Numberless instances are upon record where this course was followed, for the most part without cavil or controversy. Avarice or ambition occasionally brought an uncle or cousin to wrestle with the adoptive heir. We too have heard of struggles not dissimilar, of a disinherited Tudor superseding and beheading the successor by adoption named by the previous king, and of a Saxon monarch actually in possession overthrown by a

Norman devisee by will. But cases like these were never held to alter or settle the national law of inheritance. They were appeals to the power of moral force or of physical force, or of both combined; the convulsion passed, the legal current of the blood resumed its natural course; and the form of the visage of property and order was not perceptibly changed. Succession through the female line, in default of male heirs, has been the prevalent law of Europe as well as of Hindustan for centuries; and the indefeasibility of pretensions through the parenthetical exercise of female power to lands, honours, privileges, principalities, and powers, has prevailed as widely near the rising of the sun as beneath his going down.

It pleased the Governor-General of India, notwithstanding, to be persuaded of the contrary; and being persuaded, to proceed, with as little moral ruth as legal truth, to proclaim his right to interpret the meaning of Hindu or Moslem heirship, and to fabricate a meaning as unknown to Menu, Mahomet, or Akbar, as to Alfred, Edward III., Elizabeth, or Cromwell. In one of his earlier despatches he expounds the policy he had it in contemplation to pursue, of appropriation on the plea of lapse to the Paramount Power. "I take occasion of recording my strong and deliberate opinion, that, in the exercise of a wise and sound policy, the British Government is bound not to put aside or neglect such rightful opportunities of acquiring territory or revenue, as may from time to time present themselves, whether they arise from the lapse of subordinate States, by the failure of all heirs of every description whatsoever, or from the failure of heirs natural, where the succession can be sustained only by the sanction of the Government being given to the ceremony of adoption, according to Hindu Law." The first occasion for applying this sweeping doctrine of confiscation presented itself in 1848 in the principality of Sattara.

When the Peishwa fell in 1818, a proclamation was issued, in which it was declared that, as his usurping authority had ceased to exist, the legitimate heir of Sivají should be restored, "and placed at the head of an independent sovereignty of such an extent as might maintain the Rajah and his house;" and in the treaty of 1819 Lord Hastings had, in words of widest meaning, recognised and guaranteed the Rajah of Sattara to Pratab Singh, and his heirs and successors for ever; whether heirs of the body, heirs by adoption, or heirs by will. The Persian words which signify these different species of heirs, were inscribed in the counterpart held by the Mahratta chief. No question was ever raised as to their authenticity; but they were rendered in the English version of the treaty by simpler and more generic terms. For seventeen years the Maharajah had confessedly been among the faithfulest of feudatories. General Robertson and General Briggs, who were successively Residents at his court, uniformly testified to his worth, ability, and rectitude; and in 1835 the Board of Directors presented him with a jewelled sabre in acknowledgment of his undeviating friendship and fidelity. Subsequently a misunderstanding arose respecting certain jaghires, to which his reversionary rights were disputed by the Government of Bombay. Hurt by the neglect of his representations, he offered to refer the question unreservedly to Mountstuart Elphinstone, by whose advice he had been freed from duress on the fall of the Peishwa and restored to his ancient heritage. This was refused; further delays occurred, vexation gave place to suspicion, and suspicion to resentment, until at length his mind became possessed with the idea, that having served a temporary purpose, he and the severalty of his State were to be brought to an end. The vehemence of his objurgations piqued the Government of Bombay into a temper of hostility, and eventually into a course of proceeding which it is impossible to justify. During three years he was the object of secret inculpation, and of inquiries which drew down the censure of the Court of Directors as being "a waste of time, and seriously detrimental to the character of the Government." They were, notwithstanding, persisted in, and Pratab Singh asked in vain for a copy of the charges made against him. It was refused. He then waited alone on Sir James Carnac, the Governor of the Presidency, and offered to give himself up, and remain in captivity, surrendering "the charge of his kingdom until his innocence was established." But this was likewise declined. He was asked to sign a paper admitting his dishonour, which he passionately spurned. A lying story of his being in conspiracy with Scindia and the Nizam was confuted by Metcalfe and Stuart, then resident at their courts; but mutual distrust had become ineradicable, and his appointment of an agent to appeal for him in England, to the justice of the Company, or of Parliament, was treated as a proof of duplicity. Finally he was seized at dead of night, in his palace, and borne away under escort to a distance from the happy and prosperous country he was never to see again. What was to be done with the vacant throne? Sir Robert Grant had been told by those about him that the "erection of Sattara into a separate principality was a blunder, as it broke the continuity of British territory," and that "the present was an excellent opportunity for repairing the error." Precedents were not wanting. "The history of the British connection with India recorded the names of many chiefs and princes whom we began with advancing to honour, or at least supporting with our protection, and ended with deposing, destroying, depriving of a great part of their territories or reducing to political annihilation." But there were circumstances which rendered it just then inexpedient to destroy or annihilate this interceptive state. People would be apt to say that there was no overt act warranting forfeiture, and many countervailing circumstances. "If we awarded the Rajah any punishment which should be of material benefit to ourselves, the story of his guilt would never be believed. . . . Persons would argue that, having made use of this prince, and now considering his dominions a convenient acquisition, we had readily admitted or even suborned calumnious accusation against him as an excuse for the fulfilment of our rapacious purposes. Such would be their representation, and it would, I fear, be very generally credited."[1] Lord Auckland was then preparing the invasion of Afghanistan, and did not think it expedient unnecessarily to multiply provocations in the Western Presidency. Instead of annexing Sattara, therefore, he resolved to set up Appa Saib, the brother of the deposed prince, in his room, requiring him to renounce all claims to the disputed jaghires. When dying, Appa Saib nominated a youth of his kindred, who in due course lighted his funeral pyre, and took possession peaceably of his rank and station. His only rival to the Gudi was the adopted son of the deposed Pratab Singh, whose will, executed three years before, now became known. He died in 1847, and thus the only reasonable competition was between the two cousins by adoption. Mr Frere, the English Resident at Sattara, apprised Lord Dalhousie, that among collaterals there was "no one who would think his claim sufficiently strong to be put in competition with that of the

[1] Minute in Council, by Sir R. Grant, 30th January 1837.

adopted son of either the late Rajah or his brother; because all other relations, who might otherwise be claimants, believe both adoptions to be regular. But there were many who might have asserted their claim had no adoption taken place, and who might possibly assert it should they hear that both adoptions were invalidated; and any of them, as far as he could judge of the facts of the case before him, would, were other competitors save the British Government out of the field, be able to establish a very good *primâ facie* claim in any Court of Justice in India, to be the Rajah's heir by blood, as against the British Government in its character of heir to all who die leaving no natural heirs of their own; which appeared to him the only character in which our Government could, consistently with the treaty, lay claim to the Sattara State."

To deny the universality of adoption as a practice was as idle as to question the prevalence of Brahminical traditions; and to dispute the duty of adoption was to outrage the general sense of right and wrong in one of its chief behests. Adoption, it should never be forgotten, is not a means of merely supplying, in some occasional instance, the lack of kindred, or of inventing an heir-at-law where there is none by blood; it is ordinarily a mode of choosing among many relatives who shall stand in place of a son, not only to inherit property, but to discharge sacred obligations, and to offer up those propitiatory prayers and sacrifices for the departed soul, which none can offer but one who is duly clothed with a filial character; and without which, a long sojourn in the Gehenna of the Hindu is believed to be inevitable. The upstart claim of annexation by virtue of the doctrine of lapse was the most foolish and offensive form confiscation could be made to assume; inasmuch as it wounded every moral and religious, as well as every social and political, feeling. In the case of Sattara, it casts a retrospective glare upon the pretended conspiracy of 1837 and all the events of that time. What made the annexation of Sattara recklessly unjust even in European eyes, was the fact that Pratab Singh, whom Lord Hastings had made much ado about restoring to his ancestral throne, was himself the heir of Sivaji by the observance of the law of adoption. Twice had the descent in the male line failed, and on the second occasion it had been preserved so late as 1777 by resort to this natural, legal, and hitherto undisputed expedient. Appa Saib was a wise ruler, who laid out, it is said, eight per cent. of his income on works of public utility, and there never was an allegation of the country being misgoverned. But, in truth, one sickens in the unavailing search for plausible ground of justification, or of palliatives for wrong, so repugnant to every principle of public equity or private right.

Throughout Malwa and Rajpootana the tidings spread dismay and hate. There was no mistaking their import or their scope. All landed property held by tenure, analogous to our fee simple or fee tail, was put in jeopardy. The decencies of consistency, legality, expediency, were rent and torn. The Resident, Sir John Low, a friend of Malcolm, reported that "the confidence of the native States was shaken." Colonel Macpherson wrote from Gwalior that Scindia and other Hindu princes were thrown into "a state of great anxiety on the subject of family succession." Sir Frederick Currie also placed on record his conviction, as a Member of the Council at Bengal, that "the decision in the Sattara case caused surprise and alarm throughout India." He exposed the fallacy of those who argued against the right, because it required recognition by the Paramount Power. This was equally true with respect to heirs natural, and amounted to no more than the ordinary discretion of investiture or confirmation, which, in some form or other, has always belonged to suzerainty, whether temporal or ecclesiastical. But a discretion to guard against heedless choice, or the imposition of an incapable successor through corrupt artifice or death-bed fraud, cannot warrant the indiscretion of a usurping power to destroy for the future the very relation in virtue of which it claims to act. This, likewise, was the opinion of Sir G. Clerk, who contended again and again that adoption conveyed as clear an equitable right to recognition by the Suzerain as heirship by birth.[1]

Sir Frederick Currie's views, ably and unbendingly expressed in Council, were happily sustained by Sir Henry Lawrence as successor to Sir John Low, when, in 1852, the Governor-General meditated the application of his doctrine of lapse to the small State of Kerowli. It was the first of the Rajpoot States thus threatened, and there can be little doubt that had one of them been sacrificed, a great fear would have fallen upon all of them, and implacable feelings engendered of detestation proportionate to their dread. Intelligence reached England, moreover, of what was impending, and the India Reform Association, led by Mr Dickinson, succeeded in calling public attention in time to its impolicy and iniquity. A motion by the late Mr Blackett was threatened in the House of Commons, and the Peelite Administration, careful of the repute of one of the chief personages of their party, bade the Viceroy hold his hand.

---

[1] See the authorities and arguments on the subject, carefully collected and lucidly arranged in "Thoughts on the Policy of the Crown," by J. M. Ludlow; and in "Retrospects and Prospects of Indian Policy," by Major Evans Bell.

Thus Kerowli was reprieved, and after a period of uncertainty, prolonged through many months, adoption was recognised in favour of Madden Pâl, by whom the little State has been ever since quietly governed. Whether owing to the intercession of Sir Henry Lawrence or Sir Frederick Currie, the danger was for the time averted; but who should say what might happen when they were gone? The shock given to the Mahratta Princes, great as well as small, was not easily forgotten. "There were childless men among them, and from that time a restless, uneasy feeling took possession of them, and no man felt sure that his house would not perish with him."[1]

The residue of what was once the powerful State of Berar, had since its partition in 1805 been left to the family of Bhonsla. In 1818, the Maharajah had been deposed and banished, and in his room the next of kin to the former Sovereign was chosen by the chiefs and nobles to take his place, which he did with the full sanction and approval of the British Government. There was no dispute regarding the inheritance. Sir Richard Jenkins, who was Resident at his court, and who thoroughly possessed the confidence of his Government, at the time spoke of the "restoration of the State of Nagpore to its rank, as one of the substantive powers of India."[2] It was sheer trifling therefore to pretend that the Government had been set up by alien power, and might be superseded, when occasion served, by the like authority. Upon his demise in 1854, the Rajah being childless, the natural wish of his family and chief adherents was expressed though the Resident at Nagpore, that his successor by adoption might be duly recognised by the Supreme Power. Mr Mansel in no doubtful terms enforced the fitness of the claim. It

---

[1] Arnold, vol. ii.   [2] Bell, Retrospects and Prospects, p. 29.

was the bitter cry on all sides, he observed, that our rule exhibited no sympathy, especially for the natives of rank, and not even for other classes; that the improvement of the native princes was in our own power; and that whatever sins of mismanagement were chargeable on the past Government of the Principality, the blame was at least partly due to want of care and solicitude on the part of the representatives of the suzerain.[1] The Viceroy and his Council treated such suggestions with disdain. Mr Mansel's functions as Resident were at an end, and his advice was no longer wanted. Measures were taken to cut down pensions to the Ranees, and minutes were recorded of the value of the jewels, no more to be accounted heirlooms in a family about to be stripped of royal rank and fortune. Jeswunt Ahee Rao publicly performed the obsequies of the deceased prince, and, attended by the nobles and officers of the household, was installed in the palace of the Maharajahs of Nagpore without the semblance of contention. Suddenly in October it was surrounded by British troops—the regalia and caskets containing gems valued at £1,000,000 sterling were seized and subsequently put up to sale by auction in the Viceroy's name; the princesses and their retinue were treated as prisoners of State, and interdicted from holding any communication with persons outside their garden bounds, save through the newly appointed Commissioner sent to take charge of the dominions of our late ally; and, finally, those dominions were publicly proclaimed by Lord Dalhousie to have, by failure of heirs male, lapsed to the Central Power, and to be henceforth incorporated with those of Britain. In vain the aged Maharanee Banka Baee pleaded and remonstrated with her gallant gaolers on behalf of the ladies and children of

---

[1] Despatch, 29th April 1854.

her court; in vain she asked permission to send persons of distinction, hitherto treated with every outward mark of honour, and against whom not a breath of complaint had been ever heard, to sue for justice at Calcutta. All intercourse save through the Commissioner was for months forbidden, and effectual means were taken to prevent any evasion of the interdict. Major Ouseley was arrested on his way to Nagpore, where he was ready to offer such services as loyalty would permit, to the unhappy princesses; and certain Mahajurs, who were willing as bankers to advance funds for their release, were likewise flung into prison for their contumacy.

When the chief articles of value had been removed, and all apprehension of tumult or resistance had passed away, some of the captive nobles were allowed to approach the rifled treasure-house, and to communicate by letter with the bereaved and broken-hearted Queen, urging her in language of desperation never to acknowledge the disinheritance of her race or the annexation of her country. She contrived to send agents to England in the idle hope of obtaining justice here. Could she not await their answer ere she signed the capitulation drafted by the Commissioner, whereby pensions were offered to her helpless relatives and courtiers as the price of her nominal acquiescence? Her Vizier had died of mortification and rage, and most of those who were suspected of being able to counsel her aright, were still detained in custody. A hot breath or two strove to rekindle the embers of expiring self-respect and pride in her aged bosom; but the chill of eighty years and the feebleness of despair, quenched each spark of hope ere it could be fanned into flame; and the widow of the once feared and formidable Raghogee Bhonsla, amid tears and tremblings, was driven at length to sign a renunciation of all claims of Regency or Sovereignty on her own behalf. Even in this extremity not a word was said repudiating the legal and religious title by adoption of Jeswunt Rao. Sentries mounted guard no more; trusty garrisons were maintained at every post of the appropriated realm; trusty agents were set to watch each chief suspected of harbouring resentment, and the Civil Administration of the country was rapidly reorganised in accordance with injunctions from Calcutta. Local self-rule at Nagpore, which had lasted for generations, ceased to be; and all was over.

Not all: for the trophies of this glorious exploit were still to be displayed; and the value of the stolen goods was yet to be realised in cash. In the Calcutta *Morning Chronicle* of 12th October 1855, was read the following advertisement, which it were a pity to abate by any jot or tittle of what it has to say for itself :—

GRAND PUBLIC SALE

OF THE

NAGPORE JEWELS.

HAMILTON AND COMPANY

Have the honour to announce, that they have been favoured with the

COMMANDS OF GOVERNMENT,

To submit to Public and Unreserved Sale,

THE WHOLE OF THE

NAGPORE JEWELS,

&c. &c. &c.

These Magnificent Ornaments (the Largest and Most Valuable Collection ever exhibited in Calcutta), are now on View at Messrs Hamilton and Company's Show Rooms.

THEY COMPRISE

DIAMONDS, of Immense Size and Weight, and of Pure Water, Set as Armlets, Bracelets, Rings, and Large Diamond Drops of Various Weights. One of these Diamonds is Considerably Larger than the 'Darya-i-Noor.'

PEARL NECKLACES, Very Large and Uncommon, Single, Double, and Four-Rows, with Diamond Pendants, or Dook Dhookies.

LARGE EMERALD NECKLACES, Elegantly Carved and Polished.
SEVERAL Superb Drop-shaped DIAMONDS and Other NECKLACES.
HINDOOSTANEE EAR-RINGS, Very Handsome, Set with Diamonds and Pearls.
VARIOUS Diamond, Ruby, and Emerald JEEGAHS, SERPECHES, GOSEPAICH and RAJEHSYE, or HEAD ORNAMENTS.
A VERY Elegant Diamond TORRAH, or TURBAN ORNAMENT, Containing many Drops.
SEVERAL PEARL Ditto, Ditto.
A CHARCOBE, or ROYAL DRESS COAT, Ornamented with Beautiful Diamonds, Pearls, Rubies, and Emeralds all over.
SEVERAL GOLD and Enamelled HORSE TRAPPINGS, Set with Diamonds, Rubies, Emeralds, Cats' Eyes, and Pearls; GUNDAS; HYKULS; KULGEE; and FLOWER ORNAMENTS for HORSES' HEADS; SADDLES; CHARMAJAHS, or SADDLE CLOTHS, Embroidered with Diamonds, Emeralds, Rubies, and Pearls.
VERY Handsome Gold and Enamelled ANKOOSES, or GUZBAGS, for Driving Elephants, Set with Diamonds, Rubies, Emeralds, &c. Gauntlets, Set with Ditto, Ditto, Ditto.
GOLD and Enamelled UTTER and PAUN DAUMS, ROSE-WATER SPRINKLERS, SPICE BOXES, SURROY, WATER JUGS, KULLUM DAUNS, &c. &c., Set all over with Purely White Diamonds.
A VERY Elegant Gold and Enamelled HOOKAH, Set all round with Beautiful Large and Pure-Water Diamonds, with Chillum, Cup, Surpose, Mouth Piece, Kirrenah Mounted with Diamonds, and a Snake Embroidered with Pearls and Rubies and Large Emerald Pendants.
A LARGE number of Gold, Diamond, and Ruby Mounted SWORDS, RHINOCEROS' HIDE SHIELDS, DAGGERS, KNIVES, BOWS, ARROWS, QUIVERS, &c. &c.
SEVERAL Very Costly SWORD BELTS and KNOTS, Studded with Diamonds, Rubies, Emeralds, and Pearls.
PURE GOLD AND SILVER ORNAMENTS, viz. PAUN AND UTTER DAUNS, ROSE-WATER SPRINKLERS, SPICE BOXES, SALVERS, with Enamelled Work, WATER JUGS, &c. &c.
GOLD JEWELLERY; viz. Several Bracelets, Necklaces, Armlets, Waist Chains or Chunder Harrs, Ear-rings, Bangles, Anklets, Toe Rings, &c. &c.
ARMOUR; viz. Steel Gauntlets, Helmets, Coats, Spears, Battle Axes, Kandahs, Knives, Shields, Several of them Inlaid with Gold, &c. &c.
PLATE CHESTS, Containing English-made Silver, Electro-Plated Ware and Porcelain Dinner and Dessert Services, to Dine 100 Persons.

Can any one be at a loss regarding the impression made on the mind of every prince of India by the public sale, in the metropolis of the East, of the personal effects of one who, throughout his reign, had been our faithful ally? Can any one doubt that the advertisement was execrated in every Bazaar, and cursed in every Zenanah, as a threatening notice ostentatiously given that the picklock of despotism would be used without shame as an implement of exaction: and none could tell whose regalia or casket would next be rifled. Our historians are never weary of reprobating the sudden and summary decree of Bayonne, in which Napoleon informed the world that in the Peninsula the house of Bourbon had ceased to reign, and in reprobating the duress under which an imbecile sovereign was driven into an act of formal abdication. And many severe things have been justly said of the pictures taken from the Escurial, and of the bronze steeds borne away from the Piazza of San Marc. But at least Napoleon cannot be upbraided with stealing or selling the gems and apparel of his victims. It was bad enough to appropriate the sword of Frederick, but Napoleon, unscrupulous though he was, would have been ashamed to make away with rings and necklaces of the Prussian queen, and then to have put them up to the highest bidder among the brokers of his capital. If vice loses half its hideousness by losing all its grossness, it may likewise be said that public violence becomes more hateful when it is tarnished with the reproach of base cupidity. At the very time when the Queen's Lieutenant-General in Asia was thus playing the freebooter and auctioneer, our Foreign Secretary was addressing to the court of St Petersburg remonstrances against the sequestration of the revenues of certain Polish noblemen upon suspicion of their complicity in seditious designs. Well might the minister of the Czar scornfully retort,—" Physician, heal thyself."

Another absorption which belongs to the same period is that of Jhansi, whose chief, from having been a vassal of the Peishwa, became a feudatory of the British Government. Ragonath Rao, at his death in 1835, left a youth who was said to be his adopted son; but the latter failing to substantiate his claim, one of his uncles took possession of the Gudi without resistance by the people or interference by us. And because as Rajah *de facto*, and presumptively *de jure*, he was recognised by Lord William Bentinck as head of the State, Lord Dalhousie pretended that he had a precedent therein for rejecting any claimant by right of adoption in 1853, not—in favour of a rightful heir by blood or popular choice, but in favour simply of confiscation of the territory and its revenues. It may or may not be the duty of the Paramount Power to interfere in cases of disputed succession, but it never can be its duty or right to take advantage of a presumed or factitious flaw in the title of a particular claimant in order to shut out all the members of a family, some one of whom in the opinion of their people must be entitled to reign. Yet, this and nothing else was that which was done by Lord Dalhousie. Anund Rao was in 1853, in all due form, adopted by the dying Prince as his son and heir. The Rajah wrote to the Governor-General respectfully commending his youthful choice to his consideration and care, and asking for the recognition of his widow as Regent during the minority. He appealed to the second article of the subsisting treaty, which guaranteed the territory to heirs of his family in perpetual succession, whether heirs by descent, consanguinity, or adoption, and he trusted that, "in consideration of the fidelity he had always evinced towards Government, favour might be shown to this child." He was allowed to die in the delusion that native fidelity would be remembered. The Empire was grown so strong that the autocrat of Fort William thought it could afford to forget fidelity. The youthful Maharajah's rights were denied; the Regent Rance was assigned a palace for her prison, and Jhansi was by proclamation incorporated with the Company's possessions. Luckshim Bai grieved unforgivingly. At the first note of insurrection in 1857, she took to horse, and for months in male attire headed bands, squadrons, and at length formidable corps of the Mahrattas, until she became in her way another Joan of Arc to her frenzied and fierce followers. No insurgent leader gave more trouble to the columns of Sir Hugh Rose; but not even in desperate and deadly fight, lasting for many hours, could she be persuaded to quit the field. In the general *melée* of defeat, Luckshim fell by a random shot, but not until she had exacted terrible retribution for the wrongs and insults to her family and her country.

CHAPTER XXVI.

TAKING IN KINGDOMS.

1853—1856.

"To the evils of annexation, growing out of our insatiable love of territorial aggrandisement, we shall probably be wilfully blind, until awakened from a great national illusion by some rude shock to the fabric of our Indian finance."

—RICHARD COBDEN.[1]

SIKH and Hindu had felt alike the heavy hand of annexation. Before quitting India, Lord Dalhousie was resolved to leave indelibly his mark likewise on Mussulman States. The glory had indeed departed from them, but the after-glow of power still lingered. Gloom had long settled over them; but, in the exquisite words of the poet, "It was not darkness, but light that had died." And even this faint and fading solace of grandeur gone, and hope, whose heart was broken, destructive despotism grudged. It was not content to have overthrown, it would obliterate reproachful memorials. Unsated with supercession, it thirsted for the drops of comfort still remaining in the broken cup of bondage, and longed to appropriate what it did not want. Four Mohammedan Courts had, within the century, lent it aid from time to time, as we have seen. Each of them in turn had been undone, and all were now more or less at its mercy. The Viceroy was

[1] How Wars are got up in India, by Richard Cobden, M.P., p. 56.

a man of many gifts, but mercy was not among them. Mercy he showed none.

When English trade stood shelterless on the beach of Malabar, the Nawab of Arcot was its first friend. It lent him help against the French, and in exchange he gave it storage-room and dwelling-place. As it grew his power dwindled, and as his tulwar rusted its bayonet waxed bright. The enthymeme of usurpation need not be again recited. By the time Lord Wellesley came to renew the treaty between Madras and Arcot, "the Carnatic had been," says Mr Arnold, "immeshed in the net of our friendship and the noose of our protection." But Lord Wellesley had a soul above pettifogging oppression, and he would have disdained to take advantage of forfeited pledges. Omdut-ul-Omrah was suspected of intrigues with Tippoo Saib; and Ali Hussein, his son, inherited, it was feared, his father's infidelity. But this was not made a pretence for breaking our engagements with his house, or confiscating the revenues repeatedly guaranteed them. With Azîm-ul-Dowla a fresh treaty was made "for settling the succession to the Soubahdary of the territories of Arcot, and for vesting the civil and military administration of the Carnatic in the Company." The fourth article declared that four-fifths of the revenues were for ever vested in the Company, and the remaining one-fifth "appropriated for ever for the support of the Nawab." His son enjoyed his dignities, privileges, and emoluments, until his death in 1853, when Lord Dalhousie thought the time had arrived to let the curtain fall upon the farce of Gratitude to Arcot. The Cabinet of Lord Aberdeen and the Court of Directors assenting, he forbade Azim Jah to assume the title, and refused to pay him the stipulated fifth of the revenues, which he claimed as undisputed heir, upon the ground that when treaties are made "for ever" with feudatories, the suzerain is not bound longer than the sense of expediency lasts; or in other words, that the observance of public faith is obligatory only on one side, because the semblance of royalty, without any of the power, is a mockery of authority which must be pernicious. If anything were surprising in the misgovernment of India, it would be the audacity which could misrepresent the faded finery of Chepank Palace as keeping up illusions, even in its powerless owner, of pretendership to royalty. Royalty, in the best days of the family, had never been asserted by them. They were subordinate to the Nizam, who was himself a feudatory of the Padishah. Local authority they really had enjoyed a hundred years gone by; but it was authority which had no more to do with royalty than Hamlet had to do with Hercules. Much or little, it was all clean gone; the archives of Madras and of Calcutta could tell where. But its property and rank and titular privileges had hitherto been respected, because they had been made matters of public stipulation by the representatives of the British crown; and now the money was to be taken by force, the use of the titles interdicted by decree, and the broken covenants given to the winds.

The despotic demeanour of Lord Dalhousie towards the Native Princes was not exemplified alone in the arbitrary absorption of States on the plea of lapse from default of male heirs. The Viceroy let no opportunity escape for impressing the native mind with a sense of the autocratic will and domination of the Central Power, of which he was the mouthpiece; and his conduct towards the Nawab-Nazim of Bengal, one of the oldest of our allies in Asia, was in keeping with what had gone before. Bengal had come to be regarded as the home-farm of Empire. The treaties of 1757, 1760, and 1763 with Mír Jaffir and Mír Kasim, as we have seen, gave us the first political and territorial *locus standi*, and the engagements of 1765, 1767, and 1770 with their successors, each marked a step in the progress of encroachment upon native rule. The administrative experiments of Hastings, Cornwallis, and subsequent Viceroys, gradually withdrew from the Court of Moorshedabad even the semblance of government; but five formal treaties had acknowledged the rank, dignity, and social privileges of the Nawabs-Nazim of Bengal. By terms which indicate perpetuity of obligation, if they mean anything at all, a suitable income had been provided for the ex-ruling family, and the minutes and despatches of each Governor-General in succession were unanimous in treating the descendants of Mîr Jaffir as princes *de facto* if not *de jure*. The cession of executive functions on the one side, and their acceptance on the other, was not brought about by conquest, was not signalised by incidents of violence or victory, and was accompanied by no formal act of abdication. The process of transfer was silent, its progress was steady. It had its origin in the compacts which gave the Company command of the forces and the control of the exchequer of Bengal. With the instruments as well as the sinews of war at their disposal, they did as powerful Ministers had aforetime done elsewhere, usurped the sceptre in reality, while paying ceremonious respect to its holder. The minority of Mobaruck-ul-Dowla, the last of the heirs of Mîr Jaffir, favoured this alienation of native rule. The Governor and Council had during that time ample opportunity of consolidating the supreme authority, then resting unquestioned in their hands; and when in due course it should have reverted to the Soubahdar, they showed no disposition to yield it up, while the native community, growing used to the mandates of Fort William, knew not how to substitute those of Moorshedabad. The Nawab protested, but his complaints were unheeded, or were answered only with plausible evasion. Successive Nawabs were treated by successive Viceroys with scrupulous regard to the formalities of rank and station, but not an inch of power was restored. No attempt, however, was made to question the validity of the treaties, which were palpable acknowledgments of the rank and rights of Mîr Jaffir's dynasty. No one had contended that, although we had absorbed all power, dignity and its attendant privileges did not remain with the Princes of his house. On the contrary, Lords Wellesley, Minto, Hastings, Amherst, Hardinge, and even Lord Dalhousie himself, had penned letters and despatches acknowledging the rights "guaranteed by subsisting treaties," and promising to "uphold the interests, dignity, credit, and prescriptive privileges" of the family. In 1838, Syud Munsûr Ali Khan, the eighth in regular descent from Mîr Jaffir, succeeded while a minor to the musnud of Bengal. All the formalities of investiture, proclamation, and congratulation were duly observed with him, as with his predecessors; the Government of India officially notified to the public, its allies, and all friendly powers, that Syud Munsûr Ali had succeeded to the hereditary honours and dignities of the Nizamut and Soubahdary of Bengal, Behar, and Orissa, and was declared to have assumed the authority, dignities, and privileges thereof, and a salute of nineteen guns and three volleys of musketry was ordered to celebrate the event.

Excepting disagreements as to the appropriation of certain sums from the annual allowance guaranteed by the treaty of 1770, nothing disturbed the harmony of the relations subsisting between the past and present rulers. One of the most dearly prized of the privileges enjoyed by the

Nawabs in their regal retirement was exemption from the jurisdiction and authority of the Adawluts, and even of the Supreme Court. By a special legislative Act in 1794, they had been authorised to take cognisance and adjudicate on all matters in dispute between members of the family, the court, and the retinue of Moorshedabad; and by three subsequent enactments in 1805, 1806, and 1822, the mode of public and official intercourse with the Nawabs was regulated; and the position of plaintiff or defendant in legal suit being incompatible with the social rights of princes according to Eastern custom, it was ordained that the Governor-General's agent at the Nawab's Court should be his vicarious representative in legal process. An attempt had been made in 1834 by local authorities to set aside some of these privileges; but on reference to the Government at Calcutta, they were strenuously upheld,—Sir Charles Trevelyan recording the emphatic declaration that "the Nawab had been recognised by the British Government as an independent Prince, and that the national faith was pledged for nothing being proposed or carried into execution derogating from his honour." The Supreme Court had "no right to exercise jurisdiction over the Nawab-Nazim of Bengal," and the Advocate-General was instructed "to adopt every necessary legal means for resisting it." The Act of 1825 had been framed to prevent his being "liable to any indignity in person or property in the process of the Zillah Courts," for if his liability to the Supreme Court were admitted, there was no degree of indignity which might not be inflicted on him in contravention of the pledged national faith, and the respect obviously due to the representative of our oldest ally on this side of India.[1]

[1] Letter to H. Paulin, Esq., Company's Attorney, 20th February 1834.

The conscientious avowals of his predecessors had no weight with the haughty annexationist. To him treaties were only tentative formularies, to be ruthlessly swept away when they barred the progress of imperial acquisition. To him the fame of spreading fear was more than the credit of national faith, and humiliated races more than the plighted honour of his own nation. In 1853 an incident occurred which brought out in strong relief the overbearing nature of the Viceroy. In March of that year the Nawab was on a shooting excursion, two English officials being among the guests, when two Hindu lads were seized on suspicion of having stolen a box of jewels belonging to one of the subordinate eunuchs, and by some of these officers were beaten with such severity as to cause death. The act was undoubtedly one of gross brutality, and deserved the punishment inflicted on some of the Nawab's servants, to whom, after a long and patient investigation, it was clearly brought home; but his Highness's principal officer, Aman Ali, and others of rank, who were included in the indictment, were, after a long trial, honourably acquitted, while not a tittle of evidence was adduced tending to implicate the Nawab in the slightest degree. In trial and review of proceedings, the matter went through two courts, and after passing such an ordeal the Prince might surely be excused if he regarded the acquitted servants as innocent, and reinstated them in his retinue. This act of justice, however, drew down on him the wrath of the Governor-General, who, disdaining to notice the decision of the Adawluts presided over by English judges, addressed a violent despatch to the agent at Moorshedabad, asserting that the outrage had been committed "under the very eyes" of the Nawab, and demanding explanations why he had failed to "exert his authority to prevent so outrageous a crime, committed almost in his very presence." It should here be remarked that the evidence, carefully reviewed and criticised by English judges, had established the fact sufficiently for all unprejudiced minds that the Nawab was entirely ignorant of the cruelties practised on these unfortunate men, and that their death was circumstantially reported at the time to have taken place from cholera. Nevertheless Lord Dalhousie called on the Nawab to give an explanation of his conduct in the matter, and he determined that "measures should be taken to mark the sense entertained by Government of such proceedings, and that safeguards should be provided against a repetition of them in future." The measures thus extra-judicially resolved on were the humbling of the Prince by reducing his salute from nineteen to thirteen guns, refusing him permission to travel, stopping the amount in his civil list for travelling expenses, and appointing a police officer to accompany him on all excursions. He was also peremptorily required to dismiss the suspected persons of his household, and to "hold no further communication with them." Finally the Viceroy in Council repealed the four Acts alluded to, on the specious plea that the privileges they secured "were a serious impediment to the course of justice." It had hardly been matter for surprise if the Prince, thus insulted and oppressed in defiance of every principle of law, logic, or common sense, had looked on sullenly in the day of England's difficulty. But in common with many other Native Chiefs, he aided materially and morally Lord Canning's Government during the Mutiny. Throughout, his conduct was one of unswerving fidelity. When British power emerged, shaken but unshattered, from the storm of rebellion, to the official request to know what expense he had been at for unusual service rendered, he answered declining to receive any pecuniary return, affirming that he had done his duty, fulfilling the conditions of the treaties entered into by his ancestors." In deeds, if not in words, he repeated the reproach of his progenitor ninety-seven years before. "You have thought proper to break your engagements; I would not mine." The Government was bound in decency to acknowledge in some way this requital of good for evil; the restoration of his salute, the removal of the police inspectors, and the reimbursement of travelling expenses were therefore ordered. In other respects the Dalhousie deprivations have been maintained; the demands of the Nawab for an equitable adjustment of accounts, which the maladministration of Government agents over many years has involved in complication and confusion, and the restoration of certain moneys to which he is clearly entitled as heir-at-law, but which have been persistently sequestrated, have been refused; his rights under solemn treaties made with his family—treaties which were the title-deeds of our settlement in India only a century ago—are declared to be obsolete, and even his rank and title have been mutteringly threatened with extinction.

The year 1854 saw two more valuable provinces absorbed through other means. The subsidiary force kept up at the expense of the Nizam had long been excessive, measured by its nominal use or his ability of paying for it.[1] Lord Dalhousie admitted that it was too large, and suggested that the staff, at all events, ought to be reduced. But £750,000 were due as arrears, and no improvident willingness to raise loans at 30 per cent. held out any real hope of liquidation. The Viceroy, therefore, caused it

[1] Kaye's Sepoy War, vol. i. p. 97.

to be intimated that he would accept the fertile cotton districts of Berar, the Raichore Doab lying between the rivers Krishna and Tumbudra, together with other lands, in payment of the debt, and as security for future charges for the contingent. When the draft treaty was presented, the Nizam expostulated, asking whether an alliance which had lasted unbroken more than sixty years ought to have an ending like this. He did not want the subsidiary force; the Viceroy might withdraw it if he pleased; or he might cut down its supernumerary strength and extravagant allowances, which were merely maintained as ways of patronage by the Governor-General, and not for any benefit to him. But to ask him to part with a third of his dominions was to humble him in the eyes of his people, and to abase him in his own esteem. He had not deserved treatment so heartless, and he could not be expected to submit to it. But he was expected, and he did submit: and soon afterwards he died, leaving his son to try, as best he might, how the work of government could be carried on. The nettings of 1853 were full of cotton and opium, for the provinces newly added are among the most prolific in Southern Asia.

We are come to the last, and the most memorable of Lord Dalhousie's acts of annexation. From Clive to Auckland, every Anglo-Indian ruler had dealt with the Government of Oude as that of an independent State. It had been invaded, rifled, mutilated, sometimes aided with troops to do mischief to its neighbours, and sometimes to its own people. More than once it was flattered by the gift of expropriations from other States, and as often humbled by being compelled, not to give them back to the rightful owners, but to give them up to the Paramount Power. The undermining of native authority had indeed been pitilessly continued under all circumstances by the never failing means of an exorbitant subsidiary force. The Vizier being left every year less discretion in affairs, fell ever more lamentably under the influence of parasites, who wasted his revenues, and shut him in from all knowledge of his people's condition, and from all hearing of their complaints. It cannot be doubted that beneath the unchecked cupidity and caprice of some of the Talookdars they suffered grievously, and that portions of their fair and fertile country had in consequence become impoverished and wasted. Disorganisation had in fact become normal; and making every allowance for sinister exaggeration, it is impossible to regard the remonstrances of successive Residents at Lucknow as having been made without substantial cause. Reforms in every branch of the administration had become urgent and indispensable, and it may freely be admitted that it was the duty of the Paramount Authority to insist upon their being made. But until it can be shown that honest, intelligible, and consistent efforts were tried to redeem the local institutions, which mercenary encroachment had perverted, and to restore the local health imperialism had poisoned, there cannot be a shadow of justification for inflicting the sentence of death arbitrarily pronounced against them. To the last men of intellect and honour, who had intimate knowledge of the whole state of the case, believed that reparation was in our power, and pleaded hard that it ought to be made. But from first to last it never was seriously attempted. Things were suffered year by year to go from bad to worse, while the gripe of exaction never was relaxed, until at length, in 1856, the scandal of mismanagement was pronounced ripe, not for the pruning-knife of suzerain control, but for the axe of ruthless annexation.

When war against the Mahrattas had left the Company without a pagoda to sustain the public credit or to pay their troops, Lord Hastings bribed the Vizier with the pinchbeck title of King to give him a million sterling out of his private treasure. When war against the Afghans needed new resources, Lord Auckland made a fresh treaty requiring the surrender of half his territory to sustain additional troops. On every occasion the diplomatic engagements dictated at Calcutta and imposed at Lucknow were profuse in professions of respect for the dynasty and acknowledgment of its sovereign rights. To the last Oude was flattered with egregious assurances of friendship and consideration, until at a blow all was swept away.

When absorption and incorporation had been determined on, differences of opinion arose in the Supreme Council as to the mode of proceeding in point of form. The Viceroy affected to have scruples. He would have preferred declaring the treaties broken by the failure of Vajîd Ali to fulfil the conditions of efficient government embodied in the treaty of 1837; he would then have withdrawn the contingent, without which the city and the palace would have been left defenceless against banditti; and when insurrection and anarchy had spread alarm among the neighbouring provinces, he would have been prepared for armed intervention at the request of the King, or without waiting for it. But he has left on record a confession that this would have been a circuitous method of attaining the end which General Low, Mr Peacock, Mr Grant, and Mr Dorin thought it less dishonouring to bring about by more direct and summary means. The Board of Directors and Board of Control, when the two plans were laid before them, refrained from deciding, and left the Marquis free to do as he thought best.[1] The difficulty was like that felt by Warren Hastings on a former occasion, which Sheridan, amid the cheers of the House of Commons, declared to be that of choosing between Bagshot and Hounslow. It was, however, speedily got over by the Governor-General yielding to the more summary method urged by his colleagues. The Resident was therefore directed to inform the Prince that he had been weighed in the balance and found wanting, and that the kingdom had departed from him.

It was said by the apologists of the act, that the treaty of 1837 conferred the right to seize the government of Oude, should its native rulers fail to govern well, and that consequently no more was done in 1856 than what that bargain provided for and justified. The flimsiness of this plea has been thoroughly exposed by Major Bell. The treaty of 1837 "did not give Lord Dalhousie all he wanted. It did not give him the surplus revenues of Oude, to be disposed of as he pleased, but compelled him to account for them to the State of Oude. It gave him a right indeed to seize the government, but only for a temporary object, and bound him (in the words of the treaty) to maintain the native institutions and forms of administration, so as to facilitate the restoration of those territories to the sovereign." The Viceroy felt the pressure of these cogent terms, and tried hard to prove that because the Directors bade Lord Auckland exonerate the King from supplying an increased number of troops, the whole of the treaty of 1837 had been abrogated. Nothing can be more untrue. It was duly ratified at Fort William on the 18th September 1837; was never repudiated by the Government of the Queen, and

---

[1] Bell's Retrospects and Prospects, chap. v.

was never disallowed by the Board of Directors, whose ratification was in point of fact never deemed necessary in the case of a new treaty. "No one in India, at Lucknow or at Calcutta, ever doubted the validity and binding force of this treaty until Lord Dalhousie found that it stood in the way of his scheme of appropriating all the revenues of Oude." [1]

Sir H. Lawrence and Sir W. Sleeman both publicly expressed their conviction that the Central Government was endued by it with all the powers necessary for securing in Oude an efficient and humane administration; and Lord Hardinge, in 1847, impressively warned the Court of Lucknow that, under and by virtue of the treaty, they were liable to have the powers of government sequestered if they were not properly discharged. But sequestration is not synonymous with confiscation; and the suspension of a spendthrift's allowance does not mean the appropriation of his estate. It is not unworthy of note that Lord W. Bentinck, the most lenient and considerate of men, contemplated temporary interposition in Oude, in the hope and with the view of introducing juster and sounder principles of local administration, and that he obtained the sanction of the Court of Directors in case he should think fit to make the experiment. But who will debit his memory with contemplation of the crime perpetrated in 1856 ? We have his own clear definition of his meaning. "It may be asked of me,—when you have assumed the management, how is it to be conducted, and how long retained ? I should answer, that acting in the character of guardian and trustee, we ought to frame an administration entirely native,—an administration so composed as to individuals, and so established upon the best principles, as should best

[1] Bell's Retrospects and Prospects, chap. v.

serve for immediate improvement, and as a model for future imitation; the only European part of it should be the functionary by whom it should be superintended, and it should only be retained till a complete reform might be brought about."

CHAPTER XXVII.

TO-DAY; AND TO-MORROW?

"A feeling of discontent and dissatisfaction exists among every class, both European and Native, on account of the constant increase of taxation which has for years been going on. My belief is that the continuance of that feeling is a political danger, the magnitude of which can hardly be over-estimated; and any sentiment of dissatisfaction which may exist among disbanded soldiers of the Native Army is as nothing, in comparison with the state of general discontent to which I have referred. . . . We can never depend for a moment on the continuance of general tranquillity; but I believe that the present state of public feeling, as regards taxation, is more likely to lead to disturbance and discontent, and to be to us a source of greater danger, than the partial reduction which we propose in the Native Army can ever occasion. Of the two evils I choose the lesser."

—Lord Mayo.[1]

WHEN Parliament assembled early in 1858, the uppermost thought in the minds of all was the urgent need of remedial measures for India. A century of misrule had ended in a convulsion so terrible that the best and bravest natures shuddered at its contemplation, and the wisest and ablest servants of the State were those who said the least about it. The whole of the dreadful truth has never yet been spoken,—will never probably be spoken in our time; but enough became generally known to make men of all parties anxious, by a thorough change of policy, to take securities against the like ever happening again. Notice was formally given by ministers to the East India Company that its days were numbered. What was called the "double government" had long been

[1] Minute of the Viceroy, on Military Expenditure, 3d October 1870.

regarded as incurably evasive of responsibility, and incurably vicious in its abuse of patronage. The time had arrived when national opinion ratified the prescient condemnation of Francis, Burke, and Fox, and pronounced decisively, though tardily, that a secret Committee of the Directors of a joint-stock company should be permitted no longer to share with the Imperial Cabinet the power of nominating the rulers of our great dependency. The public voice called on Parliament to do its duty to India, as well as to portions of the empire inferior in extent, population, and importance. However it had been acquired, all political parties agreed in owning that the Queen was bound to the natives of her Empire in Asia " by the same obligations of duty which bound her to all her other subjects." These were in fact the words placed in Her Majesty's lips by Lord Stanley, when, as Secretary of State, he counselled and countersigned the memorable Proclamation, assuming the direct and unqualified government of her possessions in India. But while Parliament in its legislative capacity acknowledged and confirmed to the Crown the undivided dignity and authority of supreme administration, it did not thereby renounce or pretend to shake off the enhanced burthen of its own obligation to exact a rigorous and righteous account of all that might be done from time to time in the name of the Queen. The Statute of 1858, putting an end to the Charter of the East India Company, and declaring that in time to come no privilege of race or creed should be tolerated, and no respect of persons by reason of their lineage or place of birth be known in the eyes of the law, bade the tribes and nations of Hindustan stand forth and claim their full measure of rights and immunities, and pledged Queen, Lords, and Commons to be ready to hear and determine their plaint for justice whenever duly preferred, and to enforce reparation and restitution for wrong whenever proved.

The Royal Proclamation of the 1st November 1858, renounced solemnly all thought of further annexation.

"Whereas, for divers weighty reasons, we have resolved to take upon ourselves the Government of India, heretofore administered in trust for us by the Honourable East India Company—we do by these presents notify and declare that we have taken upon ourselves the said Government, and we hereby call upon all our subjects within the said territories to be faithful, and to bear true allegiance to us, our heirs and successors.

"We hereby announce to the Native Princes of India, that all treaties and engagements made with them by or under the authority of the Honourable East India Company, are by us accepted, and will be scrupulously maintained, and we look for the like observance on their part. We desire no extension of our territorial possessions; and while we will permit no aggression upon our dominions or our rights to be attempted with impunity, we shall sanction no encroachment on those of others. We shall respect the rights, dignity, and honour of Native Princes as our own.

"We hold ourselves bound to the natives of our Indian territories by the same obligations of duty which bind us to all our other subjects, and those obligations, by the blessing of Almighty God, we shall faithfully and conscientiously fulfil."

The Princes of India received these assurances with satisfaction, qualified only by their inability to judge how far the representatives of Majesty afar off would observe their equitable tenor. Remembering the past, they could not feel sanguine as to the future; for they were told that the preponderating will in Parliament decided who should be the Queen's ministers, and who should be her Viceroys; and they and their fathers had oftentimes appealed in vain against the haughty satraps who had been set over them. Their hopes rose when, somewhat later, Lord Canning, in his celebrated Minute regarding Adoption, explicitly laid it down that the policy of the Government would thereafter be to recognise the native rights of succession in royal and noble houses, because it had been resolved to preserve subsisting dynasties and chieftainries as essential to good government and peace. "I was astonished," he said, " at the effect produced by my declaration at Gwalior, where the announcement was received with expressions of joy like those on the birth of a prince." Scindia told the Resident that a cold wind had been blowing on him incessantly for years, from which he was now relieved. Yet, unhappily, too soon—" was it gone, and for ever, the light they saw breaking?" Hardly was the ink of the Adoption Minute dry when Government recalcitrated; and the old policy of confiscation and absorption was summarily put in force upon a new and equally untenable plea. The young Rajah of Dhar was suddenly informed that his accession to his father's titles and privileges had been disallowed, without a hearing or a trial of any description, and that his dominions were to be incorporated with those of the Crown, because, during the revolt, some of his troops had mutinied, and for a time resisted the efforts of his guardians to bring them back to discipline and loyalty. Lord Canning assigned as his only reason that he was determined to show the Durbars of the minor States that they must be held accountable if they were unable as well as if they were unwilling to restrain the misconduct of their soldiery. In reply to a question, put in the House of Commons, Lord Stanley frankly repudiated the doctrine thus laid down, which did not, he said, lie in the mouth of a Power which had been itself unable to keep its troops from mutiny; and he promised that the annexation should be reversed. His despatch reprieving Dhar and its people from the penalties of sins whereof they were guiltless in all but the name, was set at nought by Lord Canning, who directed Sir Robert Hamilton, the Resident at Indore in August 1858, to inform the young Rajah that his principality was annexed, and that his treasure and jewels were to be divided as prize-money among the troops of the column then serving before the place. He was to accompany the announcement with an intimation that while Government reserved its decision, the unfortunate family must never hope to be restored. The Resident, an upright and a fearless man, acquainted with the real circumstances of the case better than the Viceroy, expostulated against this injustice. The rulers and the people of Dhar had been faithful allies until, in the midst of the tempest of mutiny raging around them, the mistake had been committed of turning loose upon them the lawless mercenaries removed from the Nizam's country, because they were supposed to be dangerous there. Certain fanatics had seized the opportunity to foment sedition, the local Government being in the hands of a Regency; but the British Agent had throughout been on terms of constant communication with the Rajah, and had nothing to complain of in him, his relatives, or influential advisers. If he were to be deprived of his political authority, Sir Robert Hamilton pleaded hard that at least he should not be despoiled of his property. Lord Canning's pride was nettled at the rebuke he had received from the Secretary of State. He left to Colonel Durand the task of answering the remonstrance, and the decree of sequestration was pitilessly enforced. The potent influence of Mr Bright was exerted in the following session, and Sir Charles Wood, who had succeeded Lord Stanley in the India Office, sought to compromise the question by giving a pledge that, on attaining his majority, the Rajah should be reinstated, one-fifth of his territories being permanently retained by way of smart money. Two years afterwards, public notice was given throughout Malwa of the sale by auction of the family ornaments and gems— or, as it was called, of the "Dhar plunder"—valued at £80,000. After many delays upon the ground that he was not yet qualified to govern, the friends in England who had watched over the endangered rights of the Rajah had the satisfaction of hearing that he was restored.

It is deeply to be regretted that, within the last few years, the Anglo-Indian administration seems to have been drawn to thoughts of reviving the "lunatic policy of annexation."[1] It ought not to have been forgotten, indeed, that "during the perilous crisis of 1857, the most serviceable and timely aid, in men and money, was furnished by every class of native rulers."[2] Lord Canning had publicly thanked many of them for their effectual help; and, alluding to the smaller States, he admitted that "these patches of Native Government served as breakwaters to the storm, which would otherwise have swept over us in one great wave."[3] At such words each menaced and mistrustful ruler might well have said, like the captive king in the tent of Saul, "Surely the bitterness of death is past." Evil traditions, however, are insidious and strong, even when they are not respectable through age. The danger past, the old craving for more territory returned. After two partitions, a separate though protected Raj was still left in

---

[1] Mr Bright—Debate on Indian Budget, 1st August 1859.
[2] The Mysore Reversion, by Major Evans Bell, p. 2. [3] Adoption Minute.

Mysore. With prescient care the Duke of Wellington had, upon the fall of Seringapatam, warned his brother that although the treaty with the restored Rajah professed to be one of "perpetual friendship and alliance," which was to last so "long as the sun and moon endured," its terms were sufficiently ambiguous to "give ground for the belief that we gave the Rajah the country with the intention of taking it away again, when it should suit our convenience;" and he expressed his strong opinion that "the conduct of the British Government in India had not at all times been such as to induce the natives to believe, that at some time or other improper advantage would not be taken of the article in question."[1] But when the Duke was dead it was thought the time had come when advantage might be taken of the omission, in the treaty, of the words, heirs and successors. Lord Dalhousie left on record his advice, that should the reigning prince die childless, the last remnant of the ancient realm of Mysore should be forthwith absorbed; and in 1865 the Anglo-Indian Government prepared to secure the expected escheat by lapse. In that year the Rajah adopted a distant relative as his son, according to Hindu rites; the representative of the British Government being present, and the chief persons of rank and property in the State. The fact was formally notified by him in a letter to the Governor-General. Sir John Lawrence declined to recognise the validity of the adoption, and was sustained in his efforts to defeat it by the Secretary of State. But his arguments were controverted by five distinguished members of the Supreme Council, who each and all stigmatised the attempt to pervert the treaty of 1799, in a manner, as the Duke of Wellington had foretold, that would "not be creditable to us." Fortunately for

[1] Letter of Colonel Arthur Wellesley to Lord Mornington, 1799.

the honour of England and the tranquillity of India, another pen was dipped in indignation at the contemplated injustice. In a work of rare ability both as regards the matter and the manner, Major Evans Bell called the attention of the public to the history of the case, and beneath the cloud of witnesses against this miserable scheme of usurpation, appealed from the Council Board of Calcutta to the judgment of the people of England. Citing the damnatory protest of Sir H. Montgomery, who characterised the project as a "breach of good faith;" of Sir F. Currie, who declared it to be "unjust and illegal;" of Sir J. Willoughby, who termed it a "flagrant injustice;" of Sir George Clerk, who called it "the result of wild counsel, neither honest nor dignified;" of Captain Eastwick, who said "that it could not be justified by our treaty obligations, nor by the law and practice of India," he challenged the Government to defend their purpose. Party convenience rendered the season unsuitable, and thus another Native State was saved from extinction. But what sort of tenancy-at-will is this for Native Governments, on whose stability the order, prosperity, and peace of an Empire depend? Other Princes naturally and inevitably brood over these things, and feel, though they may not say aloud—*Nusquam tuta fides!* Parliament, in almost every session, is asked to enquire into some case of actual injury or threatened deprivation; and individual members, unconnected with office, are often found willing to master the details of grievance, and to declaim eloquently against evil done, if not against evil doers. But it usually comes to nothing. A political tribunal so constituted is, if possible, even more helpless than the House of Lords proved to be in 1795, to do justice between the Begums of Oude and Warren Hastings. Until suitable means are found for the trial of such causes, there will and can be no sense of security felt by the

Princes of India. But, after what has happened aforetime, and in our own time, Parliament will be inexcusable if, conscious of the reproach, yet unmindful of the shame, it neglects to make due provision for the purpose. It will, of course, be said by all the indolent and apathetic, and all who prefer the unbridled power of bureaucracy to the vindication of the national influence and honour, that the erection of a Parliamentary Tribunal fit to try issues of right, revenue, dignity, and rule, between Suzerain and vassals, is a thing impossible; if not impossible, unprecedented; and if not unprecedented, revolutionary. It is not worth while arguing about the impossibility. Most things worth doing, in our day, have been declared by official politicians to be obviously impossible, because to them the possibility was not obvious. Catholic Emancipation, the Repeal of the Corn Laws, Household Suffrage, and much beside, were each and all pronounced, on the best authority, to be things that could not be done. But they were done, notwithstanding, and the earth still goes round, and nobody feels materially the worse: a good many think they feel considerably better. As for the lack of precedents, it might be enough to say, that the case of India is one so utterly unparalleled, that the remedy sought must needs be unparalleled also. In truth, however, it is only necessary to put together maxims grounded on established precedents, in order to spell out warily and wisely all the conditions that are required: and for the nickname of revolutionary, one can hardly be expected to care, when the only object that is sought is the conservation and contentment of an empire. *Sobriquets* are easily given, but they need applicability to make them stick; and if any man can devise a method to vindicate the solemn pledge of Parliament to India, to realise the plighted faith of the Queen, and to build up steadfast faith and hope in the Princes and people of Asia, he need not trouble himself about being called a revolutionist; for he will have done the most anti-subversive thing which it is possible to conceive.

Why not then consider how a joint Committee of the Two Houses, three from each, may be chosen whenever a claim duly authenticated and verified is raised by any of the feudatories of the Crown in India? Why should the selection of three noblemen and of three gentlemen without miserable imputations of party bias be impracticable? Why should we every year see questions as pecuniarily great, and interests as morally and socially grave, referred without misgiving to a Committee in each House, to be practically disposed of, without any of the more solemn judicial sanctions with which it would be easy to invest the Tribunal thus proposed? Why should not the composition, order, and procedure of such a tribunal be regulated by statute? and why should not the co-ordinate authority of the Crown be represented in a Chairman or Assessor, to be named from amongst ex-Chancellors or Chief Justices, to guide its deliberations by the wisdom of experience, and acquaintance with the principles and practice of international law? Why should not unofficial peers and commoners deem it a high distinction to be chosen by their fellows to be daysmen between central power all but absolute, and therefore always liable to err, and local freedom, all but helpless, and therefore always liable to distrust and disaffection? Why should not such a judicature be a Court of Record, its decisions contributing to build up, as with hewn stones, carefully chosen and fitly joined together, a wall of defensive justice and right, beneath which princes and chiefs might sleep securely, and dare to resume their ancient air of dignity and self-respect, no man making them afraid?

Natives of wealth and education have been, in compliance with the Statute of 1858, admitted to the Council of each of the Presidencies. As a step in the right direction, the change ought not to be disparaged; but it would be idle to suppose that its political effect can be of any appreciable importance. At Calcutta, three or four Rajahs living in the neighbourhood are summoned periodically to meet the Governor-General and their European colleagues at the Council Board; and chiefs of secondary rank are in like manner invited to confer with the Governors of Madras, and Bombay. As a formal renunciation of the exclusiveness of alien rule, it is well; but who takes it for a participation of power between foreign authority and native will? The question is not one of numerical proportion;—that would be a childish view to take of the matter. Votes are of no value when the subjects to be voted on are settled and arranged beforehand, by one over whom the voters can exercise neither veto or control. As equerries, men of birth and opulence are gratified by being asked to ride in a pageant, or take their places at a banquet; and the opinion of political outriders is sometimes asked in courtesy about the political weather. It is even said that their deferential expression of opinion has been known to have been acted on respecting wind or rain, or the colour of a court suit. But who is fooled by such lofty condescension into imagining that grooms-in-waiting are Ministers of State? If power remains where it was and what it was, permission to assist at its ceremonies is but the politeness of centralisation, and no more.

In a subordinate sphere another step, and one that had more of the look of reality about it, was that of conferring upon natives the Commission of the Peace. At first the Ryots were incredulous, then half inclined to laugh, afterwards distrustful, but by degrees they were convinced that the Talookdar or Baboo must have paid handsomely for the right to do himself and his neighbours justice in certain small matters. When the practice shall be carried further, and some approach shall be made to the system of local justice prevailing in our own agricultural districts, where every resident gentleman of property, not as of political favour, but as of social right, is called upon to act as a magistrate, not capriciously and alone, but according to recognised principle, and in concert with others like himself, the people of India may come to believe that Government is sincere in desiring to extend some English institutions to India in substance as well as in name. For the present, it would be premature to hazard an opinion on the success of an experiment which is yet but in course of being tentatively made. In many great districts the number of persons holding the Commission of the Peace is infinitesimally small; in others the native magistrates are described as not venturing to decide in reality any question open to serious controversy.

The local administration of justice remains throughout the Non-Regulation Provinces for the most part in European hands. In the provinces of earlier acquisition, Hindus and Mussulmans have at all times been judges of subordinate courts, and much stress has been recently laid upon the admission of candidates for these appointments by competitive examination. Many who are well qualified to judge, set but a low estimate on the adequacy of such a test of fitness for judicial office. However that may be, the main fact stares us in the face, that not one in a hundred of the higher judges has been born or bred in the country whose disputes he is empowered to determine, and whose inhabitants he may fine, flog, imprison, or impoverish at his individual discretion. From the nature of things he must be a judge both of law and equity. This equity he must find for himself out of his inner consciousness; the difficulties of law are more perplexing when they arise from various codes ancient and modern, written, half-written, or not written at all, but often preserved in a kind of fossil state, now and then rubbed up for a special purpose, and thus partially made to reveal their antique qualities. When the young gentleman from England is sharp-witted and of an inquiring turn, he gets after a time to know, by the help of interpreters, what illiterate peasants, roguish witnesses, lying tessildars, and grain usurers swear, in their various dialects, for or against one another. But it takes him a long time to be able to feel sure how much of what he calls justice is not guess work, and how much of it is not behind his back compassed by corruption. It is no use blaming him for blunders that are inevitable, and wrongs he cannot help, and seldom so much as hears of. Appeal of course is said to be open (like the London Tavern), to all who will avail themselves of it, and are prepared to pay for the gratification; but the privilege, which never was general, has been materially circumscribed by the imposition of innumerable, and, by the vast majority, impayable stamp duties on every species of litigation which an exotic system of finance has rendered necessary. The enormous distances, moreover, which the bulk of suitors have to travel, and the delays at the central seats of law, which await them there, form impediments not to be overcome. In a great number of districts the Collector or district Commissioner still exercises the functions of a Vice-Chancellor and puisne judge. He is usually a soldier, with a fair disposition to do right, according to the principles of common sense, and with an ignorance of what in England we think a judge ought to know, that would be ludicrous if it were not lamentable. To-day he has to assess damages according to the customs sanctioned by Akbar; to-morrow to marshal assets in bankruptcy, conformably with the orders of Basinghall Street; and next day to settle a question of legitimacy according to Brahminical traditions. What would the people of London think if a cavalry officer were made Recorder, a colonel of marines Common Serjeant, and a first class prizeman in gunnery appointed to preside at Bow Street? But with all the fine bureaucratic talk about the protection of Parliament having been extended and applied, it is clear that, in matters of judgment, justice, and mercy, any qualifications, or disqualifications, are still deemed immaterial in India.

To seats in the Supreme Courts, native practitioners at the bar are not only now admissible, but are actually admitted; and English judges who have sat with them are forward to acknowledge how honourably and usefully they bear themselves. This is something, and it would, indeed, be much, if, beyond the Presidential cities, the fact were practically brought home to the minds of the community; but, whatever may be the code of civil or criminal law, the adjudication of ordinary disputes between man and man must be local, if it is to be prompt, cheap, and intelligible; and if it be not, it signifies comparatively little what it is, or what it is believed to be. The indigenous tribunal of Punchayet has been all but suspended by the imposition of a system of stipendiaries, whose unacquaintance with the infinite details of social life, renders them ineffably feeble in their best attempts to exercise any moral or equitable sway. The people must be idiots to reverence law so administered; but the blame lies neither with commissioners, assistants, or deputies, who have to administer as best they may the system they have found existing; it will hereafter lie at the door of

Parliament, if, having undertaken the government of an unrepresented Empire, it fails to reform the administration of justice thoroughly, and in a sense conformable to Indian public opinion.

The apologists of dis-location, and of concentration of all authority in one central hand, have always relied on its physical results as outweighing beneficially the discontent and demoralisation it palpably entails. India, for the first time, enjoys, according to them, the industrial blessing of security from the caprices of arbitrary exaction, and from the ravages of internal war. Taxation may not be always light, and it can be seldom agreeable; but, at all events, it is based on principles of uniformity and moderation, and it is not spent on Court shows, or equipments for border raids. Logically, India ought to grow fat; for, dividing the population by the total revenue, the average payment for English Government is no more than 7s. a head by 150,000,000 of people; while most of the nations of Europe pay three or four times that amount; and we, in England, bear a burthen on the average (taking into account local as well as imperial taxation) of not less than £3 a head. But the fallacy of this mode of argument is fundamental and glaring. Shelter from the ravages of local warfare is undoubtedly a great gain; so is the shelter of a twenty-feet prison-wall against the licence of marauders, and the edge of the east wind. But did anybody ever seek voluntarily such protection, or grow rich and happy beneath its shadow? A physical benefit is only entitled to gratitude, and only receives it when it may be had at a price worth paying for it. The question here is not the specific good, which, as an abstract proposition, is little more than a form of words without meaning; but whether the cataleptic trance imposed by the Paramount Power—imposed on all spontaneous local activity, warlike or peaceful—is not bought unnecessarily dear? Does rural or urban industry thrive within the precincts of the great imperial pound? Does it delve and weave, speculate and spin, with the energy and profit necessary for the accumulation and the diffusion of wealth? Are the people of India growing rich or poor? Is the taxation they pay really light or really heavy? Is the government sum in short division, which gives a quotient of a few shillings a head, as against nine times as much which we pay, a true or a fair statement of the fact, or merely a statistical delusion?

How ought this comparison of taxation to be made? We might as well take an average of the length of the tails of the dogs and horses, or of the backbones of the bipeds in human form, for the purposes of such a comparison. The wonder is how men in high office could ever have been betrayed into talking in such fashion. If taxes were paid in bone or blood, to divide their sum into the aggregate of blood and bones, might have some reason or sense in it; but there is literally no sense in a bald capitation estimate of fiscal burthens; for the only ingredients of the computation worthy of attention or care are palpably omitted. Taxes are a deduction not from men's bodies, but from their purses. If their purses are small and nearly empty, a tax of a rupee may be extortionate; if their purses are deep and full, the exaction of a £5 note may be light. If we compare the £50,000,000 of Indian revenue with the £72,000,000 of British revenue, the sole question worth asking is, how do the national incomes stand, out of which the two amounts are drawn. All else but this is mere irrelevancy and trifling. What then do we find? From the most authentic sources we gather that the total production of the Indian Empire is under £300,000,000 a year;

that of the United Kingdom is about £900,000,000 sterling. This would give a taxation of 3s. 4d. in the pound in India, and less than 1s. 8d. in the pound in England. The difference, however, between the incidence of the two burthens is enormously increased by the circumstance that nineteen-twentieths of our taxes are annually, monthly, it might almost be said daily re-spent amongst us; while of the revenues of India a large portion is exported hither to furnish us with extra means of comfort and of luxury. The manure is thus continually withdrawn from eastern fields to enrich the island gardens of the West. It has been variously estimated that, irrespective of interest on debt, six, seven, and even eight millions a year are drawn from India to be spent by Englishmen either there or at home. The process of exhaustion may be slow, but it is sure. Science, skill, care, invention, may devise means of compensation, and when they are applied systematically and permanently, we shall be able to measure their value. But is there any pretence for saying that any attempt of the kind has ever been made, or is efficiently making now? We have laid the people and Princes of India under tribute, and after a century of varied experiments, the only limit of exaction seems to be the physical capacity of the yield.

Lord Mayo says plainly, in his minutes and despatches, that the burthen of Imperial taxation has increased, is increasing, and ought to be diminished. In 1856 the total expenditure amounted to £33,378,026, and that for 1870 was £50,782,412, or an increase of more than seventeen millions sterling. Meanwhile, what is the condition of the mass of the people? By the confession of the latest authority, they are reduced to the lowest point at which existence can be maintained. Penury, with all its attendant privations, when the season is good, and pinching want bordering on destitution when the season is bad, are the only alternatives of the ryot's lot. Even this is not the worst. When, owing to exceptional causes, the harvest fails, the same dreadful consequences follow under our system of so-called civilised rule as used to happen in former times. Not five years ago six hundred thousand persons perished of starvation within three hundred miles of the capital of Anglo-India.

Even an increased taxation of 50 per cent. is insufficient to meet the expenditure. In spite of the imposition of an Income Tax, novel, unequalled, and prolific of fraud, constantly recurring deficits require to be met by fresh loans. The augmented expenditure, which augmented taxes and loans are raised to meet, consists mainly of outlay upon the army and upon public works. Ever since the Mutiny, the number of European troops has been permanently increased, and the rise of prices has greatly swollen the cost of the Commissariat. Encouragement to railways has become part of the standing policy of the Government. To stimulate agricultural industry, and to furnish means of cheap transit for goods of bulk, the increase of canals has become a duty still more imperative. Their advantages can hardly be exaggerated. At a sixth of the cost of iron roads (as iron roads are made in India), water ways can be constructed, as in the region of the Godavary, that would pay for their own cost, and diffuse the blessings of fertility around them. The growth of cotton has not spread as rapidly as was prognosticated; and the present Commander-in-Chief is of opinion that, strategically, railways can only be regarded as valuable so long as they are in our actual possession, while their establishment inevitably dislocates and diminishes the old means of transit, which cannot suddenly be re-organised on an emergency. Be that as it may, all mankind have learned to trade and travel by steam, and the least we can do for the country, whose ancient ways and works of civilisation have been half destroyed in our struggle for ascendancy, is to secure it the mechanical advantages of our own. Canals, if not railways, must be extended, however they have to be made. But communities denuded of Native power, dispirited by disappointment, and drained for generations of the accumulations of their industry, cannot be expected to make such works for themselves. We have broken the limbs of enterprise, and we must find it splints and crutches. To some extent this has been done by guarantees of interest given by the Anglo-Indian Treasury for the millions of capital expended on railways. But, when other capital for public works is wanted, the question is, to what account shall this money be charged. Mr Laing set it down as an item in the Capital Account of Empire, arguing justly that it was an expenditure indispensable to political security, and an expenditure which the debilitated and disheartened energies of the country were unable, without grievous detriment, to bear. The Home Government overruled his decision, and sooner than lend himself to a course which, as a statesman, he had pronounced blundering and oppressive, he resigned. Various expedients have been resorted to in order to choke the gaping deficit, but hitherto without effect. Mr Massey concurred substantially in opinion with Mr Laing; and being unable to induce the Home Government to sanction the framing of his budgets in the way which he thought equitable, he sought to vindicate his own consistency by arraying the necessary expenditure in a time of peace against the normal results of taxation, whereby he made both ends meet; and then, below a black line of warning, added the charge for offices, barracks, and canals, wherefrom arose the deficit to be provided for, either by borrowing, or by exceptional and oppressive taxation. It is now admitted that the outlay of millions on large permanent barracks has been worse than money thrown away. Aggregation, which proves so detrimental in Europe, is deadly in Asia. Not only in Bengal, but in the north-west provinces, these monuments of bureaucratic blundering serve only to remind the overtaxed community of one kind of jobbing on which their money has been recently spent. The merchants of Bombay, in the remarkable protest addressed by them in May 1870 to the Secretary of State against raising the income-tax to eightpence in the pound, reasonably suggested that "if the charges of constructing extensive public works of a permanent nature were met by terminable loans for fixed periods, instead of being defrayed from the current revenues, one main cause of deficit in the finances of India would be eliminated." But the recommendation has not been adopted; and fresh disclosures of the unfair and fraudulent working of the income-tax are made day after day. The bulk of the community, it is true, escape its incidence. Their discontent is secured by the heavy duty on salt, which can only be evaded by the peasantry who are fortunate enough to live near the sea, or the works where this indispensable element of life is manufactured; the former boil their rice in sea-water, and the latter mingle with it portions of the mud that has become saturated with saline particles.[1] The Duke of Argyll in 1869 pressed upon the attention of the Viceregal Council the need of securing an equilibrium, and Lord Mayo, in language equally earnest, acknowledged the expediency of military retrenchment. Pre-eminently responsible for the peace and safety of the vast dependencies committed to his charge, he avows that, even were

[1] Report of the Bombay Association for 1870.

the embarrassments of the Exchequer less urgent, we should not be justified "in spending one shilling more upon our army than can be shown to be absolutely and imperatively necessary. There are considerations of a far higher nature involved in this matter than the annual exigencies of finance, or the interests of those who are employed in the military service of the Crown. Every shilling that is taken for unnecessary military expenditure, is so much withdrawn from those vast sums which it is our duty to spend for the moral and material improvement of the people." But what are vast armies maintained for in a country so circumstanced? Danger from without there is none that, with the advantages of railways and telegraphs, half the number of troops now kept under arms would not be able to repel. But if danger be from within, is it not time that Parliament should consider whether the engrossment of Indian patronage in alien hands, and the exclusion of princes, nobles, traders, and landowners from all substantial share in the government of their country, is not a national error and a national wrong, that sooner or later may cost us very dear.

The key of the position is in the public purse. Until it is taken in hand and firmly held by Parliament, the prison doors of India's progress will never be unlocked. Misrule cannot exist without an overgrown army, and wasteful military expenditure cannot live but by misrule. From first to last the policy of conquest and confiscation has implied and required not only an amount of force which good government would not have wanted, but an amount of jobbing, under the name and pretence of military expenditure, which good government would under no circumstances have needed or allowed. Wholly apart from the enormous drain upon the profits of Indian industry, in the form of emoluments hoarded and husbanded for private use at home, the resources of the country have systematically been exhausted for the pay and keep of an excessive military establishment, of which a great portion has at all times been European. Fifteen years after the suppression of the last revolt, the standing army employed in keeping India down costs £16,500,000, a vast increase as compared with the period previous to the Mutiny, and the whole of the increase being upon European men, equipment, and stores. Lord Mayo, endeavouring to meet the suggestions of the Secretary of State, proposed to reduce the number of native troops to the extent of 7000 or 8000 men, thereby to effect a saving of £640,000 a-year; but he admitted that "serious opposition" was likely to be offered to measures of economy by the military authorities of the Government; and unless he received the most complete, prompt, and vigorous support from the Home Government, he feared "his efforts would be ineffectual." The entire force may be set down at 200,000 men, one-third being British. Two years and a half were consumed in discussions as to how even this moderate change was to be effected. The correspondence discloses the existence of anxieties entertained in the highest quarters, which it would be inexcusable for the Legislature to disregard. Lord Lawrence and Sir W. Mansfield were of opinion in 1868 that no reduction of the standing force could be safely attempted. The present Commander-in-Chief unequivocally concurs in the same view. " Our whole experience of India," he says, "should warn us that we cannot always depend upon tranquillity; that disturbances arise when they are least expected; and when they commence at one point, unless immediately checked, they are sure to be followed at others. There are considerable forces under native chiefs who may be individually friendly, but whose troops can never be relied on not to join against us."[1]

[1] Minute, 19th September 1870.

He proceeds to enumerate the quarters in which future collision might possibly arise, unreservedly pointing to the greater Native States who in 1857 remained faithful.

In the controversy of thirty years carried on between the partisans of annexation by right of lapse, and the defenders of local independence under the form of adopted heirship, hardly a word is said of the people's wishes in the matter. Parenthetically their feelings are sometimes glanced at by Sir Charles Metcalfe, Mr Frere, and Colonel Sutherland; threateningly they are noticed as adverse, and liable to become dangerous, by Sir Claude Wade. But even these clear-sighted and true-hearted advocates of the wiser and the juster ways of rule felt themselves restrained by the prevalence of opposite ideas among their superiors in office, and still more among their equals and associates in the service, from urging too openly or too often considerations which they knew would be sneered at as sentimental, and laughed at as weak and fantastic. An honest man placed in the trying position where he would fain ward off injustice from the weak, and at the same time save the honour of his country from the stain of sordid wrong, and who is conscious that, failing to dissuade those above him in authority from the evil course contemplated, he will himself be called upon to be its instrument, or to give way to a successor less scrupulous than himself,—an upright and honest man in such a case may well be pardoned if he fears to embody in a formal report sentiments of indignation and grief, which in his private confidence may overflow. To his *doctrinaire* chief in power, he feels that it were worse than useless to appeal on grounds of magnanimity or expediency. All his weight with him, and all his chance of leave to throw that weight into the scale while yet it wavers, depends upon his retaining some measure of respect with the short-sighted. He must gulp down each rising suggestion of immediate pity or of remote policy, lest the ruling spirits, inflamed by such remonstrance, should exclaim, "What have we to do with thee? art thou come to torment us with misgivings before the time?" with presages of calamity that may prove but rhodomontade, and which sound like mere romance? Many a worthy English official has had to gnaw his heart out with vexation at finding himself placed in a position of this kind; a position which he knows not how to justify thoroughly to himself, and yet which it may seem cowardice and selfishness to abandon. The consequences of the hand to mouth impolicy of fiscal exaction and territorial encroachment, weigh upon his pen and tongue by day, and trouble his sleep by night. The field committed to his care, which he would have sown with the seeds of contentment, confidence, and gratitude, he sees doomed to bring forth suspicion, anger, hatred, and the mute looking for a day of restitution. And his grief, if he be a true man, true to the honour of his race, his creed and his country, is that his hand should, in spite of himself, be used to withhold the good, and to scatter broadcast the pestiferous seed.

This may in some degree account for the silence, too seldom broken throughout the Annexation controversy, regarding its aspect in the eyes of the millions whose interests are compromised thereby. Even jurists and critics, writing independently on the subject in England, seem prone to fall into the same train of thought as their countrymen on the banks of the Ganges and the Indus. We have had able arguments in maintenance of the right of Adoption, and subtle pleadings in favour of its disallowance; both have mainly turned upon the conflict between supreme and subordinate authority; nearly every argument on the one side has been nakedly arrayed on behalf of the maintenance and extension of British rule; and nearly every argument on the other has been in deprecation of the hardship and injustice to Mohammedan Nawabs or Hindu Rajahs. Yet, even for the sake of the unhappy Princes who have been despoiled, or of those who, in their secluded palaces, listen tremblingly for the footfall of the spoiler, it would seem a hopeless task to plead for restitution, or lasting re-assurance, on grounds like these. Where or when, in the history of conquest, from the days of Cyrus or Scipio, has the rein been drawn at the undefended gate of dependant royalty? Tell the aggressor to beware of ambush; tell him there is a mine that may be fired; tell him of untameable tribes fanatically vowed to vengeance; tell him of snows to be traversed in retreat, of wells that may be poisoned, or communications that may be cut off; paint, in a word, the imprudence of being pitiless; and Native princes may get breathing time, if they be not saved eventually from ruin. But the tale of acquisition in the East is full of warnings, that no fidelity to our cause, and no obvious inability to resist our paramount sway, can afford any assurance against dethronement and denudition. Forty years long did Scindia, the Nizam, and the King of Oude, adhere unswervingly to the side of English ascendancy; and all that time they were honoured (or humoured) with recognition, as staunch and faithful allies are ever entitled to be; nevertheless, we have seen the dominions of one absolutely annexed, those of another partitioned, and the question seriously debated respecting all who are situated like the third, whether immemorial customs and traditions, regarding the law of inheritance, should not be set aside, in order that their lands and subjects should be summarily transferred to the care of a foreign satrap.

The dangerous prevalence of discontent is confessed by the Commander-in-Chief and by the Governor-General in terms so grave, that the Secretary of State has felt it to be his duty to lay them before Parliament for its information and admonition. Simultaneously with the disclosure, tidings have come of tragic events, which public conjecture ascribes to the plottings of those who desire to turn Moslem grudge and grievance to seditious account. Dr Hunter, who has made the subject his especial study, undertakes to tell us how the Wahabee conspiracy arose, how it has continued to exist, and how its ramifications spread over dissimilar and distant regions, feeding and growing upon the fruits of our misrule.[1] Some of his statements are said to be exaggerated, and some of his inferences to be too sweeping, by the wiser and wealthier sort, who have much to hazard, and nothing to hope, from insurrection.

Speaking generally of the present generation of Mussulmans in India, Colonel Nassau Lees states his belief that they are "quite prepared to accept the supremacy of the English as an evil which must be endured, because it cannot be cured. They are prepared to live as peaceably and contentedly under British rule as they would under any Mohammedan Government they are likely to see established on its ruins, provided they are considerately treated, and wisely and well governed."[2]

But are they so? The President of the Mussulman College at Calcutta answers the question fearlessly in the negative. Instead of trying to make them feel that our rule, as regards education and the protection of individual rights, is better than that which it supplanted, we have

[1] Our Indian Mussulmans. Hunter, 1871.
[2] Letter to the *Times*, 18th October 1871.

so acted as to make it difficult for the most loyally-disposed to defend us from the reproaches of their fellow-believers, and ignominious to try. Instead of furnishing them with the arguments in favour of submission, which can be founded only on appeals to a conciliatory and consistent policy, our course has been unstable, unequal, and unfair. While our growing power was weak, we affected the utmost deference for the Mogul, and the utmost regard for his authority. Even when we bought, beguiled, or bullied our way into the position of his Lieutenants, we affected to acknowledge the superiority of believers in the one true God above the worshippers of Seva and Vishnu. When all political disguise had been thrown off, and our claim to ascendancy was concealed no longer, we still continued to reiterate incessantly the pledge, that no man should have cause to fear disfavour or molestation on account of his religion, and that under the suzerainty of England, all races should be made to feel themselves equal. Of late years a different policy has been systematically adopted. The descendants of the once dominant minority find themselves the objects of peculiar and differential distrust. Whatever may have been done to conciliate the Hindus and Sikhs, nothing has been sincerely or intelligently attempted to appease the old grudge of the Mussulmans, while many new grievances have arisen, of which they have been suffered to complain without any prospect of obtaining redress. In Bengal, says Colonel Lees, their discontent is rather our fault than their own. For there "it is certainly due mainly to those unjust and iniquitous proceedings of early Indian Government, which made landlords out of Hindu collectors of revenue, and finally crystallised the injustice thus done to the community in general, and the Mohammedan portion of it in particular, by that gigantic blunder. The perpetual settlement placed the whole of India under unequal and unjust contribution."

But throughout India grievances of more recent date furnish the fanatical Wahabees with never-failing themes of taunt and adjuration to aid their plots and preparations for a Holy War.

They object that the Inam Commission unjustly deprived many of them of the lands granted to them by the Mohammedan Sovereigns of India.

That the appointment of Cazi and Government Mohammedan Law Officers, has been abolished, whereby they have been deprived of the benefit of properly constituted authorities to perform and register many of their civil rights.

That funds left by charitable and pious Moslems, for educational purposes, have been taken from them; and religious bequests (*watef*), or funds left to be devoted to the "Service of God," have been misapplied by Government, which is the self-appointed trustee for their proper administration.

That they have been elbowed out of almost all Government appointments by Hindus, and no efforts are made by Government to rectify this injustice, or to better their prospects.

That no offices under Government are open to Mussulmans learned in their own sciences, laws, literature, and languages; that, consequently, learning and learned men have disappeared, and their community is left in darkness; while the Government system of education is such that they cannot accept it, and retain the respect of their co-religionists, if even they may remain good Moslems.

But it is time to bring this narrative to a close. The words of Mr Bright, uttered twelve years ago, are still apt and true. "The question assumes every year a greater magnitude and a greater peril. We have what we have had for twenty years—deficit on deficit, and debt on debt. Some day or other it will find us out, or we shall find it out. . . . What we are now meeting is the natural and inevitable consequence of the folly we have committed. . . . But take India as it is, the Empire as it stands, and see if it is not possible to do something better with it than you have done before."[1] It will, of course, be said that the task is difficult: it is indeed so difficult that there is not a day to lose in setting about it; for if Empire in Asia is to be preserved, the thing has to be done, and that ere long. To Mr Fawcett is due the credit of having made an excellent beginning in the appointment of the Select Committee on Indian Finance. The interest with which its proceedings are regarded by all intelligent and reflecting persons in the great centres of Eastern activity, is a good omen of the practical and business-like temper of the time. The past is irrevocable. But the shaping of India's destiny in the future is still within our power.

[1] Mr Bright, Debate on the Indian Budget, August 1, 1859.

INDEX.

Abbott, Captain, 344-47.
Act of, 1873, 82, 83; pregnant clause in, 83; 126.
Adawluts, Sudder and Nizamut, 97.
Adoni, battle of, 147.
Adoption, right of, 366.
Afghanistan, 310-13, 315, 320, 330.
Agnew, Mr Vans, 338, 339.
Ahalya, 103-105.
Ahmedabad, settlement at, 11.
Akbar Khan, 314, 315.
Aliverdy Khan, 23; spirited conduct of, 243.
Ambition, English, 57.
Amherst, Lord, 293, 294.
Amyatt, Mr, 49.
Anderson, Lieutenant, 338, 339.
Annexation, completed, of India to the British crown, 41, 393, 394.
Anund Rao, 375.
Anstruther, J., on international justice, 153.
Appa Saib Bhonsla, 287, 365, 367.
Appeal, proposal to erect a tribunal of, to try Indian issues, 399, 401.
Arcot, 20, 22, 150; Nawab of, 162, 378, 379.
Argyll, Duke of, opinion of, on the present financial situation, 411, 412.
Army, Indian, its cost and strength, 411, 412; proposals to reduce, 412, 413.
Ashley, Lord, speech of, 330.
Asia, southern, states of, in time of Walpole and the elder Pitt, 3.
Asuph-ul-Dowla, 136-38.
Atkinson, R., 162.
Attaché-Extraordinary, 269.
Auckland, Lord, 308, 310, 318, 365; Lord Brougham on, 307.
Aurungzebe, 13; grandson of, 16; disintegration of dominions of, 17; 106.
Authority, paramount, assumption of, by Government, 82.
Ava, King of, 357.
Azim Jah, 378, 379.

Baillie's corps, 149, 150.
Baji Rao II., 241, 243, 287-89.
Bankers, the native, of India, 37, 38.
Baramahal, 142, 143, 190, 191.
Barlow, Sir S., 260, 262.
Barwell, Mr, 83, 125.
Bassein, treaty of, 242, 243, 245, 247.
Batavia, 266.
Beckford, Alderman, motion of, 69.
Beerbhoom, Rajah of, 76.
Bell, Major E., 399.
Benares, treaty of, 119, 121; 134, 136.
Benfield, Paul, 162.
Bengal, the chiefs of, jealousy of and rupture with the Company, 14; the Nawab of, 14; Mohammedanism in, 17; the Nawab-Nazim of, 18, 35, 36; native governments of, 37; famine, pestilence, and destitution in 1768, and its consequences, 73-77; hard exactions in, 78; affairs of Company in, 89; 237, 379.
Bengalis, the, 74.
Bentinck, Lord W., 8; Quaker simplicity, 294; appointment to governor-generalship, 296; qualifications, 297; abolition of Suttee, 297, 298; lessons of his administration, 299; and Coorg, 300; severe régime, 301-3; distrust of a free press, 303; his most important reform, 304; on the native army, 305; results of administration, 305, 306; on interposition in the affairs of Oude, 390, 391.
Berar, Rajah of, 272; cotton districts of, annexation of, 386.
Bhawalpore, Rajah of, 332.
Bill, a, of costs, 36, 37.
Bill, India, of the Coalition of 1783, 155, 156; of Pitt, 157-59, 168.
Bishenpore, Rajah of, 76.
Bishop, first, 270.
"Black Hole" of Calcutta, 28.
Bookkeeping by double entry, 28.
Bombay, 13, 183; presidency of, 232; merchants of, 411.
Bourdonnais, Le, 20.
Bourbon, Isle of, 265.
Brahmins, and Mohammedanism, 17.
Bribery, 25.
Bright, Mr, 392, 420; on India, 419, 420.
Bulwunt Singh, 134.
Burke, Edmund, 8; views of, 71, 72; oversensitiveness, 78; raillery, 88; on Nuncomar's death, 127, 128; 140; on Sir P. Francis, 157; 161; motion of inquiry, 162; 167, 168; impeachment of Hastings, 169, 170; 173, 175.
Burmah, first war with, 194-195; second war with, 353-357.
Burnes, A., 309-314.
Buxar, battle of, 51.

INDEX.

CALCUTTA, 16; panic at, 26–28; 37, 39, 41, 75, 94.
Calicut, settlement at, 12.
Cambay, settlement at, 11.
Canning, Mr, 295.
Canning, Lord, on maintenance of native states, 358; adoption minute of, 395; annexation of Dhar, 395; and Lord Stanley, 396; and the smaller States, 397.
Canora, Colonel, 346.
Carnatic, the, 20, 22, 27, 42, 148, 162, 227, 232; Nawab of, 269–270; 378.
Cartier, Mr, 66, 73.
Castlereagh, Lord, and the colonies, 7; 239.
Catherine's, Princess, marriage portion, 13.
Champion, Colonel, 119–120.
Chandernagore, French settlement at, 26, 33.
Charles II., 13.
Chatham, Lord, 7; and colonial possessions, 7; and the E. I. Company, 69; understood programme in regard to India, 69, 70; on Sir P. Francis, 158.
Cheyte Singh, 134–138, 154, 171.
Chillianwalla, 349.
Chiswick, Uncle, 86.
Chittagong, 15, 46, 49.
Chunda Sahib, 20, 22.
Chuttanatti, settlement at, 16.
Chuttur Singh, 344–348.
Circars, Five, 141.
Classes in India, relation of, to the soil, 108, 109.
Clavering, General, 83, 114, 121, 123, 127, 130, 135.
Clive, Robert, character and antecedents of, 21; expedition to recapture Bengal, 29; treaty with Suraja Dowla, 29; account of the runaway council, 30; proposal to destroy the French settlement at Chandernagore, 31, 32; dominant influence in the council, 33; perfidy of, 35; bill of costs, 36; moderation, 37; dishonesty, 39; a new dignity, 42; letter to Pitt, 42; return home, rewards, and peerage; Mir Jaffir's legacy to, 44, 53; political influence, 56; appointment as general-in-chief of the forces in Asia, 57; letter to Mr Rouse, 57; arrival in Calcutta, 59; effect on, of a tropical sun, 64; and the Directors, 65; impeachment, 78; suicide, 79; and Hastings, 87, 91, 92, 117.
Close, Colonel, 256.
Cobden, 8; on Burmese war, 356.
Colebrooke, Sir G., 79.
Committee, select, 59.
Commons, House of, and the Company, 69.
Company, East India, first charter, 11; original aims, 11; first settlement, 11, 12; first grant of jurisdiction, 12; commercial intolerance and cruelties, 12; first eighty years of, 13; "abject" submissiveness of, 13; rupture with chiefs of Bengal, 14; first attempt at aggression, 15; aims of territorial acquisition, 15; insidious doings, 16; first grant of a jaghire, 16; grant of new powers to, 19; Suraja Dowla's opinion of, 33; 39; extortion of the servants of, 47; treaty with Mir Jaffir, 49, 50; cheated by its servants, 56; farmers-general of the revenues of Orissa, Behar, and Bengal, 60; taxed by Parliament, 70; conduct of, towards Hyder Ali, 145, 146, 152; impolicy in regard to conquest, 226; dissolution of, 393.
Condore, battle of, 42.
Conscience, a troubled, 77.
Control, Board of, 159, 160, 162, 165, 203, 231, 251.
Coorg, 192, 193; annexation of, 300.
Coote, Sir E., 151.
Cornwallis, Lord, 8, 139; 153, 174, 185, 191, 193, 195; on Bengal, 197; on the conquest frenzy, 252; return to India, 252; embarrassments, 253; policy of, 255; regrets, 256; opinions as to empire in India, 257; conference with Wellesley, 259; death, 260.
Cosimbuzar, factory at, 15, 25, 26, 27.
Council, Calcutta, 27, 30. 33, 34, 35, 36, 38, 41, 44, 45, 46, 50, 59, 62; (Warren Hasting's,) 83, 114, 115, 121–124, 127.
Court, a phantom, 176, 177.
Courts, supreme, native judges in, 405.
Crisis of 1857, 397.
Crown, paramount power of, 358, 359; lapse to the, 359, 362.
Custom dues, and the Company's servants, 47, 49, 58.

DALHOUSIE, LORD, arrival, 336; embarrassments, 340; annexation of Punjab, 340, 350; and Pegu, 353, 355; policy of appropriation, 362; 368, 370, 374, 375, 377, 378, 379, 383; and the Nawab of Bengal, 383, 384; and the Nizam, 385; and Oude, 386–390; and Mysore, 398.
Deccan, the French in, 20, 23; musnud of, 141.
Delhi, and its court, 10; first English embassy to, 11; 12, 13, 18, 19, 25, 32, 60; durbar, 61; court of, 98, 99, 105, 106, 291, 292.
Despotism, Indian, not exceptional, 103.
Devecotah, fort and jaghire, 20, 21.
"Devil's brother," the, 332.
Dewan, the, of Bengal, 60.
Dewanny, gift of, 53, 60, 61, 62; 197–98, 204.
Dhar, and its rajah, 394–396; "plunder," 397.
Dhuleep, Singh, 330, 332, 333, 334, 336, 341, 343, 350–53.
Directors, court of, 26, 43, 56, 63, 65, 79, 82, 90, 154, 155, 159, 160, 164, 165, 251, 363–64, 389.
Doctrine, the, of lapse to the crown, 283.
Dost Mahommed, 310–15, 341, 349.
Dowlat Rao Scindia, 283–84.
Dundas, Mr, 154, 162, 163, 171, 172, 175.
Dupleix, 19, 20, 22; wife of, 19.
Dutch, the, in India, 2; successful struggle with the Portuguese, 10; 11, 12; and English, 30; 140, 189.

INDEX.

EDWARDES, Sir H., 339, 340, 343, 348.
Effrontery, solemn, of the Calcutta Council, 62.
Ek-Chusm-ul-Dowla, 261.
Ellenborough, Lord, 315, 316, 322, 326, 327, 329.
Elliott, Sir Gilbert, 263.
Ellis, Mr, 48, 49.
Elphinstone, General, 313-15.
English, the, in India, arrival and first outlooks of, 2, 3; their inveterate lust of conquest and territorial acquisition, 6; settlements of, at Surat, Cambay, Ahmedabad, 11; at Calicut and Masulipatam, 12; prowess in the defence of Surat, 13; at Madras, 18; at Calcutta, 19, 25.
Expenditure, excessive, 409.
Experiment, an, 335.

FAWCETT, Mr, 420.
Finances, Indian, under Hastings, 166.
Forde, Colonel, 41, 42.
Forgery, crime of, in India, 126.
Fowke and Bristowe, 131, 132.
Fox, J. C., on arbitrary rule, 1; 8, 155, 161, 167, 168, 171, 173.
Francis, Sir P., 83, 114, 121, 123, 124, 127, 130-133; speech of, 157, 158, 167, 174, 175.
France, 210; fear of, 212; 216.
French, the, in India, arrival and first outlooks of, 2; ambitious views of, 19; struggle of, with English, 19, 21; concession for peace, 22; in the Carnatic, 23; vigorous action against the English, 26; conduct of, towards the English in Calcutta, 31; at Chandernagore, 31, 33, 34, 140, 217; powerlessness of, 218.
Fuller, Mr, motion of, 70.
Fyzoola Khan, 120.

GAMA, Vasco de, 9, 10.
Game, a, not worth the candle, 231.
Gentlemen in the political line, 253.
George II., 39.
George III. and Clive, 43; and Lord Hillsborough, 83; 156, 189.
Geriah, battle at, 49.
Gwalior, 395; Maharanee of, 327, 329.
Glencoe, Massacre of, 27.
Golab Singh, 333, 347, 353.
Goodias, 96.
Goojerat, 349.
Goorkhas, war with the, 274, 276.
Gough, Sir H., 328, 340, 349.
Government, new attempt at, 66, 68; end of "double" in India, 392, 393.
Governments, separate, of Bombay, Madras, Calcutta, 81; the native, 99, 100; Mohammedan and Hindoo, 100.
Governor-General, first, and his colleagues, 83.
Govindpur settlement, 16.
Grafton, Duke of, on Indian reform, 69.

HAFIZ, Rahmet, 119.
Hardinge, Lord, 329, 331, 334, 336, 390.
Harris, General, 221, 223.

Hastings, Warren, 27, 75; character of, 80; appointment as first Governor-General, 83, 84; antecedents, 85; a Grecian, and something more, 86; a spy under Clive, 88; literary ambitions and Dr Johnson; 88; meanness and munificence of, 89; marriage, 90; at Madras, 91; at Calcutta, 91; counsel to the Directors, 94; and Anglo-Indian jurisprudence, 112, 113; object of his diplomacy, 114; and the Vizier of Oude, 115, 118; and treaty of Benares, 121; and his colleagues, 121; complaints against, 122; letter to Lord North, 123; tried and convicted by his colleagues, 125; and Nuncomar, 125, 126; tenders resignation and then withdraws it, 130; unnatural compact with Asuph-ul-Dowla, 137; condemnation and demand for recall of, 154; and the Mahratta war, 156; proposition of a peerage to, 163; resignation, 164; letter to directors, 164; administration, 165; return, 167; impeachment, 167; defence, 170; Sheridan's estimate of, 173; arraignment in Westminster Hall, 175, 177; acquittal, 181.
Hastings, Lord, on the *beau ideal* of rule, in India, 278; and Vizier of Oude, 388.
Hastings, Marquis of. *See* Lord Moira.
Hastings, Mrs, 164, 167.
Herat, siege of, 310.
Hindustan, people of, 10; beginning of conquest of, 21; secret of conquest of, 221.
Holkar, 239-41, 244, 249, 250, 260, 261, 272, 277, 278, 288.
Holwell, Mr, 27; memorial of, 45, 46.
Hooghly, the first settlements on, 16, 26; Phonsdar of, 122.
Hunter, Dr, quotation from, 66.
Hurry Punt, interrogatory of, 254.
Hyderabad, 143, 216; treasury of, 326.
Hyder Ali, 105, 142-151.

IMHOFF, Baron and Baroness, 89, 90, 130.
Imbecility, official, 414, 415.
Impey, Elijah, 86, 113, 127, 137, 138, 154, 174, 182, 183.
India in 1600, in relation to Europe, 1; effects on, of doubling the Cape, 2; present extent and population, 3, 4; present political condition contrasted with its past, in the days of Walpole and the elder Pitt, 3, 4; completed subjugation of to British sway, 4; 393, 394; first voyage, by the Cape, 9; Southern, 17; secret of conquest of, 22; bankers of, 37, 38; not a mine of fabulous wealth, 41; a new El Dorado, 53, 54; turning-point in the fortunes of, 61; stock, 56, 68, 82; economy, 266; complete pacification, 336.

JAMES I., 11.
Jehangir, 11, 289, 290.
Jeswunt Ahee Rao, 370-372.
Jhansi, annexation of, 374, 376.
Joan of Arc, an Indian, 376.

INDEX.

Johnson, Dr, and Hastings, 88.
Judicature, high court of, 82, 83, 113, 125.
Jugget Seit, 37, 38.
Juggett Singh, 253.
Jullindhur Doab, 333.
Junius, 115, 132.
Jury system, 111.
Justice, local administration of, 403–405.

KAZI of Khairpur, 318.
Keane, Sir J., 312, 313.
Kerowli, 368, 369.
Khalsa army, 332, 333; final rout, 349.
Khan Singh, 338.
Koh-i-nor, the, 352.
Kurnool, Nawab of, 273.
Kurrachee, port of, 321.

LAHORE, treaty with, 262; court of, 333; Resident of, 334, 335, 337, 340–342; British at, 337.
Lake, Lord, 248, 257, 258, 260, 261.
Lally, 42.
Lambert, Commodore, 354.
Land, its distribution and owners in Bengal, 198; revenue and its collection, 198, 199; tenure, 201–3; settlement, 205–8.
Lawrence, Sir H., 351, 390.
Lawrence, Sir J., 398.
Leadenhall Street in 1872, 82; delight at, 91, 159, 196, 231, 232; and conquest, 237, 238.
Lees, Colonel Nassau, 417.
Lucknow, court of, 19.
Luckshim Bai, 375, 376.
Lust of Christian Europe, 1, 2; of England, 6.

MACARTNEY, Lord, 152.
Macaulay, Lord, on war of sheep against wolves, 40; 114, 127, 307.
Macnaghten, Sir W., 313, 314.
Madras, authorities at, 20, 21; siege of, 42; Hastings at, 89, 91; 141, 190; garrison of, 145; 225.
Maharanee Banka Bace, 370, 371.
Mahé, siege and surrender of, 147, 148.
Mahomed Reza Khan, 58, 92, 93, 95, 96, 106, 124.
Mahrattas, the, 18, 59, 106, 116, 118, 132, 133, 143, 144–146, 152, 186, 191, 193, 217, 227, 239, 240, 245; war with the, *casus belli*, 245, 247; its objects, 247; its termination, 248, 250; 277, 282, 285, 327, 328.
Mahratta princes, the, 369.
Malartic, M., 217, 218, 221, 223.
Malcolm, Sir Jo., comparative estimate of Europe and India, 9; 20, 108–111.
"Man, the glorious little," 258.
Mangalore, treaty of, 187, 190.
Mansel, Mr, advice of, 369, 370.
Masulipatam, 12, 42, 141.
Matthews, General, in Mysore, 151, 152.
Mauritius, 265.
Mayo, Lord, on danger of excessive taxation, 392, 408, 411, 413.

M'Leod, Lord, papers of, 150, 153.
Meadows, General, 189, 190.
Mecanee, victory of, 324, 325.
Meer Roostum, 323.
Metcalfe, Col. 261, 262; confession, 265; on our empire in India, 274; 275, 279, 288, 289, 291, 303, 307, 308.
Mill, James, on Hyder Ali, 148, 149.
Minto, Lord, 264; boast of, 267.
Mir Jaffir Ali Khan, 35–37; treaty of, with the Company, 40, 41; 42, 44, 45, 49, 50; reproaches of, against the good faith of the council, 50, 52.
Mir Kasim, 44, 46, 48, 49, 51, 52.
Mobaruck-ul-Dowla, 93, 186, 187.
Mogul, the, 11; and the Company at Bombay, 13, 14; and the Company at Hooghly, 16, 18; 60, 92, 99.
Mogul Empire, disintegration of, 17, 18; 106.
Mohammedanism in India, 17, 101, 105, 107.
Mohammed Ali, 22, 196.
Mohammed Khan Talpur, 318.
Moira, Lord, 268; favour with the Regent, 269; tenderheartedness, 269; finances of, 270; sagacity, 271; and the Goorkhas, 274; administration, 276; finance, 292; return, 293; governorship of Malta, 293.
Mongheer, fall of, 49.
Montague, Mr F., 174.
Moolraj, 337–339, 348.
Moorshedabad, court of, 19, 32; durbar of, 33; courtiers of, 34; march on, 35, 36; treasury of, 37, 49; fall of, 94.
Mornington, Lady, 213.
Mornington, Lord, 213–218; on French ambition, 219; pious concern for the faith and morals of Tippoo Saib, 219, 220; 222.
Moultan, outbreak at, 338, 339; siege, 348, 353.
Mound, St Thomas', the English at, 151.
Morison, Colonel, 83, 114, 121, 123, 127, 130.
Mussulmans, the, and British rule, 417–419.
Munny Begum, 96, 122.
Munro, Sir Hector, army of, 149, 150.
Munro, Sir T., 109, 110, 190, 191, 193, 225, 228; on watching opportunities, 184; wise counsel of, 279, 280.
Mutakheren on the English, 282.
Mutiny, the conduct of the Nawab of Bengal during the, 384, 385.
Mysore, 141, 142–143, 144, 146, 189; projected partition of, 191, 222–225; rajah of, 225, 227, 228; attempted annexation of, 398, 399.

NAGPORE, annexation of, 370–372; jewels of, 370, 372, 373.
Nana Farnavis, 240.
Nana Saib, 287.
Napier, Sir C., 322–326.
Napier, Sir W., 321.
Napoleon, parallel between the aggrandising policy of, in Europe, and that of the British in India, 5, 6; 210; expedition to Egypt, 218; 374.

INDEX.

Natives, vain complaints of, 55.
Nawabs-Nazim of Bengal, 18, 60, 63, 64, 71, 92, 379-382, 383, 385.
Nizam, the, 18, 22, 42, 141, 143, 152, 191, 193, 195, 217, 225, 272, 293.
North, Lord, and the Company, 71, 82, 114, 123, 129, 153, 154.
Nuddea, Rajah of, 76.
Nudjum-ul-Dowla, 52, 53, 58, 59, 65, 93.
Nuncomar, 58, 95, 96, 106, 123, 125, 126, 127.

OATH of fealty by the grave of Runjit Singh, 332.
Official frauds, 77.
Omichund, 37-39.
Oodwa, defence of, 49.
Oude, 138, 139; Begums of, 137-139; vizier of, 139; annexation of, 389, 390.
Oude and its viziers, 18, 41, 51, 59, 115-120, 134, 138, 139, 233, 272, 386, 289.
Ouseley, Major, 371.
Outram, Major, 320, 321, 324, 325.
Oxenden, Sir E., 13.

PALMER, W., & Co., 292, 293.
Parallels, historic, 102-105.
Parliament, injunction of, 196.
Patriotism, common, of Hindu and Moslem, 100, 101.
Patna, 15, 32, 48.
Peace, native commissions of the, 402, 403.
Peel, Sir R., 331, 334.
Peers who voted in the case of Hastings, 181.
Pegu, annexation of, 355-357.
Peishwa, the, 239, 240-242, 256, 283, 285-287.
Penal laws, absence of, 105.
Pensions, English, from Louis XIV., 61.
Philip II. of Spain, 188.
Pindharries, the, 276-279, 283.
Pitt, William, and our colonial possessions, 7; letter to, from Clive, 42, 43; India Bill of, 157-159; 161, 163, 164, 171-173, 175, 211, 212, 214, 230, 252.
Plassey, battle of, 36.
Pondicherry, 147.
Poona, spectacle at, 245.
Portuguese, the, in India, 2; purely commercial aims of, 10, 11; 140.
Pratab Singh, 360, 363, 364, 367.
Presidency, the, in Calcutta, and the Soubahdar's Court, 67.
Pretab Sing, 20, 21.
Princes, native, distrust of English fidelity, 399.
Proclamation, royal, assuming the government of India in name of the Queen, 394.
Prome, fall of, 355.
Proprietors, court of, 69, 70, 251.
Proselytism, infatuation of, 17.
Punchayet, tribunal of, 405.
Punjab, 331, 336, 340, 343; annexation of, 349, 352.

Radachurn Mittre. 126.
Ragonath Rao, 374, 375.
Railways, 409, 410.
Rajahs, the, as members of the councils of the Presidencies, 402.
Raje Muhl. 36.
Rajashie, Rani of, 76.
Rampûr, battle of, 119.
Ranee Chunda, 332, 335, 336, 339-343, 353.
Rangoon, authorities of, 353-355.
Rapine, heyday of, 55, 90.
Retrenchments, 93, 94; call for military, 410.
Revenue, board of, 97.
Revolution, silent, in Bengal, 66, 67.
Richmond, Duke of, 72.
Roe, Sir Thomas, 11.
Rohillas, the, 115-120, 171.
Rohillcund, 117-120.
Rose, Sir H., 376.
Rotten at heart, the, 30, 35.
Rumbold, Sir T., 154.
Runjit Singh, 309, 310.
Russia, suspected intrigues of, 309, 310.

SAHUJI, 20.
Satara, annexation of, 362, 464.
Scinde, amirs of, 317-30, 322-324, 326, 227, 330.
Scindia, 239-241, 244, 248, 249, 261, 272, 277, 278, 288, 395.
Scott, Major, 163, 167.
Seaton, Mr. 291.
Sepoys, the, 354.
Seringapatam, 143, 216.
Servants, the Company's, 186.
Shah Alum, 51; firman of, 53, 60.
Shah Alum II., 248, 254, 290, 291.
Shah Sujah, 310, 312, 315.
Shahzada, 41.
Shelburne, Lord, 154, 155, 163.
Shere Mohammed, 326.
Shere Singh, 341, 343, 347-349.
Sheridan, R. B., 128; on the Company, 129; on Sir E. Impey, 138; 168; speech against Hastings, 172, 173; 214.
Shore, Mr, report of, 75; 81, 201, 204, 209.
Sikhs, the, 330-332, 338, 341, 347, 351.
Simla proclamation, 311.
Sirdars, the, 330, 333, 342, 348.
Sitab Roy, 95.
Sivajee, 102, 106.
Sivajî, 13.
Sobraon, 333, 334.
Somnath, gates of, 316.
Spain, dependencies of, under Philip II., 17.
Stanley, Lord, 393, 395, 396.
St George, Fort, founding of, 12; 80.
Strachney, H., on native justice, 98.
Struggle for empire in Europe, 210-212.
Succession, rights to, 359-362; Dalhousie's disregard of native law, 362.
Suja-ul-Dowla, 51.
Suraja Dowla, 24-26, 29, 33, 34, 36, 38.
Surat, taken from Portugal by the Dutch, 10, 13, 232.
Suttee. abolition of, 297.
Syef-ul-Dowla, 93.

2 E

TANJORE, 232.
Tanjore, Rajah of, 20.
Tatta, cantonments at, 320, 321.
Taxation, comparative, 406–410.
Teheran, 310, 320.
Thurlow, Lord, 163, 164.
Tippoo Saib, 150–152; character of, 187–189, 190; submission, 194–195; 212, 216, 217, 219, 221, 223, 224.
Tolerance, 105, 106.
Travancore, Rajah of, 189, 190, 195, 264.
Treaty, French and English, of 1754, 22; with Mir Jaffir, 40, 41, 49, 50.
Tribunals of justice, 178–180.
Trimbuckjee, 283, 285.
Troops, native and European, 22.

UNIT, the social, in India, 109, 110.

VANSITTART, Mr, 44, 46, 55, 57, 78.
Verelst, Mr, 66, 73, 94, 116, 127.
Vira Rejendra, 300.
Vishnu, traditions of, 17.

WAHABEES, complaints of, 419.
Watson, Admiral, 29, 31, 32, 39.

Watts, Mr, 27, 32, 33, 36.
Wellesley, Lord, administration of, an epoch, 226; advice, 227; regard for trappings of royalty, 229; love of glory, 230; expensiveness, 231; indifference to Leadenhall Street, 232; disposal of Oude, 233; military policy, 234; inexorable finance arrangements, 234, 235; his place in the history of our Indian empire, 235; and Leadenhall Street, 237, 238; scheme of a college for Indian statesmen, 238; resignation tendered and refused, 239; treaty dictated to the Peishwa, 242, 243; correspondence with the Mahratta chiefs, 245–247; extravagant rule, 251; 378. *See* Wellington.
Wellington, Duke of, on extension of territory, 210; 296; and the Rajah of Mysore, 398. *See* Wellesley.
Wheler, appointment as Governor-General, 130.
William, Fort, erection of, 16; surrender 27; 127.
Wine, new, in old bottles, 112.
Wynaad, 217, 218, 221, 222.

THE END.

www.ingramcontent.com/pod-product-compliance
Lightning Source LLC
Chambersburg PA
CBHW051740300426
44115CB00007B/636